Applications of Research in Music Behavior

Applications of Research in Music Behavior

Edited by
Clifford K. Madsen
and
Carol A. Prickett
With a Foreword by J. Terry Gates

THE ALABAMA PROJECT
Music, Society, and Education in America

The University of Alabama Press
Tuscaloosa and London

Library of Congress Cataloging-in-Publication Data

Main entry under title:

Applications of research in music behavior.

Papers sponsored by the 1984–1985 symposium, The Alabama Project; Music, Society, and Education in America, J. Terry Gates, director.

Bibliography: p.

Includes index.

1. Music—Instruction and study—United States—Addresses, essays, lectures. 2. School music—Instruction and study—Addresses, essays, lectures. I. Madsen, Clifford K. II. Prickett, Carol A. III. Gates, J. Terry. IV. Alabama Project: Music, Society, and Education in America.

MT1.A77 1987 780'.7 85-24690

ISBN 0-8173-0298-0

British Library Cataloguing-in-Publication Data is available.

Contents

Foreword

Several years ago, the School of Music at The University of Alabama began to benefit from an endowed chair, the purpose of which was to bring university students and faculty into substantive contact with nationally recognized authorities in the various disciplines of music. The 1984–85 endowment funded four residencies by experts in different foundational areas of music education. Each residency concluded with a weekend symposium at which presentations and discussions by additional experts were featured. This special yearlong series of residencies and symposia was called by the collective title "The Alabama Project: Music, Society, and Education in America."

The initial symposium, dealing with professional methodology, was led by Charles Leonhard and offered views on and challenges to the profession by Gretchen Hieronymous Beall, Robert Glidden, William Jones, and Richard Graham. Following the residency of Max Kaplan, a symposium addressing issues in the sociology of music brought together Albert LeBlanc, Barbara Kaplan, Joe Prince, and Peter Webster. The third residency, that of Clifford Madsen, and the research in music behavior symposium were the impetus for this volume. Abraham Schwadron held the final resident post and headed a symposium concerning philosophy of music education; other presenters included Malcolm Tait, J. H. Kwabena Nketia, Michael Mark, Gordon Epperson, and Charles Fowler.

The symposia prompted two volumes: the present book and *Music Education in the United States: Contemporary Issues*, which will be available at a later date. The latter work includes current information by symposia presenters augmented by other selected writers.

The Alabama Project reached not only students and faculty at The University of Alabama, in and beyond the School of Music, but also teachers and students in a variety of school systems in the state. Through the Music Educators National Conference (MENC), project resources were offered to music educators of the Southeast. Auburn University's Department of Music presented a lecture series by the four Alabama Project residents. During the residencies, more than 130 presentations, speeches, clinics, addresses, individual consultations and additional professional contacts were made. The symposia added more. In the publications, music educators are offered a current repository of exemplary theoretical writing and experimental research.

With thanks to those who made this rare experience possible, and with gratitude to those many who made it work, we submit these publications to our colleagues.

J. Terry Gates
The Alabama Project

Preface

More than a decade has elapsed since the first research in music behavior volume was published by the Teachers College Press. That first volume addressed a relatively new research area and contained twenty studies. Many of them were reprints, and, as would be expected in a pioneer effort, the quality was somewhat uneven. Even so, the book received an extraordinary response and went through several printings as it became a text for music therapy and research programs throughout the nation. Initially intended as a research sourcebook, it provided an impetus for more exacting procedures and research within applied settings and thereby helped create the climate for continued research activity.

The Alabama Project has encouraged the development of another research in music behavior volume. The present work is quite different from the first in that it contains entirely original research as well as several overviews concerning the state of research efforts and needs within selected areas. Studies from researchers who appeared on the University of Alabama campus in Tuscaloosa and presented the best of their current work have been augmented by selected research from the Sixth National Symposium of Research in Music Behavior, Fort Worth, 1985.

This volume evidences not only the burgeoning activity over the past ten years, but a diversity and sophistication not found in previous works. Additionally, many of the earlier researchers have continued to build upon their previous investigations and thereby provide that special kind of research continuity not possible over short periods of time. This book neither pretends to be representative, nor attempts to provide a complete review. It is felt that this would not be possible. Rather, it focuses on selected procedures and issues in experimental research activity that are deemed relevant and fruitful for continuing investigation.

Special thanks are expressed to The University of Alabama Press for its competence and diligence in handling the publication of this volume. Appreciation is extended to the staff and director of the Alabama Project for facilitating this endeavor. Particular gratitude is due my coeditor, who not only played a key role in coordinating the manuscript, but also continues to serve as a major source of academic and social reinforcement for all those fortunate enough to be associated with her.

C.K.M.

Applications of Research in Music Behavior

Part I
Introduction

1 Good Teaching May Be in Sonata Form

Cornelia Yarbrough

Members of the music teaching community have begun to challenge members of the research community with questions such as "What does your research have to do with my seventh-grade general music class (or band, or chorus, or orchestra)?" In addition, some music educators have expressed concern that the *art* of teaching has not been given the same intensity of study by the music research community as the *science* of teaching.

Historically, the music teacher has been viewed as an authority regarding all music subject matter, a developer of music curriculum materials, an evaluator of student performance, and a controller of classroom discipline. Each of these areas of music teaching has been given attention by the music teaching as well as the research communities, and new methodologies and strategies for teaching have emerged.

Although it is true that these methodologies have been approached scientifically, or analytically, by researchers, a careful review of extant music education research suggests that we may begin to entertain the notion that music teaching may be both an art *and* a science. Specifically, recent research in this field may illustrate that it might be both artistically and scientifically structured into classical musical forms.

For example, a review of 50 research articles suggests, if viewed creatively, that some effective music classroom and rehearsal teaching/learning situations may be in sonata form. The *Harvard Dictionary of Music* states: "A movement written in sonata form consists of three sections—exposition, development, and recapitulation (also called statement, fantasia section, and restatement), the last followed by a coda" (Apel, 1969). The purpose of this article is to explore the premise that good teaching might be artistically and scientifically structured so that it contains an exposition, development, and recapitulation.

Exposition

The exposition contains a first and second theme connected by a bridge (modulating) passage (Apel, p. 791).

The art of teaching music may involve the ability to analyze and/or compose two themes connected by a bridge. Suppose that the first theme concerns aspects of the musical task; the second theme, characteristics of the students to be taught; and the bridge, the transition (or modulation) from the musical task to the student.

The teacher, as composer of musical tasks (Theme 1), might be concerned with an a priori definition not only of long-term goals and objectives but also of daily musical tasks. Recent research contains examples of musical task analyses of conducting (Madsen & Yarbrough, 1980), rehearsal skills (Price, 1983; Thurman, 1976; Yarbrough & Price, 1981), elementary music teaching skills (Moore, 1976a; Rosenthal, 1981; Wagner & Strul, 1979), performance objectives (Abeles, 1973), and composing (Bennett, 1976; Gorder, 1980).

After composing the musical task, careful consideration should be given as to how the musical task(s) will be presented to students, i.e., the bridge between Themes 1 and 2. In composing the bridge section for effective teaching and learning, consideration of both delivery and approaches/techniques may be necessary. Teachers' delivery of musical tasks has been defined by the research community as involving personality variables, such as eye contact, body movement, facial expressions, and voice inflections (Madsen & Yarbrough, 1980; Thurman, 1976; Yarbrough, 1975; Yarbrough & Price, 1981). In addition, the importance of correct versus incorrect modeling of the musical task (Baker, 1980), the development of the teacher's ability to give prompts and other signals to initiate student behavior (Price, 1983; Rosenthal, 1981; Yarbrough & Price, 1981), and use of classroom and rehearsal time (Moore, 1981; Thurman, 1976; Wagner & Strul, 1979; Yarbrough & Price, 1981) have been the focus of current and ongoing research efforts. Other effective approaches and techniques of task presentation that have been reported in the research literature include self-analysis (Madsen & Yarbrough, 1980; Alley, 1980; Yarbrough, Wapnick, & Kelly, 1979), self-instruction (Romanek, 1974), simulation (Brand, 1977), unit study (Garafalo & Whaley, 1979), videotaped instruction, use of popular music to teach form (Grashel, 1979), use of the vertical keyboard to teach pitch to uncertain singers (Jones, 1979), various approaches to developing expressive performance (Marchand, 1975), and contingency management (Moore, 1976b).

Finally, having composed a musical task (Theme 1) and a delivery system (bridge), the teacher should be concerned with the most important theme of all, Theme 2. This theme may be the a priori analysis of the students who will be taught. This analysis might involve every variable (age, sex, experience, current knowledge, performance capabilities, and so forth) that might affect students' progress in learning the musical task. These characteristics and responses should be observed, analyzed, evaluated, and targeted before the teaching/learning interaction begins as well as during the class or rehearsal period. Research demonstrates that Theme 2 may be successfully composed via pretests consisting of student self-analysis (Alley, 1980; Madsen & Yarbrough, 1980), audiotaping of performance skills (Goodwin, 1980; Kuhn, 1977), preference and attitudinal responses (LeBlanc, 1981; Nolin 1973), cognitive and performance responses (Flowers, 1983; Geringer, 1978; Hair, 1977; Piper & Shoemaker, 1973; Van Zee, 1976), and observational techniques (Flohr & Brown, 1979; Webster & Schlentrich, 1982; Yarbrough & Price, 1981).

Thus, in the exposition section of this sonata form teaching model the teacher defines the musical task (Theme 1), describes the student to be taught through observation and other means of a priori evaluation (Theme 2), and decides how the task will be presented to the students (bridge or modulating passage). The exposition may be the most important ingredient for artistic and creative teaching because the more complete it is, the more effective the teacher, as an artist, may be in *initiating* students' successful responses to musical tasks rather than inappropriately *responding* to students' errors in interacting with the tasks.

Development

In the development section more than anywhere else, the composer is free to use his ingenuity and imagination (Apel, p. 792).

Having systematically composed or analyzed Themes 1 (musical task) and 2 (student characteristics and performance capabilities) and having decided the best way to deliver the musical task to the student (bridge section), the teacher using this sonata form teaching model would then have an opportunity to demonstrate the *art* of teaching through the development section, which takes place in the classroom or rehearsal. As in a sonata form musical composition, sonata form teaching requires interaction, variation, and modulation of the themes presented in the exposition section.

For interaction, variation, and modulation to occur in a creative teaching situation, the teacher may want to structure teaching/learning situations in which commitment and reciprocity occur. Commitment may be shown by analyzing how time is spent in the rehearsal and/or classroom. For example, what do teachers and students *do* in the presence of the musical task?

Almost every music educator has observed rehearsals and music classrooms where the commitment of the music teacher is high and that of the students is low. Table 1.1 is a typescripted excerpt of a high school band rehearsal. Several interesting things can be observed in this less than 4 minutes of rehearsal. First, the average student off-task during teacher presentation of the musical task and teacher reinforcement and feedback is 25%, and the average off-task during student performance is 8%. Second, reinforcement or feedback does not occur after every student interaction with the task. Finally, the amount of time spent interacting with the task is about equal for both the teacher (1 minute 58 seconds) and students (1 minute 49 seconds). These observations may indicate low reciprocity between teacher and student as well as high commitment on the part of each to the musical task.

Thus, although teachers allow students equal time with the task, they may completely exclude students during their own interaction with the musical task. It is perhaps overstating the obvious to say that the more time the teacher spends interacting solely with the musical task, the less time the student will be able to spend. In this situation, we may conclude that the commitment of the teacher is high and that of the students is low.

Another interesting point that can be observed in Table 1.1 concerns the teacher's delivery of the musical task. It is not always clear what the task is, that is, the verbalizations used are often very abstract and are possibly more appropriate for sophisticated, professional musicians. The problem then is twofold: how can teachers demonstrate commitment to the musical task without losing the commitment of students?; and how can teachers foster reciprocity in the classroom or rehearsal between themselves, the musical task, and the students? Or, musically speaking, how might teachers (in composing the development section) attend to Theme 1 without sacrificing attention to Theme 2? Is there a way to juxtapose Themes 1 and 2 by using the bridge section?

Two important dimensions of commitment and reciprocity that have been documented by researchers in music education are student attentiveness and attitude. These researchers have developed ways to measure commitment and reciprocity levels through behavioral observation instruments, music selection recorders, and attitude scales (Alpert, 1982; Greer, Dorow, & Hanser, 1973; Kuhn, 1975; Madsen & Yarbrough, 1980). It is yet unclear how much demonstrative music preference and attitude is necessary to affect significant music achievement. However, it has been documented that, as classroom attentiveness deteriorates to less than 80% on-task, academic learning declines (Madsen & Madsen, 1983). Furthermore, research has illustrated that overt commitment to the musical task increases as active involvement with the task increases (Forsythe, 1977; Spradling, 1980; Price, 1983).

One way to increase the level of student commitment to the musical task might be to reduce active teacher involvement with the task and increase active student participation. As composers, we might artistically emphasize the development of Themes 1 and 2 and de-emphasize the bridge (teacher behavior) section. If good teaching is composed this way, then the teacher may have to become a facilitator from Theme 1 to Theme 2, an attractive accessory to modulation (transfer of learning), and a punctuator of success. The goal for the teacher, therefore, may be economy of bridge material and generosity in student/musical task interaction.

Regarding reciprocity or shared exchanges among teachers, musical tasks, and students, patterns of student-teacher-task interactions have emerged through structured observations of high school bands, choruses, and orchestras. These patterns generally consist of three essential ingredients: task presentations, students' responses, and teacher reinforcement and/or feedback. The presence of all three ingredients in the specified order has been defined as a complete teaching cycle and is documented in music education research (Moore, 1981; Price, 1983; Rosenthal, 1981; Spradling, 1980; Thurman, 1976; Wagner & Strul, 1979; Yarbrough & Price, 1981).

These studies demonstrate that prospective and experienced music teachers find it difficult to present appropriate and accurate musical tasks consistently, allow students the right amount of time to interact with the tasks, and successfully use techniques of reinforcement.

High correlations between lack of eye contact with students (lack of teacher/student reciprocity) and off-task behavior (lack of student commitment) is further cause for concern. Closer observation reveals lack of teacher eye contact with students is a function of increased teacher interaction with the musical task (score) to the almost total exclusion of student interaction with the task (musical performance). Further support for this notion is found in high correlations between student performance time and on-task behavior. The more students are allowed to play their instruments or sing (interact with the musical task), the more attentive (committed) they appear.

If commitment and reciprocity occur, this should be recognized through reinforcement by both teacher and student. Overt recognition of commitment and reciprocity by all participants in the teaching/learning process may add a dimension to artistic teaching heretofore undefined and most appropriately residing in the affective domain.

Music researchers have collected a wealth of data concerning the effect of teacher reinforcement on student attentiveness, achievement, attitude, and music preferences (Forsythe, 1975; M. Gordon, 1979; Greer et al., 1973; Kuhn, 1975; Madsen, 1981b; Madsen & Alley, 1979; Madsen, Dorow, Moore, & Womble, 1976; Murray, 1975; Salzberg & Salzberg, 1981). Data demonstrate the power of positive feedback and reinforce the idea of the teacher as a punctuator of success. Future research might concern the effect

Table 1.1
Typescripted Excerpt of High School Band Rehearsal

Time line (Min:Sec)	Teacher Presentation of Task	Student Response	Reinforcement or Feedback
0:00	I want everyone playing. At G. Mezzo-piano. Balance.	Average off-task = 25%	
0:08		Students play. Average off-task = 8%	
0:28	Follow after me. After G, please (counts) . . . the 7th measure. The people with two half notes in that measure . . . would you play, please? I want 1, 2, and the downbeat of the next measure. Ready, and . . .	Average off-task = 25%	
0:43		Students play. Average off-task = 8%	
0:46	Again. This is horns, especially horns. Much more tenor sax as well.	Average off-task = 25%	
0:52	Once again. Listen inside. Everyone at G. Think about phrasing, please. Ready, and . . .	Average off-task = 25%	No. I'm not getting enough horn. You're not settling on the beats together. (Disapproval)

1:21		Students play. Average off-task = 8%	
2:15	The last chord needs to be more of a pyramid. Especially in trombones. Look. Here's a problem we're facing, people. The minute we put that up to fortissimo level and the minute we put it up to tempo we lose horns, we lose tenor saxes, we lose some of the baritone progressions and all of the low reeds. It's gone. The half-note segments are not there anymore. The melody becomes prime importance and it ruins the whole harmonic structure. It has to be vibrant. It has to be exciting and the only way that's gonna come off is if you people make it. Again. G.	Average off-task = 25%	
3:15		Students play. Average off-task = 8%	
3:47			Much better. (Approval)

of student reinforcement on the teacher. It might be interesting to find out how much of our music curricula is determined by the happiness level of students.

In summary, the development section may be viewed as the point in teaching time when interactions take place. Their characteristics are determined by the teacher, who is the composer of the teaching/learning process. A definition of the ideal development section is far from simple. How many tasks should be presented during a rehearsal or class? How much time should be spent in explaining the task? How much time do students need to interact with it in order to achieve musical success? How much feedback or reinforcement should be given? What about individual teacher and student differences? The answers to these questions represent an ongoing challenge to the music education research community and to the profession as a whole.

Recapitulation

The recapitulation normally contains all the material of the exposition, though usually with certain modifications in the bridge passages (Apel, p. 792).

The recapitulation section of teaching in sonata form provides an opportunity for teachers to assess the amount of student independence in interacting with the musical task by revisiting the ideas or themes outlined in the exposition. Here teachers cease to be a bridge between Themes 1 (musical task) and 2 (the student) and become instead objective evaluators.

Evaluation (recapitulation) should answer several important questions. First, can Theme 1 and Theme 2 interact without the bridge? Many music educators take pride in the fact that their students become professional musicians or very active in community music organizations. This may be attributed to the amount of independence the students have achieved in musical performance. In addition, it could reflect an increase in the repertories of music they appreciate and enjoy. Secondly, are student responses to targeted musical tasks successful? In other words, how do achievement, attentiveness, and attitude in the recapitulation compare to those in exposition?

Although the evaluation process often occurs only three times during the course of instruction—at the beginning, at midterm, and at the end—the ideal recapitulation (evaluation) may be an ongoing, constant one. Periodic quizzes, observations, audio- and videotaping may provide valuable information for the revision of the teaching composition.

Whether sonata form teaching occurs in a 10-minute time segment or across an entire year or more, the recapitulation is the key to greater understanding of the learning processes of individual students. If they cannot play their instruments, if they are not enjoying music class or rehearsal, and if they are constantly inattentive, then restructuring of the exposition and development may be necessary.

The recapitulation section may involve a complete restatement of Themes 1 and 2, providing opportunities for students to demonstrate independence in interacting with musical tasks and in transferring musical skills to other situations, and offering teachers the chance to observe and evaluate student progress. Revisiting the exposition section can be a most revealing and rewarding experience. Careful evaluation may be the key to progress in creative teaching and learning.

Coda

A concluding section or passage, extraneous to the basic structure of the composition but added in order to confirm the impression of finality (Apel, p. 181).

To entertain the idea that good teaching might be in sonata form may be just that: entertainment. However, there may be merit in considering teaching as a formal *and* artistic structure. It is apparent through study of musical forms that great compositions do not just "happen" (Bennett, 1976). Good music, like good teaching, is the result of careful planning, creative analysis as well as organization, and artistic manipulation of all the elements.

As it is impossible to make general statements regarding the whole realm of musical creation, so it may be regarding music teaching. However, it does seem appropriate now and then to reflect upon what we know based on extant research; to put our imaginations to work; and, most importantly, to strive to realize the ultimate goal: excellence in teaching.

Part II
Applications of Research: Teaching Music to Children

We are music educators—professionals offering a service (teaching music) to our clients (students) that we firmly believe will enrich and enhance their lives, as it has our own. We worked hard to become musicians because we really care about our art, and we want others to know its joy. No matter how open-minded we may strive to be, it is almost inconceivable to us that anyone exposed to the pleasure of "good" music could be anything but eager for more. And yet, most of us have known the frustration of missing the mark, of preparing a beautiful lesson that goes unlearned, of playing an extremely moving excerpt to a glazed-eyed audience. When we are trying to teach, but few are learning, where can we turn for answers?

Perhaps at least a part of the solution may lie in looking, as professionals, at our clients or students as clearly and objectively as possible, a task that is much easier to propose than to carry out. Having been sophisticated musicians for a number of years, we may find it difficult to recall what it was like to be a fourth-grade beginner who cannot remember whether the half rest is the upside-down top hat or the right-side-up one. The very fact that almost all of us were musically precocious may work against us. A junior high choral teacher who matched pitch when only a preschooler may be at a distinct disadvantage when confronted with eighth graders who have yet to learn this skill. In taking a clear-eyed look at the people we hope to teach, research techniques can help us sort fantasy from reality.

What interests children about music? What shapes their listening and playing choices? What holds their attention? Are there critical ages at which certain skills or preferences become set? When music study becomes demanding, what techniques keep students working hard, rather than turning to easier non-music pursuits? How closely tied are language development and musical responses? Are children helped or hindered by teaching about music, writing about music, or looking at graphic aids? Most importantly, what factors can be demonstrated as having such a consistent effect that applications to music students, generally, might have validity? We are all familiar with "pet theories" about music teaching, which seem to achieve magical results in isolated settings, but which fail miserably when applied to actual children in everyday classrooms. How can we separate the usable from the fluke?

The investigations that follow in Part II address these questions. They represent the work of real music educators confronted with the challenges of teaching real students. Using the stringent techniques of experimental and behavioral research, these teachers have sought answers, tested ideas, and focused on discriminating what is truly effective from what is promising, but useless. The first five studies alone involve direct observation of more than 1,400 pre-high school students and 150 undergraduates who are not music majors; Hair's paper analyzes and summarizes the findings of an additional 47 authors. Although individual students' strengths and challenges must *never* be overlooked, it may be suggested that the trends evidenced in these large groups, where extraneous influences have been controlled or counterbalanced through the rigors of experimental methodology, may serve as valid starting points, "warranted assumptions" if you will, when devising individualized teaching strategies. Music education is not only a process of helping children explore music. As the studies that follow demonstrate, it may also be the process of learning more about how children learn, through music. Each study opens as many new areas for study as the number of questions it answers.

2 Effect of Tempo on Music Preference of Preschool through Fourth-Grade Children

Wendy L. Sims

Summary

This study was designed to examine the effects of tempo on the preference responses of children from preschool through fourth grade because previous research has demonstrated that by the fifth grade tempo already functions as a strong preference determinant. A total of 247 children indicated their attitude toward each of five fast and five slow musical excerpts by marking a smiling, neutral, or frowning face. Results indicated that both of the primary variables under consideration, age and tempo, were related to differential preference responses. A strong, positive correlation was found between tempo and preference, with fast items generally receiving higher ratings. The comparison of tempo preferences by age level was also significant, $\chi^2(10, N = 247) = 47.86, p < .001$. On the basis of this analysis, it was concluded that the tendency to base preference decisions on tempo discriminations and to prefer fast tempos is probably acquired by grade four. The results of this study support extant theories of preference development, and are for the most part consistent with the research literature.

Design: Test-retest, statistical $N = 247$ Groups: 6
Statistical Analysis: chi-square, Mann-Whitney *U*, Pearson product-moment correlation, Spearman rank correlation
Reliability: .61–.84
Independent Variables: Tempo (fast or slow), grade level (preschool through fourth), order, item length
Dependent Variable: Tempo preference test responses
Music: Listening

* * *

Expanding the musical tastes of children, in an effort to create lifelong learners, participants, and consumers of music, has long been a primary goal of music education. There is still relatively little empirical research, however, that addresses the development of attitudes toward music with respect to when and how preferences are acquired. Examination of the extensive reviews of music attitude research provided by Wapnick (1976) and Kuhn (1980) reveal that this is particularly true with relation to preschool and elementary-aged children. This study was designed to contribute to the small, informative body of research available that documents several aspects of attitude development and its measurement among children in this age group. Identification of as many variables as possible that affect the acquisition of music preferences by children would be of value to music educators for consideration in determining the optimal times, best techniques, and most appropriate materials to achieve attitude-related goals.

One factor that has been found to affect preference responses of preschool, fourth-, and fifth-grade children is teacher approval. Alpert (1980), Dorow (1977), Greer, Dorow, and Hanser (1973), and Greer, Dorow, Wachhaus, and White (1973) all found that teacher approval positively affected verbal and/or behavioral preference measures. The teacher's impact on third- and fourth-grade students' preferences is also evident in responses found by Baker (1980), because preferences for appropriate or inappropriate performances were affected by the performance models presented as a part of classroom instruction.

Less conclusive results have been found in the examination of discrimination ability as a variable affecting preference. In fact, data seem to indicate that the acquisition of musical discriminations by nursery school, first-, second-, and third-grade children did not affect attitude toward the music taught (Brown 1978b; Greer et al., 1973). Based on these results, Brown (1978b) questioned whether "knowing" leads to "valuing" and concluded that "producing the ability to make discriminations in music might indeed be unrelated to such processes of valuing that find music useful in life's experience" (p. 453).

All the studies discussed above have used some form of an operant music selection device in the collection of data. These instruments record subjects' choices of stimuli presented, as well as the time spent listening to the selections. Attitude data may also be generated from verbal or written self-reports. Self-report measures used as dependent variables in preference research with young children have usually been in verbal or pictographic form (Charboneau, 1981; Kuhn, 1976).

Schukert and McDonald (1968) elicited verbal responses from preschool children in an attempt to determine whether repeated exposure to a less preferred type of music would result in a preference change. "Induced familiarity" did not seem to affect children's preference choices in this study.

Pictographic self-report scales have been used in music research with children mainly in response to questions, rather than to aural stimuli. Kuhn (1976), however, explored the use of these scales for measuring responses to a variety of musical examples by first- through third-grade students. Children were presented with sets of smiling, neutral, and frowning faces, and were instructed to mark the face that showed how they felt about each piece of music they would hear. This technique was found to measure preference with "acceptable reliability"; test-retest correlations for individual scores ranged from .431 to .830.

Rogers (1957) also found a written response to aural stimuli to be "reasonably reliable" using test-retest methodology, in a study designed to explore age and musical style as variables influencing preference decisions. Children in Grades 1, 4, and 7 were asked to indicate their preference between members of the paired comparison items presented. Results included an "overwhelming" preference for popular music, which increased with age, while preference for classical music decreased with age. These findings are consistent with those obtained through operant listening techniques by Greer, Dorow, and Randall (1974). Listening time for rock music was found to generally increase with age for their nursery school through sixth-grade subjects. No difference in preference was apparent between nursery and first-grade children, and a "pivotal time in terms of musical taste" was identified between the third and fourth grades.

Age was also used as an independent variable by Eisenstein (1979) in conjunction with musical elements identified as contributing to complexity or redundancy in listening examples presented. Data for the second-, third-, fifth-, and sixth-grade subjects were generated by both paired comparison choices and subsequent time spent listening to the example chosen. As in the previous studies described, Eisenstein found age differences and concluded that the music was "more reinforcing for lower grade than upper grade children" (p. 84). Complex and redundant conditions did not seem to elicit differential responses, however.

Several of the issues and variables identified above have been addressed in a series of studies by LeBlanc and associates, based on LeBlanc's theoretical model of preference acquisition (LeBlanc, 1979, 1981; LeBlanc & Cote, 1983; LeBlanc & McCrary, 1983), including response mode, reliability, age, style, and musical elements. Written self-report measures were used as primary means of data collection for each of these studies; each response was marked on a 7-point like/dislike continuum (for a thorough discussion of preference response mode selection, see LeBlanc, 1984). As with written response formats described previously, good reliability was found for LeBlanc's attitude scales.

The use of age as a variable was not of primary concern in this series of studies, though it was examined. All the subjects participating in these research projects were in the fifth or sixth grade, and, though LeBlanc and Cote (1983) found fifth-grade preference for jazz music higher than sixth grade, this was hypothesized to be attributable to the different type of schools each grade represented. When responses to a subsequent study were compared for fifth and sixth graders housed in the same school, no significant differences were apparent (LeBlanc & McCrary, 1983).

Style was a variable of primary interest. The effects of style found in previous research were generally confirmed by LeBlanc (1979, 1981), who found that "popular" styles tended to be rated the highest. Based on the results of these studies, the musical elements of performing medium and tempo were identified as possibly affecting preference decisions. Results of the next study, which used these as variables, indicated a significant interaction, with consistent preferences for instrumental performances and faster tempos (LeBlanc & Cote, 1983). In the most recent study reported in this series, the effects of tempo alone were examined by controlling both style and medium. Each of the four increasingly faster tempo categories received higher preference ratings; this finding led to the conclusion that "taken with previous indications it offers convincing evidence that faster tempos are preferred by this age group" (LeBlanc & McCrary, 1983, p. 292). LeBlanc and McCrary also provide a comprehensive review of tempo-related literature, most of which considered tempo "without using preference as a dependent measure."

Replication of their study with other styles and ages was among suggestions for further research made by LeBlanc and McCrary. Although their results show that, by the fifth grade, student attitudes toward music are affected by tempo, the age where tempo-based discriminations begin has not been determined. The primary purpose of this study was to examine the effects of tempo on the preference responses of children from fourth grade down through preschool in order to find out how this variable functions with younger children and in an attempt to identify when tempo becomes a basis for preference judgments.

Method

The 247 children who served as subjects for this study represented the following grade levels: preschool, $n = 34$; kindergarten, $n = 37$; first, $n = 33$; second, $n = 47$; third, $n = 49$; and fourth, $n = 47$. All children who were available for participation in both scheduled testing sessions at each testing site were included. First- through fourth-grade subjects were enrolled in a university-affiliated research school, whose student population was selected to represent a "relatively normal distribution in terms of socioeconomic factors and ability." Kindergarten and preschool subjects were obtained from several privately operated schools in the same geographic area and were selected to represent a population similar in makeup to the research school. Preschool participation was limited to 4-year-olds because pilot testing indicated that meaningful responses to the research task were not feasible for younger children.

The assessment instrument used was developed to test the influence of tempo on children's music preference discrimination. Although it was designed to tie into LeBlanc and McCrary's (1983) work, modifications were necessary to accommodate the age range investigated in the present study. A three-choice pictographic response mode similar to that used by Kuhn (1976) was selected, based on a pilot study that seemed to indicate that the younger children were not capable of responding to a larger range of choices, and that even the older children enjoyed working with the "faces." Students were instructed to mark the smiling face if they liked the music they heard, the straight face if they thought it was "okay," and the frowning face if they did not like the music. Word cues were included on the answer sheet for the children who could read. To increase the motivational value of the test form, students were allowed to indicate their response by drawing a "nose" on the selected face.

The length of the test was also determined through pilot testing. It was found that 10 items, with an administration time totaling about 10 minutes, were within the limit of the younger children's attention spans for this activity. It also became apparent that, in order for children at the ages used in this study to differentiate among responses, fairly clear discriminations were necessary, so only two categories of tempo were used. Slow items ranged from 32 to 64 beat notes per minute, and fast items from 124 to 180, as determined by professional musicians from the recordings. To control for style and medium, all selections were chosen from recorded piano works of Mozart and Beethoven (see Table 2.1). Durations varied from 11 to 30 seconds, allowing for musically logical excerpts, and in accordance with previous research, which indicated that short examples were sufficient for reliable judgments to be made (Chalmers, 1978; Kuhn, 1976; LeBlanc, 1979). Items were tape-recorded in two different orders, which were determined at random but with the stipulation that each begin with a different tempo category and that no more than two same-tempo category items occurred in succession. The two orders were used as a control, particularly for the possibility that reactions to the initial piece might influence further responses, and approximately half of the subjects were randomly assigned to each presentation order.

Table 2.1
Preference Results on First Test Administration in Order from Most to Least Preferred

Rank	Tempo/MM	Composer/Title*	Duration
1	Fast/130	Mozart/Rondo, K. 494	:13
2	Fast/174	Mozart/Sonata, K. 331, Variation VI	:11
3	Fast/180	Beethoven/Rondo a capriccio, op. 129	:16
4	Fast/124	Beethoven/Sonata, op. 13, Rondo	:16
5	Slow/64	Beethoven/Sonata, op. 13, Adagio cantabile	:15
6	Fast/159	Beethoven/Sonata, op. 10, no. 3, Presto	:23
7	Slow/64	Mozart/Sonata, K. 457, Adagio	:15
8	Slow/42	Beethoven/Sonata, op. 27, no. 2, Adagio sostenuto	:20
9	Slow/64	Mozart/Fantasy No. 3, K. 397, Adagio	:15
10	Slow/32	Beethoven/Sonata, op. 13, Grave	:15

*Artists, record labels, and numbers are available from the author.

Different methods of test administration were used to accommodate the needs of the various age levels. Second- through fourth-grade subjects were tested in groups of 10 to 14 students, first graders in groups of 5, kindergartners in groups of 2, and preschoolers individually. Whenever groups were used, subjects were seated in such a way that they could not see one another's response sheets. Students were instructed that the most important aspect of the test was for them to listen and make their own decisions, and that whatever answers they chose, as long as they were "thinking," would be acceptable. They were also asked to wait until the tape was paused between selections to answer, as suggested by LeBlanc (1984). Although help was provided with the technical aspects of response form use, no ver-

Table 2.2
Test-Retest Reliability: Trial 1 and 2 Pearson Product-Moment Correlation Coefficients and Percentage of Exact Agreements

		Correlations	
Grade	Total test	Fast totals	Slow totals
Preschool	.67	.55	.65
Kindergarten	.61	.53	.39
First	.76	.68	.77
Second	.73	.57	.74
Third	.84	.70	.87
Fourth	.79	.81	.74

bal or facial feedback to the music itself was given by the test administrators because the influence of authority figures on preference has been described earlier. To keep peer interaction at a minimum, students were not allowed to talk during testing and were told that they should be "just like good spies" and not give away their "secret" answers by sound or gesture. Identical procedures were used for the second testing, which occurred 1 week after the first. Students were instructed that they would hear "more" music and were not told that it would be the same. At no time was the word "tempo" or related terminology used by the test administrators.

Results

To compare preference responses, each "face" was assigned a numerical weighting. Smiling, neutral, and frowning ones received scores of 3, 2, and 1, respectively. "Fast scores" will refer to the summed responses to the five fast items, "slow scores" to sums for slow items, and "total scores" to sums across all items.

Test-retest reliability was examined in several ways. Three Pearson product-moment correlations were computed for each grade, comparing individuals' fast, slow, and total scores across the two trials, and are presented in Table 2.2. All correlations were significant at the .01 level, except for "kindergarten/slow," which was significant at the .05 level. A chi-square test was used to check for stability of total scores across both trials by grade level.

The number of subjects whose total scores were higher for the first administration, higher for the second administration, or the same for both administrations were compared, and no significant differences were found ($p > .05$).

For all the following analyses, results from the initial testing session only were used. According to LeBlanc (1979), this probably represents a "more natural sampling of affective behavior" (p. 261) than the retest data.

Total scores for each item were first computed separately for the two different Order of Presentation groups. Two Mann-Whitney U tests, one comparing Orders 1 and 2 using fast item totals for each grade level and the other comparing the two orders using slow item totals, indicated that no significant differences existed between orders ($p > .05$). Because order did not seem to be related to differential responses, both order groups were combined for all further analyses.

As a post hoc control for possible effects due to item length, a Spearman rank correlation comparing total preference rankings to ranked durations was completed. Item duration was not significantly related to preference ranking ($p > .05$).

Of primary interest was the effect of tempo on total preference responses by age levels, and several different approaches were used to examine these variables. The rank order of each piece by total score is presented in Table 2.1. The results of the Spearman rank correlation procedure indicated a significant positive relationship between ranked tempos and item preference totals ($r_s = .81$, $p < .01$). When Spearman rank correlation coefficients were computed to compare ranked tempos and item preference totals for each grade level, significant positive relationships at the .05 level were found for each grade level except kindergarten, which showed a non-significant, negative relationship. Coefficients obtained for each increasing grade level were: P = .66; K = −.34; 1st = .60; 2nd = .66; 3rd = .79; and 4th = .74.

Tempo preferences by age level were compared using a chi-square analysis. For each level, the number of subjects whose scores were either higher for fast items, higher for slow items, or equal for both was recorded. Results of the analysis indicated the presence of significant differences, $\chi^2(10, N = 247) = 47.86$, $p < .001$. Frequencies were converted to percentages for ease of inspection (see Table 2.3). Also found in Table 2.3 is a total preference score for each grade level consisting of the sum of all responses made, and a mean calculated by dividing each total by its n. These scores give some indication of overall attitude toward the music presented. Individual totals ranged from 30, the highest score possible given the test format, to the lowest possible score of 10.

Table 2.3
Frequencies of Preferred Tempo Categories and Overall Total Preference by Grade Level

Grade	Preference for: Fast	Slow (in percent)	No preference	*n*	Overall total	Overall *M*
Pre	47.06	8.82	44.12	34	887	26.09
Kdg	32.43	45.95	21.62	37	923	24.95
1st	33.33	18.18	48.48	33	805	24.40
2nd	44.68	34.04	21.28	47	1,117	23.77
3rd	59.18	10.20	30.61	49	1,135	23.16
4th	76.60	14.89	8.51	47	990	21.06
Total				247	5,857	23.71

Discussion

Test-retest correlations indicate that overall reliability of this measure was adequate and they were in line with reliability figures reported in previous research studies. Results of the chi-square test used to examine stability confirmed that, as a group, subjects did not seem to respond either significantly more positively or more negatively to the second testing. This may be consistent with Schukert and McDonald's (1968) results, though only one repetition was investigated in the present study.

Analyses of both item orders and item length were included as controls. Results indicate they seemed to function this way because no differential effects due to either factor were found.

Both of the main variables under consideration, age and tempo, seemed to affect preference responses. One indication of this was the strong, positive correlation between item ratings and tempo. With only one exception, totals for the fast items were higher than those for the slow items. Although no explanation is available for the one inconsistency, the rating of the highest-ranked slow selection above the lowest-ranked fast selection, this may indicate a piece-specific response rather than a response based on tempo alone.

The tempo/preference relationship was positive and significant at every grade level except for kindergarten. The kindergartners' response pattern seemed to be different from that of the other levels throughout the study, though the same test procedures and instructions were used with them as with the other grade levels. Whether kindergartners actually respond differently from children at other levels or whether their responses merely represent an anomaly of the data or subject selection cannot be explained without further research.

Some fairly definitive conclusions seem apparent from examination of the frequency analysis based on grade levels and preferred tempo categories (presented in Table 2.3). From the data, it may be inferred that the tendency to base preference decisions on tempo discrimination and to prefer fast tempos, which research has shown to be in effect by the fifth grade (LeBlanc & McCrary, 1983), is probably acquired by Grade 4. This is indicated both by the small number of fourth graders who demonstrated no preference, as well as the substantial number who preferred selections with fast tempos. These results support the theory presented by Greer et al. (1974) that a pivotal time in the evolution of musical taste occurs between Grades 3 and 4. Results of the third graders might also indicate that this is a transitional time because, though scores for 30% of these children did not seem to indicate a tempo-based preference, the scores for the remaining children were weighted almost 6:1 in favor of fast tempos.

Results of the four youngest age levels also seem to indicate that some children at all ages were making preference decisions based on tempo discrimination. Responses of second graders seem to be the most evenly spread among categories. Among both the first-grade and preschool groups, substantial percentages of children did not demonstrate a preference, and responses from the majority of those who discriminated fell into the fast category. The kindergartner's tendency to respond differently from the other age groups is again apparent because this is the only level at which the most frequent responses fell in the slow tempo category.

One final result of interest is the overall preference score for each grade level (see Table 2.3). It seems reasonable to interpret these scores as indicators of general attitude toward classical-style piano music. Attitude responses decrease with each successive age level, from the fairly high positive average responses of 4-year-olds to the somewhat neutral average responses of fourth graders. Responses of subjects in this study are consistent with trends reported in the literature reviewed. It is also interesting to note that 34 children (13.8%) responded with all smiling faces, but only 7 (2.8%) chose all frowning faces.

Based on casual observation, subjects seemed to remain on-task and make thoughtful decisions. Although it was anticipated that boredom might influence results of the second testing, this did not seem to be the case, possibly because of the limited number of examples or the children's positive reactions to the answer-sheet format. In general, this testing methodology seemed to work well for children at the age levels that were studied.

Results of preference studies have direct implications for classroom music teachers. As LeBlanc (1981) and LeBlanc and Cote (1983) suggest, in order to increase the probability for student acceptance of new styles or genres of music, it would seem logical to begin with examples that reflect characteristics of music associated with positive affect, such as fast tempos. This might be especially true for students from Grades 4 through 6, who have been shown to respond particularly strongly to this musical element. Research to identify response patterns for other musical characteristics now seems desirable.

Younger children's tendency toward more positive, less-discriminatory responses to music might be capitalized on by teachers desiring to shape preferences. Teacher approval and modeling could be used effectively, as the research indicates. These might be focused on critical points in attitude development, which appear to occur around the third grade. Data indicate that children seem to reach a "plateau" in their ability to make overt musical responses around Grade 3 as well and that the most growth occurs between Grades 1 and 2 (Petzold, 1966). It would seem particularly advisable for research in music education to address the role of the music teacher and curriculum in the development of children's musical abilities and tastes at these important primary grade levels, as well as the possibility that the quality of early music experiences might have long-term effects on musical growth.

These speculations present a variety of possibilities for future research. Further information to help pinpoint factors and timetables affecting children's acquisition of attitudes toward music, as well as exploration of how this knowledge might best be incorporated into music education techniques and curricula, would certainly be of value to the music profession.

3 Effects of Age, Sex, and Activity on Children's Attentiveness in Elementary School Music Classes

Randall S. Moore

Summary

Observation in elementary schools indicated that only 5% mean off-task occurred in music classes. Inattention ranged from 2.7% off-task during instrumental performance to 9.8% off-task in transition periods. There was high correlation of inattentiveness by boys and girls in music classes. The boys were significantly less attentive than girls during singing activities and instruction periods. More than half of the teaching time in general music was spent on only two types of activities, singing and lecture-instruction; and less time was given to discussion, listening, playing instruments, and clapping rhythms.

Music educators may reconsider how teaching time is used by giving equal emphasis to a greater variety of music learning activities. Time spent in playing instruments, discussion with students, listening, especially to teacher modeling, and rhythm exercises might be increased whereas transitions between activities should be kept to a minimum. Although student attentiveness in music classes was reconfirmed to be very high, it appears that boys may need more teacher encouragement to participate in singing and attend to lecture-type instruction.

Design: Posttest only, statistical $N = 977$ Groups: 5
Statistical Analysis: ANOVA, *t*, Pearson product-moment correlation
Reliability: .87, .88, .92
Independent Variables: Age (grades 1-5); sex (boys and girls); classroom activities (seven categories)

Dependent Variables: Attentiveness (boys and girls off-task); use of time in music classes
Music: Performance, listening, discussion, group

* * *

Student attentiveness has long been regarded as an important ingredient in music learning. Observational research has shown that teacher intervention and type of classroom activity can significantly affect student attention.

When teachers use 80% approval and 20% disapproval contingently in music classes, students become more attentive by following classroom rules (Kuhn, 1975). Madsen and Alley (1979) indicated that, when trained educators and therapists use higher frequencies and variety of reinforcement with students and clients, on-task behavior increases. Forsythe (1975) found that elementary children are generally more attentive during music classes than during non-music classes. Yarbrough (1975) discovered that high school and college choral students are more attentive during music activities and respond more favorably to conductors who are highly approving.

Additional studies have arisen from interest in the effects of specific music activities on student responses. Forsythe (1977) observed that children in elementary music classes were least attentive in preparatory, or "getting ready," time and more alert during music performance activities.

Similar findings appeared when a comparison was made of experienced versus intern teachers (Wagner & Strul, 1979) and British and American music educators (Moore, 1981). In university music classes, Madsen and Geringer (1983) replicated the results from public school studies to verify that music performance activities created low off-task behavior, teacher/student verbal interaction caused higher inattentiveness, and "getting ready" moments produced the highest inattention.

Although observational studies continue to demonstrate consistent findings in music classroom behavior, scant information is available that compares attentiveness of boys and girls in music situations. Baker (1980) found that some 8- to 10-year-old boys show different musical preferences than girls the same age. Abeles and Porter (1978) reported on the important role that sex stereotyping of musical instruments has in society and that children select to play an instrument that is oriented psychologically for their gender.

In elective, after-school music programs, one study noted the unbalanced ratio of three girls to every boy who volunteered for a community choir (Moore, 1983). Trends in general education cite the differential treatment that the two sexes receive in the classroom. Sadker and Sadker (1985) contradict the traditional assumption that girls dominate classroom discussion in reading while boys are dominant in math. These two researchers found that boys receive more teacher attention than girls in language arts, English, math, and science.

The purpose of the present study was to observe attentiveness of boys and girls in music classes to determine if any differences exist between genders across various activities and grade levels in elementary schools.

Method

Subjects were 977 children, who were observed for attentiveness in music classes in Grades 1–5. These subjects represented a variety of socio-economic backgrounds across five age groups; 50.7% were boys and 49.3% girls. The 700 minutes of data that came from 140 minutes per grade level across 32 music teachers (31 female) in four school districts represented a cross section of experience from student teachers (23%), first-year teachers (18%), and experienced teachers having more than 5 years experience each (59%).

Observation forms and procedures were patterned after ones developed by Madsen and Madsen (1983). Data were recorded at 20-second intervals on forms that contained spaces for 20-minute observations. Observers scanned the class during each interval and counted the number of boys and girls off-task. The second hand of a clock guided measurements into 15 seconds for observing and 5 seconds for recording. Group activities, teacher reinforcements, and off-task frequencies of both genders were recorded three times per minute.

To investigate off-task levels in relation to class activity, an activity code was devised to facilitate data collection. Observers wrote one code symbol to describe the activity occurring most during the observation interval next to the off-task numbers. Table 3.1 shows the activity codes and definitions used for the seven possible activities.

Two trained observers gathered data on visitations to music classes in elementary schools. To obtain these data, observers told teachers that information was sought concerning children's attentiveness in class. No mention was made of observing differential responses of boys and girls. Reliability between judges was 98% agreement for teacher activities and 88% agreement for student off-task across 20% of classes observed. Observer agreement was computed by dividing total agreements + or −1 by total agreements plus disagreements (Madsen & Yarbrough, 1980).

Results

Data from observations were computed into means across five grade levels and seven activity codes. The mean percentage of class time spent in

Table 3.1
Key to Activity Symbols and Definitions

Symbol	Activity defined
D	Discussion: recitation between student and teacher who asks questions
I	Instruction: lecture by teacher—a teacher-centered activity
S	Singing: moving lips to song text, inhaling deeply, following song from source materials
L	Listening: sitting quietly to hear live or recorded sounds
P	Performance: playing instruments such as recorders or Orff instruments
R	Rhythmic actions: clapping, dancing, or movements to music
G	Getting ready: transition preparations for engaging in a music-related activity

each activity and the corresponding off-task behavior are shown in Table 3.2.

This table shows varying amounts of class time used in each of the activities across the five grades. The general uniformity of how time was spent in each grade is surprising. A consistently larger percentage of time was given to instruction (23%) and singing (32%) than to other activities.

When comparing off-task figures to activities, higher off-task occurred during instruction ($M = 6.7\%$) and singing ($M = 6.3\%$). The highest off-task accumulated during "getting ready" transitions ($M = 9.8\%$), and the amount of time in the activity averaged less than 6% of the total time. It is remarkable that all the off-task amounts are so low (generally less than 10% each). The contrast of off-task amounts between boys and girls reveals that the former appear more inattentive than girls in most instances. In all grades (1–5) boys were consistently responsible for 66% of the off-task behavior compared to 34% for girls.

The music teachers sampled were generally very positive (79% approving) across all student groups and averaged .69 reinforcers per minute. No grade-level differences were noted when comparing rate of reinforcement and approval/disapproval ratios.

The Pearson product-moment correlation between total percent of class time per activity and total percent off-task was not significant ($r = .20$). This finding suggests that length of time spent on activities does not dictate attentiveness in music class, particularly in regard to the small amount of time spent in "getting ready," where the highest off-task occurs. Singing

Table 3.2
Mean Percent of Class-time Activity and Off-task Behavior

Grade			Activity symbol						
			D	I	S	L	P	R	G
1	% CT*		15	25	35	6	3	10	6
	% OT†	Boys	1	6.8	8.3	2.7	2.1	6.3	10.2
		Girls	1.4	2.8	2.5	7	1.6	1.7	4.4
2	% CT		20	23	36	10	3	3	5
	% OT	Boys	4.4	8.2	9.6	3.5	5.2	1.9	13
		Girls	2.8	4.6	4.7	3.7	3.4	0	6.8
3	% CT		15	25	36	7	5	5	7
	% OT	Boys	6	10.3	9.1	1.6	3.6	1.9	20.6
		Girls	2.4	5.1	3	2.3	.1	.9	12.9
4	% CT		15	23	31	13	7	6	5
	% OT	Boys	4.5	8.9	9.6	6.5	4.4	8.3	7.0
		Girls	3.8	5.2	4.8	3.3	2.7	3.6	2.5
5	% CT		19	19	23	17	6	10	6
	% OT	Boys	5.8	9.6	8.7	5.6	2.8	8.2	10.7
		Girls	3	5.6	2.7	7.8	.8	2.6	9.7
M	% CT		16.8	23	32.2	10.6	4.8	6.8	5.8
	% OT	Boys	4.3	8.7	9.1	3.9	3.6	5.3	12.2
		Girls	2.6	4.6	3.5	3.5	1.7	1.7	7.2

*Percent of class time.
†Percent of students engaging in off-task behavior.

consumed more than 30% of class time, but only 6% average off-task behavior. Performance on instruments used less than 5% of time in class, but off-task was held to below 3%.

Analysis of variance comparison of mean percent of class time spent across seven activities produced a significant result: F (6,28) = 17.7, $p < .05$. A subsequent Newman-Keuls test indicated that singing consumed significantly more time than all other activities and that talking about music (discussion and instruction) totaled significantly more time than all other events except singing.

The grade-level variable appeared to have no significant influence on off-task frequencies, F (4,65) < 1. Data suggested that first graders have the lowest off-task and fifth graders the highest.

Results of an analysis of variance indicate significant differences in off-task behavior across seven activities, F (6,56) = 11.3, $p < .05$. The Newman–Keuls comparison showed that inattentiveness during the "getting ready" category was significantly higher than all other activities. Off-task behavior was significantly greater during singing and instruction than all other activities except transition periods. Following a significant F ratio, F (1,56) = 31, $p < .05$, between boys' and girls' attentiveness, subsequent t tests revealed that boys displayed higher rates of off-task in singing, t (4) = 5.27, $p < .05$, and instruction time, t (4) = 9.84, $p < .05$. During the rest of the music class time, no other significant differences in gender attentiveness appeared. A positive correlation ($r = .87$) existed between boys and girls in off-task behavior across all seven classroom activities.

Discussion

Results of this study reconfirm findings in previous research in regard to the use of teaching time in music as well as the amounts and sources of off-task behavior by music students. Unique findings of this investigation reveal differences in the responsiveness of boys and girls to various music activities. Boys appear to pay significantly less attention than girls during instruction and singing activities. Inattentiveness by boys and girls in music classes has a high correlation ($r = .87$); the continuum goes from 2.7% off-task during instrumental performance to 9.8% off-task during transition periods. The implication for music educators would be to curtail transition periods as much as possible and increase time spent in a wider variety of music activities.

Evidence is needed in the area of inattentiveness in singing and actual singing ability. To assume that inattentive boys do not sing as well as girls is probably ill-advised. Perhaps cultural expectancies are greater forces that control social and academic behavior in the classroom than individual abilities. Research needs to be done to compare inattention and achievement levels in music.

4 The Effect of Written Descriptions on Memory of Fifth Graders and Undergraduates for Orchestral Excerpts

Patricia J. Flowers

Summary

Both fifth graders and undergraduates were able to identify whether or not they had heard given orchestral excerpts significantly beyond guessing. Although undergraduates were better than fifth graders in identifying which excerpts they *had* heard, no difference was shown between grades in identifying new excerpts. Extramusical descriptions facilitated correct identification of new excerpts better than timbre description or listening-only conditions for both fifth graders and undergraduates. It was noted that, when the undergraduates used consistent extramusical labels for repeated excerpts, more correct identifications were made than when different descriptions were given.

Positive effects of consistently using unique descriptive labels have been noted in discrimination and/or recognition of various non-verbal events. This study replicates much previous research by using distinctive labels to aid memory for orchestral excerpts. Continued research might isolate variables that could account for differences in identification of new versus repeated stimuli, investigate strategies for identifying themes or motifs presented in musical context, or suggest ways of stimulating uniqueness and consistency of description, especially for younger students.

Design: Statistical (3 × 2) $N = 330$ Groups: 6
Statistical Analysis: *t* tests, ANOVA, chi-square
Independent Variables: Listening task: extramusical description, timbre description, listening only; Grade: undergraduate, fifth grade

Dependent Variable: Correct identification of orchestral excerpts heard one week previously (new/repeated excerpts)
Music: Listening, group

* * *

Memory of musical material is important to performing musicians as well as listeners. Awareness of changes in music—such as modulation, attention to repetition, and contrast of various musical elements—all require some degree of musical memory. Therefore, finding means of facilitating this memory seems to have practical applications as well as theoretical value.

The effect of verbalization on perception or memory of non-verbal events has received much attention in diverse areas of investigation. A substantial relationship between codability and recognition of colors has been noted; many subjects indicated that they named initially presented colors, then "stored" the names to facilitate subsequent recognition (Brown & Lennenberg, 1954). Distinctive labels have been found to facilitate discrimination learning in recognition of faces, colors, and shapes (Katz, 1963; Katz, 1973; Katz, Albert, & Atkins, 1971; Katz & Seavey, 1973; Katz & Zigler, 1969; Norcross, 1958; Norcross & Spiker, 1957; Spiker, 1963; Spiker & Norcross, 1962). Verbal labels are thought to encode perceptual stimuli by encouraging attention to distinctive features (Ellis, 1978, p. 217). Thus, distinctive labels often aid memory, and common labels tend to make stimuli less recognizable.

Some studies that have specifically investigated the effect of verbal labels on memory for naturalistic sounds have found that consistent labeling on input and recognition tasks is of value in accurately identifying targeted sounds at 5-minute and 7-day retention intervals (Bartlett, 1977; Bower & Holyoak, 1973; Lawrence, 1979). Other studies have investigated encoding tasks in a musical context. In one series of experiments, Beethoven string quartet movements were used as stimulus material, and subjects were instructed to attend to a visual representation of melodic contour and/or rhythm pattern, estimate stimulus duration, choose descriptive words from a verbal checklist, or write brief descriptive phrases of affective image. In general, the visual encoding processes were most effective in promoting recognition of excerpts from these quartets; description of affective image, least effective (Dowling & Bartlett, 1981). Further, this study found that subjects responded more frequently to targeted items than related (similar) items in this musical context. Subjects were not lured by excerpts similar in melodic contour, rhythm pattern, instrumental texture, tempo, and meter. Madsen and Staum (1983) also found that non-music majors were generally able to recognize targeted melodies in a series of similar melodies that had been altered only in meter or mode. These studies have suggested that results may differ between tasks involving isolated pitches and those presenting complete musical statements.

Various written or visual tasks have been developed as a means of focusing attention on elements of music for teaching discrimination, facilitating memory, or increasing preference (Mueller, 1956; Reimer, 1967; Thompson, 1972). However, it has been suggested that attention to non-music tasks may actually draw attention away from the listening that it is intended to enhance (Geringer & Nelson, 1980). Although one study found that visual and written guides assisted fourth and fifth graders in identifying title and composer of orchestral excerpts more than listening-only (Kostka, 1984b), additional investigation seems to be needed in this area.

The purpose of this study was to investigate the effects of written descriptions or listening on fifth graders' and undergraduates' abilities to recognize orchestral excerpts when 1 week intervened between initial hearing and posttest. Extramusical descriptions were intended to be "distinctive," that is, unique for each excerpt. It was expected that timbre descriptions would often be similar because all excerpts were performed by an orchestra or combination of orchestral instruments. A listening-only group was included to allow comparison of subjects who were able to give maximum attention to the music itself with subjects who wrote extramusical or timbre descriptions. Specific research questions were: (1) Will fifth graders and undergraduates score significantly different from chance in remembering orchestral excerpts played 1 week after an initial hearing?; (2) Will a difference exist between new and repeated excerpts in students' ability to identify correctly whether or not they were played 1 week previously?; (3) Will fifth graders and undergraduates differ in their ability to identify new or repeated excerpts?; (4) Will there be any difference due to listening task on ability of students to identify new or repeated excerpts?; and (5) Will consistency of written descriptions between first listening and posttest facilitate memory of repeated excerpts?

Method

Some 180 fifth graders and 150 undergraduate non-music majors participated in this study (N = 330). The fifth graders comprised the fifth-grade enrollment at three suburban elementary schools. Each school had a full-time music teacher, and the children received music instruction at least two times per week. The undergraduate subjects were non-music majors attending a state university who were enrolled in music appreciation, music fundamentals, or music methods classes.

Musical materials consisted of 30 excerpts selected from the repertoire for full orchestra or smaller ensembles of orchestral instruments. These pieces were selected because they were assumed to be unfamiliar to most non-musicians; because they represented a diversity of timbres, styles, tempi, and modes; and because short excerpts could be isolated that concisely presented thematic material from the larger work. Students indicating familiarity with any of the chosen excerpts were dropped from the study. The length of excerpts ranged from 14 to 28 seconds and generally consisted of a complete melodic or harmonic statement. From these 30 excerpts, 20 were randomly chosen and ordered for the initial listening task. Of these 20 excerpts, 10 were randomly designated for repetition on the posttest with the 10 remaining excerpts. Thus, two tapes were prepared, each containing 20 orchestral excerpts and having 10 of these excerpts in common. These excerpts and their order of presentation are shown in Table 4.1.

Students were randomly assigned to one of three listening tasks so that each group consisted of 110 subjects (60 fifth graders and 50 undergraduates). During the initial listening task, the extramusical description group was instructed to listen to each excerpt and write a short extramusical description of the music, such as an analogy, feeling, or image that the music brought to mind. The timbre description group was asked to write a description of the timbre, such as the name of the ensemble, predominant family of instruments, or solo instrument. The listening-only group was simply told to listen to and concentrate on the music. This group had no written task, and no more specific listening instructions were given. All listening tasks were completed in groups of between 10 and 25 students. Subjects were informed that a follow-up lesson would occur the next week. However, they were not told that they would be asked to remember what they had heard.

One week after the initial listening session, subjects were played the second tape, which contained 10 repeated excerpts and 10 new excerpts. They were asked to follow the same listening procedures as in the previous week: write extramusical descriptions, write timbre descriptions, or simply listen. In addition, they were instructed to write "Yes" if they thought they had heard an excerpt in the first listening session, or write "No" if they had not heard it. Subjects were encouraged to write "Yes" or "No" for every excerpt.

At the conclusion of the posttest, papers were collected and checked for completeness. Subjects whose papers contained omissions were dropped from the study. The number of correct and incorrect identifications were counted for new ("No") and repeated ("Yes") excerpts. Further, written descriptions by extramusical and timbre description groups were compared for consistency of descriptors between initial listening and posttest on repeated excerpts.

Table 4.1
Sources of Excerpts and Order of Presentation

	Initial Listening		Posttest
1.	Poulenc, *The Model Animals,* "Death and the Woodman"	1.	Vivaldi, *Concerto in G for Flute, Strings, & Continuo,* 1st movement
2.	Saint-Saens, *Cello Concerto no. 1,* 2nd movement	2.	Saint-Saens, *Cello Concerto no. 1,* 2nd movement
3.	Beethoven, *Violin Concerto,* 1st movement	3.	Stravinsky, *Pastorale*
4.	Vivaldi, *Concerto in G for Flute, Strings, & Continuo,* 1st movement	4.	Poulenc, *The Model Animals,* "Death and the Woodman"
5.	Vaughn Williams, *Concerto for Tuba,* 1st movement	5.	Schubert, *Symphony no. 5,* 2nd movement
6.	Dvorak, *New World Symphony,* 2nd movement	6.	Bruckner, *Symphony no. 4,* 1st movement
7.	Janacek, *Taras Bulba,* "The Death of Ostap"	7.	Corelli, *Concerto Grosso no. 8 in G Minor,* 1st movement
8.	Beethoven, *Quartet in F,* op. 135, 1st movement	8.	Mozart, *Divertimento no. 2 in D Major,* 5th movement
9.	Sibelius, *Violin Concerto,* 2nd movement	9.	Prokofiev, *Alexander Nevsky,* "Russia Under the Mongolian Yoke"
10.	Mozart, *Clarinet Concerto,* 1st movement	10.	Poulenc, *Concert Champetre for Harpsichord and Orchestra*
11.	Corelli, *Concerto Grosso no. 8 in G Minor,* 1st movement	11.	Elgar, *Cello Concerto,* 4th movement
12.	Giuliani, *Guitar Concerto,* op. 30, 3rd movement	12.	Vaughn Williams, *Concerto for Tuba,* 1st movement
13.	Lajtha, *Symphony no. 4,* op. 52, 3rd movement	13.	Beethoven, *Violin Concerto,* 1st movement
14.	Prokofiev, *Lieutenant Kije Suite,* "Troika"	14.	Tedesco, *Concertino for Harp,* op. 93, 2nd movement
15.	Stravinsky, *Pulcinella,* (11. Allegro)	15.	Vivaldi, *Concerto no. 9 in D Minor* (oboe & strings), 3rd movement

16.	Elgar, *Cello Concerto*, 4th movement	16.	Schubert, *Symphony no.* 5, 2nd movement
17.	Bach, *Brandenburg Concerto no.* 2, 1st movement	17.	Nielsen, *Woodwind Quintet*
18.	Schubert, *Symphony no.* 5, 3rd movement	18.	Beethoven, *Quartet in F*, op. 135, 1st movement
19.	Rossini, *La Scala di Seta*	19.	Lajtha, *Symphony no. 4*, op. 52, 3rd movement
20.	Elgar, *Serenade in E Minor*, op. 20	20.	Beethoven, *Piano Concerto no. 4*, 2nd movement

Results

Prior to making comparisons based on grade level or listening task, the total number of correct answers on the 20 posttest excerpts was assessed for each subject and mean scores for each group were compared by t tests to a chance score of 10. It was found that all groups scored significantly above chance in identifying new and repeated excerpts. Mean total scores and standard deviations are presented in Table 4.2.

It was of further interest to determine whether a difference existed in correct identification between new and repeated excerpts. Dependent t tests were computed for each group, and it was found that fifth graders responded significantly more correctly on new than on repeated excerpts (listening-only: t (59) = 4.90, $p < .001$; timbre description: t (59) = 4.66, $p < .001$; extramusical description: t (59) = 5.76, $p < .001$). Undergraduates writing extramusical descriptions were also more correct in identification of new over repeated excerpts, t (49) = 2.22, $p < .05$. However, no significant difference was noted for undergraduates in listening-only or timbre-description conditions, t (49) = .80; t (49) = .94, respectively. Because all fifth-grade groups as well as the undergraduate extramusical description group were significantly more correct in identifying what they had *not* heard than what they had heard, all subsequent group comparisons were made separately for new and repeated excerpts.

Analyses of variance compared grade level (fifth graders and undergraduates) and listening task (extramusical description, timbre description, and listening-only) for new and repeated excerpts. On the 10 repeated excerpts, a significant difference was found for grade level, F (1, 324) = 27.08, $p < .01$; the undergraduates gave more correct answers than fifth graders. There was no significant difference due to listening task, nor was there a sig-

Table 4.2
Correct Identification of Total Posttest Excerpts

	Listening-only		Timbre description		Extramusical description	
	Undergraduates	Fifth graders	Undergraduates	Fifth graders	Undergraduates	Fifth graders
M	14.26*	13.57*	14.18*	13.20*	15.38*	14.37*
s	2.07	2.62	2.73	2.40	2.33	2.05
n	50	60	50	60	50	60

* ($p < .001$).

Table 4.3
Correct Identification of Repeated Excerpts on Posttest

		Listening-only	Timbre description	Extramusical description	Total
Undergraduates	*M*	6.98	6.84	7.34	7.05*
	s	1.70	2.19	1.67	1.87
	n	50	50	50	150
Fifth graders	*M*	6.10	5.70	6.15	5.98
	s	1.64	1.96	1.94	1.85
	n	60	60	60	180
Total	*M*	6.50	6.22	6.69	6.47
	s	1.72	2.13	1.91	1.93
	n	110	110	110	330

*Undergraduates scored significantly higher than fifth graders.

nificant grade × listening task interaction. Mean correct scores and standard deviations for repeated excerpts on the posttest are presented in Table 4.3.

Analysis of responses to new excerpts on the posttest revealed no significant differences due to grade level or grade × listening task. A significant difference was found due to listening task on new posttest excerpts, $F\ (2, 324) = 6.01$, $p < .01$. Subsequent comparisons of group means (undergraduates plus fifth graders) showed that students writing extramusical descriptions were significantly more correct than those under listening-only conditions, $t\ (324) = 2.19$, $p < .05$, or timbre description, $t\ (324) = 2.05$, $p < .05$. There was no significant difference between listening-only and timbre-description groups, $t\ (324) = .14$. Means and standard deviations for correct scores on new posttest excerpts are presented in Table 4.4.

A final consideration was whether students were more often correct when they gave consistent descriptions on the initial listening task and the posttest than when they gave different descriptions for the same excerpt. A 2 × 2 contingency table was produced for each description group on consistent/inconsistent description and correct/incorrect identification for the 10 repeated excerpts. Computation of chi-square analyses revealed a significant relationship between correctness and consistency of description for the un-

Table 4.4
Correct Identification of New Excerpts on Posttest

		Listening-only	Timbre description	Extramusical description	Total
Undergraduates	*M*	7.28	7.34	8.04	7.55
	s	1.65	2.44	1.55	1.94
	n	50	50	50	150
Fifth graders	*M*	7.47	7.50	8.22	7.73
	s	1.75	1.87	1.49	1.83
	n	60	60	60	180
Total	*M*	7.38	7.43	8.14*	7.65
	s	1.70	2.14	1.51	1.83
	n	110	110	110	330

*Extramusical-description group scored significantly higher than listening-only or timbre-description groups.

dergraduate extramusical description group, χ^2 (1, N = 50) = 21.82, $p < .001$. More correct responses were made than would have been expected when consistent descriptions were given; conversely, more incorrect responses occurred than would have been expected when different descriptions were given for repeated excerpts. No significant differences existed at the .05 level for any other group of undergraduates or fifth graders who produced written descriptions.

Discussion

The memory task presented to subjects in this study did not at first appear to be an easy one: listen to orchestral excerpts one time only, then identify these excerpts from a series of somewhat similar excerpts 1 week later. Some subjects expressed uncertainty when presented with the posttest listening task and undoubtedly guessed on excerpts for which they were unsure. However, both fifth graders and undergraduates were able to identify whether or not they had heard given excerpts significantly beyond guessing. This corroborates previous research, which found that even unsophisticated listeners seem to possess good ability to remember musical stimuli.

It is interesting that all fifth-grade groups and the undergraduate extramusical group were significantly better at identifying new over repeated excerpts; that is, they were better able to say "No" to what they had not heard than "Yes" to what they had heard. Possibly, the subjects forgot some of the repeated excerpts, but were not lured by the new excerpts on the posttest, resulting in more "No" than "Yes" responses. Perhaps subjects had a propensity to say "No" when unsure, thus increasing the opportunities for being correct on new excerpts. This is speculative, however, and future research might address degree of certainty and differences in distinguishing new from repeated excerpts.

When comparisons were made on repeated excerpts, it was found that undergraduates were better able to remember what they had heard than fifth graders and that none of the listening tasks seemed to effect remembering better than others. However, no significant difference existed between undergraduates and fifth graders on *new* posttest excerpts. In fact, fifth graders scored somewhat higher than undergraduates, though this was not significant.

In comparing listening tasks, it was noted that the extramusical description groups performed better at each grade level on both new and repeated excerpts. However, significant differences occurred due to listening condition only on new excerpts. It seems that extramusical descriptions may help subjects determine what they have *not* heard more than what they *have* heard. No significant differences existed between timbre-description and listening-only groups, which indicates that writing descriptions did not focus attention away from the music more than simply listening. It was observed that greater variance occurred under timbre-description conditions. Perhaps these timbre descriptions, which were often similar among many different excerpts, helped some students and hindered others, which resulted in a greater spread of scores.

In comparing consistent/inconsistent descriptions and correct/incorrect identifications, no relationship was found between correctness and consistency of descriptors for the timbre-description group. However, for the undergraduates, producing the same extramusical descriptions on initial hearing and posttest for repeated excerpts resulted in more correct responses. Perhaps this is attributable to the relative uniqueness of descriptions for each excerpt compared to the overall similarity of descriptions produced by subjects in the timbre-description group. It seems that older subjects may be more consistent than fifth graders in applying distinctive descriptions to repeated excerpts and that, when this is the case, they are more accurate in making correct identifications.

In summary, it was found that most subjects identified what they had not heard better than they remembered what they had heard; older students remembered better than fifth graders; there was a tendency for extramusical description to facilitate memory, especially in identification of new excerpts and when labels were used consistently; and writing similar descriptions for many different excerpts (timbre description) tended to produce greater variance than listening-only or extramusical description. These data corroborate previous studies suggesting that musical stimuli presented in gestalt are memorable even to subjects not trained in music and that distinctive labels may facilitate memory when used consistently.

Future research might consider the effect of uncertainty on subjects' responses, isolate variables that could account for differences in identification of new versus repeated stimuli, investigate strategies for identifying themes or motifs presented in musical context, and suggest ways of stimulating uniqueness and consistency of description, especially for younger students.

5 The Use of Behavioral Contracts In Music Instruction

David E. Wolfe

Summary

This study examined the use of contingency contracts in private piano instruction to assist students in improving daily practice. Two female students, 9 and 10 years old, and one male student, 9 years old, participated in the project. An individual contract was prepared for each of the participating students. A multiple baseline design across subjects was implemented to assess the effect of the use of contracts on practice behavior. Results showed that, during the contract condition, the amount of daily practice time per week was increased by each student as compared to baseline figures. Follow-up data were collected 4 months following termination of the contracts.

The use of contingency contracting can help the private studio instructor identify instructional objectives, individualize teaching programs, and develop a systematic process for assessing and rewarding student progress. These components of teaching seem essential in stimulating maximum student output as well as encouraging regular and consistent music achievement.

Design: Single subject—multiple baseline $N = 3$
Graphic Analysis: Average number of minutes practiced per week
Independent Variable: Behavioral contracts
Dependent Variable: Practice behavior: average number of minutes practiced per week
Music: Performance, individual

* * *

The use of behavioral, or contingency, contracts in education and therapy is certainly not new. These contracts have been systematically employed in motivation management of human behavior for the past 50 years by numerous professionals: classroom teachers, social workers, physical fitness personnel, marriage counselors, and special educators, to name just a few. However, there seems to be a paucity of reported applications of their use in music environments.

A contingency contract is an agreement written between two or more persons (e.g., teacher and student, therapist and client) that states behaviors the involved parties will perform and the consequences that will result. The document clearly specifies behaviors and rewards (Hall & Hall, 1982). Rationale for the use of contracting assumes that persons may be more willing to learn or change their behavior if the *what* and *how* of learning have been mutually agreed upon by the student or client and the teacher or therapist. This rationale is founded on the expectancy theory of motivation, which states that, if students know what is expected from them and want to do it, they probably will (DiSilvestro & Markowitz, 1982; Madsen & Madsen, 1983; Polczynski & Shirland, 1977). In other words, when given a desired objective and a clear understanding of how to meet it, the person will become motivated to strive to reach it. The use of contracts also seems to: assist in clarifying objectives; provide for individualization; permit student self-evaluation; stimulate cooperation or negotiation between student and teacher; and facilitate assessment of student or client progress (Quinto & McKenna, 1977; Riegle, 1978).

The literature is replete with descriptive and experimental studies detailing the various applications of contingency contracting. Contracts have been used in high school and college classes to encourage students to complete course requirements. Various courses in nursing (Kruse & Barger, 1982; Lord & Palmer, 1982; Paduano, 1979; Schoolcraft & Delaney, 1982), health education (Sutherland, 1982; Wilson & Eisenhauer, 1982), writing skills and public relations (Leahy, 1980; Stephens & Motes, 1980), physiology (Burkett & Darst, 1979), and business (Polczynski & Shirland, 1977) have incorporated agreements between students and teachers to foster course-requirement completion and improvement in academic grades. Contingency contracts have also been successfully used in classroom situations to increase appropriate on-task behaviors (Arwood, Williams, & Long, 1974; Ciminillo, 1980; Smaby & Tamminen, 1981) and to improve productive work and study habits (Goldman, 1978; Kelley & Stokes, 1982).

Written agreements between participants and instructors have been employed in the area of physical fitness. Bonanno, Dougherty, and Feigley (1978) as well as Mather, Nixon, and Corbet (1978) used contracts to increase individualized programs of physical activities. Courses in tumbling and aerobic exercising have used written documents to assist participants in self-improvement (Wysocki, Hall, Iwata, & Riordan, 1979; Youngberg & Jones, 1980). Weight-reduction programs have also routinely employed contracts with clients (Mann, 1972; Ross, 1976; Vance, 1976).

Other areas of application are in the professional fields of social work, counseling, special education, and therapy. Social service settings have used contracts to improve family interaction (Framer & Sanders, 1980; Jones, Magura, & Shyne, 1981; Patterson, 1971; Saxon, 1979; Stuart, 1971), to resolve conflicts between spouses (Jacobson, 1977; Weiss, Birchler, & Vincent, 1974), and as a method of intervention with abusive mothers (Wolfe, 1981). Educators have relied on contracts to assist special-needs students in achieving self-determination and work experiences (McCadden & Despard, 1980; Munro, 1981). Various therapy professionals have also employed agreements in drug-addiction programs (Hall, Cooper, Burmaster, & Polk, 1977), group psychotherapy settings (Corder, Haizlip, Whiteside, & Vogel, 1980), and foster homes (Upper, Lochman, & Aveni, 1977). Other uses of contracts have been noted in counseling environments (Cochran, 1980), independent study courses (DiSilvestro & Markowitz, 1982; Worby, 1979), and practicum situations with student teachers (Lux, 1979; Rose, Koorland, Lessen, & Reid, 1978).

Few articles have reported the use of contingency contracts in music instruction, but they have suggested positive results (Obenshain, 1980; Spradling, 1979; Wolfe, 1984). Based on the limited employment of this well-founded process in the area of music to motivate individuals toward constructive change, this study examines the use of well-constructed contracts in private piano instruction to assist students in improving daily practice.

Method

Subjects

Two female students, 9 and 10 years old, and one male student, 9 years old, participated in the study. All three were enrolled in a university-affiliated Youth Conservatory. Two of the students had taken private piano instruction for 1.5 and 4 years, respectively, and were considered by their instructor to be "beginning intermediate" pianists. The remaining student had received 3 years of private piano instruction and was judged to be an "advanced beginner." Because the private instructor was concerned with having the students practice more consistently, as well as increase the amount of time practiced daily, these particular students were selected for the study. Parental consent was obtained for each student, and the parents agreed to monitor the daily practice.

Preceding the experimental phase of the project, the instructor, along with each student, prepared a "reinforcement menu" (see Wolfe, 1984), consisting of items to be used as rewards. They included: school supplies, such as pencils and rulers, posters, sticker collections, and gift certificates to McDonald's.

Contract Construction

An individual contract was prepared for each of the participating students. Components of the contracts consisted of a goal; practice routine for the student to follow; practice requirements; and benefits to be received when conditions of the contract were met. The terms of the contract were discussed between teacher and student, and, during those initial negotiations, both of them were able to suggest appropriate conditions and rewards. When terms were agreed upon, the contracts were signed by student and teacher and were sent home for parents to sign. For a more detailed description of contract construction, see Wolfe (1984).

Individual Criteria

Contract conditions for each student were unique. Conditions for Student 1 stipulated that she practice at least 1 hour for 6 out of 7 weekdays and record the exact amount of time spent daily. The contract also stated that, during the daily practice, she should memorize music for at least 10 minutes (following a teacher-constructed memorizing process). At the weekly studio lesson, she was also required to perform four sightreading pieces with correct fingerings, counting, and notes (no mistakes). The private instructor was responsible for judging the accuracy of the performance requirement.

Student 2 was requested to practice a minimum of 1 hour 45 minutes for 5 out of 7 weekdays, and to record the exact amount of time involved. In addition to the practice-time requirement, this particular student was to identify and write at the top of each new piece of music the key signature and period of music in which the piece was composed, as well as to pencil in the measure numbers throughout each piece. Musical terms that appeared in each new selection were also to be defined and written in the music. The instructor carefully checked during each weekly lesson to determine that all these items were completed.

Conditions for Student 3 stated that he was to practice at least 1 hour for

5 out of 7 weekdays and to record the exact amount of time expended. The terms included in the contract also requested that he practice the first 15 minutes of each daily session on finger technique. At the weekly studio lesson, he was to perform at least one assigned piece of music (chosen by the instructor) and make no more than two mistakes related to notes, rhythm, and dynamics. The instructor judged and scored the accuracy of the performance. It can be noted from reviewing the above criteria that the conditions of the contracts not only emphasized the quantity of time practiced, but were also concerned with addressing the problem of the quality of time spent at the piano.

Experimental Design

A multiple baseline design across subjects (Hall, 1974; Hersen & Barlow, 1982) was implemented to assess the effect of the use of contracts on practice behavior. During baseline conditions, concurrent recordings were made of the same behavior (practice time) across the three students. The experimental condition (contract usage) was begun, with Student 1, following an initial 2 weeks of baseline. The contract condition was then successively applied to Student 2 after 3 weeks and Student 3 after 4 weeks of baseline recording.

Procedures

Each student was to record the exact amount of time spent in practice each day. Parents of each child agreed to make certain that recorded practice time was accurate by signing the weekly practice record. This record was then reviewed with the private piano instructor at the weekly lesson, and the instructor was responsible for judging the remainder of the conditions of the contract ("quality" items) following the student's performance during the lesson. When practice conditions of the contract were met, the instructor gave the student an agreed-upon reward. An additional reward could also be obtained by the student when the "quality" criteria were reached. This routine was followed each week by the private instructor throughout the experimental condition for each student.

Results

An examination of the graphed data (Figure 5.1), as well as the figures in Table 5.1, show that Student 1 averaged 55 minutes daily of piano practice

Figure 5.1
Average Daily Practice Time per Week, in Minutes

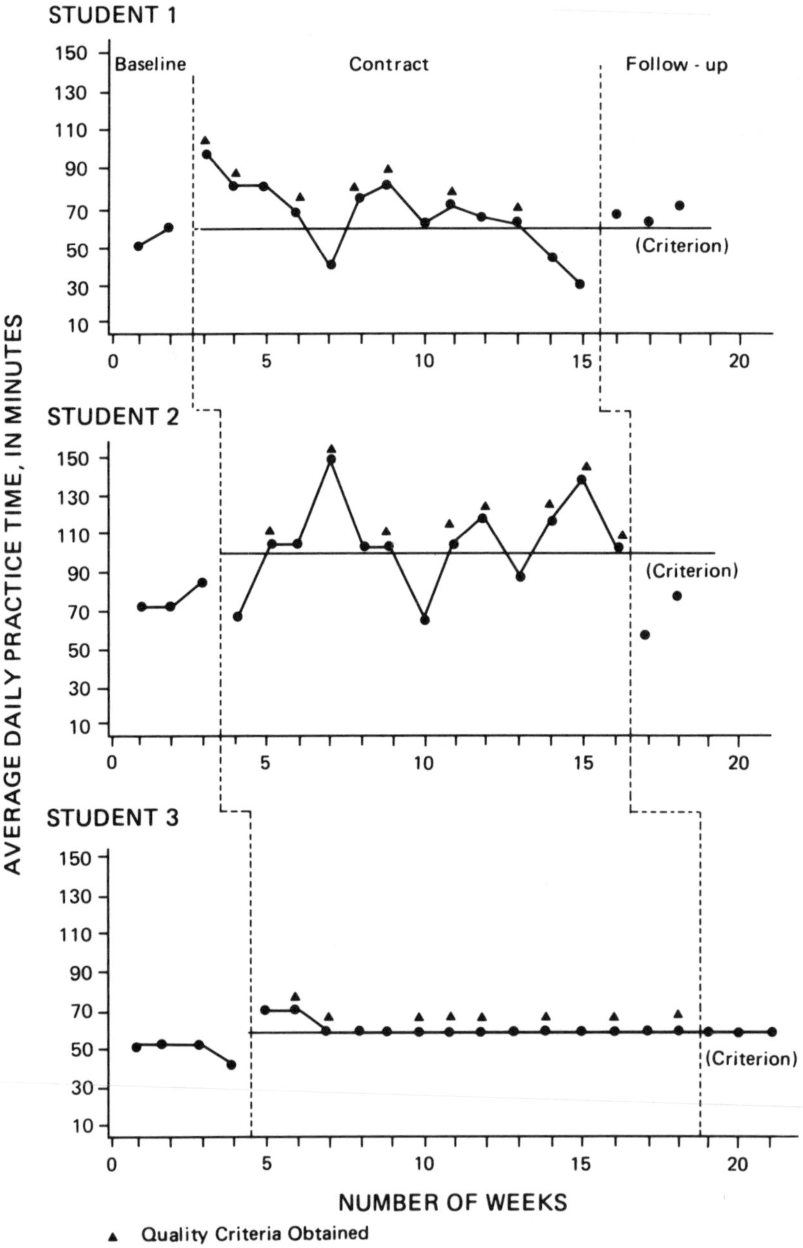

Table 5.1
Average Daily Practice Time, in Minutes

	Baseline condition	Contract condition	Follow-up
Student 1	55.41	67.81 (60*)	67.27
Student 2	76.00	109.23 (105*)	70.60
Student 3	49.75	61.75 (60*)	60.00

*Criterion

per week during the baseline and 68 minutes during the contract condition. Baseline average for Student 2 was 76 minutes, and, during the contract period, it increased to an average per week of 109 minutes of daily practice. Figures for Student 3 show an average of 50 minutes during baseline and 62 minutes of practice recorded during the use of the contract.

Number of weeks in which the students met individual performance criterion ("quality" variable) during the contract condition were: 7 out of 13 weeks (54%) for Student 1; 8 out of 13 weeks (62%) for Student 2; and 8 out of 14 weeks (57%) for Student 3. Follow-up data were collected on each student's practice time 4 months following the termination of use of the contingency contracts. Average daily practice time per week during the follow-up for each student was: 67.27 (Student 1); 70.60 (Student 2); and 60.00 (Student 3).

Discussion

It would appear from reviewing the graphed data (Figure 5.1) and the supporting figures contained in Table 5.1 that each student, during the contingency contract condition, did increase the amount of daily practice time each week, and all were fairly consistent in meeting the stated practice criterion. For the weeks during which this particular criterion was not met for Students 1 and 2, it was noted in the practice schedule that the student either was physically ill during a portion of the week or was reported to be out-of-town with family members. Judging from the number of asterisks scattered throughout the contract phase, students reached their individual performance requirements (quality criteria) during the majority of weeks. It should be noted, after reading the performance requirements of Students 1 and 3, that these criteria permitted few performance mistakes. Based on these high expectations, the frequency of reaching these performance objectives may be considered adequate.

The follow-up period of this study occurred 4 months after terminating the use of the contracts. Judging from the data points for Students 1 and 3, practice criterion continued to be reached without use of the structured contract and the associated rewards previously gained during the project. A decrease can be noted in the follow-up data for Student 2. However, an uncontrolled variable would seem to have influenced the results. Parents of this particular student requested that the amount of her daily piano practice be reduced because she not only was involved in private piano instruction, but also was taking ballet lessons, was a regular and avid skier, and was involved in numerous other school and church activities. The follow-up data reflect the parents' request.

It would seem that use of contingency contracting in music instruction has unlimited potential in assisting the private studio instructor in identifying instructional objectives, individualizing teaching programs, structuring and providing for student rewards, and in developing a systematic process of assessing student progress. These components of teaching seem essential in fostering maximum student output as well as encouraging regular and consistent music achievement. Because few investigations have been made in this particular area, research into various aspects of contingency contracting remain to be conducted. Only through careful examination of the processes of contracting can the most productive methods of utilization in music instruction be obtained.

The author extends his appreciation to Laura G. Zisette and her Utah State University Youth Conservatory students for participating in this study.

6 The Effect of Three Evaluation Procedures on the Rehearsal Achievement of Eighth-Grade Band Students

William Zurcher

Summary

Achievement was significantly higher ($p < .05$) when students recorded their own daily numerical grades (A) than when they received no feedback (B). Daily numerical grades (A) also resulted in significantly higher achievement ($p < .001$) than daily teacher-issued letter grades (C).

This study indicates that daily teacher-issued letter grades are not specific enough to change behavior. Because so many grading systems utilize letter grades, further research is urged in music and other subject areas to structure task-specific measuring systems.

Design: Withdrawal (ABCA) $N = 63$ Groups: 1
Statistical Analysis: Correlated t tests (two-tailed), Pearson product-moment
Interobserver Reliability of Student Entries: .98
Independent Variables: A. Student-recorded/teacher verified daily numerical grades; B. No feedback; C. Teacher-issued daily letter grades.
Dependent Variable: Grade means (0–100)
Music: Performance, group

* * *

Periodic attention has been given in various state and national music educators' magazines to the problem of grading instrumental musicians in an objective manner. However, all these articles have used a letter-grading system that is determined, for the most part, by the completion (or noncompletion) of certain music projects or tasks by the end of the marking period (Bibzak, 1975; Ross, 1975). No articles are known to have addressed the possibility of determining achievement on a daily basis. Behavior analysis research, on the other hand, has yielded a large body of evidence which shows that evaluations can be made not only on a daily basis, but also moment by moment. In numerous studies, significant differences in achievement have been shown between periods in which a token economy is in effect and periods in which no feedback is given. Less attention, however, has been given to converting token economies into letter grades.

Greer (1980) devised a self-recording Personalized System of Instruction (PSI) that can be used to determine grades. Zurcher and Greer (1980) showed that such a system could change behavior in a junior high school band. However, no study is known to have investigated whether differences exist between daily student-recorded credits and daily teacher-issued letter grades or between no feedback and daily teacher-issued letter grades.

Ross (1975) has outlined some of the problems associated with the grading of instrumental students. After pointing out the unfairness of determining grades on a single measurement, such as a test or tryout, he lists some of the typical grading systems in current use: issuing all "A"s (to encourage students to continue in the organization); grading according to where a student sits ("A" for first chair, "B" for second chair, "C" for all others); and objective point systems (which Ross believes are often too complex and confining). Ross urges a grading method where everyone, as a starting point, receives a "C" by completing five basic attendance and performance steps. A grade of "B" is earned by finishing an additional three (out of ten) steps; and a grade of "A," another three (out of fourteen) tasks.

Bibzak (1975) suggests three possible grading methods: a *checkoff system,* in which every student begins with an "F" and works up to the desired grade (or a second version, which Bibzak believes is "considerably more optimistic," in which each student begins with an "A" and falls lower for each task not completed); a *blanket system,* where every student receives a "B," but can do something extra to earn an "A"; or a *contract method,* in which the student signs a contract to complete a certain number of tasks to earn the desired grade.

Because the present study compared student-recorded/teacher-verified credits to no feedback and to daily teacher-issued letter grades, a brief review of literature in the area of student-recording is in order. Glynn, Thomas, & Shee (1973) employed self-control techniques in a class where a high level of on-task behavior had already been established using externally administered reinforcement procedures. The study determined that second graders, using self-control techniques, maintained high levels of on-task behavior previously established. The study offered a conceptual base for the analysis of self-control: self-assessment, self-recording, self-determination of reinforcement, and self-administration of reinforcement. However, the study did not determine the accuracy of student record-keeping in detail. The investigators report that the procedures functioned because student accuracy was sufficiently reinforced by verbal comments of both the teacher and pupils. In a later study, Ballard & Glynn (1975) substantially increased rates of responding in storywriting by adding self-determined and self-administered reinforcement to self-assessment and self-recording procedures.

Broden, Hall, & Mitts (1971) state that the effectiveness of self-recording procedures is improved when used in combination with established reinforcement procedures. Their study used self-recording with two eighth-grade students to increase study behavior in one student and to decrease, to some degree, talking aloud behavior in the other. Seymour & Stokes (1976) found that self-recording increased targeted behaviors for three girls in a maximum-security institution, but did not effect change in a fourth girl. In a study using self-evaluation by adolescents in a psychiatric hospital (Santogrossi, O'Leary, Romanczyk, & Kaufman, 1973), this technique did not reduce disruptive behavior because the lack of controls on self-recording made it possible for the students to misbehave and still receive the backup reinforcers by inaccurately recording high self-evaluations. Also, Fixen, Phillips, & Wolf (1972) reported that self-recording without contingent backup reinforcers did not improve room-cleaning behaviors of predelinquent boys.

Using learning principles outlined by Greer (1980), a Personalized System of Instruction (PSI) was established by Zurcher (1980) for the Baldwin Harbor, New York, Junior High School band. The system utilized self-recording forms (tally sheets), which students used to enter credits (points) as they were earned in 23 categories. These forms were turned in to the instructor for verification of accuracy and correction (if necessary). These earned credits were then converted to letter grades and attitude marks for report cards. The credits could also be spent (without affecting marks) for various music and non-music backup reinforcers elected by the students (Zurcher & Greer, 1980). The present study was designed to determine if differences exist between daily self-recorded/teacher-verified credits, no feedback, and daily teacher-issued letter grades.

Method

Experimental Setting and Subjects

The subjects for this study were the entire eighth-grade band (63 members) at a junior high school in Baldwin, New York, an upper-middle-class community of approximately 35,000. The students ranged in age from 12 to 13 years. All but seven of them had at least 68 weeks of previous experience with the PSI program. The enrollment of the seventh- and eighth-grade junior high school was 1,019.

The PSI Program and Token Economy

Earned Credits. The band rehearsed every other day for one period. Up to 100 credits could be earned by students during each rehearsal for being on time (10), bringing their instruments (20) and band music (10), posture (10), being on-task (20), taking instruments home after rehearsal (20), and taking band music home (10). Credits were also earned for weekly lessons (Zurcher, 1975) and marking-period performance examinations, but these credits were not included in the analysis because these aspects of the program were recorded by the teacher rather than the student. All the credits described above were used to determine report-card grades every 12 weeks by dividing the number of credits earned by the total number possible. In addition, credits in nine other categories were earned during rehearsals and lessons to determine attitude marks for report cards. The results (which paralleled the grading results) are not presented here.

Students kept track of their own earned credits on a printed tally sheet (Zurcher, 1980). Reliability of student entries was assessed by the instructor, a student teacher, and several band officers who kept contemporary records of students who were not eligible for credit in the various categories. Student tally sheets were collected daily to verify and correct student entries. Interobserver reliability of student entries was 98%: [agreements / (agreements + disagreements)] × 100%.

Credit Redemption. All credits earned by the students could be spent (without affecting grades or attitude marks) for various music and non-music backup reinforcers. Various amounts of credit could be spent for music activities, such as receiving a lesson on a second instrument (taught by a qualified student who earned credits for teaching); practicing a second instrument; taking a second instrument home; checking out additional music; borrowing cassette recorders; borrowing cassette tapes of band parts, lessons, or solos; borrowing solo music plus tapes of solo accompaniments; checking out extra-credit projects; and borrowing cassette tapes of jazz.

Credits could also be spent for non-music activities, such as being excused from band rehearsals; receiving permission to be late for rehearsal; leaving band rehearsals early; receiving academic help from a fellow student; borrowing recordings of drama or comedy; staying in the music area before school, during free time, or after school; or other student-selected activities approved by the instructor. A previous study (Zurcher & Greer, 1980), showed that students overwhelmingly elected to spend their credits for music rather than non-music reinforcers.

Experimental Design

The study utilized a withdrawal (A_1 B C A_2) behavioral design. Data were taken during 22 rehearsals.

Phase A_1. During the initial phase of the experiment, students (using printed tally sheets) kept daily records of their earned credits during five consecutive rehearsals. The tally sheets were turned in at the end of each rehearsal. Using seating charts, the instructor, the student teacher, and band officers kept contemporary records of students who did not earn credits in each category. These charts were used to verify and (if necessary) correct student tally sheets, which were then returned for the next rehearsal. Earned credits could be spent at any time.

Phase B. During this phase, students did not have tally sheets and had no feedback on credits being earned for six consecutive rehearsals. They were told that the grading method remained exactly the same except that the instructor would keep track of their grade and attitude credits. The instructor, student teacher, and band officers again used seating charts to ascertain credits not earned, and the instructor transferred this information to tally sheets that were not available to the students. They were told that they were still earning grade and attitude credits that could be spent.

Phase C. During this phase of six consecutive rehearsals, the instructor (again using seating chart records kept by him, the student teacher, and band officers) kept contemporary records of credits on tally sheets that were then converted to letter grades (A, B, C, D, F) and attitude marks (1, 2, 3, 4). These letter grades and attitude marks were entered on another form and distributed to students at the beginning of each rehearsal to provide feedback regarding the previous rehearsal. Again, they were told that they were still being graded for the same items and that they were still earning credits that could be spent.

Phase A_2. This phase of five consecutive rehearsals was a return to the conditions of phase A_1.

Table 6.1
Differences between Treatment Mean Scores

	Treatment	N†	M	SD	r	t
A_1	Daily credits	63	92.71	7.06	.60	2.02*
B	No feedback		90.74	9.21		
A_1	Daily credits	63	92.71	7.06	.62	4.07**
C	Daily letter grades		89.30	8.70		
B	No feedback	63	90.74	9.21	.72	1.75
C	Daily letter grades		89.30	8.70		
C	Daily letter grades	62	89.34	8.74	.58	3.58**
A_2	Daily credits		92.74	7.89		
B	No feedback	62	90.75	9.29	.47	1.79
A_2	Daily credits		92.74	7.89		

†One subject was eliminated from A_2 comparisons because of illness.
*$p < .05$
**$p < .001$

Results

Analysis of correlated t-test values for a two-tailed test indicate that rehearsal achievement in phase A_1 (daily self-recorded/teacher-verified credits) was significantly higher ($p < .05$) than phase B (no feedback). Phase A_1 achievement was also significantly higher ($p < .001$) than phase C (daily letter grades). No significant difference existed between phase B (no feedback) and phase C (daily letter grades). Analysis of data from phase A_2 (daily self-recorded/teacher-verified credits) showed a significant reversal ($p < .001$) of the downward trend of phase C (daily letter grades). No significant difference occurred between phase A_2 and phase B (no feedback). The reliability of students' self-recording was 98%. There were 5,142 agreements and 99 disagreements.

As shown in Table 6.1, the mean scores for each phase were relatively high, which is consistent with previous data (Zurcher & Greer, 1980). The mean for phase A_1 (daily credits) was 92.71%, phase B (no feedback) was 90.74%, phase C (daily letter grades) was 89.3%, and phase A_2 (daily credits) was 92.74%.

An analysis of each category of earned credits was made to determine the percentage of adherence to established criteria. Figure 6.1 shows clearly where treatment changes occurred. The only categories to remain relatively

Figure 6.1
Mean Grade per Rehearsal and per Treatment
Rehearsal grade mean (solid line)
Treatment grade mean (broken line)

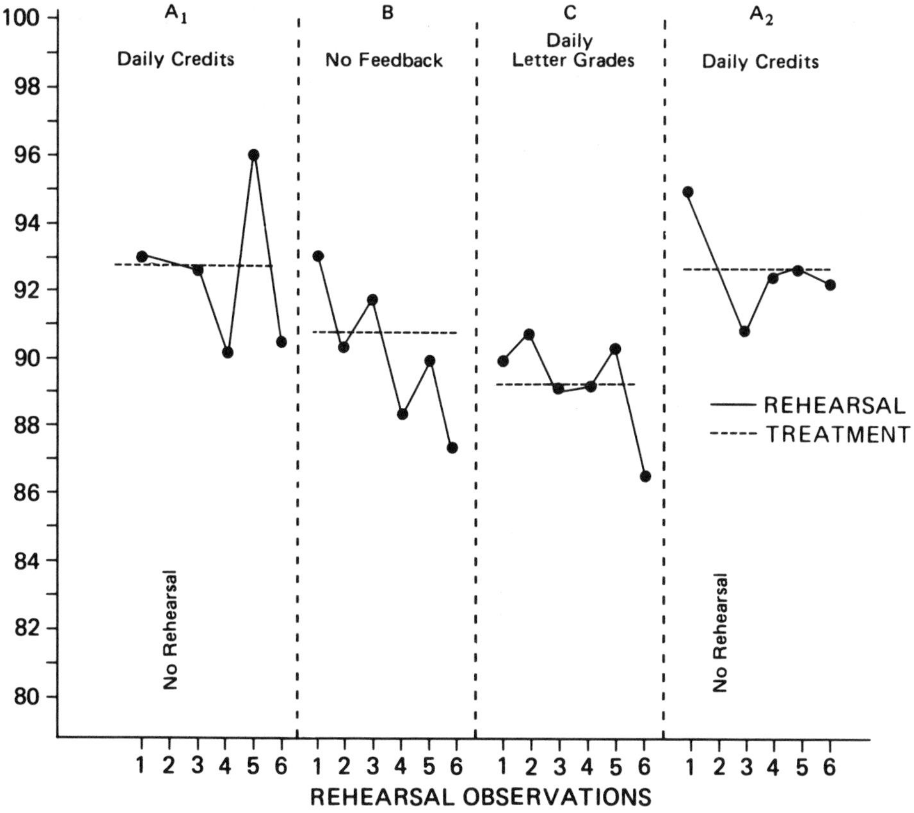

stable over the four phases were position, instrument and music present for rehearsal, and instrument taken home. Consistent with overall treatment differences, the largest changes in the four phases occurred in the categories of music taken home (A_1-85%, B-75%, C-61%, A_2-84%) and on-task behavior (A_1-94%, B-88%, C-83%, A_2-96%). One category ran counter to overall results: on time (A_1-82%, B-93%, C-95%, A_2-87%).

Discussion

The elimination of external variables is the single largest problem in conducting experimental research over a long period of time in an educational setting. Two contrasting variables that were present during phase C (daily letter grades) were the annual spring concert and performance examinations to determine seating for the concert. One might have expected a high percentage of students to take music home and to be on-task during this phase. Just the opposite occurred. The decrease in on-task behavior, however, is consistent with other behavioral research that shows decreasing levels of on-task behavior during periods of no feedback. In all four phases, the instructor approved on-task behavior and said nothing to off-task students, but entered off-task marks on the seating chart as they occurred. Apparently, daily letter grades were not specific enough to provide feedback, whereas self-recording provided immediate feedback.

The decline in music taken home during phase C (daily letter grades) was entirely unexpected and inconsistent with previous preconcert experience. Students may have believed that this aspect of the grading system was not being checked (in spite of daily announcements that the credit system was still in operation), or it may be that they believed they were prepared for the performance examination and concert so that they could ease up on practice. One cannot rule out the additional possibility that other school commitments may have interfered.

An explanation for lower on-time behavior during phases A_1 and A_2 (daily credits) is not readily apparent. A number of students were late on several occasions. It is possible they were delayed by their previous teacher because of a lab or gym activity and elected to receive no credit rather than go back to the teacher for a late pass, thus delaying them even more. The possible presence of prior treatment effects and other external variables, which may have had some effect on the results, suggests the need for a replication of this study in order to eliminate, as much as possible, these variables.

Behavior analysis research has shown that self-recording procedures when used in combination with contingent reinforcement can change targeted behaviors. This study indicates that daily teacher-issued letter grades are not specific enough to change behavior to the degree desired. Because so many of our grading systems utilize teacher-issued letter grades, further research in music and other subject areas is urged in order to structure task-specific grading systems that will operate effectively with differing populations.

7 Children's Responses to Music Stimuli: Verbal/Nonverbal, Aural/Visual Modes

Harriet I. Hair

Summary

This study summarizes recent research on children's verbal/nonverbal, aural/visual responses to music stimuli.

* * *

One of the most important developments in music research during recent years has been the growth of studies focusing on the music perception, music ability, and musical growth of young children. The increasing number of articles in research journals and texts on the psychology of music document this trend (Shuter-Dyson & Gabriel, 1981; Deutsch, 1982; Hodges, 1980; Radocy & Boyle, 1979).

In attempting to understand children's musical development, many researchers have examined the types of responses they give to music stimuli: verbal, nonverbal, visual, performance (singing or playing), kinesthetic (motor or gestural), or affective. This paper concentrates on recent research based on the verbal/nonverbal response modes of children and briefly discusses the aural/visual modes.

A recurrent problem for teachers and researchers dealing with the musical growth of young children has been the use of traditional music terminology and concepts that are confusing or possess no meaning for them. The accepted linguistic meaning of a word they learn initially may not be the same as the musical meaning associated with that word. This is particularly evident in studies dealing with pitch and tonal direction.

For example, children learn the words "high" and "low" in relation to space. Only later do they learn to associate them with pitch. Researchers have established that children can make aural discriminations among musical sounds long before they can use the appropriate music terminology for labeling these differences.

Numerous approaches have been used in investigating the identification and development of music concepts in children. Recent studies have given children appropriate descriptors (McDonald, 1974; Rost, 1976; Zwissler, 1971), avoided or discouraged verbalization (Schevill, 1971; Scott, 1978), asked children to make judgments and then explain their rationale (Botvin, 1974; Bettinson, 1976), used aural/visual tasks (Zaporozhets & Elkonin, 1971; Olson 1978), examined the reinforcement value of music for cognitive learning tasks (Greer, 1978; Greer, Dorow, & Wolpert, 1978), and used non-verbal performance tasks (Van Zee, 1976; Hair, 1977). Taebel (1974) found that the test scores of children who were told exactly what attribute to listen for did not vary significantly from those who were asked to provide their own explanation of the change in the music.

How important are verbalizations about music? Is the ability to verbalize about music an important part of music behavior? Some claim that it is not. However, it is interesting to note the numerous studies that depend on the subject's understanding of verbal instructions or descriptions in the research task or testing procedure. Yet, too often the researcher has not given due consideration to the language that he uses nor to that which children use in describing music phenomena.

Studies in the anthropology of music by Merriam (1964) and Blacking (1973) provide strong justification for research on verbal response modes. Merriam (1964) states that verbal behavior plays an important part in the music process:

> [Music] sound has structure, and it may be a system, but it cannot exist independently of human beings; music sound must be regarded as the product of the behavior that produces it. The level out of which this product arises is behavior, and such behavior seems to be of three major kinds: [physical, social, and verbal]. . . . Verbal behavior is concerned with expressed verbal constructs about the music system itself. (pp. 32, 33) . . . Concepts about music are basic to the ethnomusicologist who searches for knowledge about a music system, for they underlie the music behavior of all peoples. Without an understanding of concepts, there is no real understanding of music. (p. 84)

Thus, talking about or conceptualization about music may be more important in our understanding of the music process than many researchers in music education may have believed. Blacking (1973) suggests that it may also involve the musicality or musical ability of individuals. He claims that what is labeled as musical in one culture may not be in another. What we consider as necessary traits in a musical person may not be so judged in a non-Western–music culture.

In addition, Blacking states that "because sensory discrimination is developed in culture, people may fail to express any distinction between musical intervals which they can hear, but which have no significance in their musical system. . . . They may not know the special terms [to use in describing the sounds]" (p. 6).

The implications of these statements are that labeling the differences between intervals of sound or melodic direction is not based solely on physiological or acoustic rationales, but is influenced or dominated by our musical, cultural, and language biases. The statements also imply that findings of researchers should be limited to the culture and/or subcultures to which their subjects belong.

Verbal and Nonverbal Response Modes

Research in children's discrimination of pitch concepts shows that they can make discriminations on non-verbal tasks at very early ages. Chang and Trehub (1977) found that 5-month-old infants showed a "startle" response (changes in heart rate) to melody with altered contour, but not to a transposed melody.

Kessen, Levine, and Wendrich (1979) demonstrated that, after a few brief training sessions, babies under 6 months of age can learn to match pitches, singing back the pitches sung to them. The babies sang successful matches two-thirds of the time, and a large proportion of these were "nearly in tune."

Zaporozhets and Elkonin cited two Russian experiments in *The Psychology of Preschool Children* (1971, pp. 31–32). In studies of children 3 to 5 years old, Yendovitskaya (1958, cited in Zaporozhets & Elkonin, 1971, p. 31) used arm movements to indicate pitch relationships. Repina (1961, cited in Zaporozhets & Elkonin, 1971, p. 32) trained children to associate high and low tones with the sounds and visual representations of small and large animals. In the United States, Scott (1978) designed a set of boxes that would produce sounds when lifted. She stated that preschoolers were capable of demonstrating their understanding of pitch concepts (register, melodic contour, and interval size) by manipulating the sound boxes.

In studies of verbal responses by preschool children, analogous terms have been used in teaching the concept of pitch. McGinnis (1928) used the labels "Daddy Bear" and "Baby Bear" for low or high tones. Williams, Sievere, and Hattwick (1932) called one end of the piano keyboard "high or upstairs" and the other "low or downstairs." Jones (1979) found that for second-, third-, and fourth-grade children a vertical keyboard was effective in improving aural/vocal skills and an understanding of the concept of pitch direction. Zwissler (1971) taught first-grade children to use the terms "up and down," and they appeared to understand these terms. Yet, when they were tested, many children used other terminology in the pitch tasks.

Van Zee (1976) studied the aural discrimination, performance on a keyboard instrument, and verbal responses of kindergarten children to pitch and rhythm concepts, (i.e., melodic contour, duration of tones, and rhythm patterns). She found that children were more efficient in demonstrating their understanding of musical terms than in verbally describing them. She discovered that the most frequently confused terms were those associated with musical pitch, and that kindergarten children did not employ a common characteristic vocabulary. She stated that the musical terminology commonly used with these children is not necessarily a part of their vocabulary, but must be learned. She suggested that verbal responses do not necessarily develop concurrently with perception. This is consistent with the findings of numerous researchers.

Dowling (1982), in discussing the developmental pattern in melodic information processing, proposes the following sequence:

> the baby's ability to distinguish gross features such as contour and pitch level, to the 5-year-old's grasp of tonal scales and ability to discriminate key changes, to the adult's ability to detect small changes of interval size. There seems to be a hierarchy of features, and the sequence of human development follows that hierarchy closely (Pick, 1979). (p. 415)

The same researcher states that the establishment of pitch as a directional dimension is not a relatively late phenomenon in a child's development in the light of Chang and Trehub's results:

> What is true is that first graders have trouble with their language description of pitch direction as Zimmerman and Sechrest (1970); Pflederer and Sechrest (1968); and Hair (1977) have documented. Words like "up" and "down" are very difficult for children of 5 or 6 to learn to apply to pitch in the way we adults do. (p. 419)

Hair (1977) investigated the ability of first-grade children to discriminate tonal direction on verbal and non-verbal tasks. Children were not given any cues about vocabulary, but used their own words to describe how the music moved. On the non-verbal tasks, they played tonal patterns on the resonator bells that matched those played by the investigator.

An analysis of the types of responses given by the children on the spoken test showed that 35% were verbal, 39% were gestural, and 26% were a combination of verbal and gestural. Both Hair and Van Zee (1976) found that a large percentage of the subjects gave overt or gestural responses in addition to or in lieu of verbal responses.

In Hair's study, directional responses were given by 66% of the participants. However, some of these responses were considered to be incorrect (i.e., sideways and north). The fact that these children did appear to understand the concept of direction may mean that they could learn to associate traditional music terminology with tonal direction if proper teaching techniques were determined. Only 5% used the traditional music terms "up and down" or "high or low" correctly.

On the performance test, 97% of the subjects played three or more items correctly, and 51% played five or more of the six items correctly. Thus, apparently, many of them could perceive a difference between tonal patterns and could match ascending and descending patterns without being able to verbalize correctly the concept of tonal direction. These findings are consistent with research cited earlier in this paper.

Children learn the words "up and down" and "high and low" in relation to spatial concepts. The idea of "up and down," with regard to musical sounds, is based on a temporal rather than spatial phenomenon because the musical connotation of these terms is derived from the frequency of vibrations in a tone. The abstract usage of these concepts in music parlance apparently has little logical meaning or relation to the spatial concepts that are familiar to the young child. Apparently, it is illogical to assume that young children can label tonal direction without music training. The frequent practice in public school music education of offering only a one-half hour music period per week, as was the case for the children in this study, does not seem to provide enough training to make these concepts meaningful to a child of this age. More research is needed to determine the amount and the type of music training required to make the concepts of tonal direction meaningful for first graders.

Webster and Schlentrich (1982), based on studies by Hair (1977) and Scott (1978), investigated the ability of 4- and 5-year-old children to discriminate pitch direction using one of three modes of response: verbal (spoken); gestural; and performance-based, using resonator bells. Initially, the subjects were instructed to say "going up or down," to point or play upward or downward. The investigators found no statistically significant differences among the response modes. However, in analyzing the scores, the rank order of modes was performance-based, followed by gestural, then verbal. For the small percentage of children who had the highest possible score and who thus were judged to understand clearly the concept of pitch, the type of response mode did not appear to make any difference.

Children seemed to prefer and enjoy the performance tasks more than the others. Webster and Schlentrich suggested more experiences for preschoolers using non-verbal, performance-based response modes. They concluded that, in teaching children, the model of experience to concept to verbalization may provide the best avenue for future investigations of musical learning.

Hair (1981) compared the vocabulary of children in Grades 2, 3, and 4 with that of college students, music and education majors. Subjects were asked to listen to different presentations of a well-known melody and to write a word that described the characteristic change in each playing. Hair found that, when correctly describing music concepts, subjects of all ages used consistent and traditional terminology. However, when incorrect terms were chosen, little similarity in vocabulary existed between children and adults. The number of different words given per concept ranged from 23 to 72. Yet, only 1 to 5 words per item were common to both children and adults.

Children in these grades correctly labeled the concepts of tempo and dynamics. Scores of subjects with additional age and training showed no significant improvement on these items. Children had difficulty in labeling the concepts of pitch, rhythmic change, and timbre. They did not have adequate vocabulary to describe the concepts of minor mode or harmony.

In comparing scores of children and adults, one should note that the groups of children consisted of a random sample of ability levels. One might assume that the adult collegiate subjects had a higher ability level than the normal population. The college students' larger vocabulary may have made their choice of words more confusing. The fact that the adult groups scored higher only on the items related to more abstract or technical terminology suggests that new means must be sought to compensate for children's inadequate grasp of traditional terminology. As Hitchcock (1942) suggested, perhaps sound-descriptive terms would be more appropriate for children than the traditional vocabulary. Most educators assume that it is important for children to label music concepts verbally. Further investigations need to determine how linguistic skills evolve and function in relation to music perception. Researchers should continue exploring how much and when associative training is needed before conceptual labels for aural stimuli become meaningful.

In a replication of this study with music therapists and trainable mentally retarded (TMR) students (mental age 5 to 7), Hair and Graham (1983) found similar results. When correctly describing music, both groups used consistent terminology. When incorrect terms were given, no vocabulary was common to both groups. The TMR students repeated many of the same words across the different test items. Their low test scores resulted from their inappropriate use of terms, not their lack of vocabulary.

Flowers (1982) compared the written verbal responses of third- and fourth-grade children and undergraduate non-music majors in their overall pattern of descriptions of musical elements. Most of the children gave responses referring to extramusical, timbre, or tempo characteristics, and the college students referred to extramusical, tempo, and pitch/melody. The responses of children were more limited in the number of categories used in describing music than college students. The former tended to evolve a single approach to describing all the music selections. If they chose to refer to one concept, other conceptual categories of descriptions were generally omitted.

Farnsworth (1969), in citing research by Schoen, Gatewood, Mull, and others, stated that synonymous words will be used with some consistency to describe Western music if the listeners are drawn from roughly the same subculture. He felt: "The degree of agreement is little affected by differences in listener intelligence, tested musical aptitude, musical training, or age level (if above the sixth grade)" (p. 80).

Vocabulary of older children was investigated by Utley (1973). In developing his music perception test, he used words already familiar to the children, not the language used by trained musicians. He asked junior high school students (Grades 7 through 9) to listen to music and to describe it in their own words, using "non-technical" terms. He found substantial agreement among the choice of vocabulary of the various groups and that the words used by one group were "readily understood" by the others (p. 45).

Hair (1982b) designed a study to investigate the vocabulary of children in lower grades and the same grades as those cited by Farnsworth and Utley. She examined the vocabulary that children in Grades 4 through 7, college students, and university faculty members used when asked to write 10 descriptors for a given music concept word. Although there was more similarity in the vocabulary of adults and children of these ages than with younger children, important differences remained in the vocabularies of these groups. The number of words common to children and faculty was much smaller than the number common to children and college students. Thus, the faculty chose the least similar vocabulary to that of the children. Adults tended to give more synonymous and technical terms, and the children gave more purely descriptive vocabulary.

Many children and some adults did not respond at all to the more technical musical terms. For example, for the concept "timbre," nearly half of the children and a fifth of the college students gave no response. For the concept "minor," 37% of the children, 14% of the college students, and 12% of the faculty did not respond. Either they had no understanding of these concepts or no additional descriptors for these terms. The lack of similarity in vocabulary between faculty and children underscores the critical need for educators to be more conscious of these differences in designing appropriate teaching strategies, textbooks, and research projects that will make the traditional music vocabulary meaningful for children.

Implications of the findings of these research studies on verbal responses are: (1) Children can demonstrate understanding of musical concepts (via playing or singing) earlier than they can give correct verbal labels; (2) Children use the same vocabulary as adults for concepts they understand, but quite different descriptive vocabulary otherwise; (3) More effective methods must be found to teach the meaning of music terminology to young children; (4) The tendency of young children to decide on one single approach to responding should be investigated further; (5) The more training an adult has, the less descriptive and more technical vocabulary he or she uses in describing music concepts; and (6) Non-verbal, gestural responses of young children need further investigation.

Aural and Visual Response Modes

Most of the traditional research studies and tests focusing on aural and visual tasks in music have presented motionless graphic representations of the directional movement of aural stimuli. Schevill (1969) asked second-grade children to identify melodic direction by matching aural stimuli with visual representations of lines, windows in a house, or bouncing balls that indicated "up and down." Simons's tests (1976) presented directional arrows to indicate the melodic direction of sounds the student heard. Norton (1979) had children circle pictures in a booklet to denote responses to aural examples of melodic direction.

Zaporozhets stated that in Repina's study (1964) visual representations of large animals were associated with low sounds and those of small animals with high sounds. As Karma (1979) stated, "The whole system of notation is a spatial analogy of a thing not originally spatial" (p. 51).

In earlier studies, there had to be a cross modal transfer between the aural and visual discrimination of the stimuli as well as between the discrimination of tonal movement through time and of the concept of direction implied by the motionless visual image. The question is posed that these latter variables may have confounded the results of previous research dealing with tonal direction.

Recent advances in computer technology facilitate the programming of sequential and simultaneous graphics and sounds. Thus, the researcher can control the variables of sound and graphic representations with regard to rate of presentation, length of stimulus, interstimulus time, and spatial relationships.

Studies by Olson (1978, 1981) and Hair (1982a) have produced similar findings concerning cross modal transfer between the aural and visual response modes. Olson used traditional motionless music notation; Hair, moving and stationary graphics presented by a microcomputer.

Olson (1978) asked first-grade subjects to judge whether or not stimuli perceived across aural and visual sensory modes, or within the aural mode, were the same or different. The stimuli consisted of short melodic phrases and contour-line graphs. These graphs resembled the stairstep models found in many elementary music books. Subjects were asked to judge whether the stimuli were the same or different when perceived aurally then visually, or visually then aurally. In addition, they were asked to match stimuli within the aural mode. Results indicated that matching aural stimuli with aural stimuli was significantly easier for first-grade children than either the visual/aural or aural/visual task. No significant differences were found between the visual/aural or aural/visual tasks.

Later in his longitudinal study, Olson (1981) retested the same subjects in Grades 3 and 5. He found that the tasks maintained their relative order from the first to fifth grades. The rank order of means showed the aural/aural task highest, followed by the visual/aural, and the aural/visual task. The differences between the intersensory tasks were still not significant. Olson concluded that teachers should begin teaching basic concepts within the aural sensory mode to children in the primary grades.

In a study of children in Grades 1 through 4, Hair (1982a) examined the ability of children to discriminate between same or different directional patterns through aural and visual tasks presented on a microcomputer. The visual stimuli consisted of moving or stationary graphics that resembled quarter note heads placed in the intervallic positions found in traditional notation. The aural stimuli consisted of two, three, or four tone patterns.

The children scored higher on the aural/aural matching tests than on any of the visual and aural test combinations. These results supported Olson's findings. The subjects scored significantly better on the aural moving graphics tests than on the aural stationary graphics tests.

The addition of the visual dimension, so long thought to aid in the discrimination of melodic direction by children, did not appear to help them. It is generally accepted that children learn the concept of visual spatial direction earlier than that of aural, tonal direction. This study included children of ages and abilities in which these concepts should have been developed. Yet, the moving visual and aural combinations seemed to be most effective with the fourth graders and the high and middle ability groups. The only group that appeared to be helped by the stationary visuals were the fourth graders. This occurred only when the aural presentation preceded the visual.

The amount of differences found for ascending versus descending items and for the number of tones within an item did not appear to change across grade level, ability, or gender.

In teaching music to young children, one must continue to search for a meaningful link between the aural and visual concepts of direction. This research implies that teachers should teach first the aural/aural matching; secondly, the moving visual and aural tasks; and, thirdly, the stationary visual and aural combinations. The most difficult task for these children was in associating tonal direction with stationary visual images. This task is certainly analogous to the problems children encounter in reading a musical score. The research of both Hair and Olson cautions teachers about assuming that children are ready or able to make cross modal transfers between the aural and visual modes.

Bettinson (1976) studied 7-year-old children to determine whether or not a relationship existed between the ability to conserve standard, visually presented Piagetian tasks and the ability to conserve melodic, aurally presented tasks. She found no significant relationship between these two abilities. She felt that this might be because the mental processes involved in aural perception were more complex than in visual perception. In addition, she suggested that the lack of appropriate musical terminology may have been another reason for a 7-year-old child's lack of reasoning abilities on the melodic conservation test.

Norton (1980) investigated first-grade children in two similar studies. She stated that "the relationship between auditory conservation and visual-tactile conservation was not significant in either the San Antonio study (1980) or the Akron study (1978)." She felt that this relationship was minimal enough "to imply that the constructs underlying these thought processes were not exactly the same" (p. 215).

Webster and Zimmerman (1983) investigated the effects of using graphic (dashes), traditional, or no notation on the conservation of rhythmic and tonal patterns of second- through sixth-grade children. They concluded that the visual notations were a significant aid for the children in both the rhythmic and tonal tasks and that this was particularly true for the older ones. They implied that the musical background of the children may have influenced this finding and that this should be carefully screened in future research.

Forsythe and Kelly (1985) investigated the effects of pairing visual and aural stimuli on the aural discrimination of fourth graders. They devised a listening test in which rhythmic and pitch relationships of short musical phrases were represented visually by a teacher moving one hand across a chalkboard simultaneously with each melodic phrase. Rhythmic realizations were precise, and pitch relationships were proportional to the steps and skips in each melody. The researchers found that visual cues were most effective in helping students from schools in low socio-economic areas that had no music specialists. Children in schools in high-income areas that had music twice a week did slightly better on the aural/aural presentations.

Implications of the findings of these research studies on aural/visual response modes are: (1) Children initially learn aural discriminations better within the aural mode than across modes; (2) The capacity or process of responding aurally or visually may be quite different; and (3) Aural and visual conservation appear to have no significant relationship.

Implications for Future Research

What are some of the considerations and implications for the future of research with children and music? Music education research should involve both field and laboratory studies. The most important results will arise from a sampling of both types of research environments. We must seek to have a balance between the two. The need to control sounds and variables within a lab situation is always tempting, but it excludes the reality of the environment in which a child learns. If we are trying to discover how learning occurs, then it seems self-evident that we must do research in the situation in which the learning takes place. We can learn from the ethnomusicologist who goes into the field to take samples of the music he hears and to analyze it according to the culture in which he finds himself.

The types of musical examples used in research studies with children should include timbres as well as melodic and rhythmic patterns that are found in the children's repertoire. In some cases, synthesized sounds or music of the violins found in test examples may not be the sounds that these children know and thus this may influence their perceptions of the music examples being tested. Many anthropologists feel that our sensory perceptions of pitch and rhythm are influenced by our cultural biases and expectations of sound.

Communication should be better between researchers and authors of textbook series for young children. Many teaching strategies and curricula presented by the textbook series need to be investigated by music education researchers. For example, most textbook series base their curricula on a conceptual approach to music. Emphasis is placed on providing students with a variety of music activities that will give them an experiential basis on which to form and label concepts according to traditional music terminology. Yet, the use of music terminology continues to be a problem in studies with young children, and many teachers question whether or not they are successful in teaching concepts. Investigations should be made to determine the ages when certain concepts are taught most effectively.

Leonhard and Colwell (1976) state:

> Most of the research dealing with the relationship between age level and skill is focused on the earliest age at which the skill (concept) can be learned, rather than on the age after which the skill is increasingly difficult to acquire. (p. 9)

Shuter-Dyson and Gabriel (1981) theorize: "What would seem most important to find out is the optimum age or level at which the child should receive the opportunity of acquiring the skill in question, and the best sequencing of musical learnings" (p. 102).

In addition, most textbook series and music educators advocate a multisensory approach to learning music for young children. The assumption is that involving more than one sensory mode will enhance learning. Visual and aural analogies are found throughout the elementary textbook series. Yet, relatively few research studies in music education have investigated the efficacy of this assumption.

Researchers need to investigate: (1) whether children learn music more efficiently within the aural mode or across modes; (2) whether there is a stage in the learning process when cross modal transfer enhances or inhibits aural learning; and (3) whether some children are more visually versus aurally oriented. Once these questions have been answered, more effective teaching strategies could be designed.

Research will need to consider the effects that the media and technology have on young children. The emphasis on visual stimuli and on non-verbal manipulative responses, added to the decrease in time spent reading and writing or in verbally interacting with family and peers, may pose new problems for language studies of young children.

Research procedures with young children will be greatly influenced by the rapidly developing computer technology. Moving and color graphics, random access to sounds, instruments that interface with the computer, interactive voice synthesis, and touch sensitive screens will open new avenues for research dealing with visual and aural dimensions.

Researchers need to be able to work together in teams or consortiums on a continuing basis. Major funding and research time allocated by universities in cooperation with foundations and/or the government are needed to allow for long-term projects. Joint research projects involving music researchers and psychologists should be designed. Centers for research on the musical characteristics of children should be established to provide electronic data bases that would be available to educators and researchers. More continuity and replication among research projects is needed to build a more precise picture of the development of musical characteristics of children. Only then can a theory of music education and more effective teaching strategies be formulated.

Part III
Applications of Research: Teaching Future Teachers

Almost all music educators, no matter what their specialty, become involved in the teacher training process for future music educators. Besides the obvious role of college professors, most music teachers who have even a few years of experience serve as models for observations, supervisors of student teachers, and members of peer-review committees. In many parts of the country, the number of hours undergraduate music education majors devote to direct contact with practicing professionals is being increased substantially. Therefore, the issues involved in improving undergraduates' skills are of vital interest to *all* music educators, not just to college faculty members. Just as we care deeply about teaching children music, we are all concerned with teaching those who will themselves teach children.

"Good teaching" and "abundant learning." Those two phrases sum up our aspirations for young music educators' classes. However, our dreams do not always come true. The nightmare of turning classes or ensembles over to student teachers who, despite course work and observation, seem totally unprepared to handle the situation haunts each of us. They have read their texts, watched us teach, listened to our advice, and even attempted to evaluate their own work in some fashion, but somehow those things have not always done the trick. Is teaching people to improve their teaching skills an impossible task? Is ineptitude invincible? The research in Part III indicates, happily, that the answer may be, "Not at all!"

The studies in this section represent efforts to isolate the elements of preparation and observation that lead to an obvious improvement in selected teaching skills. Some of these skills are quite basic, the type we all too often assume anyone who had been a direct observer of teachers, that is, a student, for more than a dozen years would incorporate automatically. Nevertheless, again and again these basic skills are lamented as lacking in undergraduate teachers. Many of us have assumed that technological innovations such as videotape, which allows a student to watch himself or a master teacher, would alleviate the problem; we have been confused by the mixed results obtained. What are the critical factors that separate productive observation and preparation, evidenced by improved teaching and abundant learning, from wastes of time? What must we, as teachers of future teachers, include in these processes to ensure that those who will become professional colleagues are adequate for the task?

Part III offers guideposts: methods for directing observation so that it becomes truly useful, a model to encourage and assist a student to assess his or her own progress, and suggestions for adjusting the emphasis of lesson-plan preparation. These studies represent the fruits of systematic investigations of the efficacy of teacher training tasks, both traditional and innovative. As in Part II, the results of controlled studies, using objective, verifiable dependent measures and encompassing several hundred subjects from music and elementary education backgrounds, may be considered to be valid for adaptation and application by those of us in direct contact with teachers in training. Although absolute truth may be as elusive in teacher education as in other aspects of life, it is perhaps not out of line, as earlier proposed, for results of studies with such breadth to serve as warranted assumptions for future work.

The need for further research, extending the germs of ideas explored in this section, is implicit in this body of work. As we learn more and more, we become better and better at teaching future teachers.

8 Behavior Checklists and Videotapes versus Standard Instructor Feedback in the Development of a Music Teaching Competency

Charles E. Furman

Summary

This study evaluated the effects of four feedback conditions on the development of a single musical competency: leading group singing using guitar accompaniment. These feedback conditions occurred after weekly progress demonstrations in class. The four conditions—checklist, videotape replay, checklist plus videotape, and standard instructor feedback (contact control)—addressed pinpointed accompanying skills, the percentage of 3-second intervals that were musically accurate, and the percentage of 3-second intervals in which song leading was correct. A questionnaire assessed students' attitudes toward videotaping and self-perceptions of their guitar accompanying skills. Posttest analysis indicated that the Checklist Only and the Videotape and Checklist groups attained significantly higher scores on the behavior checklist and on song leading scores, though no significant differences occurred among any groups on musical accuracy. Although questionnaire results indicated that attitudes toward videotape were positive, in evaluating their own accompanying skills, students in the Checklist Only group outscored all others and mentioned a greater number of specific behaviors.

The overall finding that the use of a checklist alone was as effective as its use in conjunction with videotape is discussed in the light of other studies. It appears that using technology effectively and efficiently requires precise techniques, and that both electronic instrumentation and traditional instructor feedback may need reevaluation as potent teaching methods for guitar accompanying skills.

Design: Statistical, with comparison group (n = 39) N = 74 Groups: 4
Statistical Analysis: ANOVA, t test Reliability: .92–.94
Graphic Analysis: Performance accuracy by experimental group
Reliability: .92–.94
Independent Variables: Four feedback conditions: video only, checklist only, video and checklist, contact control
Dependent Variables: Leading singing using guitar: musical accuracy, song leading skills, checklist scores, free-response self-evaluation, evaluation of instructor
Music: Performance, individual

* * *

Literature in music therapy and music education indicates the desirability of training specific competencies in therapists and teachers using operationally defined specifications. Competencies have been defined as skilled, overt behaviors (Madsen & Yarbrough, 1980) that musicians must demonstrate in their respective settings to achieve educational or therapeutic goals. Educators in the fields of music education and music therapy are presently designing strategies to develop these music teaching competencies most efficiently.

The use of videotape as feedback has been shown to be an effective tool in skill enhancement, particularly when utilized in conjunction with a focusing mechanism (Fuller & Manning, 1973; Hanser & Furman, 1980; Hosford & Johnson, 1983; Madsen & Alley, 1979; Moore, 1976b; Prickett, 1983b; Yarbrough, 1976, 1978; Yarbrough, Wapnick, & Kelly, 1979). The use of videotape as a research tool allows for objective gathering of data for later analysis and viewing by multiple observers.

Accompanied group singing is one activity in which future teachers and therapists may expect to spend a great deal of time (Alley, 1978; Baird, 1958; Braswell, Decuir, & Maranto, 1980; Braswell, Maranto, & Decuir, 1979; Fleming, 1953; Hylton, 1983; Jellison, 1979; Stegall, Blackburn, & Coop, 1978). Singing songs, in fact, was one activity during which correct client response rate was the highest, compared with other types of activities led by student music therapists (Alley, 1982). The popularity and practicality of guitar as an accompanying instrument for group singing has also been noted (Boyle, Hosterman, & Ramsey, 1981; Cassity, 1976; Eisenstein, 1974; Etzkorn, 1964; Madsen & Madsen, 1968; Michel, 1971). This review of literature has not yielded a published competency-based, operationally defined procedure for the acquisition of song leading skills using guitar for accompaniment.

The purpose of the present study was to examine the value of videotape as feedback in the development of a single competency: guitar accompanying of group singing in compliance with predetermined definitions contained in a behavior checklist.

The investigation consisted of four treatment conditions imposed on the weekly guitar song leading performances of students enrolled in a beginning guitar class: videotape feedback with a behavior checklist, videotape feedback only, behavior checklist feedback only, and contact control in which nonspecific instructor feedback was presented. Dependent measures consisted of: scores from the behavior checklist, music scores representing the percent of each performance that was musically acceptable, song leading scores representing the percentage of each performance during which correct song leading/teaching behaviors were demonstrated, student ratings of the course and instructor, and a questionnaire that assessed attitudes of the students toward videotape feedback. Specific questions the study sought to answer included the following:

1. Will feedback conditions differentially affect individual and/or group student performance of guitar song leading skills?
2. Will feedback conditions differentially affect acquisition of a fine motor musical skill, that is, guitar performance?
3. Will feedback conditions differentially affect the development of the conducting-like song leading skills, apart from the guitar skills?
4. Will feedback conditions differentially affect student attitudes toward the course, the instructor, or the videotaping process in general?
5. Will feedback conditions differentially affect students' self-evaluation of their individual guitar skills?
6. Will music majors perform or achieve differently than non-music majors enrolled in the same beginning guitar course?
7. Will the use of a partially subjective measure, that is, the behavior checklist, yield acceptable reliability when used by trained observers?

Method

Subjects

Seventy-four university students, 29 men and 45 women, who were enrolled in eight sections of a one-semester beginning guitar course, participated in the study. On the basis of enrollment figures, the eight sections were grouped in pairs to form four experimental groups of approximately equal size. Each pair of sections was randomly assigned to one of four feedback conditions for the semester. Thirty-nine students, enrolled in six additional sections of the class during the same semester, served as a posttest-only comparison group for the study.

Course Content

One instructor taught all eight sections included in the four experimental conditions. A syllabus was given to each student that outlined course requirements, provided grading guidelines, and specified the textbook to be used. The text for the course was *Guitar Songbook with Instruction,* by Beverly McKeown (1975). The objectives of the course included learning the I, IV, and V^7 chords of four major keys, elementary right-hand strumming and picking techniques, and group singing accompaniment skills. Each week, the instructor presented lecture/demonstrations of new material to be learned, modeling each skill correctly for all classes. Each class section was given time at the beginning, intermittently throughout, and at the end of each class period to practice new skills and review old ones. Each student played a "checkup" weekly. For each checkup, a student sat in front of the class and played the chords of a song, specified by the instructor, while leading the class in singing. The checkups provided the opportunity for students to overcome anxiety and to integrate new skills through repeated practice.

Although classes were randomly assigned to treatment conditions, they were still intact classes. For this reason, the first checkup was designated as pretest to compare the groups before beginning the treatment period in order to assess possible bias. The pretest was videotaped after the third class period to allow students to learn the rudiments of guitar playing, to acclimate to the instructor and classmates, and to ensure that enrollment counts were final after the university drop/add period.

At the end of the semester, two checkup examinations, follow-ups 1 and 2, were videotaped the week following the posttest checkup for each student. Follow-up 1 was a song specified by the instructor; follow-up 2, one chosen by the student. Including follow-ups, then, each student performed 11 checkups during the semester.

Throughout the semester, identical lesson plans were used for all eight experimental sections. The six sections comprising the comparison group, however, were taught by five different teachers, each using their individual course outlines and lesson plans. Course objectives for all 14 sections were similar, but not identical.

Independent Variables

In all classes, students were called upon in random order to perform their checkups. The feedback conditions were implemented as follows:

Checklist Only feedback group. During, and according to, each student's performance of the specified checkup song, the instructor marked yes/no to the 15 items of the behavior checklist, which is described subsequently. After all students in the class completed their checkups, the instructor distributed the marked behavior checklists to the respective individuals. After several minutes, the checklists were collected.

Beginning with checkup 5, each student was presented with an unmarked checklist before the checkups began. After each playing, several minutes were allotted during which the students recorded yes/no responses to the checklist items indicating their perception of their own performance. After the performances were completed, the instructor distributed marked checklists containing the instructor's evaluations as before. Students were then able to compare their own evaluations with those of the instructor. All checklists were collected.

Videotape Only feedback group. During each student's performance of the specified checkup song, the instructor videotaped the performance. After all the checkups were completed, the instructor moved the videotape unit to an adjacent office. Students viewed their tapes individually with the instructor, who gave no specific feedback, but merely nodded to observations made by the students.

Videotape and Checklist feedback group. During each performance of the specified checkup song, the instructor videotaped the performance and marked yes/no to the 15 items on the behavior checklist. After all students in the class completed their checkups, the instructor distributed the marked behavior checklists. Students viewed their tapes individually with the instructor.

Beginning with checkup 5, the instructor withheld the marked checklist containing the instructor's evaluation until after the students viewed the tape of that day's performance. When they entered the office to view their tapes, they were given an unmarked checklist on which to record their evaluations as they watched their tape. The instructor gave the premarked checklist to the students at the end of their viewing. They then compared their own evaluation with that of the instructor.

Contact Control (standard instructor feedback). During each performance of the checkup song, the instructor wrote two comments about it on a free-response feedback sheet. The comments were accurate concerning the performance, but nonspecific in nature, according to a predetermined list of comments devised by the instructor. The list included expressions such as "Be more musical," "Show more enthusiasm," "You're improving," and so on. After all students had performed, the instructor distributed the comment sheets to them.

Dependent Variables

Behavior checklist scores. A behavior checklist was constructed in consultation with a panel of three experts, teachers having from 4 to 10 years of experience teaching guitar classes. Fifteen behaviors were pinpointed that the panel deemed desirable for effective accompanying using the guitar (see Figure 8.1). The checklist was piloted and revised in a previous study using 59 students (Furman & Greenfield, 1983) to ensure its practicability for use in the present investigation.

Scores on the behavior checklist were the calculated percentage of the 15 items that students demonstrated acceptably. Ten percent was deducted from the percentage correct for either of two incompatible responses, as shown on the bottom of the form. Reliability on the behavior checklist scores was achieved using trained observers in the actual classroom for those groups that were not videotaped across all checkups. Trained observers watched and evaluated selected taped performances of those groups whose performances were consistently videotaped.

Music scores. Interval recording was used to determine the percentage of 3-second intervals during which a musically acceptable performance was demonstrated (Killian, 1981). Correct musical performance was defined as: playing the correct chords, playing loudly enough to be heard, and playing in the correct meter, without lapses, throughout the entire interval. A Plato®-assisted program was used by the instructor to record the acceptability or nonacceptability of each interval during a post hoc viewing of the videotapes (Greenfield, 1982). Reliability observations were obtained simultaneously and independently by a trained observer using a paper/pencil form.

Song Leading scores. Interval recording was used to determine the percentage of 3-second intervals during which acceptable song leading skills were demonstrated. Previous studies have pinpointed eye contact as a teaching-related skill directly related to group attentiveness to conductors (Yarbrough, 1975; Yarbrough & Price, 1981) and music therapists (Greenfield, 1980). Correct song leading was defined as: eye contact with the singers as a group, singing with the group, and continuing the right-hand strum pattern on the guitar, without lapses, throughout the entire interval. The same computer-assisted program was used as described previously. The 3-second intervals employed in determining both the music scores and the song leading scores were dictated by the constraints of the computer hardware, but are consistent with the 3-second minimum of eye contact required for a correct response by Madsen and Yarbrough (1980).

Figure 8.1
Behavior Checklist

Name______________________________

Date_______________________________

GUITAR SONGLEADING

1. YES NO Sat up straight.
2. YES NO Guitar was in vertical plane, not horizontal.
3. YES NO Sat down and began playing without hesitation.
4. YES NO There was an absence of nervous mannerism and/or chatter.
5. YES NO Played correct chords. (If error, kept strum going: yes no)
6. YES NO Changed chords without pausing during the song.
7. YES NO Played loudly enough to be heard.
8. YES NO Sang with the singers throughout the entire song.
9. YES NO Smiled.
10. YES NO Maintained eye contact with the singers. (No more than *two* brief interruptions of eye contact.)
11. YES NO Used thumb-brush, thumb-pluck, or finger pick pattern.
12. YES NO Gave *correct* starting pitch.
13. YES NO Played introduction pattern.
14. YES NO Introduction was in the same tempo as song was sung.
15. YES NO Cued in singers verbally ("ready, sing") or visually (head lifted as "upbeat" preparation).

☐ Chewing gum ☐ Started song more than once

Questionnaire. A questionnaire was devised to determine the attitude of the students toward the videotaping process and its use as feedback. The questionnaire included a free-response section in which students were asked to describe their own guitar accompanying skills in terms of proficiencies and deficiencies. The form was administered to students in the four experimental groups at the end of the semester.

Student Instructional Rating System (SIRS). A standardized rating form was administered to students in the four experimental groups to quantify their attitudes toward the course, the materials, and the instructor of each class. The 32 items are categorized in six information areas: instructor involvements, student interest, instructor interaction, course demands, course organization, and individual student data.

Experimental Design

The experimental design is conceptualized as a pretest-posttest control group design with the addition of an unmanipulated, posttest only, comparison group. The follow-up measures comprise a means for evaluating treatment effects transferred beyond the time frame of the study. The subject matter covered, that is, development of musical skills, constitutes a changing-criteria element across and throughout all treatment conditions.

Results

Performance Measures

The checklist scores, music scores, and song leading scores were derived directly from performances at the weekly checkups. Group means for pretests and posttests of the experimental and comparison groups are displayed in Table 8.1. Group means for both follow-ups of the experimental groups are presented in Table 8.2. Reliability between the instructor's ratings and those of the trained observers was calculated by dividing agreements by agreements plus disagreements (Madsen & Madsen, 1978; Madsen & Moore, 1978). Reliability observations were obtained for 39% of all performance scores. Interobserver reliability was .93 on checklist scores; .92 on music scores; and .94 on songleading scores. Reliability between students and the instructor averaged .94 on the applicable checklist scores. One student was absent for the taping of the pretest and one student was absent for both follow-ups, yielding 73 instead of 74 students in those comparisons.

Pretest checkup. The analysis of pretest scores revealed no significant differences among experimental groups on any of the three performance measures. Therefore, these data were not considered as covariates in the analysis of posttest scores (Campbell & Stanley, 1963).

Posttest checkup. The analysis of posttest scores revealed significant differences among experimental groups on checklist scores, F (3,70) = 8.45,

Table 8.1
Mean Scores on Pretest/Posttest Performance Measures: All Groups

	Pretest scores			Posttest scores			
	Checklist	Music	Song leading	Checklist	Music	Song leading	N
Experimental groups							
Video and checklist	52.78	74.00	8.33	88.05	89.95	68.74	19
Video only	56.24	82.77	3.88	75.29	92.18	18.71	17
Checklist only	56.74	84.42	8.52	88.26	94.11	72.21	19
Contact control	57.37	85.74	7.47	78.05	95.53	21.69	19
(one teacher)						Total	74
Comparison group							
Teacher A				66.29	79.00	11.57	7
Teacher B				78.91	84.55	17.00	11
Teacher C				67.75	60.50	31.50	4
Teacher D				69.70	86.40	24.70	10
Teacher E				59.43	83.86	0.00	7
(five teachers)						Total	39

Table 8.2
Mean Scores on Follow-up Performance Measures: Experimental Groups

	Follow-up 1			Follow-up 2		
	Checklist	Music	Song leading	Checklist	Music	Song leading
Video and checklist	73.53	76.16	39.32	71.32	79.11	45.11
Video only	68.00	76.12	11.35	71.06	90.24	10.06
Checklist only	79.69	88.89	41.11	79.11	86.26	38.74
Contact control	67.28	70.28	5.89	71.44	86.33	7.39

Table 8.3
Mean Posttest Checklist Scores

Video only	Contact control	Video and checklist	Checklist only
75.29	78.05	88.05	88.26

Note: Underline indicates no significant difference at .05 level, according to Scheffe's method (Avner, 1980).

$p < .001$, and on song leading scores, F (3,70) = 18.5, $p < .001$, but no significant differences among groups on the music scores, F (3,70) = 1.22, $p > .05$. The effect of the feedback conditions accounted for 26.6% of the total effect on the checklist scores and 44.2% of the total effect on the song leading scores, according to the eta-square method.

A subsequent comparison of checklist score means determined that the Video and Checklist Group and the Checklist Only Group attained significantly higher scores on the checklist than the Video Only and Contact Control Groups (see Table 8.3). A subsequent comparison of song leading score means determined that the Video and Checklist Group and the Checklist Only Group again attained significantly higher song leading scores than the Video Only and Contact Control Groups (see Table 8.4).

Mean posttest scores of the comparison group on all three performance measures are listed in Table 8.1 for visual comparison only. No statistical analyses were used to compare performances of the experimental groups with the comparison group.

Follow-up 1. The analysis of follow-up 1 scores revealed significant differences among experimental groups on all three performance measures: checklist scores, F (3,69) = 3.45, $p < .05$; music scores, F (3,69)

Table 8.4
Mean Posttest Song Leading Scores

Video only	Contact control	Video and checklist	Checklist only
18.71	21.69	68.74	72.21

Note: Underline indicates no significant difference at .05 level, according to Scheffe's method.

Table 8.5
Mean Follow-up 1 Checklist Scores

Contact control	Video only	Video and checklist	Checklist only
67.28	68.00	73.53	76.69

Note: Underline indicates no significant difference at .05 level, according to Scheffe's method.

= 3.19, $p < .05$; and song leading scores, $F\ (3,69) = 7.18$, $p < .001$. The effect of the feedback conditions accounted for 13.1% of the total effect on the checklist scores; 12.2% on the music scores; and 25.3% on the song leading scores, according to the eta-square method.

A subsequent comparison of follow-up 1 means determined that the Checklist Only Group attained significantly higher scores on the checklist than the Contact Control Group. No other checklist score comparisons revealed any significance (see Table 8.5). A subsequent comparison of music score means on follow-up 1 determined that the Checklist Only Group again attained significantly higher music scores than the Contact Control Group; no other music score comparisons revealed significant differences among groups (see Table 8.6). A comparison of song leading score means on follow-up 1 determined that the Checklist Only and the Video and Checklist groups significantly outperformed the Video Only and Contact Control groups on the song leading measure (see Table 8.7).

Follow-up 2. The analysis of follow-up 2 scores revealed no significant differences among experimental groups on checklist scores or on music scores.

Table 8.6
Mean Follow-up 1 Music Scores

Contact control	Video only	Video and checklist	Checklist only
70.28	76.12	76.16	88.89

Note: Underline indicates no significant difference at .05 level, according to Scheffe's method.

Table 8.7
Mean Follow-up 1 Song Leading Scores

Contact control	Video only	Video and checklist	Checklist only
5.89	11.35	39.32	41.11

Note: Underline indicates no significant difference at .05 level, according to Scheffe's method.

Table 8.8
Mean Follow-up 2 Song Leading Scores

Contact control	Video only	Checklist only	Video and checklist
7.39	10.06	38.74	45.11

Note: Underline indicates no significant difference at .05 level, according to Scheffe's method.

Table 8.9
Mean Checklist Scores on Checkups 1-7: Experimental Groups

Checkup	1	2	3	4	5	6	7
Video and Checklist	57.31	72.70	77.50	76.25	74.89	81.32	80.38
Video Only	62.65	73.53	75.19	73.53	69.50	66.87	70.65
Checklist Only	64.68	75.20	86.45	76.25	82.30	89.12	80.00
Contact Control	57.65	72.35	82.06	71.11	72.29	76.79	66.67

Figure 8.2
Group Average Checklist Scores

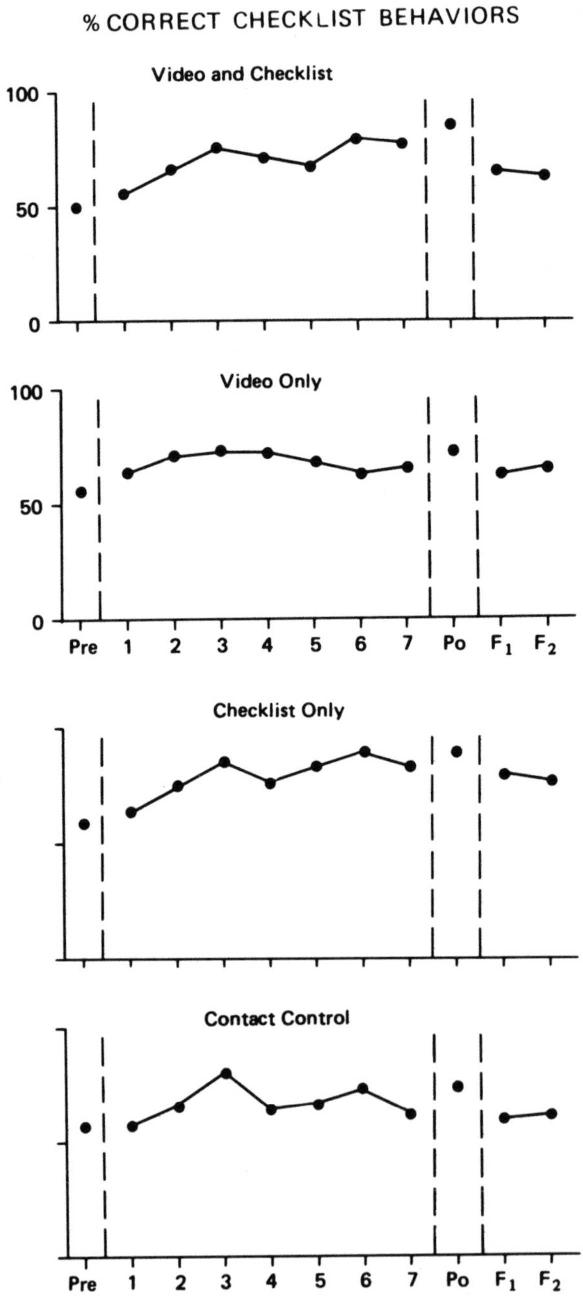

Table 8.10
Mean Music Scores on Checkups 1-7: Videotaped Groups

Checkup	1	2	3	4	5	6	7
Video and Checklist	70.74	61.80	73.61	83.10	75.44	76.16	75.56
Video Only	76.94	85.14	75.75	80.53	75.37	84.44	82.06

The analysis of song leading scores on follow-up 2 did reveal a significant difference among experimental groups, $F\ (3,69) = 10.38$, $p < .001$. This difference should be interpreted with caution, however, because the group scores failed the preliminary F_{max} test for homogeneity of variance. The performance task for follow-up 2 was self-selected, versus the previously instructor-selected song material, creating disparity in the quality and difficulty of the musical selections. According to the eta-square method, the feedback effect accounted for 31.1% of the total effect on the song leading scores. A subsequent comparison of song leading score means on follow-up 2 indicated that the Video and Checklist Group and the Checklist Only Group attained significantly higher song leading scores than either the Contact Control or Video Only groups (see Table 8.8).

Graphic analysis. Behavior graphs that plot group scores are presented to illustrate the effects of the experimental conditions on skill development and learning through time (Madsen, Greer, & Madsen, 1975, p. 1). Checklist score means for all experimental groups on checkups 1 through 7 are listed in Table 8.9. Checklist score means for pretest, posttest, and follow-ups are presented in Tables 8.1 and 8.2. Group checklist means for all checkups are presented graphically in Figure 8.2. Music score and song leading

Table 8.11
Mean Song Leading Scores on Checkups 1-7: Videotaped Groups

Checkup	1	2	3	4	5	6	7
Video and Checklist	6.16	19.95	39.28	35.85	32.94	63.74	47.31
Video Only	12.53	24.43	29.00	12.76	5.19	13.40	5.41

score means for two experimental groups on checkups 1 through 7 are listed in Tables 8.10 and 8.11. Group means of music and song leading scores for all checkups are presented graphically in Figures 8.3 and 8.4. Music and song leading scores for checkups 1 through 7 are shown only for the Video and Checklist and the Video Only groups because the other groups were not videotaped during the intervening checkups.

Music majors versus non-music majors. The scores of music majors were compared with the scores of non-music majors on the three performance measures—checklist scores, music scores, and song leading scores—for pretest, posttest, and the two follow-ups. Two-tailed *t* tests were used in all 12 analyses. Results were all non-significant.

Non-performance Measures

Questionnaire. Part one of the questionnaire served to gather background information about the individual students and to assess attitudes toward the videotaping process. Attitudinal information, from the applicable questionnaire items, is summarized in Figure 8.5.

Part two of the questionnaire was students' free-responses regarding the strengths and weaknesses of their own guitar accompanying skills. The two-part essay question was scored on a 0 to 100 scale, 10 points being scored for each discrete point presented. Reliability scoring was obtained for 20% of the responses, yielding .93 agreement between the raters. Mean scores on the essays were 45.8 for the Contact Control Group; 50.6 for the Video Only Group; 64.2 for the Checklist Only Group; and 48.9 for the Video and Checklist Group. An analysis of variance indicated a significant difference on the essay-content scores: $F\ (3,69) = 4.63, p < .01$. A subsequent comparison of means indicated that the Checklist Only Group scores were significantly higher than the Contact Control Group scores, but no other comparisons revealed significance (see Table 8.12). The frequency of actual checklist items appearing in students' essays are shown, by group and by item, in Table 8.13. The checklist items were mentioned with significantly higher frequency in the essays of the Checklist Only Group than any other experimental group, $\chi^2\ (3,\ N = 74) = 23.69, p < .001$.

Student Instructional Rating System (SIRS). Standardized SIRS forms were administered to all eight class sections participating in the study. The forms were tabulated according to the four experimental conditions. The mean SIRS ratings are shown in Table 8.14, which includes departmental

Figure 8.3
Group Average Music Scores

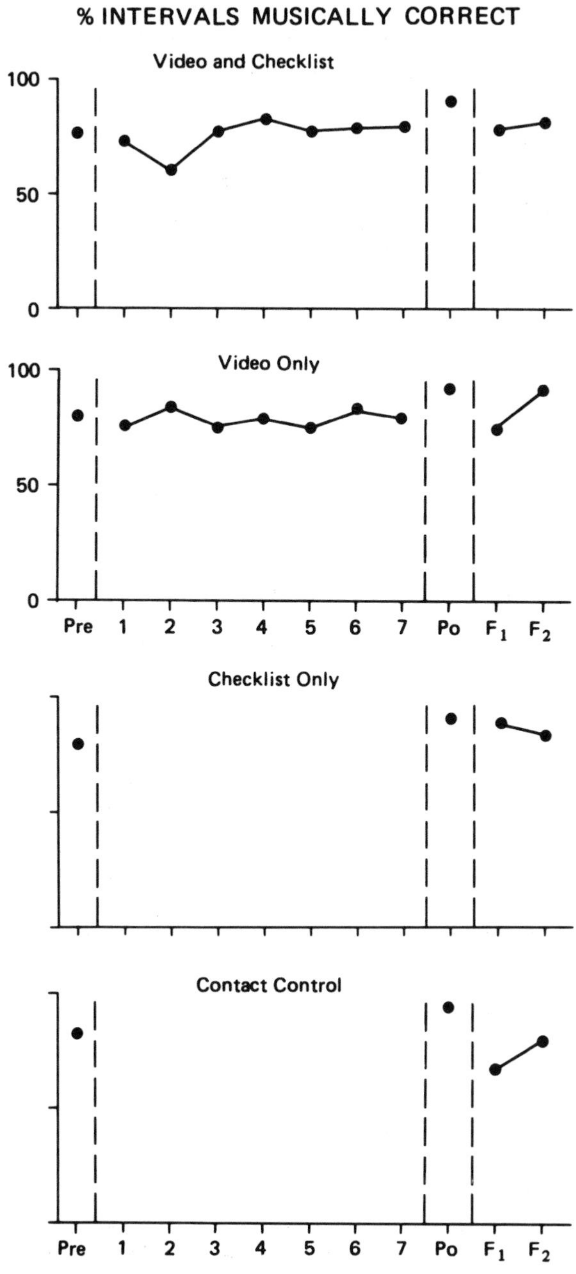

Figure 8.4
Group Average Song Leading Scores

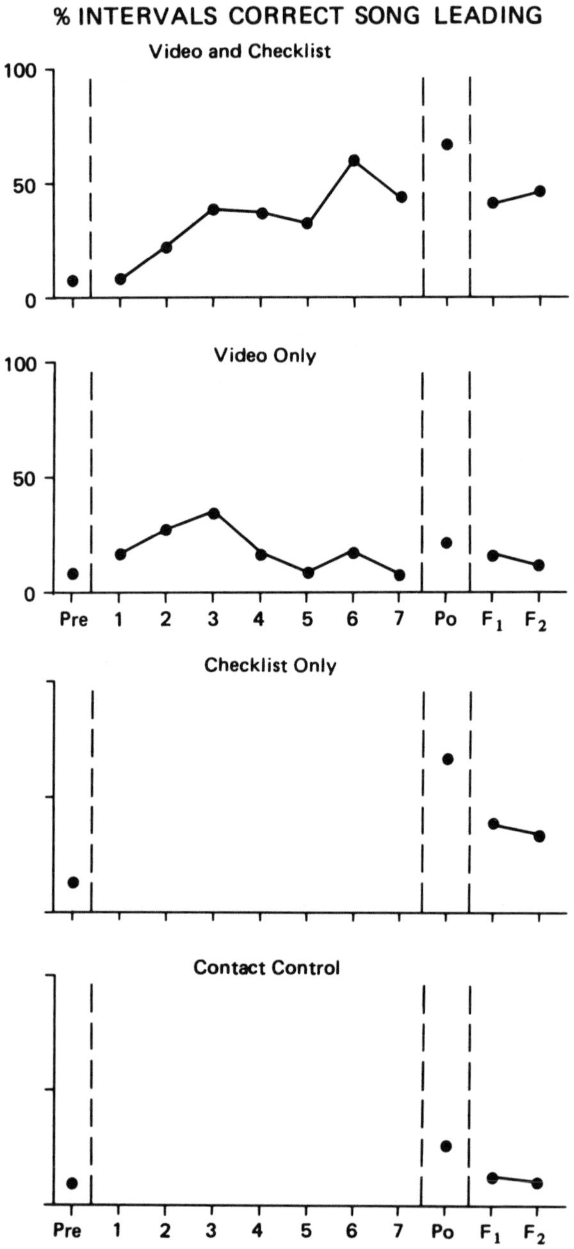

Figure 8.5
Summary of Attitude Toward Videotape Feedback

"If you were signing up for another guitar class, and you knew of the availability of videotape equipment beforehand, would you":

48% Choose a section using videotape over all other sections.

45% Choose any class. Videotape would make no difference in my decision.

7% Avoid any section using videotape.

"Do you feel that videotape feedback was/could be advantageous to you?"

	Yes	No
Students in classes that were videotaped	80%	20%
Students in classes that were NOT videotaped	94%	6%

ratings—other faculty teaching similar courses at the same institution—for visual comparison. An analysis of variance revealed no significant difference among experimental groups in their ratings of any of the evaluation areas included on the form.

Discussion

Performance Measures

On pretest performances, no significant differences were found among the four experimental groups in the analysis of the three performance measures: checklist scores, music scores, and song leading scores. Analysis of

Table 8.12
Mean Essay Content Scores

Contact control	Video and checklist	Video only	Checklist only
45.8	48.9	50.6	64.2

Note: Underline indicates no significant difference at .05 level, according to Scheffe's method.

Table 8.13
Summary of Items from Behavior Checklist Mentioned in Self-analysis Section of Questionnaire

Items	Contact control	Video only	Checklist only	Video and checklist	Total
1. Sat up straight	0	0	2	0	2
2. Guitar was in vertical plane, not horizontal	0	0	0	0	0
3. Sat down and began playing without hesitation	0	0	0	0	0
4. There was an absence of nervous mannerisms and/or chatter	2	1	5	1	9
5. Played correct chords. (If error, kept strum going: yes no)	12	12	17	13	54
6. Changed chords without pausing during the song	5	2	4	4	15
7. Played loudly enough to be heard	1	0	2	0	3
8. Sang with the singers throughout the entire song	1	2	4	3	10
9. Smiled	0	0	3	1	4
10. Maintained eye contact with the singers (no more than *two* brief interruptions of eye contact)	3	5	11	6	25
11. Used thumb-brush, thumb-pluck, or finger pick pattern	11	10	13	6	40
12. Gave *correct* starting pitch	1	0	3	2	6
13. Played introduction pattern	1	0	1	1	3
14. Introduction was in the same tempo as song was sung	1	0	6	0	7
15. Cued in singers verbally ("ready, sing") or visually (head lifted as "upbeat" preparation)	0	0	2	0	2
Totals	38	32	73	37	—

Table 8.14
Mean SIRS Ratings with Departmental Comparison

	Video and checklist	Video only	Checklist only	Contact control	School of Music
Instructor involvement (items 1 – 4)	1.49	1.67	1.44	1.49	1.66
Student interest (items 5 – 8)	1.64	1.62	1.34	1.56	1.81
Student-instructor interactions (items 9 – 12)	2.27	2.17	1.89	2.06	2.05
Course demands (items 13 – 16)	4.36	4.07	4.22	4.19	3.78
Course organization (items 17 – 20)	1.58	1.76	1.47	1.54	1.86

posttest performances indicated that the Checklist Only Group and the Video and Checklist Group achieved significantly higher scores than the other experimental groups on the checklist measure and the song leading measure, but not on the music measure.

Analysis of the performance scores on a follow-up checkup determined the following: the Checklist Only Group significantly outperformed the Contact Control Group on the checklist measure and the music measure, but no other comparisons revealed significant differences; the Checklist Only Group and the Video and Checklist Group both achieved significantly higher song leading scores than the Video Only and Contact Control Groups.

Analysis of performance scores on a second follow-up, which featured self-selected song material, revealed no significant differences among experimental groups on checklist scores or music scores. The Checklist Only Group and the Video and Checklist Group achieved significantly higher song leading scores than the Video Only and Contact Control Groups, though group variances were highly disparate.

The use of the checklist in feedback conditions was effective in increasing scores on the checklist itself and on song leading, regardless of whether or not videotape feedback was also employed. In all cases but one, where the Checklist Only Group and the Video and Checklist Group together outperformed the other experimental groups, the Checklist Only Group consistently achieved the higher scores of the two groups. This is consistent with pretest scores, in which the Video and Checklist Group obtained slightly lower scores, across all three performance measures, than the Checklist Only Group.

The Video Only Group and the Contact Control Group appear to have performed similarly throughout the study. The Video Only Group received less actual instructor feedback than the Contact Control Group. The latter group received two non-specific comments about performance from the instructor after each checkup. This condition, though not a true "control" situation, was intended to approximate the type of feedback often received by students in similar music classes and to avoid the ethical issues associated with a no-feedback condition. The Video Only Group, however, received only acknowledgment from the instructor of their own observations about their videotaped performances.

The differences among groups on the checklist, as a dependent measure, are not as dramatic as other comparisons, for example, the song leading scores. This suggests that the checklist is more useful as a teaching tool than as a discriminating evaluation instrument. Interobserver reliability on the checklist was acceptable, and the student-teacher agreements were higher than expected (.94). The yes/no format of the checklist may, in part, account for the high reliability because it requires only agreement on whether a response occurred rather than on its quality. Additionally, the students using the checklist had received instructor feedback, via the form, a minimum of four times before they were asked to evaluate themselves. Use of the checklist possesses several advantages over the other feedback conditions from an instructional point of view. First, the checklist was, by far, the quickest and most efficient method of relaying feedback to students. It required no additional equipment and virtually no writing. Second, its use structured a relatively high positive/low negative feedback format, which was directly contingent on correct behavior and very immediate to their occurrences. That is, by checkup 1 or 2, most students were already achieving above 70% correct behaviors from the checklist, resulting in proportionate positive feedback. Third, the checklist provided consistency of feedback from week to week. This would seem to be a desirable quality for feedback in the development of any new skill.

The music scores for most students stabilize between 70% and 90% accuracy throughout the study and appear to have improved little. This misrepresents the actual improvement and skill acquisition that did indeed occur. The development of a musical skill is, by its nature, a changing-criteria performance task. The pretest required the student only to play through a song, using the most elementary strum. The singers were cued in by the instructor. Subsequent checkups added criteria to the performer's task, requiring the incorporation of more difficult strumming as well as picking patterns; and being entirely in control of the singing situation, from starting pitch to cutoff. Neither the checklist nor the videotape feedback affected the music scores noticeably. It may be that learning to play a new instrument well is more dependent on modeling and practice than on any feedback system.

Three seconds, the interval used for recording correct music and song leading scores, seems to be a notably short period of time, but it is actually quite a long period when one realizes that one verse of many folk songs takes less than 1 minute to sing and subtle differences are observable even within the 3-second intervals.

The song leading scores evidenced the most dramatic improvement of the three performance measures. The differentiation among experimental groups was also the most marked on this variable. Of the three behaviors required to occur continuously for an interval of song leading to be classified as correct—eye contact, singing with the group, and right-hand strumming—eye contact was the behavior most often absent. Likewise, it was one of the most frequently missed items on the behavior checklist. Yarbrough and Price (1981) showed a direct relationship between lack of eye contact and group off-task when observing conductors. Eye contact, then, would seem to be an important skill for educators and therapists who lead group singing, which is much like conducting, but with an accompanying instrument. Many students did, in fact, increase their frequency of looking up at the group, but the duration increase was inadequate for the change to be documented by either the checklist or the song leading scores. Memorization of the folk songs was not stressed in preparing for the checkups. Requiring memorization might have improved eye contact considerably, especially because observation of the student performances suggests that looking at the songbook may be more a function of habit than of need.

The use of videotape recording equipment for data collection in studies of this type is admittedly more cumbersome and intrusive than paper/pencil observations. As the literature suggests, however, the accuracy gained by having a permanent record that may be viewed by multiple observers is undeniable. Only once during the study did equipment fail to the extent that data were lost. A unique facet of the study was the use of a computer program (Greenfield, 1982), using the PLATO® system to collect and analyze data obtained from the interval recording of the taped observations. This would not have been possible had videotape recording not been used.

The finding that music majors did not outperform non-music majors on pretest, posttest, or either follow-up is in contrast to the frequent complaints by music majors regarding their placement in a class with non-majors. An analysis of the cumulative years of instrument study by music majors and non-majors, that is, 4 years of piano and 2 years of flute equal 6 cumulative years of music study, reveals that music majors averaged 11 cumulative years of study and non-music majors averaged 5 years. Although music majors may be expected to have many years of music study, the average of 5 years of music study by non-majors indicates that college students outside the field of music are not necessarily musically naive.

The students in classes taught by the five other teachers demonstrated many of the same skills as those in the experimental groups (see Table 8.1). The fact that comparison group scores were slightly lower than experimental group scores was most likely attributable to the effect of testing, that is, the pretest of the experimental group, on the learning of the four feedback groups. It is not unlikely that the instructor of the experimental groups taught the classes with the nuances of the dependent measures in mind. This is in accordance with studies which show that groups rate highest in specific areas which are consistently emphasized (Moore & Kuhn, 1975). In addition, other instructors had had their classes perform checkup-type exams only four to five times before the posttest was given. Experimental groups had performed eight checkups before the posttest.

Non-performance Measures

A summary of the attitude items from the questionnaire indicated quite positive attitudes of students toward the use of videotape feedback in their classes. Most of them felt that videotape feedback was, or could be, advantageous to their learning. About half stated that they would choose a section in which videotape feedback was available, over another section, if they were aware of that beforehand. Slightly less than half the students said that videotape availability would make no difference in their section choice. A very small percentage indicated they would avoid a section if videotape feedback were to be used. Only one student who had been in a videotape feedback group was included in the latter category. The reason most frequently mentioned for desiring video feedback was that of "being able to see my mistakes/strengths." The aspects most frequently mentioned as disadvantages of videotape feedback were nervousness and fear.

In evaluating their own guitar accompanying skills, the Checklist Only Group outscored the other experimental groups in the number of discrete points made in their analyses. This group also mentioned overwhelmingly more checklist items than any other group, including the Video and Checklist Group. This finding bears further consideration in light of the fact that the Checklist Only Group outperformed the other experimental groups on numerous measures. The use of a focusing agent for learning has been shown to be effective in related literature. The group that had both checklist feedback and videotape feedback did not excel above groups having other types of feedback. It may be that videotape feedback is actually more useful in providing an overall picture of the entire music lesson or therapy session, and that the development of a single novel skill is somehow impeded by the presentation of too much feedback. Perhaps the checklist alone provides a focus for skill improvement without diverting one's attention to other behaviors not germane to the competency under study. The written essays of the Checklist Only Group seemed more limited to checklist behaviors than the essays of the Video and Checklist Group, which included a somewhat greater variety of other observations as well.

Responses on the standardized SIRS rating forms were uniformly favorable, and no significant differences existed among the experimental groups. A slightly more desirable rating was attained for the items grouped as Student-Instructor Interactions (see Table 8.14) in the Checklist Only Group, as compared with the other feedback groups or the departmental comparison. Possibly, the efficiency and dispatch that use of the checklist facilitated, by comparison with the other feedback methods, allowed students to perceive that the instructor had more time for discussion and answering questions.

Uncontrolled Variables

Variables that were uncontrolled in and unexplained by the study include a time-of-day effect and an individual treatment effect. The constraints of utilizing intact classes in the study precluded balancing of treatment groups to control for possible effects caused by class time on the learning or on the instruction. Although it seems unlikely that the time-of-day alone could account for some of the more dramatic pre-post changes evidenced, the possibility of its confounding the results cannot be completely discounted.

Inspection of the performance scores of individuals clearly demonstrates that the effect of feedback conditions is remarkably inconsistent within groups. This phenomenon is most evident when comparing topographies of individual song leading scores within the Video and Checklist Group and of the Video Only Group. The treatment effect, though obviously apparent for some students, is non-existent for others.

Contrary to expectation, the scores on follow-up 2 tended to drop, despite the performance of a self-selected song. It is a tribute to the integrity of most of the students that, given an opportunity for free choice, most did not choose the "easiest" songs in the textbook. Rather, they picked those that were favorites, many of which were quite challenging, and a few of which were beyond the skills of the student.

Implications

The use of the behavior checklist alone was as effective as its use in conjunction with videotape feedback in improving the guitar accompanying skills of students in the beginning guitar classes. This finding, as with any from a single investigation, should be generalized to other learning settings with prudence. Further research and replication need to be conducted for determining the most effective and advantageous use of focused videotape feedback in music therapy and music education training. Additional investigation should seek to verify those variables that are the most crucial for successful accompanied song leading in applied settings.

9 The Effect of a Focused Observation Task and Its Transfer on the Analysis of a Kindergarten Music Class by Pre-senior versus Pre-internship Music Education/Therapy Majors

Jayne M. Standley

Dianne G. Greenfield

Summary

Results demonstrated that, during treatment, pre-interns demonstrated better observation skills and scored significantly higher than the pre-seniors on the overall focused observation task (Mann-Whitney U, critical $U = 82$, obtained $U = 21$, $n_1 = 17$, $n_2 = 18$, $p < .01$). Analysis of postnarrative responses showed that pre-interns transferred these observation skills and scored substantially better than pre-seniors on specific versus ideational comments ($M = 75\%$, 62%, respectively), number of sequences cited ($M = 2.6$, 1.6), and reinforcement identified ($M = 1.5$, .24). Pre-seniors, however, scored better than pre-interns on one variable: the percent of student versus teacher comments ($M = 43\%$, 36%).

Pre-interns generally scored higher than the pre-seniors on all variables across initial observation opportunities, but repeated viewing of the same material caused a decrease in scores for pre-interns while creating an increase for pre-seniors. These differentiated responses may have implications for teacher/therapist training programs, especially for activities immediately prior to internship. As students near the end of the program, they may achieve less benefit from repetitive, casual observation opportunities such as those in traditional field experiences.

Design: ABA'CB' $N = 35$ Groups: 2
Statistical Analysis: Mann-Whitney U
Graphic Analysis: Percentage of observation responses by type and total observation scores
Reliability: .97, .98, .96

Independent Variables: Analysis of student behavior, antecedent and consequent events, identification of contingent relationships
Dependent Variables: Number of student behaviors, number of antecedent/behavior/consequent sequences, number of contingencies observed
Music: Performance, group

* * *

Educators, assuming accountability to be a personal responsibility, are directly concerned with evaluating pupil progress and its relationship to their classroom endeavors. Those preparing music teachers and therapists attempt to verify both acquisition of knowledge and mastery of the complex ability to assist others to learn.

A strong research base exists in this profession and has contributed much knowledge about effective teacher/therapist preparation. Systematic pursuit of improved methodology for competency-based music education/therapy has been an ongoing process and has occurred at many levels. Research into the acquisition of specific competencies (Alley, 1980; Greenfield, 1978; Hanser & Furman, 1980; Madsen & Yarbrough, 1980), the effect of specific competencies on pupil/client responses (Forsythe, 1975; Kuhn, 1975; Madsen & Alley, 1979; Moore, 1976a; Murray, 1975; Price, 1983; Yarbrough & Price, 1981), and the development of observational techniques for competency acquisition and evaluation (Gonzo & Forsythe, 1976; Madsen & Madsen, 1983; Madsen & Yarbrough, 1980; Yarbrough & Price, 1981) has been prolific and well documented.

Brown and Alley (1983) investigated entry-level skills and tracked persistence through the degree program. Brand (1977) compared pre-intern music education majors with their supervising teachers before and after the teaching experience on the variable of classroom management beliefs and skills. Wagner and Strul (1979) compared these two groups and undergraduate music education majors and quantified the amount of time spent pursuing various classroom activities. Few other studies have as yet pursued differentiated competency acquisition across curricular requirements and the related area of years of study. When do different types of learning activities function most effectively (i.e., lecture vs. demonstration, scholarly tasks vs. practicum assignments)? How do repetitive tasks function across time and multiple teachers, goals, settings, and evaluation modes (i.e., writing papers, taking tests, observing music interaction)? How much of a specific skill is transferred immediately upon acquisition versus across time? What are the competency differences between entry and exit levels of the curriculum?

The purpose of this study was to identify competency differences between pre-senior undergraduates and pre-intern music education/therapy majors in an observation task, specifically how they viewed and described a music interaction; how they acquired a novel, focused observation task; and how they immediately transferred elements of the focused observation task to the initial observation mode.

Method

Subjects for this study were 35 music education/therapy majors; 17 were pre-senior undergraduates with a mean of 3.3 semesters of college study and 18 were senior or certification/graduate students in their final semester of college study prior to internship. All subjects were asked to view a 6½-minute videotaped music lesson being conducted with a kindergarten class of nine children, aged 4 to 5 years. The observation task was in three phases and consisted of a baseline viewing period, followed by an observation period designed to focus on student behavior, antecedent and consequent events, as well as identification of contingent consequences, and ending with a final baseline viewing period to evaluate transfer.

During the initial observation period, subjects viewed and analyzed the first 4 minutes of the videotaped music lesson in two 2-minute excerpts. Subjects were given the following directions:

> You will have 2 minutes to watch the tape. Remember everything you see and hear. When the tape ends, you will have 2 minutes to write down everything you remember. Watch and remember. Do not write until I tell you. Begin watching.

After Observation 2, subjects were reshown Observation 1 and given 2 minutes to correct or add to their original responses. Red pens were used on the second trial so that responses following first versus second viewings could be differentiated.

The focused observation task covered the final 2½ minutes of the lesson plan and was divided into fifteen 10-second observation intervals. Subjects were given a data sheet with response space for each of the 15 intervals (see Figure 9.1) and the following instructions:

> You will watch the tape for 10 seconds and focus on what the students are doing. At the end of 10 seconds, the tape will stop and you will have 50 seconds to write. First write down what you saw the students doing. Use a different line for each *different* student behavior. Then, for each student behavior you observed, write down what happened just before and immediately after the behavior you saw. If the event after was some form of teacher behavior, decide

Figure 9.1
Focused Observation Data Form

Example	Event before	Student behavior	Event after	Contingent
1				yes/no/?
				yes/no/?
2				yes/no/?
				yes/no/?
3				yes/no/?
				yes/no/?
4				yes/no/?
				yes/no/?
5				yes/no/?
				yes/no/?

> if you thought this teacher behavior was contingent upon the student behavior (i.e., had a cause/effect relationship with it). If you thought the event after teacher behavior was contingent upon the student behavior, slash *yes;* if you thought it was not contingent, slash *no;* if you could not decide about a contingent relationship, slash *?*.

Subjects were verbally given one example of a contingent teacher response and one example of a noncontingent teacher response, and questions about the data form and the directions were answered. The observation task then began. Each excerpt required a total of 1 minute and began with the videotape in the pause mode. The researcher said, "Observe," and started the tape. At the end of 10 seconds, the researcher pressed the pause switch and said, "Write in interval ____." After 40 seconds of writing time, the researcher said, "Decide on contingencies," waited 8 seconds and said, "Look up." This cycle continued through 15 intervals without stopping. At the end of this task, subjects were reshown the two minutes of Observation 2 and subsequently given 2 minutes to correct or add to their original responses while using red pens. Subjects were told to transfer as many elements of the focused observation task as they could to this final response.

Equipment for this study consisted of a Sony Betamax portable video cassette recorder (SLO-340), a Sony black-and-white receiver (TV123), a Sony AC power adapter (AC-340A), a Hanhart stopwatch (Super-DBGM 7016 145), and a Scotch brand Beta cassette (L-500) videotape with all observation excerpts previously timed and dubbed in according to sequence of use.

The videotaped music lesson was viewed repeatedly by two independent, trained observers, and a script of its auditory and visual content developed for purposes of scoring subjects' responses. Each observation phase was analyzed for rate and type of teacher feedback, percentage of students on-task, and minutes spent in type of activity (see Table 9.1).

Lesson content of the focused observation task was analyzed according to the form described previously, and a total of 40 distinct student behaviors were identified. (Reliability across all lesson content analyses was .97 with agreements/agreements plus disagreements.) The focused observation form was subsequently scored. One point was awarded for each student behavior identified, one point for each sequence (i.e., an event before and event after identified correctly for the student behavior cited), and one point for correct determination of contingent relationship. A total score of 120 was possible on this instrument. A 33% sample of Focused Observation Forms was randomly selected and scored according to these criteria by two independent trained observers; the resulting reliability was .98.

The narrative responses following Observation Excerpts 1 and 2 and their repetition were quantified according to four variables that were operationally defined as:

Table 9.1
Analysis of Videotaped Music Lesson Content

	Observation 1	Observation 2	Focused observation
Teacher			
Approval	12.5/min	6/min	13/min
Disapproval	0	0	0
Reinforcement errors	0	1.5/min	0
Student			
On-task	96%	74%	96%
Activity			
Talking	76 sec	120 sec	69 sec
Singing	42 sec	0	0
Playing instruments	0	0	52 sec

1. *Number of Student versus Teacher Comments.* Narrative sentences were classified and counted according to the noun or implied noun serving as the subject of the sentence. Student sentences included references to students; children; a specific child by name, location, or action; group; plural pronouns, such as they or their; or behavior or responses attributable to the students, such as "singing was slower than the teacher." Teacher sentences included references to teacher; leader; therapist; the student or she, when followed by an action attributable to the teacher according to the script of the videotape; or judgments implying leadership, responsibility for the lesson, or under direct control of the teacher such as, "the lesson plan was too advanced for these children." A sentence was defined as narrative that contained a noun or implied noun and an action verb. Multiple sentences were quantified according to the number of phrases meeting the above criteria. All other narrative, such as isolated words, nonsentence phrases, or sentences not attributable to the teacher or students, was considered to be "other" and not quantified.
2. *Number of Specific versus Nonspecific Comments.* According to the above sentence criteria, all sentences were reclassified and quantified as specific: a fact or event that was observable, measurable, and veri-

fiable according to the script of the videotape; non-specific comments or ideas were defined as "all other" sentences, including inaccurate statements, personal beliefs, opinions, concepts, and so on.

3. *Number of Sequences.* A sequence was defined as any two juxtaposed sentences, one of which was categorized as "teacher," the other "student."
4. *Type of Reinforcement.* All teacher feedback was quantified in the categories of verbal, contact, or facial approval, disapproval, or reinforcement errors, according to Madsen and Madsen (1983).

The narrative response to the repetition of Observation 2 was further classified according to type of transfer. Transfer was operationally defined as any response from the focused observation task quantified according to the criteria above and occurring in the repetition of Observation 2 at a rate greater than or equal to a 50% increase above the highest frequency of that response in any of the three prior narratives. Transfer, therefore, was categorized according to an increase in sequences, specificity, contingencies (reinforcement), student comments, or ideas, or categorized as "none" if no increases occurred.

A 33% sample of all narrative responses scored independently according to the criteria above by two independent, trained observers yielded an overall reliability of .96.

Results

A total of 35 music education/therapy majors, 17 of whom were pre-senior undergraduates and 18 of whom were in their last semester of study prior to internship, participated in this study. They viewed and wrote a narrative about a kindergarten music class in two 2-minute excerpts. This task was repeated for both excerpts, but, prior to the Observation 2 repetition, subjects participated in a 15-minute focused observation task. They were then told to transfer as many elements of this task as possible to the repeated viewing of the second excerpt. The narratives for initial and repeated viewings were quantified according to student versus teacher comments, specific versus idea comments, number of sequences cited, and type of teacher reinforcements. The focused observation task was scored according to numbers of student behaviors identified, number of sequences containing correct event before and event after responses, and number of correct contingency determinations. The narrative following the repeated viewing of Excerpt 2 was quantified for type of transfer from the focused observation task.

A total score of 120 was theoretically possible on the focused observation task based on the content of the videotape and total number of separately

Table 9.2
Mann-Whitney U Test on Focused Observation Scores

	M	Sum of ranks	Obtained *U* value	Critical *U* value
Pre-seniors	28.9	234	225	
Pre-interns	39.3	396	81*	82

*Significant for $n_1 = 17$, $n_2 = 18$, $p < .01$.

identifiable student responses. Pre-intern scores ranged from 57 to 27 with a $M = 39.3$. Pre-senior scores ranged from 45 to 6 with a $M = 28.9$. This difference between groups was statistically significant on the Mann-Whitney *U* Test ($n_1 = 17$, $n_2 = 18$, $p < .01$), as can be seen in Table 9.2.

Narrative responses were quantified and graphed in Figures 9.2, 9.3, and 9.4, which show percent of student versus teacher comments, percent of specific versus idea comments, and number of sequences cited, respectively. All three graphs have several relationships in common:

1. Pre-interns were initially higher on Observation 1 than pre-seniors across all three variables.
2. Repeated viewing of Observation 1 caused a decrease in scores of pre-interns and an increase in scores of pre-seniors across all variables.
3. Both groups increased their scores between Observation 2 and the repeat of Observation 2.
4. The scores for the repeated Observation 2 were substantially higher than those of any prior observation (i.e., indicative of some transfer as per the definition of this study) on every variable except for specificity for pre-interns.

The graphs reveal additional interesting comparisons between the two groups:

1. Little difference existed between pre-interns and pre-seniors on the percentage of time spent watching the students versus the teacher in a musical interaction (Figure 9.2) and this rate remained quite low even after focusing on student behavior for 15 minutes (repeat Observation 2).
2. Pre-interns exhibited much higher rates of specificity than did pre-seniors (Figure 9.3) on all four observations. In a related study that asked subjects to translate ideas into observable and measurable behaviors, Madsen (1983) found that adults and young adults correctly did so only 59% of the time. It is interesting to note that pre-interns in this study were somewhat more "specific" than that, and pre-seniors were somewhat less so.

Figure 9.2
Percent Student versus Teacher Comments

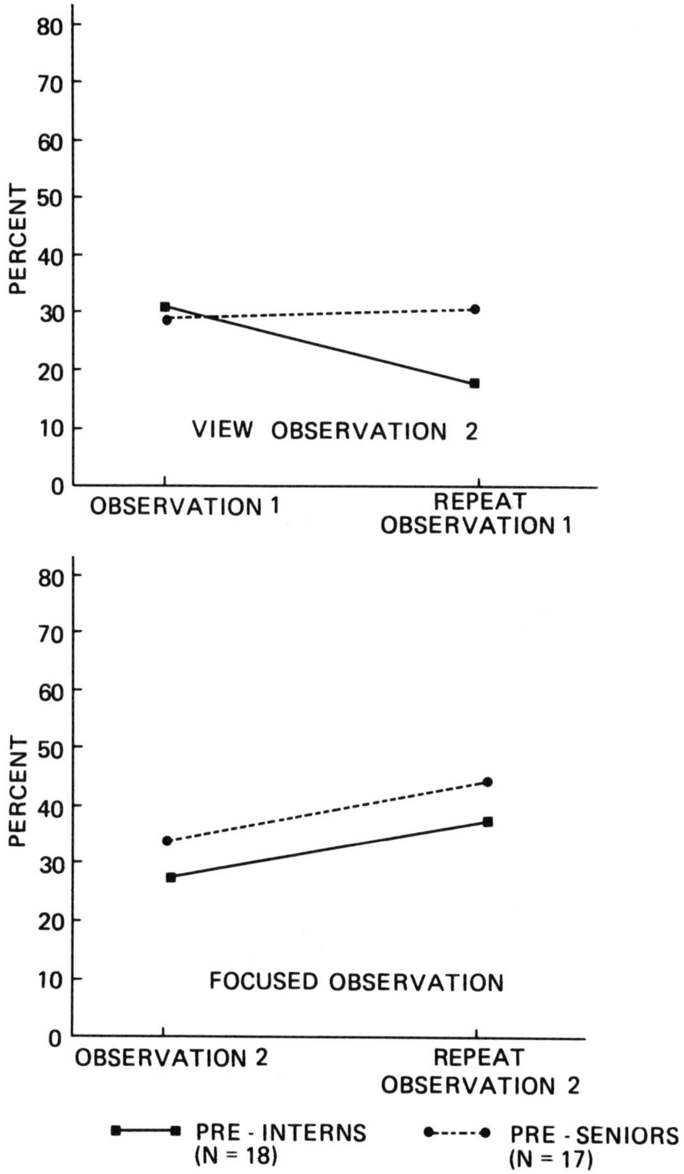

Figure 9.3
Percent Specific versus Non-specific Comments

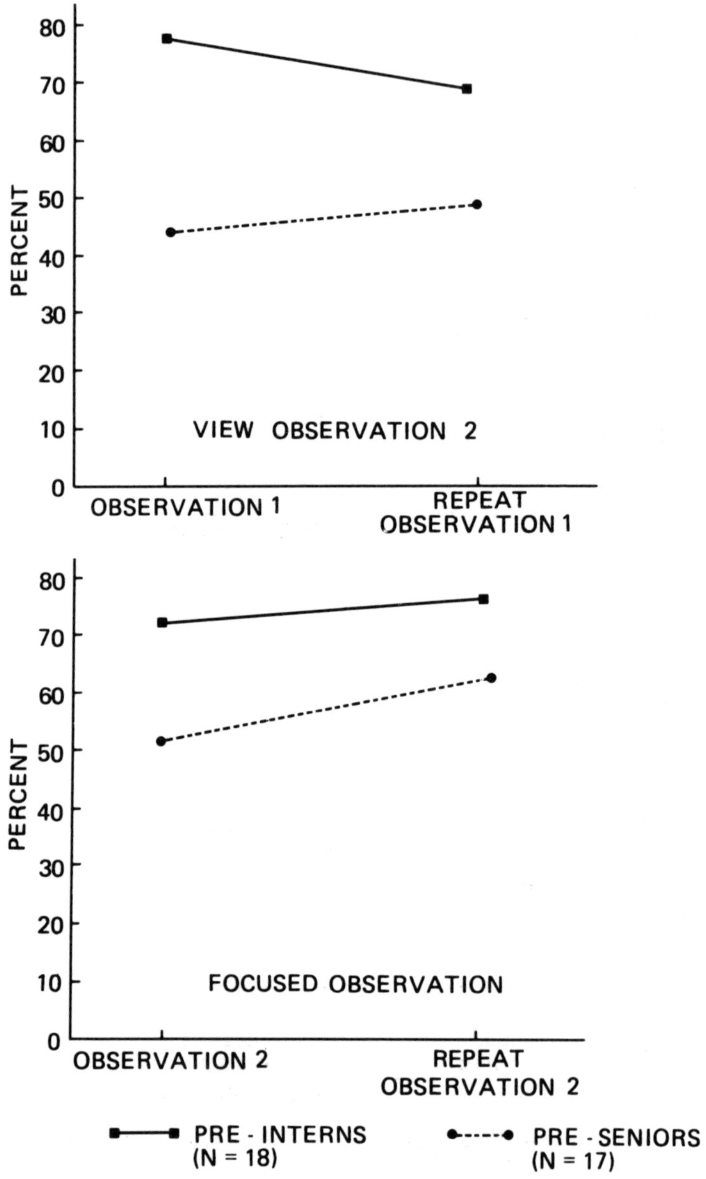

Figure 9.4
Mean Number of Sequences Cited

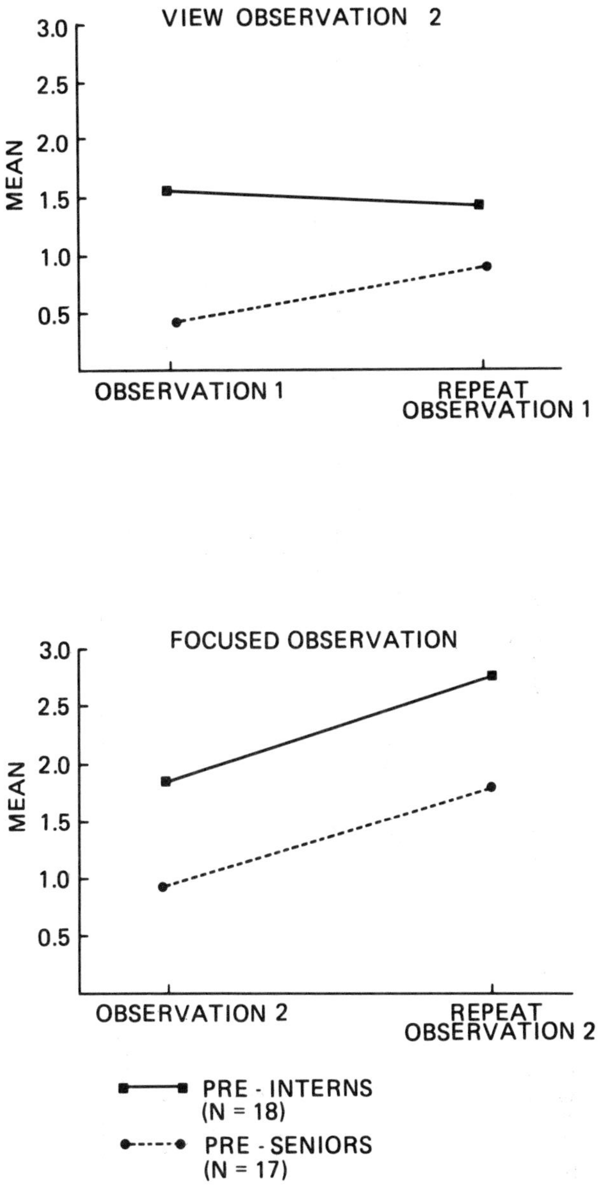

Table 9.3
Percent Type of Teacher Reinforcement Identified

	Pre-interns ($N = 18$)			
	Observation 1 ($N = 59$, $M = 3.3$)	Repeat observation 1 ($N = 26$, $M = 1.4$)	Observation 2 ($N = 37$, $M = 2.1$)	Repeat observation 2 ($N = 27$, $M = 1.5$)
Approval				
Verbal	85	73.0	87	78
Contact	5	11.5	8	15
Facial	7	4.0	5	0
Approval error	3	11.5	0	7

	Pre-seniors (N = 17)			
	Observation 1 (N = 13, M = .75)	Repeat observation 1 (N = 9, M = .53)	Observation 2 (N = 5, M = .29)	Repeat observation 2 (N = 4, M = .24)
Approval				
Verbal	85	100	100	75
Contact	0	0	0	0
Facial	15	0	0	25
Approval error	0	0	0	0
Total approvals on videotape	Observation 1		Observation 2	Focused observation
70	25		12	33

3. Pre-interns cited substantially more sequences of events than did pre-seniors (Figure 9.4).

Table 9.3 shows the identification by type of teacher reinforcement. Again, pre-interns are substantially better than pre-seniors at identifying reinforcement across all observations. Mean scores for pre-interns ranged from a high of 3.3 on Observation 1 to a low of 1.4 on its repeat. For pre-seniors, scores ranged from a high of .75 on Observation 1 to a low of .24 on the repeat of Observation 2. The videotape script analysis revealed that a total of 71 verbal, facial, and content approvals occurred, with those in Observations 1 and 2 repeated; this made a grand total of 107 opportunities to observe the teacher reinforcing the students. Mean rates of reinforcers described were exceedingly low, considering that both groups spent the majority of time watching the teacher.

Table 9.4 shows the amount and percentage of type of transfer identified in the narrative following the repeat of Observation 2. A total of 43 transfers was made by the 35 subjects, with the two groups having virtually the same means (1.3 and 1.2). Use of sequences was the primary transfer made.

Discussion

Evaluation of global concepts of human behavior, like teaching or therapy, can be facilitated by delineating the component parts in terms that are specific enough to be observable and measurable. Educators participating in the current trend toward competency-based teacher/therapist training are familiar with the process of identifying specific learning objectives based upon analysis of the delineated task, preparing and implementing learning activities specific to the objectives, and evaluating the subsequent results in criteria-referenced format. Prolonged pursuit of these endeavors leads to the realization that, though many students achieve the desired competencies, others do not. Despite careful planning and design, accumulated activities intended to produce a global competency may not necessarily do so. Exposure to such activities may not produce "learning," or the ability or inclination to spontaneously use such skills in future contexts. Competence achieved in one setting may not meet criterion when transferred to a slightly different setting.

This study revealed that pre-intern scores decreased on a repeated viewing of a videotape without focused observation objectives and that pre-senior scores increased. Both groups increased substantially on the repeated viewing following the focused observation objective. This differentiated response may have implications for teacher/therapist training programs, es-

Table 9.4
Percent Type of Transfer

Transfers	Pre-interns (N = 18)	Pre-seniors (N = 17)
Sequences	27	32
Specificity	19	27
Contingencies	19	9
Student comments	8	14
Ideas	12	9
None	15	9
N = 43	n = 23 M = 1.3	n = 20 M = 1.2

pecially for activities prior to internship. As students approach exit from the program, they may achieve less benefit from open-ended observation during field experiences. Such experiences may function to reinforce biases or existing beliefs, not to teach new information or analytical skills. The anecdotal report of narrative scorers seemed to indicate that the pre-interns were perceived as responding to the repeat of Observation 1 with new material (as opposed to corrected or more specific material) and that this new material appeared to be more judgmental in nature.

Figure 9.2 reveals that both groups spent most of their time observing and writing about what the teacher did, even immediately after focusing on student behavior in a 15-minute directed observation task. This would seem to suggest that the teacher/therapy training activities to which the pre-interns have been exposed across the entire curriculum have not yet "taught" the importance of not only knowing what teachers do, but also knowing how their actions affect their pupils.

An additional finding of this study that seems noteworthy is the low rate of reinforcement identification, revealed in Table 9.3. Out of 107 opportunities to observe teacher approvals, the pre-intern group identified from 1.4 to 3.3 approvals per viewing on the average, and the pre-senior group identified from .24 to .75 approvals. Again, it should be remembered that, the majority of time, both groups wrote teacher-oriented comments. Did they not see the reinforcement, not think it important enough to comment on, or not perceive it as a teacher technique affecting the children?

A recent study by Madsen and Duke (1985b) investigated graduate and undergraduate music therapy/education majors' perception of teacher approval/disapproval given to elementary students versus the actual classroom events. A substantial discrepancy was discovered between actual and perceived events by both groups and between the two majors. The authors concluded that these differentiated aspects of perception influence greatly the study of effects.

Students' perceptions are highly individualized and affect their responses to learning activities. It is apparent that teacher assumptions about "why" a particular activity is initiated, that is, to teach a particular objective, may be fallacious for some students. In actuality, the activity may not *function* in the way intended by the teacher.

To what extent do music education/therapy majors benefit from open-ended observation tasks or repetitious observation tasks? How can learning activities be improved to assist these majors in moving from a teacher orientation to a student orientation while observing? To what extent can group classroom settings be adapted for the differentiated perceptions of individuals? These issues warrant further investigation.

10 Observation of Applied Music Instruction: The Perceptions of Trained and Untrained Observers

Robert A. Duke

Summary

This study compares the perceptions of musicians trained in the delivery and recording of academic and social feedback with those of non-musicians who had not received such training. Subjects observed one-to-one instruction in applied music.

Both trained and untrained observers varied considerably in their perceptions of events, even within highly specific and controlled circumstances. Of particular interest are the extreme variability *within* each of the groups and the similarity between group responses concerning proportions of time devoted to various lesson activities and the assessment of teacher behavior. The data illustrate observers' propensity to direct attention to teacher behavior to a greater extent than to student behavior.

The ability to recognize, identify, and accurately record the cause-and-effect relationships associated with teaching and therapy is an essential component of useful observation. It appears necessary that appropriate dependent measures regarding the assessment of effective teaching be specified.

Design: Posttest Only $N = 100$ Groups: 2
Statistical Analysis: t tests Reliability: .93
Graphic Analysis: Bar graphs of ranges, medians, and inner quartiles for subject estimations of proportions of total lesson time and teacher time devoted to various activity categories
Independent Variables: Music therapy/education majors with behavioral training versus education (non-music) majors with no behavioral training

Dependent Variables: Content and frequency of written statements; estimations (%) of proportions of total lesson time and teacher time devoted to various activity categories

* * *

Music therapy and music education share a number of common elements concerning the nature of activities employed in the teaching process. As evidenced by the large and increasing number of hours of field experience and practica that are included in most teacher/therapist training programs, it appears widely accepted that a considerable amount of time should be devoted to fieldwork in which students are afforded opportunities to become familiar with the settings, tasks, and responsibilities associated with these professions. Recently, many state legislatures have actually mandated increasing "hands-on" time during teachers' pre-internship instruction. The inclusion of such experiences early in courses of study has proven to be beneficial, not only providing diagnostic and predictive information (Brown & Alley, 1983), but also offering a glimpse of what one actually *does* as a professional teacher or therapist.

The degree to which students in music therapy and music education actively participate in field experiences as opposed to passively observe seems to vary across disciplines, states, and programs. Regardless, a major portion of field experience involves the observation of working professionals. Although a disparity exists in the quality of teaching or therapy among situations and professionals observed, it is often assumed that students are capable of making discriminations concerning the effectiveness and appropriateness of techniques, and, subsequently, incorporating these techniques into their own repertoire. Even more basic, and perhaps a good deal more consequential, is the implicit assumption that students are able to accurately (i.e., reliably) perceive what is actually taking place during an observation.

Previous research concerning various factors that may influence the perceptions of individuals has demonstrated differential effects attributable to expectations (Jones, Worchel, Goethals, & Grumet, 1971; Miller, 1976), primacy (Jones & Goethals, 1972; Jones, Goethals, Kennington, & Severance, 1972), sexual bias (Taynor & Deaux, 1973; Feather & Simon, 1975), level of physical arousal (Clark, Milberg, & Erber, 1984; Hornberger, 1960), emotional state (Isen & Shalker, 1982; Murray, 1933; Schiffenbauer, 1974), and the relationship of the observer to the one(s) being observed (Frye, Rawling, Moore, & Meyers, 1983). Studies focusing on third-party observations of academic and social feedback have revealed differences among observer perceptions related to inconsistencies between verbal and nonverbal behavior (Tyson & Wall, 1983), the apparent level of competence of the feedback recipient (Strenta & Kleck, 1982), as well as previous observer training and the instructional goals of the observer (Madsen & Duke, 1985a, 1985b).

The present investigation compares the perceptions of individuals trained in the delivery and recording of academic and social feedback with those of individuals who had not received such training. In contrast to previous work concerning observers' perceptions of feedback in music (Madsen & Duke, 1985a, 1985b), in which subjects observed large classroom settings, the present investigation employed a relatively limited situation in which only two individuals (student and teacher) were visible to the observers.

Method

The responses of undergraduate and graduate music education and music therapy majors ($n = 50$) participating in a course concerning observational techniques in music were compared to those of undergraduate education majors who had no previous applied music background ($n = 50$) and who were enrolled in music education courses designed for non-music majors. In light of previous research using videotape viewing, which specifically addressed subjects' perceptions of approval and disapproval teacher responses, it was decided to test the perceptions of subjects viewing a film of an actual individual applied lesson.

The videotape presented both the applied instructor and student on a split screen through the use of two synchronized video cameras. An accompanist was present during the lesson, but was not in view. The lesson focused upon two contrasting sections of a work for solo bassoon and piano. The piece was nearly "performance-ready" in that note accuracy and rhythmic accuracy were greater than 90 percent, and the student and accompanist had developed relative uniformity of phrasing and articulation.

To define the actual recorded events, the 26-minute stimulus tape, edited from a 1-hour lesson, was analyzed across 10-second intervals using observation instruments developed by Madsen & Madsen (1983) and adapted for one-to-one applied music instruction by Kostka (1984a). Of the total number of recorded intervals, 50% included student musical performance; 24%, performance by the teacher. Verbal instructions/explanations and reinforcement by the teacher were recorded in 58% of the intervals, and 2% of the intervals included student verbalizations. Of the intervals that contained some type of teacher behavior, 23% included verbal approval and 17% verbal disapproval. Intervals during which the teacher gave instructions or explanations comprised 72% of the total number of intervals involving teacher behavior, and 30% of the teacher-related intervals included performance demonstration by the teacher. There were no mistakes of reinforcement (i.e., teacher approval to inappropriate student behavior or teacher disapproval following appropriate student behavior). In 13% of the total intervals, the teacher stopped musical performance in progress. Because many intervals contained more than one analysis category, the total percentage exceeds 100%.

The videotaped lesson was presented to the trained subjects during the final week of a one-semester class in behavior modification in music. A classroom designed specifically for the use of audiovisual equipment was used for the presentation. All subjects received the following verbal instructions:

> You will see a 26-minute videotape of an applied music lesson. As you observe the session, notice as much as you can about what is going on, and write brief statements about what you see. Consider the following: Setting, Teacher Behavior, Teacher/Student Interactions, Lesson Organization, Student Musical Behavior, Student Social Behavior. Once again, make as many clear and succinct observations as you can, and write them down as you watch the tape.
>
> If you have any questions, ask now.

At the conclusion of the presentation, subjects were asked to estimate the percentages of time devoted to each of the activity categories described above as well as estimate the proportion of the teacher's time devoted to Approval, Disapproval, Instructions/Explanations, and Musical Performance. In addition, subjects listed any previous teaching, counseling, or leadership experience and were encouraged to record any other comments or impressions regarding the lesson.

Results

The accuracy and uniformity of subjects' estimations of the proportions of time devoted to various aspects of the lesson varied across the eight response categories. Tables 10.1 and 10.2 present the group means and standard deviations for the estimated percentages of total lesson time devoted to Student Talk, Teacher Talk, Student Performance, and Teacher Performance, and the estimated percentages of the teacher's time spent giving Approval, Disapproval, Instructions/Explanations, and Performance Demonstration.

Significant differences occurred between the trained and untrained group means concerning the proportion of the total lesson time devoted to Student Talk ($p < .001$) and Teacher Talk ($p < .001$), with the trained subjects' estimating a higher proportion of Teacher Talk and a lower proportion of Student Talk than the untrained subjects. No significant differences were found between the groups concerning the proportions of total lesson time

Table 10.1
Group Mean Estimates of Proportions (%) of Total Lesson Time

	Trained (n = 50)		Untrained (n = 50)			
Activity (actual percentage)	M	(SD)	M	(SD)	t	p
Student talk (01)	1.47	(2.94)	4.24	(4.53)	3.63	.001
Teacher talk (44)	46.18	(14.21)	34.92	(15.30)	3.81	.001
Student performance (36)	42.32	(14.95)	47.72	(21.57)	1.45	*
Teacher performance (19)	11.57	(6.65)	9.72	(5.89)	.95	*

*$p > .05$.

devoted to Student Performance ($p > .05$) and Teacher Performance ($p > .05$). In the estimations of Teacher Time devoted to Approval, Disapproval, Instructions/Explanations, and Performance Demonstration, no significant differences existed between the groups ($p > .05$).

It may be observed that both groups' mean estimations were often quite close to the actual proportions of time spent during the lesson. Regarding feedback given by the teacher, however, both trained and untrained subjects underestimated the percentage of teacher approval and greatly overestimated the percentage of teacher disapproval.

The variation among perceptions *within* groups is of particular interest in the present investigation. Figures 10.1 and 10.2 present the range, median, and inner quartiles for both groups' estimations of each aspect of total lesson time and teacher time. The extent of variation within the groups of trained and untrained subjects is quite similar across most of the activity categories.

Table 10.2
Group Mean Estimates of Proportions (%) of Teacher Activity

	Trained (n = 50)		Untrained (n = 50)			
Activity (actual percentage)	M	(SD)	M	(SD)	t	p
Approval (16)	11.83	(10.66)	12.94	(9.03)	.56	*
Disapproval (12)	24.14	(19.16)	29.46	(17.93)	1.43	*
Instructions (51)	49.34	(16.74)	43.06	(16.84)	1.87	*
Performance (21)	16.41	(9.68)	14.40	(7.46)	1.16	*

*$p > .05$.

Figure 10.1
Range, Median, and Inner Quartiles for Trained and Untrained Subjects' Estimates of Proportions of Total Lesson Time

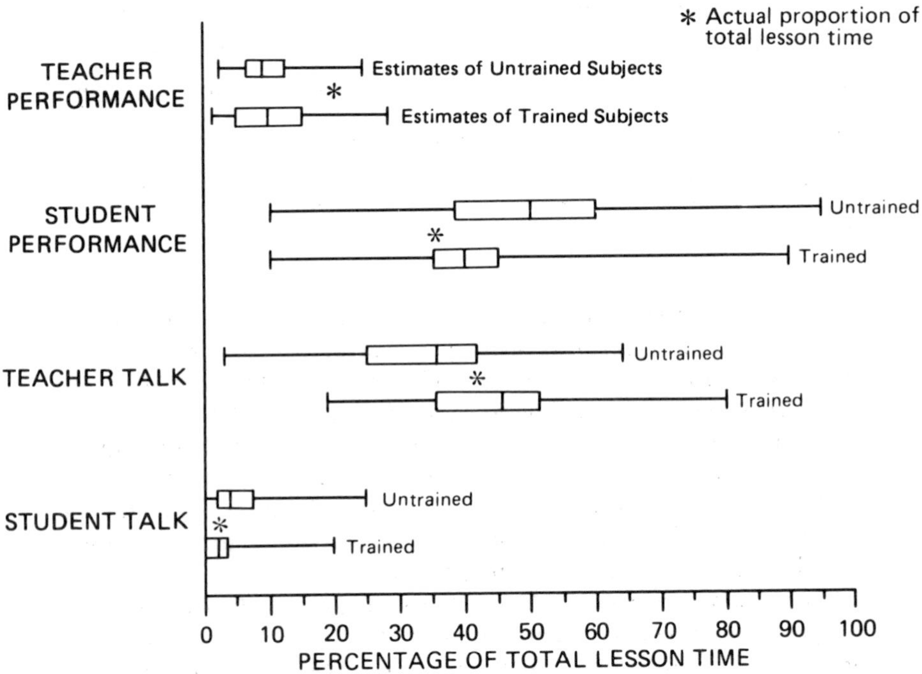

Only in the estimations of Student Talk and Student Performance are the group variances unequal, $F\ (49,49) > 1.98$, $p < .01$, the smaller variance occurring within the trained group.

Subjects' written statements concerning observations made during the course of the film were analyzed according to focus of attention: the teacher, the student, or "other." Each of these three categories was further divided into statements that were evaluative in nature (i.e., those which contained no factual information about the observation) versus those that were written descriptions of observed events. Finally, evaluative statements were categorized as to valence (positive/negative), and factual statements were identified as descriptions of Approval responses, Disapproval responses, or neutral information.

Two independent judges completed the classification of subjects' written observations. Interjudge reliability was calculated for each subjects' set of

Figure 10.2
Range, Median, and Inner Quartiles for Trained and Untrained Subjects' Estimates of Proportions of Teacher Activity

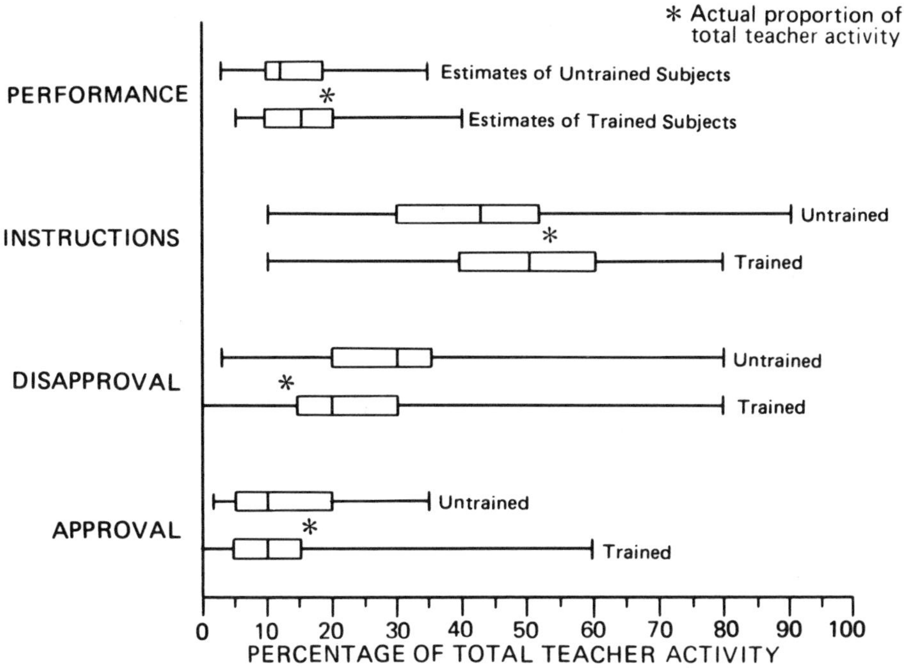

responses by dividing the number of agreements by the total number of observations. The mean reliability across subjects was .93.

Table 10.3 presents the frequency in each of the categories for all subjects. It appears that the focus of attention in both groups was primarily directed toward teacher behavior, though the proportion of responses concerning the teacher, student, and other aspects of the lesson varied between the trained and untrained groups, χ^2 $(2, N = 100) = 113.88$, $p < .0001$. The ratio of teacher-related versus student-related statements was 2.8:1 in the trained group and 4.3:1 in the untrained group.

Trained and untrained subjects also varied in the number of statements recorded across the 10 response categories, χ^2 $(9, N = 100) = 293.35$, $p < .0001$. Untrained subjects recorded a higher proportion of evaluative comments than the trained observers; a greater number of positive evaluations were also recorded by the untrained group. It is interesting to note

Table 10.3
Frequency of Written Statements

	Trained (n = 50) Focus			Untrained (n = 50) Focus		
Content	Teacher	Student	Other	Teacher	Student	Other
Evaluation						
Positive	62	23		72	22	
Negative	59	19		49	16	
Observation (factual statement)						
Approval	159	58		28	5	
Information	1,267	497		197	43	
Disapproval	202	22		44	4	
Total	1,749	619	39	390	90	54

that, in both groups, factual statements concerning Disapproval given by the teacher outnumbered statements concerning teacher Approval, though, during the course of the lesson, Approval responses by the teacher were actually more frequent than Disapproval responses (Approval/Disapproval ratio = 1.35:1).

It appears that both trained and untrained subjects vary considerably in their perceptions of observed events, even within highly specific and controlled circumstances. In addition, it seems that observers may focus their attention to a much greater extent upon teacher behaviors as opposed to those of students.

Discussion

In addition to the time estimations and specific written observations of the private lesson, subjects were encouraged to write "additional comments" following the completion of the observation task. These responses less readily lend themselves to quantification and statistical comparison. However, the written comments offer additional support to the notion that even subjects specifically trained in techniques of observation and who are familiar with the observation task may evidence a great disparity among perceptions concerning an observed activity.

Comparisons of several examples of the comments written by the trained observers further illustrate the variability among the perceptions of events. Concerning the student's musical performance, several subjects indicated that there was "not a lot of improvement" because the student "seemed to become more and more frustrated since he was constantly bombarded with criticism," but other subjects thought that the "student seemed to get a lot out of the lesson because one could *hear* the change in his performance" and "the teacher succeeds in getting the student to respond *musically.*" Several subjects perceived the lesson as a "very negative experience (in that) the teacher modeled (performed) constantly for the student," and others indicated that the teacher "let the student continue to play" and that "the teacher did much listening; I'm sure this is a credit to his instructing." Several subjects noted that the "teacher often stopped and corrected one problem and then immediately stopped again for another problem," and others perceived that "the teacher doesn't stop the piece to make comments, which I think is good because he is encouraging creativity."

As might be expected, subjects' evaluative statements and observations written during the course of the videotape evidenced similar differences. Within the group of trained observers, some subjects thought that the "teacher's goals for the student seemed clear. Combination of talking/playing demonstration was effective," but others thought the teacher was "hooked on himself—didn't instruct well—could only demonstrate." Specific techniques employed by the teacher were considered to be useful by some and annoying by others: "(Teacher) directs while allowing student to continue playing; this seems to let the student 'reinforce himself' through the music" versus "the teacher's movements during the student's performance were distracting to the student." Differences among trained subjects' perceptions of teacher approval were also reflected in comments which indicated that "criticism is given constructively, and positive reinforcement is also given," compared to suggestions that "the teacher gives shallow praise after criticism." Trained subjects' overall evaluations of the lesson ranged from "I was frustrated just watching the lesson" to "this was an ideal behavioral situation." Similar discrepancies appear among the observations and post hoc comments of the untrained subjects.

The lack of accuracy and congruity among subjects having identical training with regard to a common experience appears extremely important in relation to the implicit assumptions cited earlier concerning observation. Although several of the group mean estimations were close to the actual times spent in the various activity categories, the variance within each of the groups seems to warrant concern and further investigation by those involved in the education of therapists and teachers. It should be remembered that the trained subjects in the present study were enrolled in an observation class; had completed at least four independent observations, one with a reliability observer; and had previously demonstrated proficiency in counting selected teacher and student behaviors across 10-second observation intervals using student and teacher observation forms (Madsen & Madsen, 1983). These data underscore the necessity of pinpointing observable behaviors to be recorded during observations in order to ensure accuracy and reliability. It appears that subjects who attend to ill-defined aspects of behavior within even a limited context may not be able to accurately record details or formulate reliable evaluations.

In relation to establishing and implementing appropriate criteria for evaluating the effectiveness of instruction, some disagreement occurred among subjects regarding what was believed to be the nature of the task. In both groups, individuals' written statements concerning the teacher greatly outnumbered student-related observations. In addition, few subjects in either group cited the musical performance of the student (which may be considered the goal of the lesson) in relation to the instructions, demonstrations, and feedback given by the teacher. Very few of the trained subjects made any reference to teacher instructions/feedback and subsequent improvements in student performance, which may suggest that the observers' dependent measure for effective teaching was not necessarily student progress.

It is interesting to consider the great amount of time in which all music professionals have been involved in various aspects of music instruction, as students, teachers, and observers. However, effecting appropriate instructional/feedback techniques remains a difficult task for pre-internship as well as practicing professionals, after perhaps thousands of hours of observation and participation. The ability to recognize, identify, and accurately record the cause-and-effect relationships associated with teaching and therapy is an essential component of useful observation. This line of research suggests a need for further examination of the variables that may influence observers' perceptions of teaching/learning situations. In addition, it appears necessary that one specify appropriate dependent measures regarding the assessment of effective teaching.

11 The Effect of Self-Monitoring on the Rate of a Verbal Mannerism of Song Leaders

Carol A. Prickett

Summary

This study examined the effect of self-monitoring and its associated reactivity (a change in a behavior's rate when quantification begins) on the rate per second of a distracting verbal mannerism that occurred when education students attempted to teach a song to the class. The distracting mannerism consisted of saying "OK" in contexts other than direct approval. General admonitions to the entire class to decrease this verbalization had no effect, even though each student reviewed a videotape of his or her teaching in which the rates averaged 5.66 per 30-second interval. However, when asked to count the number of times "OK" was said on the tape, 78% of the students' rates decreased immediately. Other distracting mannerisms evident on the tape, but not directly monitored, showed no change. The reactive effect appeared to be strongest for those students whose initial rates were the highest and weakest for those who said "OK" only rarely.

The self-monitoring technique appeared to produce an immediate and dramatic change in the rate of the distracting and inappropriate mannerism, especially for those students whose need was greatest. The instructor's role was that of guide and reinforcer, rather than critic. Nevertheless, the instructor's role in targeting a behavior for self-monitoring seemed critical because general reminders and watching oneself, without specific directions, produced no noticeable effect.

Design: Multiple baseline $N = 18$ Groups: 3
Reliability: Mean = 96%; Range = 90%–98.5%
Statistical Analysis: Friedman two-way analysis of variance

Independent Variables: Watching a videotape of oneself teaching a song; general admonitions to the entire class by the teacher; counting one's own verbal mannerism rate
Dependent Variables: Rate of the verbal mannerism; percentage of session time spent in verbalization
Music: Performance, group

* * *

Instructors of college courses designed to prepare future teachers to use music in the classroom frequently address not only the mastery of subject matter by their students, but also the effectiveness of the students' teaching presentations. The identification and modification of teachers' behavioral excesses or deficits that impair the presentation of subject matter have been the focus of innumerable treatises. Although the technique of simply instructing a person to increase or decrease a particular behavior has not been shown to produce a noticeable change, social praise, financial incentives, auditory cues, and direct intervention have been used successfully (Cossairt, Hall, & Hopkins, 1973; Harris, Bushell, Sherman, & Kane, 1975; Van Houten & Sullivan, 1975). Self-monitoring, that is, counting one's actions, has been associated with observable behavior change (Saudargas, 1972; Thomas, 1972; Van Houten & Sullivan, 1975). The usefulness of self-monitoring and self-evaluation in the instruction of future music teachers has been demonstrated in a number of settings (Alley, 1980; Furman, 1984; Madsen & Yarbrough, 1980; Moore, 1976a; Prickett, 1983b; Stuart, 1979; Yarbrough, Wapnick, & Kelly, 1979).

Reactivity, or the characteristic change in rate which occurs when quantification of a behavior begins, has been proposed as the primary usefulness of self-monitoring as a behavioral technique (Nelson & Hayes, 1981). The most drastic change in rate frequently occurs immediately after self-monitoring begins and has been labeled a "reactive surge" (Nelson & Hayes, 1981). The reactive change may be maintained through continued self-monitoring. However, if self-monitoring is discontinued or if no transitional program is available to introduce reinforcers that will maintain the behavior change, reversion toward the original rate may occur (Broden, Hall, & Mitts, 1971; Prickett, 1983b).

Factors that appear to influence the strength of reactivity are the specificity of the behavior, the number of behaviors being observed, the initial rate of the behavior, personal values, and motivation to change (Hayes & Cavoir, 1977; House & Kinscherf, 1979; Johnson & White, 1971; Kazdin, 1974; Lipinski, Black, Nelson, & Ciminero, 1975; Prickett, 1983b). Reactivity has not been shown to be affected by the reliability of self-monitoring (Herbert

& Baer, 1972; Lipinski & Nelson, 1974; Nelson & McReynolds, 1971), though accuracy appears to improve with training in observation (Bolstad & Johnson, 1972; Fixsen, Phillips, & Wolf, 1972).

Among the behaviors successfully adjusted through self-monitoring are nervous tics (Ollendick, 1981) and the rate of verbal approval given by teachers or students coaching other students (Saudargas, 1972; Prickett, 1983b). If increasing positive verbalizations is a goal for education students, so too is the decrease of inappropriate verbal mannerisms. The term "OK," used when no evidence exists that it was intended as reinforcement, has been observed to occur with a high frequency during music teaching sessions (Prickett, 1983a), even in students whose speech is relatively fluent in conversation or in class discussion. The present study investigated the use of self-monitoring and its possible resultant reactivity as a technique for decreasing this verbal mannerism during a song leading and teaching session.

Method

Subjects

Eighteen undergraduate elementary education majors enrolled in a junior level music education class served as subjects. Seventeen were female; one was male. A course in music fundamentals, or its equivalent, is a prerequisite. Approximately 80% of the class reported never having seen themselves on videotape. No one had received observation training.

Design and Procedure

A multiple baseline design was used. During baseline, each student taught a song to the entire class by rote and, in private, watched a videotape of this teaching. Treatment consisted of teaching the song, watching the videotape, and counting the number of times "OK" had been said. Thirteen students taught five songs each; five others, four songs apiece.

On the first day of the semester, the instructor taught the class a song by rote, distributed a handout breaking this teaching task into 21 separate steps, and reenacted teaching the song to illustrate each step. Students were instructed to adhere to this model and cautioned to avoid distracting mannerisms such as saying "OK." Nine days elapsed between this demonstration and the first class meeting where each student taught a song. Songs 2, 3, and 4 were taught at intervals of 48 hours, 72 hours, and 48 hours, respectively. Because of inclement weather, the final song was not taught until a full week later. At the end of each day's teaching, the class as a whole was exhorted to work to reduce the number of times "OK" was said during a presentation. During teaching, no accompanying instrument was allowed, nor any cue sheets.

For each teaching session, students taught their songs to the entire class. The sequence of presentations was rotated so that the stress of teaching early, midway, or late in the hour was distributed equally among all students. The only feedback given during class consisted of polite, nonsubstantive comments by the instructor.

Students individually came to the instructor's office for private viewing of their portions of the tapes. The instructor watched the tapes alongside them. All of them kept their appointments. Told at the outset that the instructor felt they deserved to decide for themselves how well they had taught, they received no feedback other than a nonsubstantive comment, such as, "I hope you saw plenty of things which pleased you." Only one student was seen to watch the tape with the model task analysis in hand.

The tape-review procedure remained unchanged for subsequent viewings, until the time came for a particular student to self-monitor the number of "OK"s said in any context. This technique was presented by the instructor's saying, "Your teaching is coming along, so now we can polish some of the fine points." The instructor gave students a form for recording "OK"s, demonstrated making a tote mark each time the verbalization occurred, and pointed out the place to write the total. Self-monitoring students watched their tapes one time. The instructor concluded the session by telling students to keep their slips until called for, that they would be asked to count again in the future, and that it was up to them to decide who, if anyone, should know their rates. It should be noted that students' beginning dates for self-monitoring (i.e., after Song 2 or Song 3 or Song 4) were assigned by chance rather than by any relationship to the rate of "OK"s or to general teaching effectiveness.

Results

Videotapes were reviewed by two independent observers and the number of times each student said "OK" was recorded. Observer reliability averaged 96%, and any discrepancy as great as two was double-checked. The number of seconds spent in singing (either by the song leader alone or by the song leader and the class) versus non-singing (i.e., verbalization) was noted. The mean percentage of time spent in verbalization by those who began self-monitoring after Song 2 (Group I), after Song 3 (Group II), and after Song 4 (Group III) is depicted in Table 11.1. Across time, the decrease in time spent

Table 11.1
Mean Percentage of Session Time Spent in Verbalization

	Session				
	1	2	3	4	5
Group I	49.1	46.5	41.1	40.8	38.7
Group II	38.6	33.3	37.8	28.7	29.8
Group III	49.3	41.2	39.7	35.0	34.9
All groups	45.6	40.3	39.5	34.8	34.5

talking was consistent in all groups, and a Friedman two-way analysis of variance indicated this might not have been merely chance alone ($\chi^2_r = 253.58, p < .001$).

The rate of "OK"s per second was calculated, using the number of seconds devoted to verbalization, because the mannerism never occurred during singing. The mean number of "OK"s per second for each group during each session is shown in Figure 11.1. Table 11.2 translates these means into the rate per 30 seconds; 79 of 85 song leading sessions incorporated 30 or more seconds of verbalization. A Friedman two-way analysis of variance did not detect a significant trend in these rates attributable to an order effect ($\chi^2_r = 7.46, p > .10$).

Figure 11.2 portrays the individual graphs of the 4 subjects whose average rates for the first two presentations were the highest in the class, and Figure 11.3 illustrates the rates of the 4 subjects whose averages in the initial song leading were the lowest.

Fifteen students returned some or all of their self-monitoring slips, allowing 28 reliability comparisons with the external observers' counts to be made. The range of agreement was 0% to 100% ($M = 70\%$), with 13 comparisons meeting a 90% or better reliability criterion.

Discussion

The decrease in the rate of the verbal mannerism, from averages above 5 per 30 seconds during the first two baseline sessions to 2.8 per 30 seconds after everyone had self-monitored, appears to be noteworthy. As shown in Figure 11.1, the change appears to be related to the onset of self-monitoring. The mean drop in rate after the first self-monitoring session was .093 per

Figure 11.1
Comparison of Group Means of Rate of "OK"s

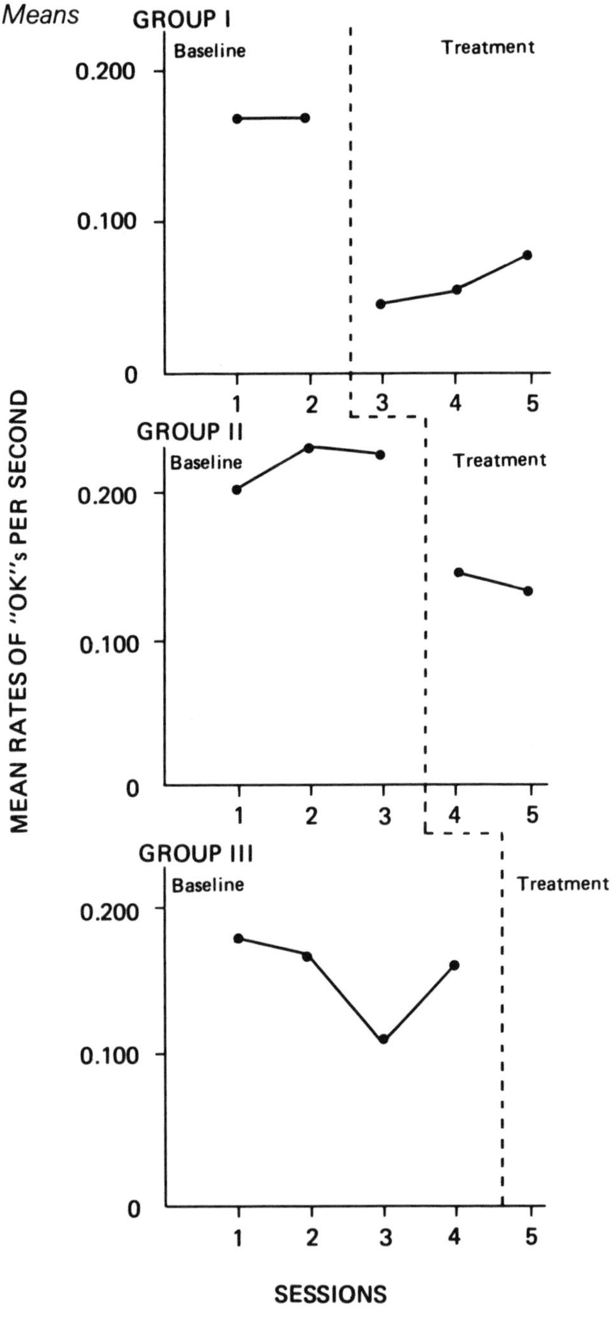

Table 11.2
Mean Rates of "OK"s per 30-Second Intervals

	Session				
	1	2	3	4	5
Group I	5.19	5.16	1.47*	1.65*	2.40*
Group II	6.09	6.99	6.78	4.29*	3.96*
Group III	5.46	5.07	3.27	4.92	2.73*

*Treatment

second or 2.8 per 30 seconds, even taking into account that 4 subjects actually increased .052 per second or 1.5 per 30 seconds.

Although the percentage of time spent talking went down slightly with each session, it should be pointed out that nothing was said to the song leaders about the amount of time involved in verbalization. Also, this decrease seems unrelated to the introduction of self-monitoring or to changes in the rate of the mannerism.

General admonitions to the class as a whole to cut down on mannerisms such as saying "OK" produced no observable effect. Seeing oneself on tape, saying "OK" as frequently as once every 4 seconds, appears to have made no difference without actually counting. Aspects of the teaching task, such as giving the correct starting pitch or calling on one student by name, varied little from session to session; adherence to the original model neither improved appreciably nor deteriorated for any song leaders. Except for one subject who gave up chewing gum after seeing herself on tape, other distracting habits such as foot-shuffling, balancing on one foot, or hair twirling continued unabated. Subject 11 (see Figure 11.2), who gave up gum, did not respond reactively to counting "OK"s.

As in the studies cited previously, the accuracy of the self-monitoring was unrelated to the strength of the reactive surge. The self-monitoring technique was effective, even though the subjects had not been trained in observation and had almost no experience in seeing themselves on tape.

Examination of Figures 11.2 and 11.3 illustrates a differential effect noted in earlier studies already cited. Song leaders whose baseline rates were quite high tended to react strongly, as evidenced by the drastic drop in rates, and students whose initial rates were lower had very mixed results. It appears that the greater the discrepancy between an observed rate and what is perceived to be the ideal, the greater the reaction.

Figure 11.2
Performance of Four Subjects with Highest Mean Baseline Rates

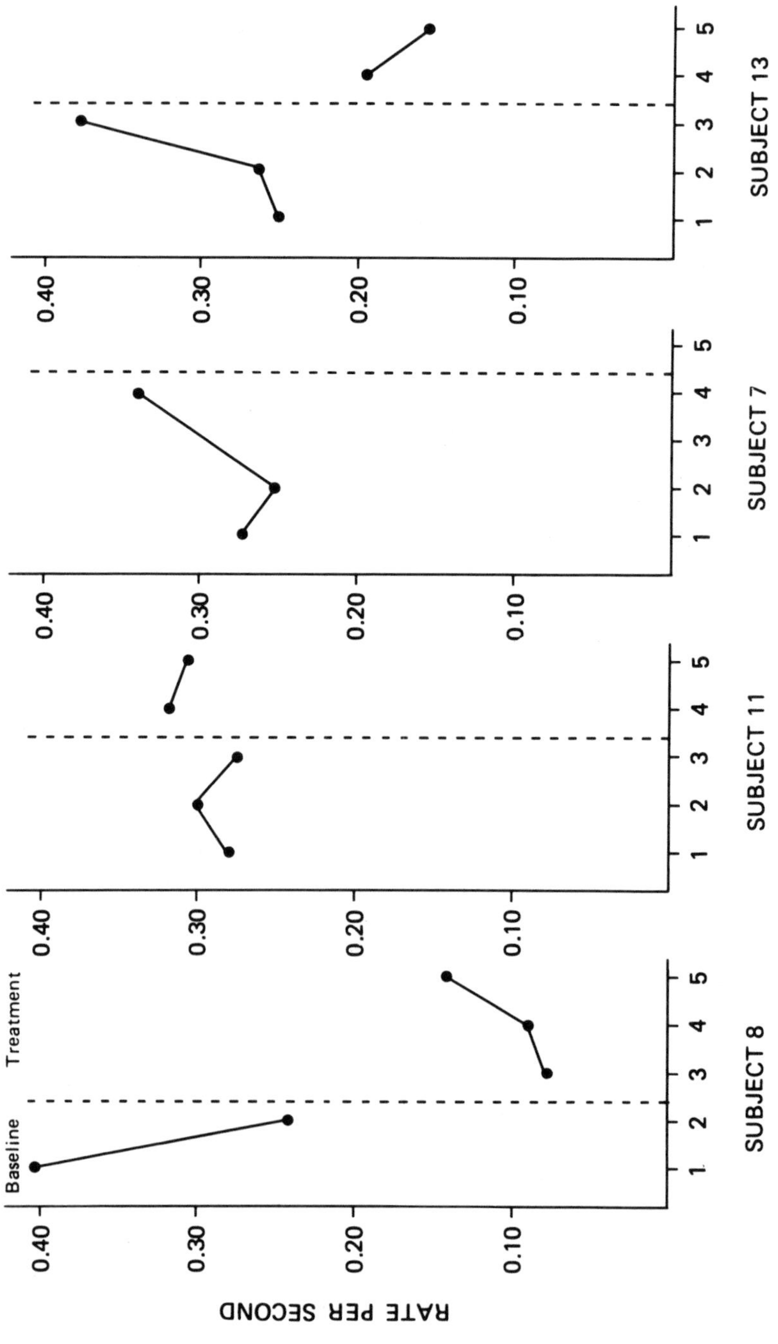

Figure 11.3
Performance of Four Subjects with Lowest Mean Baseline Rates

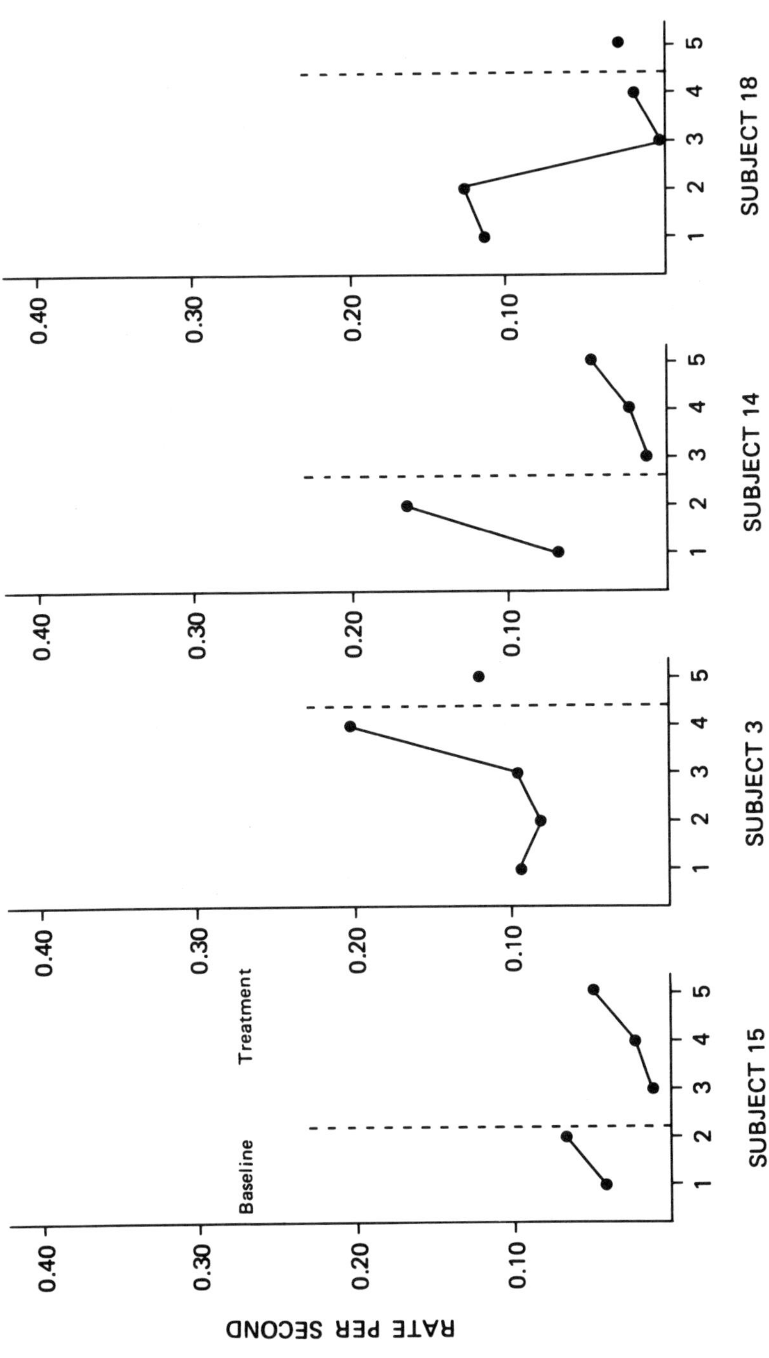

The change in rate for Group III was less pronounced than for the other groups. Three of the six students in this group missed a baseline teaching session, interrupting the sequence of song leading and viewing that was constant for members of the other groups. Additionally, the delay between self-monitoring and the subsequent session due to bad weather may have lessened the effect of self-monitoring. Finally, a fourth group member, Subject 18 (see Figure 11.3), had spontaneously dropped to a rate of zero during a baseline session, making the overall contrast less distinct.

As an efficient technique for decreasing a behavioral excess that detracts from music teaching (e.g., a verbal mannerism), self-monitoring has several strengths. Reactivity, if it occurs, tends to happen immediately. Its greatest effect is on the behavior of those whose behavior is farthest from the ideal. The technique is uncomplicated and requires little equipment or training for effective use. Further, self-monitoring is a technique that allows students to be given credit for their improvement; it may be suggested that this may contribute to students taking more responsibility for their professional development. Lastly, the instructor's role may shift from critic toward guide and reinforcer. The quick turnaround brought on by reactivity can be an occasion for immediate praise and encouragement.

Nevertheless, the instructor's role in targeting a behavior to be self-monitored appears to be essential. Simply watching oneself, even coupled with general reminders to reduce a behavior, had no noticeable effect, either on the mannerism mentioned or adherence to the instructional model or to other blatantly distracting mannerisms. In the case of excessive behaviors that the student actually may think are a part of the teaching role, such as negative or sarcastic comments to children, the instructor would need to reteach the value or ideation prior to introducing self-monitoring because it seems it is the disparity between one's self-monitored behavior and one's ideal that influences the strength of reactivity.

12 Verbal Training Effects on Teaching Units: An Exploratory Study of Music Teaching Antecedents and Consequents

Judith A. Jellison

David E. Wolfe

Summary of Study:

Because research suggests that it is important that undergraduate students learn how to plan for, and ultimately increase, the use of reinforcement and complete teaching units, it then becomes necessary to identify specific training procedures to bring about the increases. Once effective training procedures can be established, additional questions regarding effects of single-component training on the teaching unit may be examined.

Design: Exploratory pre-post $N = 36$ Groups: 3
Statistical Analysis: ANOVA
Reliability Range: .88–.98
Graphic Analysis: Descriptive graphic analysis
Independent Variables: Antecedent training (questions and directives); consequent training (general and descriptive approval); contact control (organization training)
Dependent Variables: Antecedents (questions and directives); consequents (general and descriptive approval); teaching units (complete and incomplete)
Music: Performance (teaching), individual

* * *

Prior to the late 1960s, teaching, as well as professional education and teacher training, was largely an intuitive process. However, because of the outpouring of research on teacher behavior and student learning during the past decades, data have become available that clearly describe how teachers may structure effective learning environments for students.

One specific teaching model has been presented by Becker, Engelmann, and Thomas (1971). Teaching units are described within the model and consist of the teacher presenting task signals, stimulating a response, and providing appropriate response consequences. The first two of these steps are defined as preceding stimuli or pre-task and task components, respectively, and the third step is defined as the consequent stimuli or post-task component. Research has demonstrated the effectiveness of this model in teaching mathematics and English (Becker & Engelmann, 1976; Berliner & Rosenshine, 1976; Brophy & Evertson, 1974; Rosenshine, 1979). In addition, teaching units have been observed in high school choral rehearsals (Yarbrough & Price, 1981) and have been found to result in musical performance gains and high student attitude ratings in symphonic band rehearsals (Price, 1983). The basis for the teaching unit is a behavioral three-part teaching process that may be defined as: antecedent stimuli, student response, and consequent stimuli.

One specific part of the teaching unit that has received considerable attention in music education and music therapy research has been the effect of teacher/therapist reinforcement (consequent stimuli) on student behavior. A vast amount of literature on this teacher behavior and its importance to undergraduate training programs in teaching and therapy has appeared in major research journals, as well as in several texts (Greer, 1980; Madsen, Greer, & Madsen, 1975; Madsen, 1981a; Madsen & Yarbrough, 1980).

Antecedent stimuli (task signals—the first step in the three-step unit) have received little to no attention in the music research literature. In teaching units, these stimuli may take the form of teacher questions or directives and may be considered as opportunities for the student response to occur. In educational areas outside of music, research has focused primarily on teacher questioning and various hierarchical levels (Redfield & Rousseau, 1981; Winne, 1979), duration of student response (Dillon, 1981), patterns of solicitation (Wright & Nuthall, 1970) and the correspondence between teacher questions and student questions (Mills, Rice, Berliner, & Rousseau, 1980). A few studies have suggested that the frequency of questions that a teacher asks is related to student learning (Brophy & Evertson, 1976), with higher rates of questioning being associated with higher student achievement. Good and Brophy (1974) attribute high rates of questions and subsequent high student achievement to teachers who are well organized and who have well-managed classes and therefore are able to spend most of their time actively teaching students.

From the literature, it would seem important that teachers in training learn how to plan for, and ultimately increase, the use of antecedents, reinforcement, and complete teaching units in preparation for classroom teaching. Effective training procedures to bring about the increases have not been identified. A preliminary study by Wolfe and Jellison (1984) indicated that written practice was not sufficient to bring about significant increases in these components. Once effective training procedures can be established, additional questions regarding effects of single-component training on the teaching unit may be examined.

The purpose of this exploratory study was primarily to examine training procedures designed to increase the frequency of teacher antecedents (spoken questions and directives) and teacher consequents (spoken approval). Measurements were taken on six variables, two each within the following three categories: antecedents (spoken questions and statements), consequents (spoken general and descriptive approval), and teaching units (incomplete and complete). Overall effectiveness of the training procedure on the selected training variable was evaluated as were possible effects of training on one variable on the frequencies of untrained variables.

Method

Design and Dependent Variables

Six dependent variables were measured across three training conditions (Antecedent, Consequent, and Contact Control/Organization) using a pretest/posttest design. The six variables were categorized within three areas relating to teaching units or teaching unit components. Definitions of the variables by categories are listed below:

Verbal Antecedent. Teacher question and/or directive that specifies an academic and/or social task for student(s) and that is followed by a response wait time (minimum 1 second). Verbal antecedents may be in the form of questions or directives.

Verbal Consequent. Spoken words, phrases, and sentences that occur immediately following a correct student response and that may increase the probability of the future occurrence of that response. Consequents may be in the form of general approval (praise that does not include or describe the specific behavior being praised) or descriptive approval (praise that includes or describes the specific behavior being praised).

Approval Teaching Unit. A sequence of teacher-student-teacher behaviors consisting of the following components: teacher question or directive, student(s) response, and teacher verbal approval (general or descriptive). Teaching units may be complete (consisting of all three components) or incomplete (consisting of the first two components).

Procedure

Forty-three undergraduate students enrolled in a methods course for the elementary music classroom participated in the study. They were enrolled across three sections of the course; two sections were designated for elementary education majors and one section for music education majors. Students from each of the three sections were randomly assigned to three verbal training conditions (antecedent, consequent, or organization). All testing as well as training was conducted within the context of the regular classroom setting for the particular class section. Subjects met as large groups in their respective class settings for pretest and posttest teaching and in small groups according to condition assignment for training sessions. Small groups were comprised of approximately 4 to 5 subjects, with three groups (training conditions) per class section. All 43 subjects participated in the training sessions. However, absences during pretest, posttest, or training sessions, as well as random selection of subjects to structure groups of equal size, resulted in 12 subjects per training condition with $N = 36$. Of the 36 subjects, 12 were music education majors (4 per condition) and 24 were elementary education majors (8 per condition).

Pretest teaching was conducted within a week preceding training sessions, and posttest teaching was conducted within a week following them. Dates, times, and teaching lessons were randomly assigned to each subject, with 3 to 4 subjects teaching per testing day. Printed instructions and lesson assignments were distributed approximately 4 days prior to the first day of teaching. Subjects had opportunities to ask questions for clarification of teaching assignments. General instructions for both the pretest teaching and posttest teaching were identical. Subjects were instructed to teach for at least 10 minutes and were informed that they would be videotaped throughout the teaching. Date, lesson, and teaching times were indicated on the printed instructions. Subjects were instructed to teach "the best you can, using the techniques that you have been taught in this class so far." Subjects were to teach the objective indicated on the assigned lesson and to use the procedures from the lessons as "guidelines." In addition to general instructions, the posttest subjects were instructed to demonstrate skills in the specific area in which they had been trained the previous week. For the posttest teaching, a summary sheet in the form of a checklist and specific to the skill area was attached to the printed instruction.

All lessons used in the testing and training procedures were selected from a single publication (Madsen & Kuhn, 1978). From the 40 available published lessons, 20 were selected to form an initial lesson pool. Lessons that suggested limited opportunity for teacher-student interaction (i.e., extended record listening) were eliminated in the selection process. The pool was used for the random selection and assignment of lessons to students from each class. A selected lesson was used only once per class per testing session. Each subject was assigned different lessons for pretest and posttest sessions. Because a major purpose of the study was to determine the effectiveness of the training procedures, the lesson selected and assigned to a subject for the posttest session was the same one used by that subject throughout the training session.

To gather further information regarding generalization effects of the training procedures, the music education majors ($N = 12$) taught an additional lesson in elementary classrooms of public schools throughout the community. No particular materials or instructions were given subjects for this teaching situation. Students were videotaped throughout their teaching for video analysis of the same six variables observed in the pretest and posttest teaching setting.

Training Sessions

Prior to the structured training sessions, all subjects received approximately an hour of instruction on the teaching unit (i.e., teacher asks a question or gives a directive, student responds, teacher gives approval for correct responses). Following this preliminary instruction, all subjects participated in four days of training specific to condition assignments.

Subjects assigned to the Antecedent Training Group and the Reinforcement Group were instructed to specify observable academic and/or social behaviors in their statements. Criteria for the training of questions and directives were derived from the literature, which suggests that questions and directives should be specific, concise, pertinent to the lesson, and include a "wait time" for the response to occur (Brophy, Rohrkemper, Rashid, & Goldberger, 1983; Groisser, 1964; Mills, et al., 1980; Redfield & Rousseau, 1981; Rowe, 1974; Wright & Nuthall, 1970). Criteria for the training of verbal reinforcement with specific emphasis on descriptive verbal approval were derived from research literature suggesting that statements of praise that include or describe the behavior being praised are more effective than general praise to increase academic student learning (Brophy, 1981; Fuego, Saudargas, & Bushell, 1975; Horton, 1975; Novak & Hammond, 1983; Realon, Lewallen, & Wheeler, 1983).

Subjects in the Contact Control Group were instructed to develop overall organization and clarity skills. This group was defined as the Organization Training Group. Criteria for training were based on research projects that identify teacher organization and clarity skills as important to student learning (Luiten, Ames, & Ackerson, 1980; Rosenshine, 1968; Schuck, 1981; Smith & Land, 1981; Wright & Nuthall, 1970).

Four training sessions of approximately 50 minutes each were conducted within the context of the regular class session. Subjects who were absent for 2 or more days of training were permitted to participate in the sessions, but data from these subjects were not included in the analysis. The sessions were designed for discrimination and verbal (written and spoken) practice of the assigned teaching variable. The sessions were structured to successively approximate the whole group posttest teach. Training sessions were labeled as follows: video observation and discrimination training, written practice, spoken practice, and small-group teaching.

Video observation (Day 1). Subjects received packets of information containing general instructions and an observation form. The trainer informed the participants that they would receive training designed to improve teaching skill in one particular area. They were also informed that assignment to skill area was randomly determined and that opportunities for training in the other areas would be provided in future weeks. Subjects read the general instructions for observation, which included pertinent definitions and examples. Questions were answered and the viewing of the demonstration tape was begun.

Observation forms were simple in design. The form for organization observation was a checklist of 13 organizational skills, including those designated for training (identifies the purpose of the session; gives an overview of the content; presents definitions of new terms, concepts, and principles; and provides clear and simple examples for difficult and abstract concepts). The subjects checked "Yes," "No," or "Not Applicable" for each skill observed. Subjects in the Antecedent Group were asked to count, by marking on the form, the number of occurrences of questions and directives (academic or social). Those in the Reinforcement Group, using the same procedure, counted the number of occurrences of verbal approval (general, descriptive academic, and descriptive social).

Written practice (Day 2). Subjects received training packets, consisting of instruction sheets, work sheets, and a copy of a lesson randomly selected from the initial lesson pool. Following the distribution of materials, groups met in separate areas for training. Subjects were instructed to write statements or phrases that might be used throughout the teaching of their particular lesson. Subjects in the Antecedent condition wrote 10 questions (5 academic/5 social) and 10 directives (5 academic/5 social). Subjects in the Reinforcement condition wrote 10 descriptive verbal statements (5 academic/5 social). Subjects in the Organization condition wrote statements specific to the purpose of the class session: an overview of the content; definitions of new terms, concepts, and principles; and clear and simple examples to clarify abstract and difficult ideas. Statements were written on work sheets that were checked throughout the session to ensure that the subjects understood the task. In addition, people in the Antecedent and Reinforcement groups wrote combination social and academic statements. For example, a combined statement for the Antecedent Group could be: "I want you to quietly [social] take out your recorders and play the notes [academic] that I point to." An example for the Reinforcement Group could be: "Terrific. You took out your recorders so quietly [social] and played all the notes correctly [academic]." The statements were discussed by group members for feedback and revision. All sheets were collected at the end of the session and examined to detect any errors in the subjects' understanding of the skill or specific written task.

Spoken practice (Day 3). Work sheets from the previous day were returned to individual subjects. Group members met to discuss, review, and revise statements. Subjects practiced saying the statements and then proceeded to another room to record the statements on a cassette recorder labeled according to group condition. Subjects were alone throughout the recording procedure. They stated their names and then spoke the written statements into the microphone. After recording, they worked individually on the assigned lesson in preparation for teaching. Papers and tapes were collected at the end of the session and examined to detect possible errors in the subjects' understanding of the skill or specific spoken task.

Small Group Teaching (Day 4). Written statements and lessons from the previous session were distributed. Subjects were given approximately 10 minutes to study the lesson and their written statements in preparation for a 5-minute small group teach. The small group teach was defined as a rehearsal of the beginning of the lesson. Subjects were instructed to incorporate statements they had written or other statements that would reflect the designated skill. Groups were located in separate rooms and a timekeeper was assigned to each of them. To keep all groups working on their task, they were informed that the entire session would be tape-recorded. The audiotapes were later reviewed to ensure that the subjects understood the task and were rehearsing throughout the entire session. At its end, they received instructions for posttest sessions. They were permitted to keep all work sheets and were instructed to review them in preparation for the posttest teaching.

Observation

Videotape recordings of the pretest, posttest, and generalization teaching were used for the measurement of the six variables: questions, directives, general approval, descriptive approval, incomplete units, and complete units. Antecedent and reinforcement variables were recorded as they occurred for the first 10 minutes of each of the recordings. Excluded from the observational data were questions, directives, and approval that were not relevant to the academic material or general classroom social behavior. Also excluded were words such as "OK" and "All right" when they appeared to be nonfunctional to the teaching sessions. Antecedent and approval statements were recorded as either incomplete (antecedent only) or complete (antecedent and approval) units. Only approval units were recorded. Approval statements that appeared to occur independent of an antecedent statement were recorded and included in the total approval data, but not included in the unit data.

Videotapes were observed by a single observer unaware of the subject-to-condition assignment. Reliability observation was conducted by a second independent observer for 16 videotape recordings, or 44% of all recordings. Tape recordings for reliability were randomly selected from pretest and posttest recordings; eight recordings were selected from each testing period.

Results

Observer reliability on pretest and posttest videotape data were computed for each of the six variables by dividing the number of agreements by the total number of agreements plus disagreements. Percentage of agreement for questions = .98, directives = .88, general approval = .88, descriptive approval = .96, incomplete units = .95, and complete units = .88. The range for observer reliability across dependent variables was .88 to .98.

Separate one-way analysis of variance procedures were used to determine differences across each of the three verbal training groups for each of the six variables: questions, directives, general approval, descriptive approval, incomplete units, and complete units. Separate analyses were conducted for both pretest and posttest scores. No significant differences were found among the three groups prior to or following training. Pretest and posttest mean scores and standard deviations for each group are presented in Tables 12.1, 12.2, and 12.3.

Because no significant differences were found among the three training groups, data were graphed by major (elementary or music) to identify possible patterns in training effects for each of these two groups. Mean scores for the total number of antecedents, reinforcement, and complete units for each of the training conditions are presented by majors in Figures 12.1 and

Table 12.1
Mean Scores and Standard Deviations for Antecedent Training Group

	Pretest		Posttest	
Variables	*M*	*SD*	*M*	*SD*
Antecedents				
Questions	22.17	(11.79)	20.67	(8.03)
Statements	9.75	(4.99)	9.00	(6.90)
Total	31.67	(12.35)	29.67	(9.67)
Consequents				
General approval	9.67	(8.21)	8.67	(3.87)
Descriptive approval	3.08	(3.20)	5.92	(4.48)
Total	12.75	(8.80)	14.58	(6.68)
Teaching units				
Incomplete	19.92	(6.32)	15.83	(5.97)
Complete	11.75	(9.16)	13.58	(6.46)

Table 12.2
Mean Scores and Standard Deviations for Consequent Training Group

	Pretest		Posttest	
Variables	*M*	*SD*	*M*	*SD*
Antecedents				
Questions	23.83	(9.49)	27.17	(17.19)
Statements	8.58	(6.63)	6.83	(6.66)
Total	32.42	(11.29)	34.00	(14.53)
Consequents				
General approval	9.75	(5.85)	10.25	(5.51)
Descriptive approval	7.75	(5.03)	11.95	(10.88)
Total	17.50	(8.77)	22.20	(13.22)
Teaching units				
Incomplete	16.25	(7.79)	15.17	(6.95)
Complete	16.17	(8.75)	18.92	(12.01)

Table 12.3
Mean Scores and Standard Deviations for Organization Training Group

Variables	Pretest *M*	Pretest *SD*	Posttest *M*	Posttest *SD*
Antecedents				
Questions	18.50	(9.67)	25.00	(11.00)
Statements	9.17	(7.30)	12.17	(9.30)
Total	27.67	(12.78)	37.17	(12.13)
Consequents				
General approval	6.75	(5.71)	12.92	(5.47)
Descriptive approval	6.83	(7.46)	8.75	(5.83)
Total	13.58	(10.25)	21.67	(5.37)
Teaching units				
Incomplete	15.67	(7.20)	16.83	(9.84)
Complete	12.00	(9.80)	20.25	(5.61)

12.2. Mean scores for the total number of general verbal approvals and descriptive verbal approvals used by elementary education majors are presented in Table 12.4.

Discussion

Results of analyses across groups indicate that the groups were generally very similar in their use of questions, directives, general approval, descriptive approval, incomplete, and complete teaching units at the beginning of training as well as following training. However, when the data are separated and graphed by subjects' majors (See Figures 12.1 and 12.2), different patterns emerge for the three training groups. Considering these differences, the following discussion will focus on the descriptive graphed data as presented by majors.

In analyzing the elementary education majors' data (Figure 12.1), it would appear that both reinforcement training and organization training were effective in increasing the subjects' use of antecedents, reinforcement, and complete teaching units. It should be noted that little to no change is observable in the curves for the Antecedent Training Group across mean

Figure 12.1
Mean Percentages of Antecedent, Consequent, and Complete Training Unit Responses for Elementary Education Majors under Three Training Groups

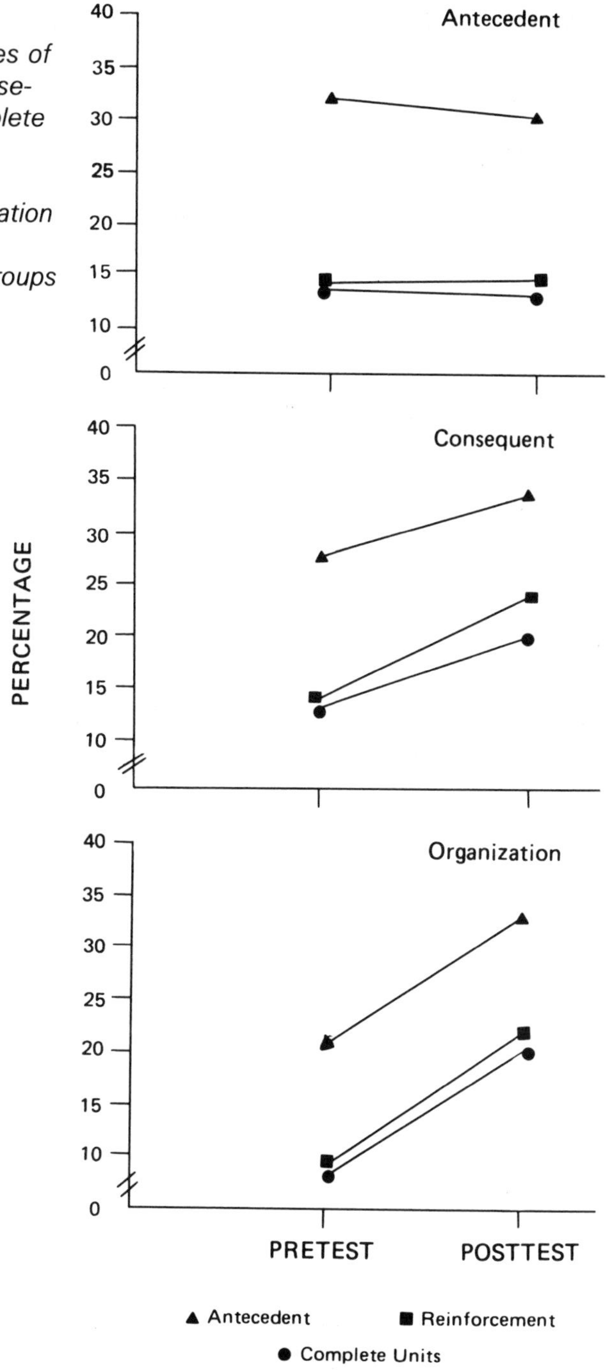

Figure 12.2
Mean Percentages of Antecedent, Consequent, and Complete Teaching Unit Responses for Music Education Majors Under Three Training Groups

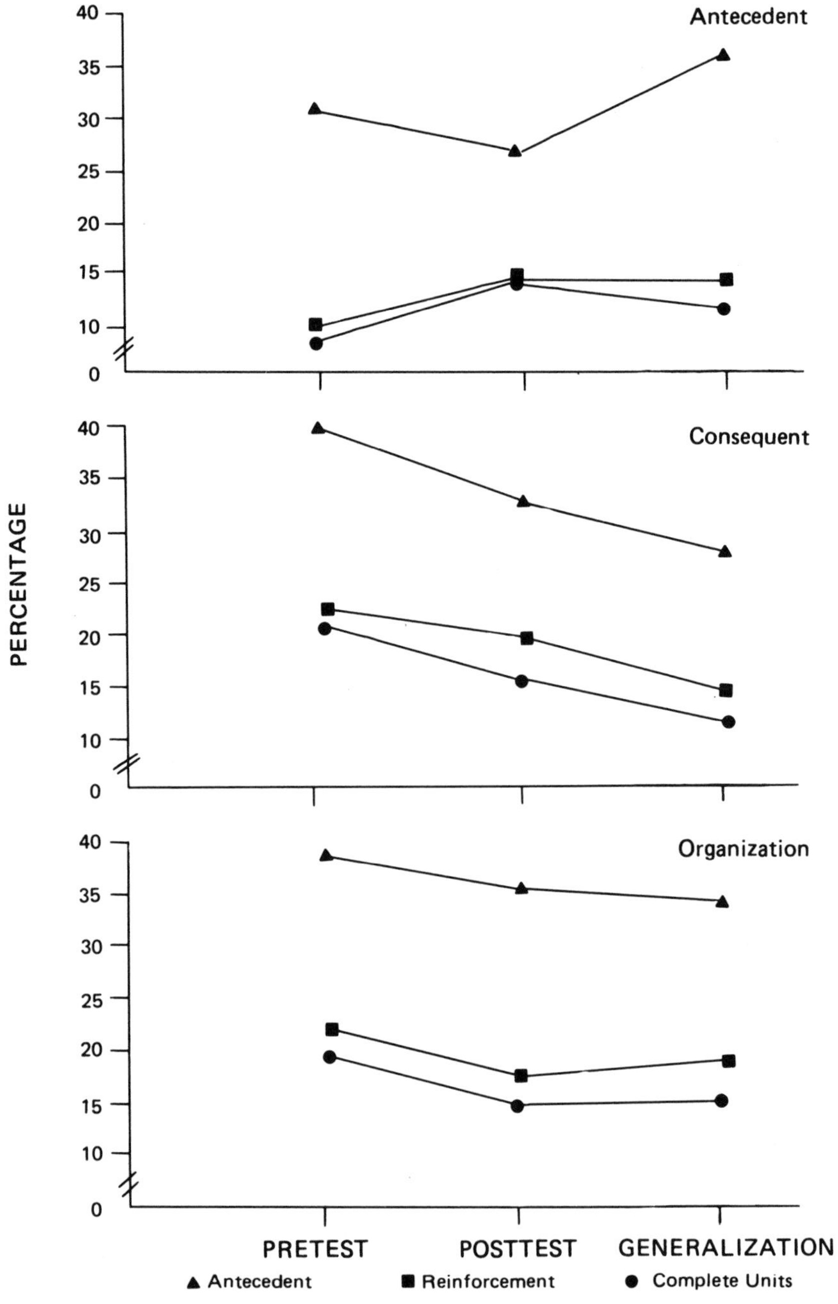

Table 12.4
Mean Percentage of General Approval and Descriptive Approval Consequents for Elementary Education Majors under Three Training Conditions

Conditions	Variables		
	General	Descriptive	Total
Antecedents			
Pretest	11.13	3.25	14.38
Posttest	8.88	5.89	14.77
Consequents			
Pretest	8.00	6.88	14.99
Posttest	10.13	14.50	24.63
Organization			
Pretest	3.38	5.75	9.13
Posttest	13.25	8.00	21.25

scores for these variables. No increases are indicated for antecedents for this group, though the group was trained on antecedents. A possible ceiling effect should be considered given the high pretest score for the antecedent variable for the Antecedent Training Group. Without significant increases in antecedent frequency for this group, effects of an increase on untrained variables for the elementary education majors cannot be determined from these data. However, regardless of the specific training area or major, the frequency of antecedents was higher than that of either reinforcement or complete units. These data suggest that training to increase the frequency of antecedents may be unnecessary. Perhaps future research on antecedents as components within the teaching unit should focus on quality (i.e., brevity, clarity). A high frequency of questions and directives does not appear to ensure completion of more teaching units.

A breakdown of the reinforcement data (general and descriptive) for elementary education majors (Table 12.4) indicates that the training procedures for increasing descriptive verbal approval were effective in increasing both descriptive and general verbal approval. Although subjects in the Organization Group received no training on verbal reinforcement, increases were evident in their use of both descriptive and general approval, and substantive increases were noted for general approval.

Increases in components of the teaching unit for the Organization Training Group (elementary education majors) were unexpected. These data initiate questions concerning the importance of time spent with the subject matter in preparation for teaching. Subjects in this group were asked to verbalize the purpose of the lesson, furnish an overview, and provide definitions of terms with clear examples for abstract and difficult ideas. Subjects in the Organization Group had more time and verbal training with the subject matter of music itself than those in the other groups. The relationship of training on the subject matter and subsequent use of approval teaching units merits additional study.

The data from music education subjects are presented in Figure 12.2. When Figures 12.1 and 12.2 are compared, decreases in posttest mean scores are indicated for every variable for the Reinforcement Training Group as well as the Organization Training Group for the music education majors, and increases are noted for these same variables for the elementary education majors. Differences can also be observed when comparing data from the Antecedent Training Group by majors. Considering that these data constituted one-third (12) of all data ($N = 36$) for analysis, statistical findings of no significant differences should be considered cautiously. Motivational factors and experience with young children may have affected these data because several music education majors were specializing in secondary music education. Additional speculations would not be meaningful given the small number of music education subjects ($N = 4$) in each of the three training conditions. Although it may be of some interest to examine the generalization data for the music education majors, again the small size of N combined with the inconsistencies of the pretest and posttest data with the larger group of elementary education majors would preclude further discussion.

In summary, data from this exploratory study on teaching units would suggest that, for elementary education majors, verbal training (written and spoken) on either approval statements or organization and clarity statements specific to the subject matter is beneficial to increase the frequency of use of questions and directives, general and descriptive approval, and complete teaching units. Also, for these majors, similar training on antecedents only does not appear to provide the same benefits if the frequency of questions and directives are initially high at the beginning of training. Data for music education majors from this study are inconclusive. Regardless of major or training, all students used more antecedents than reinforcement or complete teaching units throughout the teaching. Training to increase antecedents seems unnecessary, and frequency of antecedents does not appear to function as an opportunity for increased student responses and ultimately increased teacher reinforcement. Training time appears best spent in increasing use of descriptive and general reinforcement. Future research may be conducted to examine the quality of antecedents as components within the teaching unit as well as knowledge of subject matter as a variable affecting the use of both reinforcement and complete teaching units.

13 A Model for Personal Evaluation

Amy Brown
Alice-Ann Darrow

Summary

This investigation attempted to provide a self-advisement model for music education and music therapy students as well as to identify possible differences in the needs and self-assessment skills of these two groups. Two goals were: to establish a baseline regarding freshmen student ability to assess their own past achievement in specific professional competencies; and to assess freshmen student capacity for making judgments concerning acquisition and improvement. Students were asked to assess their own achievement on a 1-to-5 scale in a random selection of music education and music therapy competencies as well as to describe a plan for acquisition where necessary. Results indicated that most freshmen appear to have acquired the ability to assess their own achievement, but are unprepared to make judgments concerning acquisition or improvement in these competencies. Implications for faculty advisement of students, assignments, and planning are discussed, and a model, adaptable to a number of university settings, is provided.

Design: Tabular, comparison groups $N = 30$ Groups: 2
Tabular Analysis: Means, percentages
Independent Variables: Levels and majors of students; checklist
Dependent Variables: Ratings of perceived competencies in band, vocal/choral, or music therapy skills; formulation of a plan to acquire skills that are deficient

* * *

This study is an attempt to create a means through which freshmen music education and music therapy students may become sensitized to the problem of student attrition, and to offer guidelines toward persistence through university studies. Two decades of educational research concerning attrition has yielded valuable yet sometimes contradictory and disparate findings. The dimension of the problem is demonstrated by Pantage and Creedon (1978) and Cope and Hannah (1975) in reports that summarize 25 years of data relating to personal characteristics found among college dropouts. In these reports, some studies conclude that they are autonomous, mature, intellectual, creative, committed, critical, nonconforming, and unconventional. In other studies, dropouts are said to be irresponsible, anxious, impulsive, rebellious, unstable, unimaginative, aloof, disagreeable, immature, impetuous, self-centered, uncooperative, likely to overemphasize pleasure, resentful of regulations, lacking self-sufficiency, and uncertain about the future.

More reliable information has resulted from studies concerned with academic achievement; standardized admission tests (SAT, CEEB) and grades are widely accepted as accurate predictors of student persistence. Dimitroff (1974) considered these to be the *only* consequential variables. Numerous studies in the literature, however, deny such predictive power to academic factors and classify them as unstable when considered alone (Morrissey, 1971; Sexton, 1965; Eckland, 1964; Iffert, 1957).

Of the many entry variables statistically analyzed to determine their ability to predict one year persistence/dropout, high school grade point average (GPA) and class rank have frequently been the highest (Pantage & Creedon, 1978; Fetters, 1977; Astin, 1975; Summerskill, 1962). Astin (1977) found a correlation of .29 between college persistence and high school GPA out of a multiple correlation of .42 for all freshmen characteristics.

In a recent study of private colleges, 5,000 students matriculating from an initial applicant pool of 25,000 were followed for one year. Within individual colleges, persistence to the sophomore year was only slightly related to freshman academic performance and was remarkably unpredictable on the basis of any preadmission measure, such as high school GPA, SAT/ACT scores, and student demographics and characteristics (Willingham & Breland, 1982).

Most studies prior to Willingham and Breland have found a significant correlation between college performance and attrition (Ramist, 1981), student involvement in extracurricular activities (Astin, 1977), and student commitment to a degree with expectations for its completion (Astin, 1975). In addition, Astin, a primary investigator in this area, has found that students who are interrupted in any way during their four years of college resemble dropouts more than persisters; private colleges have lower dropout rates than public ones; colleges in the Northeast and South have lower dropout rates than those in the West and Southwest; and attending a highly selective college results in a lower undergraduate GPA but increases satisfaction with college and does *not* increase the chances of dropout.

Ramist's review of research (1981) generally concluded the following effects for the many other variables studied: persistence seemed to be enhanced by a student being from a state contiguous to that of the institution; by similarity between the relative size of the college and the student's hometown; by provision of parental financial aid; by participation in a federal work-study program; by opportunity for research involvement at the undergraduate level; by receipt of Reserve Officers' Training Corps (ROTC) benefits; by residence in a dormitory (but not for women in a coed dorm); by an advanced level of parental education; and by interaction between faculty and students (Pascarella and Terenzini in a 1979 study found a correlation of .24 between faculty contacts and student persistence). Attrition seems to be increased by loans (especially for male freshmen); full-time employment at the freshman and sophomore levels; marriage (for females); and receiving veteran benefits. No effect on persistence has been conclusively documented for amount of tuition, personal savings, age, sex, or parental income.

In addition to specified college board and grade point averages, schools and departments of music add music performance proficiency levels to admissions requirements. It is not known whether this additional factor, however, functions as an indicator of student potential to complete undergraduate studies in music education and music therapy. In fact, until recently, no reports in the research literature isolate students in schools of music.

The impetus for the present study resulted from the findings of one that monitored the academic careers of music education majors (Brown & Alley, 1983). The project represented data analysis across four years in a continuing study of music education student attrition and persistence through an undergraduate program of studies. The purpose was to develop predictive instrumentation and criteria for admission to the music education major as well as provide data-based guidelines for faculty-student interactions that might contribute toward student persistence. That study also represented the first attempt to apply the findings of persistence research to the field of music education specifically as well as to track individual students across the duration of study in the original college site rather than through only the first year of college study, which is customary in persistence studies.

Results indicated that jury grades at the end of the first year of study rank second only to the known academic variables as predictive of student persistence; music theory grades after the first year and basic studies GPAs also emerged as significant predictors. These findings strongly suggest that early intervention plans and refurbished advisement guidelines should consider the vital periods of faculty-student interaction to be at the beginning of the second term of study to identify problems, and immediately prior to the end of the first year of study to help students define the results of their first year.

Based upon the above four years of study, the most available facility toward curtailing attrition in music education programs appears to be the faculty-student interactions that take place during advisement sessions. This finding seems to transfer readily to music therapy students because the initial course of study for both groups is almost identical at the Florida State University, where the project was conducted. Also, over the past three years, the close identity of music education and music therapy has been obvious in the required course "Orientation to Music Education/Music Therapy."

Both music education and music therapy students need to know specifically that low applied music grades during the freshman year do not portend favorably toward the completion of degrees in music; that competence in music theory is vital; and that basic studies are more than addenda to be dismissed with little interest. This kind of information is no doubt given by advisers in general discussion during registration when students are first-time entrants, and periodically when it seems necessary. The problem seems to lie in the fact that time mitigates against the possibility of advisers functioning as constant reminders to students of the competencies that must be acquired and maintained. Advisers are also professors who prepare lessons and teach, serve on committees, perform research, direct theses and dissertations, conduct workshops, attend professional meetings, and engage in the time-consuming involvements required for student recruitment and job placement. Too often students who need advice return for consultation only after problems become serious. How then might the process of faculty/student advisement function most effectively and realistically toward supporting student persistence through degree programs in music therapy and music education?

This study attempts to answer that question and investigates the possibility that a most efficient advisement technique might be to teach students to become their own advisers after the initial faculty consultation. Essentially, it seems that freshmen need to be prepared, beyond the knowledge of required competencies, to relate personally to each competency and to determine how it might be acquired or increased. The present investigation, therefore, is intended to serve as a pilot study that helps to establish a baseline regarding the ability of freshmen to assess their own achievement in specific music therapy and music education competencies; and to assess and detect possible differences between freshmen music education and music therapy student capacity for making judgments concerning competency acquisition and improvement.

Method

Thirty freshmen students declaring a major interest in music therapy and thirty declaring a major interest in music education (15 band and 15 choral) served as subjects. All were enrolled in "Orientation to Music Education/ Music Therapy," a required course for all music therapy and music education freshmen. The music education students were given a list of band or vocal/ choral music education competencies that had been drawn from *The Profession Speaks: Music Teacher Competencies* (1981). This publication, prepared by the Florida Music Educators Association (FMEA) Music Teacher Competency Task Force and published by the FMEA, consists of a set of "generic competencies" for all music teachers, as well as 22 performance, aural, visual, and cognitive competencies for band and 22 for vocal/choral specialists. The music therapy students were given a list of 19 music therapy competencies that had been identified by Alley (1978) in a survey of music therapy professionals. The competencies are shown in Table 13.1.

All students were asked to assess their own achievement levels in each competency on a 1-to-5 scale, ranging from very incompetent to very competent, and also to describe a plan for acquisition or improvement in space provided following the numbered scale. The responses to 7 of each set of 22 band and 22 choral music education competencies and the responses to 8 of the 19 music therapy competencies were randomly selected to be utilized in the present pilot project.

Results

Raw data and mean student perceived achievement levels for each of seven vocal/choral teacher competencies, seven band teacher competencies, and eight music therapist competencies were completed.

Plan for Acquisition responses and percentages for student self-ratings in the 1-to-3 range (very incompetent–somewhat competent) on a 5-point scale were also assessed for each competency. Student acquisition plans seemed to divide into three categories: specific, general, and none. Specific plans are defined as those that provided course titles or numbers; general plans, such answers as "work," "study," "experience"; and no plan, "none" or no answer.

Thirty music education (15 band and 15 choral/vocal) subjects rating themselves on a 1-to-5 scale generated 210 ratings, of which 158 (76%) fell within the 1-to-3 range, and would require a plan for acquisition. Forty-five ratings (29%) were followed by specific plans; 35 (22%), by general plans, and 78 (49%), by no plans for acquisition.

Table 13.1
Music Education Competencies

Vocal/Choral	Band	Music therapy
1. Plays simple piano accompaniments and vocal parts.	Demonstrates tone production and explains embouchure development and control, breathing process and breath control, volume of the oral cavity, posture and holding position of mouthpiece/reed, and methods of producing vibrato.	Ability to relate to atypical or handicapped individuals in a natural and comfortable way.
2. Sings at sight, without accompaniment, vocal solos and individual vocal lines from selected choral scores.	Demonstrates articulation and explains starting and stopping the tone, methods of tonguing, and performance of basic articulations.	Ability to assess and develop remediation strategies for clients with mental health problems, developmental disabilities, physical handicaps, geriatric problems, medical conditions, behavior disorders, and communication problems.
3. Sings individual vocal lines from choral scores while other voice parts are sung or played (e.g. sings the bass line while the soprano, alto, and tenor parts are performed).	Demonstrates the fundamentals of performance for the standard percussion instruments and explains holding and playing positions, developing performance and techniques, and necessary tuning procedures.	Basic understanding of the use of music as a stimulus, consequate, or conveyor of information in a learning-theory paradigm.

4. Demonstrates knowledge of diction by singing at least three of the following languages: English, Latin, German, Italian, French, and Spanish.	Demonstrates ability to read in each of the seven clefs.	Ability to perform task analysis on a specific behavior.
5. Indicates, through conducting gestures, timing of breath to facilitate vocal entrances.	Marches, using various styles: high and low knee bends and stride steps.	Ability to develop data collection procedures for basic therapeutic objectives.
6. Demonstrates skill in subdividing meter patterns and conducting music in compound and changing meters.	Marks off a practice area, using correct measurements of a standard football field.	Ability to recognize changes and patterns in the client's behavior and significant events in the therapeutic process.
7. Identifies and recognizes characteristics and ranges of the voice in its various maturation levels.	Performs basic twirling fundamentals for baton as well as large and small flags.	Ability to evaluate treatment results and write concise progress reports.
8. Demonstrates knowledge of the principles of vocal production.	Lists repertoire of wind instrument literature at the selected level of instruction that will provide a comprehensive study of music for the instrumental student.	Ability to utilize experimental research techniques to document cause-effect relationships in therapy.
9. Recognizes and guides the changing voice.	Demonstrates knowledge of wind instrument transposition.	Basic understanding of the human developmental process.

Table 13.1, *continued*
Music Education Competencies

Vocal/Choral	Band	Music therapy
10. Demonstrates knowledge of repertoire appropriate for choral groups representing various levels of maturation and achievement (children's choruses, young adolescent voices, advanced high school choruses), combinations of voices (treble, changing, changed, mixed, etc.), and solo voices.	Critiques recorded instrumental ensemble performance while following the musical score.	Knowledge and understanding of various psychotherapies currently in use.
11. Selects and prepares choral scores for rehearsal.	Identifies fingerings/slide positions and explains principles based on overtone characteristics for all brass instruments.	Basic repertoire of music therapy strategies with various client populations.
12. Extracts and creates from the scores vocal warm-ups that relate to the technical and expressive structure of the works.	Identifies fingerings based on overtone characteristics for each woodwind instrument. Explains the fingering relationships for different woodwind instruments.	Ability to function as a leader of a client group and to shape group behaviors.
13. Plans rehearsals that include basic music history, music theory, and sightsinging as an integral part of classroom activity, both independently and in the context of a given choral score.	Discuss care and maintenance of standard instruments and related accessories.	Awareness of client rights, confidentiality, and agency/state/federal treatment laws.

14. Detects and correctly diagnoses vocal, rhythmic, melodic, and harmonic problems occurring during a rehearsal.	Selects and prepares instrumental scores for rehearsals.	Ability to design a comprehensive music therapy program in a standard patient site, including delineating role of music therapist in overall therapeutic milieu; developing and utilizing resources; designing patient-referral criterion and procedures; setting departmental standards and evaluating the program.
15. Diagnoses and corrects problems related to resonance, breathing, and phonation heard in performance (rehearsal): total group sound; individual sectional sound.	Paces a rehearsal with a concern for accomplishment.	Understanding of the appropriate content of client records.
16. Identifies problems of intonation heard in performance (rehearsal: intervals in melodic and harmonic contexts; sustained or repeated pitch maintenance, vowel discrepancies).	Identifies and demonstrates effective methods for teaching and developing technical facility, articulation, and rhythmic precision in an instrumental ensemble.	Ability to interact effectively with peers, supervisors, administrators, and families of clients.
17. Diagnoses problems of harmonic balance heard in performance (rehearsal).	Identifies intonation problems unique to each brass and woodwind instrument and prescribes corrective procedures.	Ability to participate in an interdisciplinary team to design client programs.
18. Identifies problems related to diction.	Diagnoses instrumental performance problems of an individual player and/or ensemble and prescribes corrective procedures.	Basic understanding of professional ethics in human services.

Table 13.1, *continued*
Music Education Competencies

Vocal/Choral	Band	Music therapy
19. Recognizes stylistic characteristics of musical periods viewed in an unidentified score.	Plans rehearsals that include basic music theory, music history, and sight-readings as an integral part of classroom activities, both independently and in the context of a given instrumental score.	Ability to explain music therapy to other professionals and laymen.
20. Improves the musical realization of a choral score during a rehearsal (phrasing, rhythm and tempo relationships, and harmonic relationships, including balance).	Selects method books and ensemble studies appropriate for the musical development of students at the specified level of instrumental study.	
21. Paces a rehearsal with concern for accomplishment.	Demonstrates knowledge of repertoire appropriate for instrumental groups and solo instruments representing various levels of maturation and achievement.	
22. Constructs and defends a vocal/choral curriculum that will meet the needs of students.	Devises instruction charts for marching band.	

Thirty music therapy subjects rating themselves on a 1-to-5 scale generated 240 ratings, of which 185 (77%) fell within the 1-to-3 range, and would require a plan for acquisition. Forty-seven ratings (19%) were followed by specific plans; 21 (9%), by general plans; and 179 (72%), by no plans for acquisition.

Table 13.2 shows the correspondence between the perceived competency mean for each of seven vocal/choral teacher competencies, seven band teacher competencies, and eight music therapist competencies, and the plans for acquisition of each.

Discussion

It is not surprising that upon self-evaluation, which is traditionally high (Brown, 1978a; Greenfield, 1978), 76% of music education and 77% of music therapy student responses in this study ranged within the "very incompetent" to "somewhat competent" area of the rating scale. The competencies were structured for beginning music teachers and therapists, not students, and it may be speculated that, knowing this, most students were not inclined to avoid "very incompetent" in reference to themselves. The 24% and 23%, respectively, competent and very competent ratings may still warrant attention.

Except for the "very competent" performance of fundamental twirling techniques for baton and flags that would result from specific training, the (52 = 24%) 4 and 5 ratings may result from music education student services as assistants to high school band and choral directors. Close affiliation with the teacher, coupled with the leadership activities, may have reinforced these students to the degree that they were unable to discriminate their own actual capabilities from those of the accomplished teachers.

Among music therapy respondent self-ratings of 4 or 5 (competent-very competent), 45% were given to competencies 1 and 12. Both these competencies imply comfortable feelings when interacting with handicapped people. It would seem that a much larger percentage of potential music therapists might consider themselves competent at least in this area; the small percentage arouses not a little curiosity concerning the career choice of these students.

The question "Compared to whom?" may also account for some high perception ratings in the data. All freshmen are untrained evaluators, mostly exposed only to comparison with the abilities of their high school peers. It is suspected, therefore, that the baseline established in this pilot study regarding student ability to self-assess achievement in music education and therapy competencies may correlate favorably with data provided by a larger sample of freshmen students.

Table 13.2
Correspondence between Student-perceived Competence and Plan for Acquisition*

Band

Competency no.	Perceived Competence mean	Plan for Acquisition Yes	No
4	2.0	.47	.53
7	1.86	.26	.53
8	2.33	.26	.73
14	3.0	.13	.53
16	2.73	.19	.60
20	2.66	.26	.46
22	2.80	.40	.33

Vocal/Choral

Competency no.	Perceived Competence mean	Plan for acquisition Yes	No
5	3.06	.53	.13
6	2.86	.46	.13
9	2.26	.40	.40
13	2.60	.60	.20
16	3.20	.47	.27
19	2.53	.53	.27
21	3.13	.40	.27

Music Therapy

Competency no.	Responses	Perceived Competence mean	Plan for acquisition Yes	No
1	16	1.43	4 (.13)	12 (.40)
3	21	1.30	8 (.26)	13 (.43)
5	26	1.36	10 (.33)	16 (.53)
8	27	1.80	8 (.30)	18 (.60)
9	23	1.83	9 (.30)	14 (.46)
11	28	1.56	11 (.36)	17 (.56)
12	20	1.36	6 (.20)	14 (.46)
17	23	1.60	8 (.26)	15 (.50)

*Because only responses 1 to 3 (very incompetent–somewhat competent) were analyzed, percentages do not equal 100.

The 49% "no plan" responses and only 29% specific plans for acquisition of music education students and the respective 72% and 19% figures for music therapy majors speak clearly to the issue of student capacity for making decisions concerning competency acquisition. The notable difference between the two groups of student responses in this area may reflect the absence of consequential previous exposure of incoming freshmen to the field of music therapy and seems to warrant further investigation. Most of the freshmen in this sample, however, entered these programs with no plan for competency acquisition and no apparent facility for discovering how a plan might be developed. All were given one week to complete the assignment. Students who answered with course numbers and titles "somehow" found and consulted the music education and music therapy curriculum guides. Why were they not utilized by the others? Curriculum is the major source of discussion during faculty advisement of students.

Perhaps the initial advisement session with each freshman student should include direct emphasis upon the necessity for a plan to finish school and also upon the function of curriculum guides and university bulletins. Each entering student is experiencing the exuberance that results from a carefully laid plan successfully completed. Universities conscientiously lay out that plan and communicate it to high school students.

Faculty advisers, despite the desire to be helpful, cannot and perhaps should not be constantly involved in the lives of freshmen students. The advisement process, however, is the single vehicle through which the faculty attempts to relate on a one-to-one basis with students "about school." This vehicle is perhaps most appropriately charged with the task of initiating a persistence device for freshmen. Perhaps faculty should consider teaching freshmen students during this crucial, limited time what the data indicate concerning student persistence through a program of studies. Freshmen should know that only 38% of students were still pursuing the degree program in the fourth year and that first-year performance was shown to be most crucial (Brown & Alley, 1983).

Also, curriculum guides and bulletins are often provided for students. Perhaps they should be instructed during initial advisement periods that these documents must be studied to develop a Plan for Acquisition; and that all students must become their own advisers. Herein may lie the initial step toward their understanding in tangible terms that the freshman year is not an end but a beginning. A condition should be structured through which students intelligently plan toward their completion of the degree. How can we know that they are doing so? We might ask them.

Colleges and universities traditionally provide formal orientation into the various fields that students choose to pursue. A specific plan to extend the planning process already begun during advisement might be included among the objectives for study in these orientation courses for prospective music educators and music therapists. Previous work (Brown & Alley, 1983) seems to suggest the feasibility of a "course work type" approach for student understanding of persistence problems. Also, the assignment to develop a Plan for Acquisition toward specific competencies seems practicable. Such assignments would provide faculty with opportunities for intervention when needed, and provide students with a model for personal evaluation—initiating progress toward becoming their own advisers.

Part IV
Applications of Research: Preference and Perception

Music has a reputation for possessing universal appeal, though a moment's scrutiny of this reassuring idea can raise major questions. Which music? To whom does it appeal? Under what circumstances? The issue of musical preference, its flexibility and its amenity to molding, is of vital interest to us as music educators. We spend a great deal of our professional time not only teaching performance skills but also trying to teach people to "appreciate" types of music to which they may never have listened voluntarily before.

Do some forms of music have more or less mass appeal, while others are only an acquired taste? Are the criteria that shape our choices the same for all types of music, or do they vary? Does a liking for certain styles of music necessarily preclude liking certain other styles? To what extent does formal musical training influence our choices? In Part II, Sims raised the issue of critical ages at which preferences for certain tempos may become set. Are all later choices determined by experiences in the primary grades? Do people actually listen to the music we say we are teaching them to appreciate? If so, how can we teach this efficiently? If not, why are we persevering?

Interwoven with the many questions concerning preference are questions about what is being perceived when music is playing. In the disciplines that examine human behavior, it has long been understood that hearing and perceiving music are not quite the same thing. For musicians, of course, perception is the critical issue. Do trained musicians and non-musicians perceive the same aspects of a performance? Does the intricacy of a melody affect a listener's perception? When listening to a chorus, what influences the perception of the balance of the voices? Are tempo perceptions of popular music different from those of formal, traditional art music? How closely do experts agree on tempo choices?

The work presented in Part IV attempts to address some of these issues and invites further exploration in the future. The creative ways the researchers have developed to explore what are basically unobservable phenomena deserve mention. The systematic, verifiable investigation demanded by a research format is not alien to the study of issues such as preference or perception as it might at first appear to be. Finding the manifestation, no matter how subtle, of an internal reaction requires sensitivity and keen powers of observation. It is to be hoped that readers of these studies will feel encouraged to develop equally innovative ways to assess the many unsolved puzzles of musical perception and preference.

14 The Effect of Tempo, Meter, and Melodic Complexity on the Perception of Tempo

Terry L. Kuhn

Summary

Ornamented versions of melodies were identified as being faster than plain versions, which suggests that melodic rhythm requires less cognitive abstraction than does beat. This finding suggests that melodic rhythm is an easier concept and should be taught before beat. This study has implications for content sequencing of basal series and music methods texts.

Design: One group with multiple observation $N = 175$
Statistical Analysis: Chi-square by item
Reliability: Kendall *W* with groups conceptualized as judges
Independent Variables: Tempo, meter (melody), melodic complexity
Dependent Variables: Correct/Incorrect identification of tempo change
Music: Listening, group

* * *

The purpose of this experiment was to test the effect of three potential influences on the perception of tempo. The task was presented as a series of paired comparisons. In each paired comparison, subjects were asked to indicate whether the tempo of the second example of each item was faster, slower, or the same as the tempo of the first example. The three elements examined were tempo, meter, and melodic complexity. At the outset of the experiment, it was hypothesized that subjects would be able to correctly distinguish tempos of 92 and 108 beats per minute in a direct comparison. It was also hypothesized that tempo perception would not be influenced by duple or triple beat groupings. Lastly, it was hypothesized that there would be no difference between plain and ornamented versions of the melodies.

Definitions

Beat consists of points in time separated by equal durations. Beat is usually perceived as a pulse that is generated by musical sounds and can be synchronized with a muscular response. Beats are represented with periods and durations with curved lines in the following diagram:

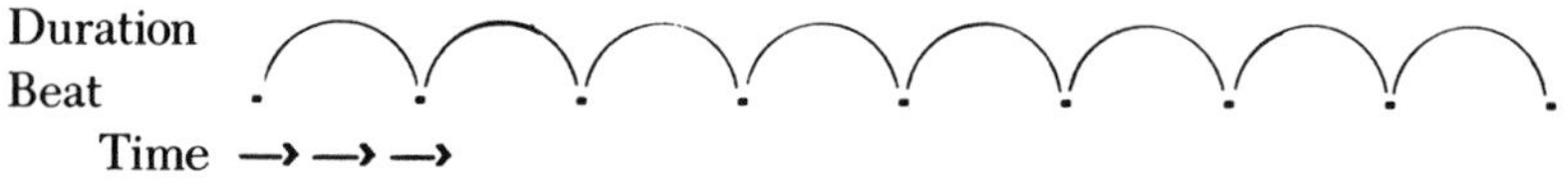

Meter is created as beats are combined into groups of twos, threes, or fours. Although two, three, and four are the normal groupings, beats can be grouped by other numerical values as well:

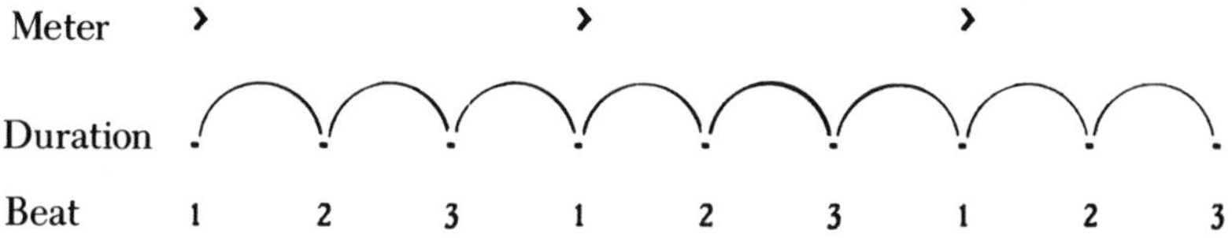

The perceptual references for the identification of beat groupings are created by differential dynamic emphasis on the beats within a group, by agogic displacement of durations within groups of beats (Ferencz, 1983), and by pitch and timbre changes on some instruments.

The number of beats per minute is called *tempo*. Faster tempos have shorter durations:

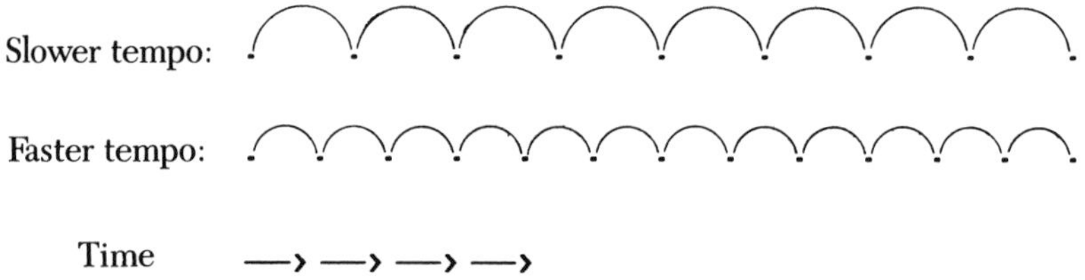

Melodic rhythm is a general term that refers to the occurrence of independent durations in time. This is the rhythm associated with the melody of the musical stimulus. The following lines represent durations of different lengths, and the note values indicate those same durations:

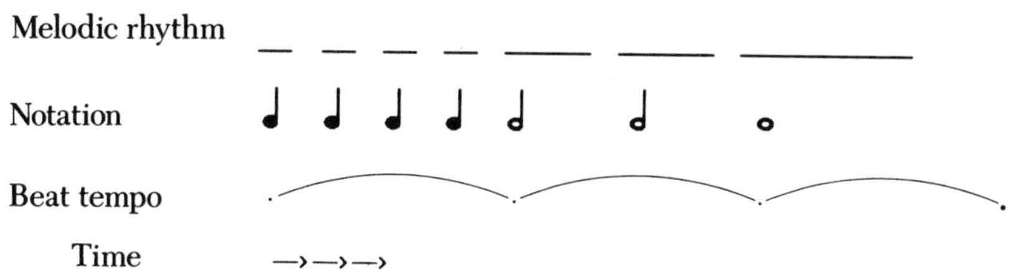

Tempo perception studies have shown professional musicians to be keenly aware of tempo modulations (Kuhn, 1977). They were able to identify tempo decreases faster than tempo increases. An expected tendency for subjects to accelerate tempo during performance when asked to perform an easy melody or to keep steady beats has also been noted in the literature (Drake, 1968; Kuhn & Gates, 1975). Groves (1966) found that age and grade levels affected the motor responses to rhythmic relationships.

Method

Subjects

Subjects for this study were 53 second-grade students, 51 fourth-grade students, and 55 sixth-grade students from a suburban middle-class elementary school. Sixteen undergraduate students enrolled in a music fundamentals class at a large Midwestern university also participated.

Independent Variables

The three variables under investigation were tempo (slow = 92 and fast = 108), meter (duple and triple), and ornamentation (plain and ornamented). Two plain melodies were created from pre-existent sources, and then an ornamented version of each melody was prepared. One melody was in duple meter, and the other was in triple meter. The two tempos were chosen because they were still appropriate for a musical performance, yet were easily distinguishable. To represent three variables, each at two levels, required the creation of eight unique examples. Each example was paired with itself and each of the other seven examples to form 36 test items.

Ornamentation

Two versions of each melody were created for the test items. The plain version was unadorned and moved entirely in beat-note values, quarter

Figure 14.1
Examples Used in Test Items

Melodies 1 and 5

Melodies 2 and 6

Melodies 3 and 7

Melodies 4 and 8

notes in this case. The ornamented version maintained the outline of the plain melody and added subdivided rhythms, passing tones, upper and lower neighbor tones, and arpeggiated figures. Melodies 1 and 5 were identical except for tempo (1 = MM 92; 5 = MM 108). The same relationship held for examples 2 and 6, 3 and 7, and 4 and 8. See Figure 14.1.

Stimulus Tape Preparation

An audiotape recording of the 36 test items was prepared. The melodies were performed on an Apple Model IIe computer with an ALF Products Apple IIe–compatible music synthesizer card and software tape 13-2-1B. Voice announcements were recorded with a Sony ECM-170A electric condenser microphone. The electrical signal from the microphone and the synthesizer were routed into a Sony MX-510 mic-line mixer and then to an ONKYO TA-

Table 14.1
Characteristics of the Eight Musical Examples

Example	Tempo	Meter	Ornament
1	S	D	P
2	S	D	O
3	S	T	P
4	S	T	O
5	F	D	P
6	F	D	O
7	F	T	P
8	F	T	O

Tempo: Slow (S)
Fast (F)
Meter: Duple (D)
Triple (T)
Ornament: Plain (P)
Ornamented (O)

2055 stereo cassette tape deck (wow and flutter = 0.035% WRMS). The same tape deck was used for all recording and playback.

Table 14.1 identifies the abbreviations used in the remaining tables.

Response Mode

After each item was played, subjects were instructed to circle whether the tempo of the second example was faster, slower, or the same as the tempo of the first example.

Results

The results section is grouped into tables by the number of elements that were different for the two examples in each item. In Table 14.2, a significant proportion of subjects correctly identified the tempo for every item in which the two examples were identical.

In Table 14.3, the items in which one element was changed between the two examples in each item are presented. Subjects correctly identified three

Table 14.2
Test Items in Which Examples Were Identical

1	12	13	17	25	26	29	34

of the examples in which tempo and meter were the only element to change, but incorrectly identified every item in which ornamentation was the only element to change. The majority of subjects failed to correctly identify Item 21 as slowing down. There was no apparent explanation for this one anomaly in the data.

Table 14.4 presents data for items in which two elements changed. When tempo and meter changed, the subjects correctly identified the tempo of the item. When tempo and ornamentation changed, two items were identified correctly and two were not. It should be noted that the tempo in Items 8 and 9 went from slow to fast while the ornamentation went from ornamented to plain. Items 3 and 27 changed from slow to fast and from plain to ornamented simultaneously. All the items in which the tempo remained constant but the meter and ornamentation changed were incorrectly identified.

It is interesting to note that when all three elements, tempo, meter, and ornamentation, changed simultaneously, two of the items were identified correctly and two were not (see Table 14.5). In the cases of Items 11 and 30, the tempo changed from slow to fast while the ornamentation changed from ornamented to plain. There was congruence in the change of elements in Items 15 and 16 with tempo changing from slow to fast and ornamentation changing from plain to ornamented.

Table 14.6 shows the test item; the two examples paired for each test item; the correct answer; the total number of responses on each item for each of the three possible answers; the tempo (fast or slow), the meter (duple or triple), and the ornamental version (plain or ornamented) for the first and second examples of each pair; the number of changes between the first and

Table 14.3
Test Items in Which One Element Changed between Examples

Contrasted Element	Items			
Tempo	5	21*	31	33
Meter	2	6	18	19
Ornamentation	22*	28*	32*	35*

*Items answered incorrectly ($p < .05$).

Table 14.4
Test Items in Which Two Elements Changed between Examples

Contrasted Elements	Items			
Tempo and meter	4	20	23	36
Tempo and ornamentation	3	8*	9*	27
Meter and ornamentation	7*	10*	14*	24*

*Items answered incorrectly ($p < .05$).

second examples of each pair; the chi-square value computed on the slow, same, fast response categories; and the Kendall Coefficient of Concordance value of *W*, which indicates the degree of correlation among the proportions of responses made by the four age groups. The chi-square value was computed to answer the question "Were the responses spread randomly across the three alternative choices?" The answer was a resounding "No!" Subjects answered with a preponderance of responses favoring one of the choices. In answer to the query of whether or not data from the four age groups should be collapsed, the Kendall Coefficient of Concordance *W* shows the agreement that exists among the proportion of responses made by the different groups. This indicator of concordance, ranging from 0.75 to 1.00, tends to be conservative compared to parametric correlation figures and justifies the combination of data among the four age groups.

Results indicate that items which required subjects to conserve and remember the beat tempo and compare it to a conserved memory derived from a second example were answered with the ornamentation element being the discrimination stimulus. On Item 21 the *only* element changing was tempo; nevertheless, the tempo identification was incorrect!

Discussion

The finding that subjects were able to identify examples performed at 108 beats per minute as being faster than examples performed at 92 beats per

Table 14.5
Test Items in Which Three Elements Changed between Examples

11*	15	16	30*

*Items answered incorrectly ($p < .05$).

Table 14.6
Item Construction and Subjects' Responses on Tempo Discrimination Task

Test item	Examples	Correct answer	Responses S	Responses N	Responses F	Tempo 1–2	Meter 1–2	Ornamentation 1–2	No. of variables changes	Chi-square*	Kendall W
1	5–5	N	5	169	1	F–F	T–T	P–P	0	315.06	0.90
2	8–6	N	21	107	47	F–F	T–D	O–O	1	66.70	0.90
3	1–6	F	3	7	165	S–F	D–D	P–O	2	292.71	1.00
4	8–2	S	157	14	4	F–S	T–D	O–O	2	251.19	0.90
5	8–4	S	143	28	4	F–S	T–T	O–O	1	189.27	1.00
6	7–5	N	16	155	4	F–F	T–D	P–P	1	241.52	0.78
7	2–3	***N***	167	4	4	S–S	***D–T***	***O–P***	2	303.65	0.77
8	2–5	***F***	148	15	12	***S–F***	D–D	***O–P***	2	206.83	0.75
9	4–7	***F***	149	18	8	***S–F***	T–T	***O–P***	2	212.24	0.81
10	1–4	***N***	6	10	159	S–S	***D–T***	***P–O***	2	260.72	0.78
11	2–7	***F***	155	10	10	***S–F***	***D–T***	***O–P***	3	240.29	0.75
12	1–1	N	7	166	2	S–S	D–D	P–P	0	298.30	0.80
13	4–4	N	3	157	15	S–S	T–T	O–O	0	251.57	0.90
14	6–7	***N***	165	3	7	F–F	***D–T***	***O–P***	2	292.71	0.75
15	1–8	F	1	4	170	S–F	D–T	P–O	3	320.72	0.90
16	3–6	F	3	8	164	S–F	T–D	P–O	3	287.33	0.84
17	2–2	N	1	165	9	S–S	D–D	O–O	0	293.12	1.00

[illegible]	[illegible]	N	21	152	2	S–S	T–D	P–P	1	228.70	0.90
19	4–2	N	17	131	27	S–S	T–D	O–O	1	136.64	0.90
20	6–4	S	157	10	8	F–S	D–T	O–O	2	250.37	0.78
21	5–1	***S***	69	104	2	***F–S***	D–D	P–P	1	92.10	0.75
22	3–4	***N***	4	9	162	S–S	T–T	***P–O***	1	276.56	0.78
23	7–1	***S***	109	61	5	F–S	T–D	P–P	2	92.89	1.00
24	5–8	N	8	5	162	F–F	D–T	***P–O***	2	276.42	0.78
25	3–3	N	9	163	3	S–S	T–T	P–P	0	282.01	0.90
26	7–7	N	10	161	4	F–F	T–T	P–P	0	271.35	0.90
27	3–8	F	4	3	168	S–F	T–T	P–O	2	309.27	0.77
28	5–6	***N***	3	8	164	F–F	D–D	***P–O***	1	287.33	0.81
29	8–8	N	5	158	12	F–F	T–T	O–O	0	255.85	0.84
30	4–5	***F***	149	18	8	***S–F***	***T–D***	***O–P***	3	212.24	0.78
31	6–2	S	144	26	5	F–S	D–D	O–O	1	192.49	0.90
32	1–2	***N***	4	31	140	S–S	D–D	***P–O***	1	177.75	1.00
33	7–3	S	97	75	3	F–S	T–T	P–P	1	82.88	0.81
34	6–6	N	3	155	17	F–F	D–D	O–O	0	241.97	1.00
35	7–8	***N***	2	9	164	F–F	T–T	***P–O***	1	287.53	1.00
36	5–3	S	135	36	4	F–S	D–T	P–P	2	159.92	0.90

Note: Items answered incorrectly are shown in boldface ($p < .05$).

S = Slower N = No Change F = Faster

Tempo: Slow (S) Fast (F) Meter: Duple (D) Triple (T) Ornament: Plain (P) Ornamented (O)

*Critical value of chi-square at .05 level = 5.99.

minute when all other aspects of the stimuli remained constant comes as no surprise. Past studies of tempo modulation have indicated that a difference as great as 16 beats per minute should be distinguishable.

The finding that meter did not influence tempo perception was also expected. The concept of meter requires one additional layer of abstraction beyond the concept of beat. Whereas beat subdivision may influence tempo perception, meter would not.

An important finding of this study was the significant difference found between ornamented and unornamented versions of the same melody. Such a finding not only suggests a need for further experimentation; it also suggests several implications for the teaching of music. Further experimentation should include tasks that require a physical response from subjects. The physical response should be designed to define the beat. Implications for the teaching of music include the idea that melodic rhythm requires *less* abstraction than does beat. If this is the case, then the sequencing of concepts should present melodic rhythm before beat.

Speculation about reasons that ornamented versions were perceived as being faster than plain versions of melodies suggest several hypotheses. The plain versions of the melodies moved in notational values equal to the beat. It is possible that more sounds occurring in the same duration give the impression of greater speed. If that is the case, it suggests that tempo perception is influenced by melodic rhythm.

Beat is an abstraction that requires the perceiver to first process melodic rhythm, and then to abstract the pulse based on perception of melodic rhythms that can be patterns based on the divisions of beats or based on the combination of beats or parts of beats. It was surprising to find such marked agreement among the various age levels studied. The cross section of second-, fourth-, and sixth-graders and undergraduates all showed very similar response patterns to the test items.

Other areas of further study should probe perceptual accuracy of subjects while performing either a simple motor response (such as clapping) or a musical instrument. The effect of rhythmic accompaniments added to these unadorned melodies is also worthy of investigation. The direct question of whether or not subjects could more accurately reproduce beats or melodic rhythm should be followed up. Results of this study suggest that those responsible for planning musical experiences designed to develop perceptual awareness should create a sequence of instruction that introduces melodic rhythm before beat.

Special thanks for assistance is extended to Patrick C. Boyden and Ramsel L. Yoho, of the Kent State University Computer Assisted Instruction Center.

15 The Effect of Musical Excerpts on Tempo Discriminations and Preferences of Musicians and Non-musicians

Cornelia Yarbrough

Summary

This study demonstrates that the unaltered tempo of a musical excerpt affects *tempo discrimination* (for fast musical excerpts, all groups discriminated faster tempos better; for slow musical excerpts, all groups discriminated slower tempos better) and *preferences* (for fast musical excerpts, slower tempos were preferred; for slow musical excerpts, faster tempos).

Responses to tempo in music have been categorized in prior research as performance, discrimination/perception, and preference. How we perform tempo, how we discriminate it, and how we prefer it would seem to be important issues for applied music instructors, music theoreticians, and sociologists. In addition, it would seem appropriate to determine whether these responses are categorical, that is, whether they are mutually exclusive, or whether they have some sort of relationship to one another. For example, does the ability to perceive/discriminate tempo affect the ability to perform it? And should we take preferences for tempo seriously if they are based on inaccuracy in discrimination and/or performance? Finally, must one first be able to perceive tempo absolutes accurately in order to discriminate tempo changes?

Design: Statistical-counterbalanced $N = 400$ Groups: 4
Statistical Analysis: chi-square, ANOVA
Independent Variables: Two excerpts by Mozart (one of a fast tempo and one of a slow tempo); two excerpts by Chopin (one of a fast tempo and one of a slow tempo)

Dependent Variables: Correct tempo discriminations (re: whether second playing was faster, slower, or same tempo); preferences for faster or slower version/increased or decreased tempo
Music: Listening, individual

* * *

Research in tempo discrimination has involved perception of gradual increases and decreases in tempos of both metronomical and musical excerpts and discrimination of tempos of musical excerpts in comparison with one another (slower than, faster than, or the same tempo). Results have demonstrated that both musicians and non-musicians perceived decreases in the tempos of metronomic beats better than increases (Kuhn, 1974; Madsen, 1979); musicians perceived an increase in the tempo of a musical excerpt by J. S. Bach more accurately than tempo decrease, but did not perceive similarly when listening to three other compositions of differing styles and tempos (Wang, 1983); and string students perceived tempo increases more accurately than decreases (Wang & Salzberg, 1984). Thus, perception of tempo has been studied through differing media in the context of awareness of change in tempo across time. As such, data have yielded mixed results that are as yet unexplained.

Using different procedures in which musical examples were presented to subjects in three or more discrete tempos (e.g., slow, moderate, and fast), researchers have yielded other interesting data. Wapnick (1980a) compared subjects' tempo discrimination within both musical and metronomic mediums. He concluded that subjects were more accurate in discriminating tempo sameness for metronomic examples than for musical examples. In addition, his results indicated that scores were higher for fast tempos than they were for moderate or slow tempos.

In studies concerning pitch and tempo discrimination, Geringer and Madsen (1984, 1985) noted subjects' apparent discrimination among musical excerpts in completing the tasks of discriminating pitch and tempo. As in other research, tempo-increase examples were more correctly identified than tempo-decrease examples. A subsequent study used familiar band excerpts and corroborated these results (Madsen, Duke, & Geringer, 1984). It was suggested that the accuracy of subjects' discriminations was influenced by the content and context of each musical example.

Tempo preferences have been for faster rather than slower tempos in previous research. Geringer (1976) found that subjects listening to recorded orchestral music preferred faster tape speeds relative to the unaltered recordings. Because these preferences could have resulted from higher pitch levels, faster tempos, or brighter timbres, Wapnick (1980b) attempted to isolate pitch, tempo, and timbre effects. Subjects in his study indicated preferences for faster tempo in more familiar pieces when pitch level and timbre were controlled. A recent study using popular music as stimuli demonstrated that subjects of all ages (fifth grade through college) preferred the original, unaltered tempo version of each popular excerpt to any of the alterations of tempo (Geringer & Madsen, 1985).

Extensive research ($N = 304$) with fifth and sixth graders (LeBlanc, 1981; LeBlanc & Cote, 1983; LeBlanc & McCrary, 1983) has shown that the faster the tempo, the higher the preference ratings. A control limitation of these studies, as stated by LeBlanc, was that various tempos of the same excerpt were not compared.

Although ability to perceive tempo seemed to increase with maturation and musical training (Dorhout, 1980) in one study, others have shown that accuracy in tempo discrimination is not related to age or musical training (Geringer & Madsen, 1984; Madsen, 1979).

In summary, data from previous research in tempo discrimination and preference indicate mixed results that suggest a strong effect of musical examples used as stimuli (e.g., Bach vs. Chopin, style of composition, familiar vs. unfamiliar, metronomic beats vs. musical excerpts). Therefore, the purpose of this study was to determine the effect of musical excerpts on tempo discrimination and preference of musicians and non-musicians.

Method

Four hundred musicians and non-musicians participated in the study: students enrolled in graduate and undergraduate music degree programs at Syracuse University ($n = 100$); non-music major graduate and undergraduate students at Syracuse University ($n = 100$); tenth-grade public school students ($n = 100$); and older adults from the Syracuse, New York, community ($n = 100$).

The 300 non-musicians each had less than 2 years of private or group music study. Music majors represented almost the entire population of the School of Music at Syracuse University. Graduate and undergraduate non-music majors represented nearly every college and school of Syracuse University at every advanced educational level (i.e., bachelor's, master's, doctoral). Tenth graders were randomly selected from the entire tenth-grade population of a large suburban high school. Older adults were selected from churches, exercise classes, secretarial pools, custodial workers, a large medical complex, and from other professional groups such as teachers, lawyers, and accountants.

Music majors were an average age of 22.32 years and had received an average of 8.38 years of musical training; non-music majors, 20.71 and 1.07, respectively; tenth graders, 15.06 and 1.83; and older adults, 39.8 and .70.

Piano music excerpts used for stimuli were selected from those used in a previous study (Wapnick, 1980a). Four musical examples, all of solo piano music, were chosen, each lasting approximately 22 to 30 seconds. Of the four examples, two were of a fast tempo and two were of a slow tempo (one in each by Chopin and Mozart) as judged by members of music faculty in the previous study (Wapnick, 1980a). The specific excerpts were:

Composer and Title	*Pianist*	*Record Cat. No.*	*Tempo Indication*
	Slow excerpts		
Mozart/Sonata, K. 282, 1st movement, measures 1–3 plus	C. Eschenbach	DGG 2720 031	Adagio
Chopin/Etude, op. 10, no. 6, measures 1–6	V. Ashkenazy	Hall of Fame 520	Andante
	Fast excerpts		
Mozart/Sonata, K. 280, 3rd movement, measures 1–37	C. Eschenbach	DGG 2720 031	Presto
Chopin/Sonata in b, 2nd movement, measures 1–60	V. Cliburn	RCA LSC-3194	Molto Vivace

Master tapes were made of each of the four excerpts at the following speeds: unaltered, 18% faster, and 18% slower. Tapes were recorded using a BIC 960 turntable, Sony TC K55II cassette deck, GAS Thalia preamplifier, Technics SE-9060 amplifier, and Lexicon Corporation Varispeech Model II speed/time compressor/expander. The compressor/expander allowed the tempo of recorded examples to be increased or decreased without altering the pitch level. Table 15.1 shows the length of altered and unaltered excerpts in seconds.

Two experimental tapes were prepared so that half of the subjects heard each of the four excerpts three times on each tape. Excerpts were presented in pairs for the purpose of comparison. Both the first and the second members of each pair (12 pairs per tape) were presented to subjects in tempo unaltered, increased (18% faster), and decreased (18% slower) conditions. Across the 24 stimulus pairs, each excerpt was presented six times: two times with the comparison tempo slower than the first tempo; two times with the comparison tempo faster; and two times with the comparison

Table 15.1
Length of Altered and Unaltered Excerpts in Seconds

Excerpt	Tempo decreased	Unaltered	Tempo increased
Fast Mozart	26	22	18
Fast Chopin	35	30	25
Slow Mozart	32	25	20
Slow Chopin	32	27	22

tempo at the same tempo as the first. In addition, when the comparison tempo was a different tempo (slower or faster) from the first tempo, the increased and the decreased conditions were each presented once as the comparison tempo and again as the first tempo. The unaltered condition was presented twice as the first tempo and twice as the comparison tempo. The "same" tempo presentations of each excerpt consisted of the increased and decreased conditions each in both first and second positions (see Table 15.2).

Thus, the tempo comparisons of same (0), faster (+), and slower (−), the versions of each excerpt that were unaltered, increased (18% faster), and decreased (18% slower), and the four musical excerpts were cast in a counterbalanced experimental design. Members of each pair were separated by 5 seconds of silence. Ten seconds of silence followed each pair.

Subjects were tested in small groups of 10 to 15. Half of them heard experimental Tape I; the other half, experimental Tape II. After removing watches or other timepieces, subjects listened to 12 pairs of musical excerpts. Each pair consisted of two conditions of the same musical excerpt, differing (or not differing) from each other solely in tempo. Pitch, timbre, and expressive elements were kept constant through use of a speech compressor. The task of subjects was twofold: first, they were to decide whether the second presentation of the musical excerpt was slower, faster, or the same tempo as the first presentation; and, second, they were to indicate which tempo (that of the first presentation, that of the second presentation, or neither tempo) they preferred. Space was provided on the answer sheet for subjects to indicate other perceived changes or to make comments.

General information collected from each individual prior to the experiment included age, sex, musical status (musician or non-musician), major instrument, and years of formal music study. Each session took about 20 minutes to complete.

Table 15.2
Presentation Order and Correct Responses

Presentation order		Correct response
Tape I		
1. Fast Mozart:	Increased–Increased	0
2. Slow Chopin:	Unaltered–Increased	+
3. Slow Mozart:	Decreased–Decreased	0
4. Fast Chopin:	Increased–Unaltered	–
5. Slow Mozart:	Unaltered–Increased	+
6. Fast Mozart:	Unaltered–Decreased	–
7. Fast Chopin:	Unaltered–Decreased	–
8. Slow Chopin:	Unaltered–Decreased	–
9. Fast Mozart:	Unaltered–Increased	+
10. Slow Mozart:	Decreased–Unaltered	+
11. Slow Chopin:	Increased–Increased	0
12. Fast Chopin:	Decreased–Decreased	0
Tape II		
1. Slow Mozart:	Increased–Unaltered	–
2. Fast Mozart:	Decreased–Decreased	0
3. Fast Chopin:	Unaltered–Increased	+
4. Slow Mozart:	Increased–Increased	0
5. Fast Mozart:	Decreased–Unaltered	+
6. Slow Chopin:	Decreased–Unaltered	+
7. Fast Chopin:	Increased–Increased	0
8. Fast Mozart:	Increased–Unaltered	–
9. Slow Chopin:	Decreased–Decreased	0
10. Slow Mozart:	Unaltered–Decreased	–
11. Fast Chopin:	Decreased–Unaltered	+
12. Slow Chopin:	Increased–Unaltered	–

Faster (+) Same Tempo (0) Slower (–)

Table 15.3
Analysis of Variance for Correct Tempo Discrimination

Source of variation	*df*	Sum of squares	Mean square	*F*
Between	3	211.02	70.34	22.91*
Within	396	1215.62	3.07	
Error	399	1426.64		

*$p < .01$

Results

Total correct tempo discrimination responses were analyzed using a one-way analysis of variance. Results demonstrated a significant difference between musicians and non-musicians (see Table 15.3). Subsequent comparison of means using the Newman-Keuls multiple range test showed a significant difference between musicians and all other non-musician groups, but no significant differences among the three non-musician groups (see Table 15.4). Furthermore, of the total possible correct responses, musicians scored 64.83% correct and non-musicians scored 50.92% correct.

Musicians discriminated among the categories slower, same, and faster tempo (χ^2 (2, N = 100) = 17.15, $p < .001$) and made more correct responses for faster tempo. Non-musicians also discriminated among the categories slower, same, and faster tempo (χ^2 (2, N = 300) = 31.44, $p < .001$) and made more correct responses for faster tempo (see Table 15.5).

Both musicians and non-musicians discriminated among the four musical excerpts. Musicians gave more correct responses for the fast Mozart excerpt and fewest correct responses for the fast Chopin excerpt (χ^2 (3, N = 100) = 35.73, $p < .001$). Non-musicians gave most correct

Table 15.4
Summary of Newman-Keuls Multiple Comparison Procedure for Tempo Discrimination Means

Music majors	Tenth graders	Non-music majors	Older adults
7.78	6.22	6.13	5.99

Note: No significant difference existed among the three underlined means.

Table 15.5
Frequency of Correct Tempo Discriminations for Slower, Same, and Faster Comparison Tempos

Group	Slower	Same	Faster	Total correct
Musicians (n = 100)	264	210	304	778
Non-musicians (n = 300)	610	514	710	1,834

responses for the fast Mozart, but fewest correct responses for the slow Mozart excerpt (χ^2 (3, N = 300) = 98.55, $p < .001$). Table 15.6 presents the frequency of correct tempo discriminations by musicians and non-musicians for each of the four musical excerpts.

It is interesting to note that all groups discriminated across the various comparison tempos, with both musicians and non-musicians perceiving the faster comparison tempo better for fast excerpts (χ^2 (2, N = 400) = 121.47, $p < .001$) and the slower tempo comparison better for slow excerpts (χ^2 (2, N = 400) = 39.56, $p < .001$). Table 15.7 is a summary of the number of correct responses for slower, same, and faster comparison tempos of fast and slow musical excerpts.

Preference responses for correctly discriminated tempo changes were counted. A total of 161 "no preference" responses were given when the comparison tempos were different. When they were the same, 724 "no preference" responses were made. The remaining 1,727 preference responses for faster/slower comparison tempos or increased/unaltered/decreased tempo conditions were analyzed.

Although more subjects indicated a preference for the first presentation when asked to indicate a preference for either the first or the second, this may have been attributable to the prevalence of the unaltered tempo con-

Table 15.6
Frequency of Correct Tempo Discriminations for Four Musical Excerpts

Group	Fast Mozart	Fast Chopin	Slow Mozart	Slow Chopin
Musicians (n = 100)	250	145	165	218
Non-musicians (n = 300)	571	389	364	510

Table 15.7
Frequency of Correct Tempo Discriminations for Slower and Faster Comparison Tempos within Fast and Slow Musical Excerpts

	Fast excerpts			Slow excerpts		
Group	Slower	Same	Faster	Slower	Same	Faster
Musicians (n = 100)	115	110	170	149	101	133
Non-musicians (n = 300)	235	253	472	375	261	238
Total	350	363	642	524	362	371

dition (see Table 15.2). It should be noted that, when tempos were the same, "no preference" responses were given; when tempos were different, preferences for the first or second versions were expressed. By disregarding the same (0) examples in Table 15.2, one can see that the unaltered version appears in every example. This problem was foreseen and resolved by counterbalancing and by considering the unaltered tempo condition a control for preference responses. That is, preferences for unaltered tempo as an absolute, rather than comparison, tempo were disregarded. In addition, a comparison between subjects' preferences for slower comparison tempos versus faster comparison tempos and their preferences for increased versus decreased tempo conditions was made (see Table 15.8).

When analyzing preference responses, one might consider two very different *a priori* assumptions. On one hand, it might be assumed that subjects' preferences were for a tempo in comparison with another tempo. They might be judging whether the second tempo version is "better than" the first tempo version. On the other hand, it might be assumed that subjects had in mind an optimum tempo and preferred it regardless of other versions with which it might be paired for purposes of comparison. This study was designed to make possible an analysis under both assumptions.

When data were analyzed under the assumption that subjects were making preference responses by comparing the tempo of the first presentation with that of the second, results for fast excerpts showed more preferences for slower tempos by both musicians (χ^2 (1, N = 100) = 24.36, $p < .001$) and non-musicians (χ^2 (1, N = 300) = 10.5, $p < .01$). Results for the slow excerpts showed that the responses for musicians were not significantly different from chance (χ^2 (1, N = 100) = 1.36, $p > .05$) but indicated a preference tendency toward the faster comparison tempo; non-musicians demonstrated more preferences for the faster comparison tempo (χ^2 (1, N = 300) = 29.08, $p < .001$).

Table 15.8
Frequency of Preference Responses by Musicians and Non-musicians for Fast and Slow Musical Excerpts

	Fast excerpts				Slow excerpts			
Group	Slower	Faster	Decreased	Increased	Slower	Faster	Decreased	Increased
Musicians (n = 100)	179	97	65	35	123	142	37	52
Non-musicians (n = 300)	361	279	111	123	210	336	51	176

When data were analyzed under the assumption that subjects were making preference responses for absolute rather than comparison tempos, results for fast excerpts indicated that more preferences were expressed by musicians for the decreased tempo condition (χ^2 (1, N = 100) = 9, $p < .01$); and that non-musicians' preference responses were not significantly different from chance (χ^2 (1, N = 300) = .61, $p > .05$), with a preference tendency toward the increased tempo condition. Results for the slow excerpts showed that musicians' preference responses were not significantly different from chance (χ^2 (1, N = 100) = 2.52, $p > .05$), with a tendency toward preferences for the increased tempo condition; non-musicians indicated more preferences for the increased tempo condition (χ^2 (1, N = 300) = 68.84, $p < .001$).

Of the total 400 subjects, only 64 made comments. Those comments concerned the extreme difficulty of the task (20 comments), dislike of classical music (10 comments), enjoyment of the music and the experiment (15 comments), complaints about the quality of the recording (6 comments), guesses about the purpose of the experiment (6 comments), and complaints about the experiment (7 comments).

In summary, for the tempo discrimination task, musicians made significantly more correct responses than non-musicians. Both groups discriminated tempo changes differently for fast versus slow musical excerpts. For fast musical excerpts, all groups discriminated faster tempo comparisons better; for slow musical excerpts, slower comparison tempos. Overall more correct responses were made for faster tempos. Both groups discriminated among the four musical excerpts, with more correct responses for the fast Mozart example.

Preference responses for relative tempos (faster versus slower) generally matched preference responses for absolute tempos (increased tempo condition versus decreased tempo condition). In addition, data for all subjects seemed to indicate preferences for slower tempos when the excerpt had a fast tempo in its unaltered state and preferences for faster tempos when the excerpt had a slow tempo in its unaltered state.

In conclusion, though all groups discriminated the faster tempo better for fast musical excerpts, preferences were for the slower tempo. And, though all groups discriminated slower tempos better for the slow musical excerpts, preferences were for the faster tempos.

Discussion

The question of the "right" tempo for a piece is a favorite one among musicians, listeners, and critics. Discrepancies in tempo among performances of a particular work are often explained as being conditioned by external factors,

> e.g. the size and reverberations of the concert hall, the sonority of the instruments, or the size of the orchestra. Such explanations, however, account for only minute modifications, and not the startling differences often found among performances. These are purely a matter of interpretation, and the differences encountered in the interpretation of tempo are no greater than those in style, phrasing, and orchestral treatment. Generally, it can be said that, where the classical repertory is concerned (Mozart, Beethoven, and especially Bach), modern conductors and performers play the fast movements too fast and the slow ones too slowly (Apel, 1969, pp. 836–837).

Conductors and performers recognize the importance of tempo selection in terms of performance accuracy and overall effect. Recognition of true beat or takt as the pulsation that underlies phrase rhythms irrespective of time signatures or number of notes in the phrase is a common basic skill taught to every beginning student of music. The pursuit of true beat continues throughout the career of every professional musician.

It would seem important to examine the relationship of the ability to discriminate changes in beat duration to the ability to discriminate changes in tempo. That is, if one defines beat as the most influential unit of tempo, then it might follow that the duration and/or prominence of a beat might determine the ability of listeners to discriminate changes in tempo. Thus, to teach people to discriminate tempo changes, one would teach them to focus on beat.

If, however, beat subdivisions are defined as the most influential units of tempo, then teaching someone to discriminate tempo changes might follow a different course. For example, consider a hypothetical musical excerpt, 60 seconds long, with 60 beats (each with a duration of 1 second). If the beats are performed without subdivision, the tempo of the excerpt might be perceived as slow. As more notes fill the space between beats, that is, the more the beat is subdivided, the faster the tempo of the piece might be perceived.

Attempts to isolate beat duration as the most influential unit affecting subjects' perception of tempo change have yielded interesting results. Studies using metronomic clicks as stimuli have shown that both musicians and non-musicians perceived decreases in the tempos of metronomic beats better than increases (Kuhn, 1974; Madsen, 1979). It may be important to observe that, in order to increase the tempo of metronomic clicks, one must decrease the duration of each metronomic beat. Conversely, to decrease the tempo, one would increase the duration of each metronomic beat. Thus, another interpretation of these results might be that subjects perceived increases in beat *duration* better than decreases.

The perception of tempo change has also been studied by using musical excerpts as stimuli. Data demonstrated that musicians perceived tempo increases more accurately than decreases for the most part (Wang, 1983; Wang & Salzberg, 1984). However, it was noted that musicians did not perceive increases in tempo better across *all* musical examples (Wang, 1983). Rather, it appeared that examples of differing styles and tempos affected subjects' subsequent perception of changes in the tempos of the examples. It was further conjectured that beat subdivision might play a role in subjects' ability to perceive tempo change.

The role of both beat and beat subdivision in tempo discrimination may have been demonstrated in a study by Wapnick (1980a) in which subjects were asked to estimate the amount of tempo change between the first and second playing of a musical excerpt. When the tempo of the second playing was less than twice as fast/slow as the first playing, subjects overestimated tempo increases/decreases; and, when more than twice as fast/slow, subjects underestimated. It is not clear whether or not the unaltered tempos of the various musical excerpts affected the tempo estimations of the subjects. However, alterations in the true beat that might have occurred in this study might have affected the number of subdivisons of the beat. That is, doubling the duration of the beat might have doubled the number of beat subdivisions, thus causing an overestimation of tempo increase.

Rather than argue the relative importance of beat versus subdivision of beat in tempo discrimination, it would seem more appropriate to consider both as influential units of tempo. It is beat duration that determines the speed of beat subdivisions; and it is the speed of these beat subdivisions that may determine performance accuracy and overall effect. Thus, to separate these units of tempo in future research would seem to be counterproductive.

The purpose of this study was to determine the effect of musical excerpts on tempo discriminations and preferences of musicians and non-musicians. Results suggest that future researchers should first control for the unaltered tempo of the musical examples, that is, whether they are of a fast or slow tempo; and, secondly, investigators should be concerned with how familiar subjects are with the musical examples.

Regarding the first point, previous research has demonstrated that subjects (both musicians and non-musicians) expressed more preferences for faster tempos and discriminated them better. Although tempo discrimination data from the present study replicate overall the ability of subjects to discriminate faster tempos better, there was an apparent effect on this ability due to the difference in the unaltered tempos of the musical excerpts used. For fast excerpts, subjects discriminated faster tempos better; for slow excerpts, slower tempos. Preference data were not analyzed overall because preferences were counted only for correctly discriminated items; subjects correctly identified more of the fast Mozart excerpt; subjects preferred fast excerpts to be slower; and, therefore, a bias toward a preference for slow tempos would result. In this study, preferences were for slower excerpts to be faster and for faster excerpts to be slower.

Data from this study suggest that, in contrast to data from prior research, the ability to discriminate faster tempos more correctly will not necessarily result in a preference for them. On the contrary, though all groups discriminated faster tempos better for fast musical excerpts, they preferred slower tempos; and though they discriminated slower tempos better for slower excerpts, they preferred faster tempos. It would seem that tempo discrimination and tempo preferences occur as separate, mutually exclusive events. On the other hand, if Apel's conjecture that "conductors and performers play the fast movements too fast and the slow ones too slowly" is correct, then performance and discrimination may be closely related.

Regarding the second point, familiarity with the musical excerpts, it should be noted that previous research used familiar musical examples, but this study used relatively unfamiliar ones. In previous research, data demonstrated no difference between musicians and non-musicians in total correct tempo discriminations and significantly more correct identifications of tempo increase examples. In contrast, the present study showed significant differences between the total correct responses of musicians and non-musicians. These results may highlight musicians' ability to make musical transfers from familiar to unfamiliar music better than non-musicians.

Accordingly, it might be hypothesized that, for musicians and non-musicians, the most transferable musical concept is that of beat or pulse. Interestingly, the fast Mozart excerpt had the most prominent pulse and was discriminated most correctly by both musicians and non-musicians. It appeared that both the length of time between beats and the presence of *rubato* were disturbing to subjects. Several musicians commented that "rubato made it hard to maintain a beat." One subject said, "When the tempo gets so slow that you want to fall asleep, then it's very hard to discriminate."

Apparently, the twofold task of, first, discriminating whether the second tempo is slower than, the same as, or faster than the first tempo, and, second, indicating a preference for one or the other (or neither) is a very difficult one. It was surprising that musicians were only 64.83% right and non-musicians, only 50.92%. Only 1 out of the 400 subjects received a perfect score. Of the 64 subjects making comments, 20 complained about the extreme difficulty of the task.

In conclusion, responses to tempo in music have been categorized in prior research as performance, discrimination/perception, and preference. How we perform tempo, how we discriminate it, and how we prefer it would seem to be important issues for applied music instructors, music theoreticians, and sociologists. In addition, it would seem appropriate to determine whether these responses are categorical, that is, whether they are mutually exclusive or whether they have some sort of relationship to one another. For example, does the ability to perceive/discriminate tempo affect the ability to perform it? And should we take preferences for tempo seriously if those preferences are based on inaccuracy in discrimination and/or performance? Finally, must one first be able to accurately perceive tempo absolutes in order to discriminate tempo changes? Future research in applied music should prove interesting indeed.

16 A Comparison of Tempo Selections by Professional Editors, Pianists, and Harpsichordists in Bach's *Well-Tempered Clavier,* Book I

Joel Wapnick

Summary

This was one of the first studies to examine the behavior of professional musicians regarding tempo selection. It found that, for the *Well-Tempered Clavier,* Book I: 1) editors selected faster tempos than those played by pianists and harpsichordists; 2) pianists performed fast works faster than did harpsichordists; 3) pianists performed slow works slower than did harpsichordists; and 4) most importantly, the variability was great in tempos chosen by pianists and harpsichordists.

It is unclear how results may have been affected by musical style, the fact that the subjects were professional artists and editors, and the fact that data from performers consisted of studio recordings rather than recordings of live performances.

This study questions the assumption that there is a narrow band of acceptable tempos for each of these pieces; and also has implications for the teaching of performance practice to students because few studio teachers and their students are probably aware of the great diversity shown by artists in their tempo selections of this music.

Design: Statistical $N = 17$ Groups: 3
Statistical Analysis: ANOVA
Reliability: Pearson product-moment correlation
Independent Variables: Editors, pianists, and harpsichordists in editions and recordings of Bach's *Well-Tempered Clavier,* Book I.
Dependent Variables: Tempo selections made by the above three groups
Music: Performance, group

* * *

Experimental research dealing with musical tempo has focused on three main areas: discrimination, performance, and preference. Discrimination studies have examined factors related to subjects' ability to identify subtle temporal increases and decreases both within ongoing musical excerpts (Kuhn, 1974; Madsen, 1979; Wang, 1983; Wang & Salzberg, 1984) and when comparing an excerpt with a version of itself that has been speeded up or slowed down (Freeman, 1981; Kuhn, 1985; Wapnick, 1980a; Yarbrough, 1985). Performance studies have dealt with both the degree to which subjects have slowed down or speeded up during performance (Kuhn, 1975, 1977) and with the magnitude of "artistic" deviations from tempo as performed by professional musicians (Seashore, 1938). Research relating tempo with preference has examined children's and undergraduate music majors' relative preferences for slow, moderate, and fast tempos both in an absolute sense and with respect to original unaltered tempo (Geringer & Madsen, 1985; LeBlanc, 1981; LeBlanc & Cote, 1983; LeBlanc & McCrary, 1983; Wapnick, 1980b).

One aspect of tempo that has as of yet received little attention is the systematic study of tempo selections made by professional musicians. Scant information is available concerning the degree to which different performers agree among themselves concerning the tempo at which a particular piece should be played. It is widely believed that for any piece (even those with specific metronomic indications) a range of acceptable tempos exists, and that such a range may be adjusted upward or downward depending upon a number of conditions (e.g., acoustical properties of the concert hall, qualities of the instrument(s), and so forth) (Donington, 1960; Palmer, 1981). This statement perhaps expresses the obvious: any piece that is played too slowly will drag, and any piece played too quickly will not be heard clearly. What is unknown, however, is how large a range for a "typical" piece of a given genre and style delineates acceptable tempo selection. We do not know, for example, what the ratio of two tempos is, given that one tempo is the "fastest acceptable" and the other is the "slowest acceptable" for a given work.

The question of magnitude of agreement among professionals concerning tempo selection is a potentially important one from a pedagogical point of view. A teacher may have a smaller or larger internal "acceptable range" for a given work than that established from a number of different artist performances. Suppose, for example, that a student is told by the teacher that the tempo is too slow. Suppose also that 30% of musicians who recorded the work played it even more slowly than did the student. It would seem that three possible conclusions could be drawn: the teacher was incorrect; the 30% of musicians who played the piece even more slowly than the student were incorrect; or the teacher was imprecise in his instructions, that is, the tempo was acceptable, but the student did not exhibit enough control over other performance parameters to perform the piece properly at the tempo selected. Although the issue of the "correctness" of a given tempo cannot be resolved through empirical methodology, it may still be of some value to both the teacher and student to know the range of tempos chosen by professional musicians for performance of a given work.

The present study consisted of a statistical analysis of recommended and performed tempos in one particular work: J. S. Bach's *Well-Tempered Clavier*, Book I. Tempos for each of the 24 preludes and fugues were selected by professional editors, harpsichordists, and pianists. The two purposes of the study were to examine the magnitude of variability in tempo selection among these professionals and to determine if systematic differences existed among the three groups.

Method

Subjects

Data from five editors, seven pianists, and six harpsichordists were analyzed in this study. The editors had all produced editions of Bach's *Well-Tempered Clavier*, Book I. The pianists and harpsichordists had each made a complete commercial recording of this collection. Persons whose data contributed to the study are listed in Table 16.1.

The data, which consisted of metronomic indications for the beginnings of each of the 24 preludes and fugues, were compiled by Willard Palmer, an editor of the *Well-Tempered Clavier*, Book I (Bach, 1981, pp. 218–219).

Equipment

Equipment used to record seven preludes and fugues consisted of a Luxman model L-3 integrated preamplifier-amplifier, a Dual 1224 turntable, and a BIC T-1 cassette tape recorder. Maxell UD tape was used.

Procedure

The recorded music consisted of Prelude and Fugue no. 19, played by Wanda Landowska; Preludes and Fugues no. 20 and no. 21, played by Gustav Leonhardt; Prelude and Fugue no. 22, played by Glenn Gould; Preludes and Fugues no. 10 and no. 11, played by Joerg Demus; and Sviatoslav Richter's recording of Prelude and Fugue no. 3.

Table 16.1
Subjects Whose Data Contributed to the Study

Editors:

- Bartok
- Bischoff
- Czerny
- Hughes
- Mugellini

Pianists:

- Joerg Demus (Westminster W9332/3)
- Edwin Fischer (Les Gravures Illustres 2C 061-01300/1)
- Glenn Gould (Columbia D35573)
- Friedrich Gulda (MPS 4921550-0)
- Joao Carlos Martins (Connoisseur Society CS 2014, 2025, and 2043)
- Sviatoslav Richter (Melodiya/Angel SRC 4119)
- Rosalyn Tureck (Decca DL 710120/21)

Harpsichordists:

- Martin Galling (Vox SVBX 5436)
- Malcom Hamilton (Everest 3134/6)
- Ralph Kirkpatrick (Deutsche Grammophon LPM 18 844/45)
- Wanda Landowska (RCA VCM-6203)
- Gustav Leonhardt (Harmonia Mundi HM 20309-13)
- Anthony Newman (Columbia M2 32500)

These recordings were used solely to determine the reliability of Palmer's metronomic indications for pianists and harpsichordists. Each of the 14 pieces listed above was heard, and an estimated metronomic indication was assigned to each. Estimates were made independently of those given by Palmer. Although these estimates were consistently slightly higher than were Palmer's, the Pearson product-moment correlation between the scores was .99.

For purposes of analysis, data from preludes and from fugues were tabulated separately. Each piece was treated as if it were a subject undergoing three treatments (assigned metronomic indications by editors and indications derived from pianists' and harpsichordists' recordings). Means and means of standard deviations were tabulated for preludes and fugues, and these data are shown in Tables 16.2 and 16.3.

Results

Four one-way repeated measures analyses of variance were used to assess treatment effects. Two analyses (one for preludes and the other for fugues) compared mean metronomic indications for the three groups. The other two (again one for preludes and one for fugues) compared mean group standard deviations. Analyses of means were undertaken to determine if systematic differences existed across the three groups. The purpose of the analyses of standard deviations was to examine whether differences occurred in groups' consistency for their tempo selections.

Results from the analysis of variance of tempo means for preludes are shown in Tables 16.4 and 16.5. These tables reveal that editors advocated tempos that were significantly faster than those selected by pianists or by harpsichordists ($p < .01$), and that pianists played the preludes faster than did harpsichordists ($p < .05$).

Results from the analysis of variance and the subsequent Newman-Keuls test for mean fugal tempo were similar in that editors again advocated faster tempos than did the instrumentalists ($p < .01$). No difference occurred between the tempos selected by harpsichordists and pianists, however (see Tables 16.6 and 16.7).

Preludes and fugues in which there was at least a 10% difference in tempos selected by pianists and by harpsichordists were analyzed further to determine if these relative differences interacted with absolute tempo. The particular preludes and fugues analyzed are shown in Tables 16.8 and 16.9. Note that metronomic indications have been transformed to numbers representing occurrences per minute of the smallest-unit note (other than those used for ornaments) in each piece. This transformation was necessary to be able to compare pieces written in duple and triple time with each other.

A t test was run on the data in each of the above two tables. Results indicated that the difference between the mean tempo of preludes played faster by pianists than by harpsichordists and the mean tempo of preludes played faster by harpsichordists than by pianists approached significance ($t = 1.86$; $df = 11$; $p < .10$). The result was in the same direction and more pronounced for fugues: the mean tempo of fugues played faster by pianists than by harpsichordists was significantly greater than was the mean

Table 16.2
Tempo Means (in Beats per Minute) and Standard Deviations for Preludes in the Well-Tempered Clavier, *Book I*

	Editors		Pianists		Harpsichordists	
Prelude	*M*	*SD*	*M*	*SD*	*M*	*SD*
1	106.8	9.5	70.0	13.6	71.5	12.4
2	124.0	14.1	109.6	27.9	96.3	20.3
3	87.2	4.4	90.9	9.4	83.7	12.2
4	96.0	6.9	92.3	19.5	89.0	11.4
5	133.2	5.0	136.0	16.0	118.7	13.5
6	78.0	5.3	78.9	6.0	73.0	9.6
7	77.0	7.4	66.5	19.4	71.0	22.1
8	91.2	12.8	63.4	11.4	83.5	11.4
9	84.2	7.1	74.6	15.3	71.0	6.8
10	69.0	9.7	50.6	12.2	55.0	13.7
11	80.8	4.4	79.0	8.7	63.5	12.4
12	55.0	4.8	45.0	14.4	43.3	3.3
13	96.8	8.2	78.6	21.1	89.3	9.0
14	102.4	6.7	105.7	15.6	79.0	7.1
15	93.6	7.8	93.1	8.2	79.3	9.2
16	55.4	8.7	41.9	6.4	39.8	6.4
17	103.0	6.0	94.9	12.6	88.7	9.3
18	129.6	6.8	116.6	12.7	116.7	23.0
19	82.4	6.1	89.4	17.2	71.8	8.6
20	83.2	3.3	84.0	12.2	68.3	9.1
21	78.4	3.6	85.1	6.4	72.8	2.7
22	87.2	7.2	64.3	12.7	77.7	8.0
23	79.0	2.0	77.6	13.4	61.2	11.9
24	82.6	19.1	65.1	13.2	81.7	31.0
M	89.8	7.4	81.4	13.6	76.9	11.9

Table 16.3
Tempo Means (in Beats per Minute) and Standard Deviations for Fugues in the Well-Tempered Clavier, *Book I*

	Editors		Pianists		Harpsichordists	
Fugue	*M*	*SD*	*M*	*SD*	*M*	*SD*
1	62.9	4.0	49.3	10.9	71.5	12.4
2	80.8	1.8	75.7	11.0	74.0	7.4
3	97.6	4.6	96.6	7.1	89.0	14.0
4	52.8	5.0	47.9	11.6	52.8	9.9
5	69.0	9.1	58.7	6.4	62.2	4.0
6	70.2	2.7	63.9	14.6	73.2	9.8
7	99.2	9.1	90.0	8.6	83.3	13.2
8	72.8	1.8	63.4	6.4	64.3	16.4
9	107.2	5.9	101.7	9.8	86.0	11.8
10	123.2	7.0	105.0	20.0	92.7	14.6
11	61.2	5.0	58.7	2.8	55.3	7.3
12	63.6	2.5	52.0	10.5	50.7	9.1
13	78.4	5.4	63.0	7.2	73.3	12.6
14	93.8	7.4	65.4	8.3	75.3	22.6
15	70.2	7.9	68.9	5.7	58.8	2.0
16	68.0	11.0	58.1	8.6	64.8	20.7
17	61.5	3.0	64.1	15.8	56.0	11.2
18	58.7	5.4	55.9	18.9	62.8	11.0
19	64.8	4.5	69.9	16.1	75.5	10.1
20	69.0	3.0	77.6	15.8	72.8	8.7
21	104.0	14.7	92.7	15.1	80.7	5.9
22	55.2	4.4	43.2	5.6	53.3	10.0
23	60.8	1.5	58.1	13.5	66.5	11.2
24	48.4	3.3	46.3	16.1	39.0	9.9
M	74.7	5.4	67.8	11.1	68.1	11.1

Table 16.4
Analysis of Variance for Tempo Means, Preludes

Source	Sum of squares	*df*	Mean square	*F*	*p*
Total	30361.7	71	—	—	—
Preludes	25770.9	23	—	—	—
Groups	2065.3	2	1032.7	18.81	.001
Error	2525.5	46	54.9	—	—

tempo of fugues played faster by harpsichordists than by pianists ($t = 2.53$; $df = 13$; $p < .05$). In view of the fact that the preludes and fugues that were played faster by pianists than by harpsichordists tended to be fast pieces, and that the preludes and fugues played faster by harpsichordists than pianists tended to be slow or moderate pieces (see Tables 16.2 and 16.3), the following conclusions appear to be justified: pianists played fast pieces at a faster tempo than did harpsichordists; and pianists played slow pieces at a slower tempo than did harpsichordists.

Tables 16.10 and 16.11 show the analysis of standard deviations for preludes. The significant main effect in Table 16.10 was apparently attributable to the editors' greater homogeneity of opinion concerning tempo selection when compared to either of the other two groups. No significant difference existed regarding the mean standard deviation of pianists versus harpsichordists.

The analysis of standard deviations for fugues is shown in Tables 16.12 and 16.13. Once again, editors agreed among themselves to a greater degree than did either pianists or harpsichordists, and no difference was manifested between pianists and harpsichordists in this respect.

Table 16.5
Summary of Newman-Keuls Multiple Comparison Procedure for Tempo Means, Preludes

Editors	Pianists	Harpsichordists
89.8	81.4	76.9

Note: All differences were significant: editors versus harpsichordists and editors versus pianists at the .01 level; pianists versus harpsichordists at the .05 level. Numbers represent beats per minute.

Table 16.6
Analysis of Variance for Tempo Means, Fugues

Source	Sum of squares	*df*	Mean square	*F*	*p*
Total	20759.1	71	—	—	—
Fugues	18050.1	23	—	—	—
Groups	742.5	2	371.3	8.67	.001
Error	1966.5	46	42.8	—	—

The 13 instrumentalists selected what might be regarded as a wide range of tempos for many of the preludes and fugues in the *Well-Tempered Clavier.* Standard deviations averaged 16.2% in size of their corresponding means, and in 10 preludes and 5 fugues one or more performances was played at least twice as fast as one or more of the other performances. Although a few performers tended to play characteristically slowly (e.g., Landowska and Hamilton) or rapidly (e.g., Fischer and Newman), the overall finding of considerable variability in tempo selection did not appear to be the consequence of one or two particularly bizarre performances. As shown in Table 16.14, 10 of the 13 instrumentalists performed a tempo in at least one prelude or fugue that was half or twice as great as that chosen by another of the instrumentalists.

Discussion

Perhaps the most surprising result of this study was the degree of variability in tempo selection evidenced by both pianists and harpsichordists:

> The wide divergence of supposedly knowledgeable opinion . . . could be the subject of a long discussion. Prelude no. 24 is a particularly interest-

Table 16.7
Summary of Newman-Keuls Multiple Comparison Procedure for Tempo Means, Fugues

Editors	Pianists	Harpsichordists
74.7	67.8	68.1

Note: No significant difference existed between the underlined means. Other differences are significant at the .01 level. Numbers represent beats per minute.

Table 16.8
Mean Tempo for Preludes in Which There Was a Minimum 10% Difference in Tempos Selected by Pianists and Harpsichordists

Pianists faster		Harpsichordists faster	
Prelude	Beats per minute	Prelude	Beats per minute
2	438.4	8	334.0
5	544.0	13	535.8
11	474.0	22	155.4
14	422.8	24	326.8
15	558.6		
19	357.6		
20	504.0		
21	680.8		
23	310.4		
M:	476.7		338.0

Table 16.9
Mean Tempo for Fugues in Which There Was a Minimum 10% Difference in Tempos Selected by Pianists and Harpsichordists

Pianists faster		Harpsichordists faster	
Fugue	Beats per minute	Fugue	Beats per minute
9	406.8	1	286.0
10	420.0	4	211.2
15	413.4	6	292.8
17	256.4	13	293.2
21	370.8	14	150.6
24	185.2	16	259.2
		18	251.2
		22	213.2
		23	266.0
M:	342.1		247.0

Table 16.10
Analysis of Variance for Tempo Standard Deviations, Preludes

Source	Sum of squares	*df*	Mean square	*F*	*p*
Total	2382.3	71	—	—	—
Preludes	1114.2	23	—	—	—
Groups	490.6	2	245.3	14.51	.001
Error	777.5	46	16.9	—	—

Table 16.11
Summary of Newman-Keuls Multiple Comparison Procedure for Means of Standard Deviations, Preludes

Editors	Pianists	Harpsichordists
7.4	13.6	11.9

Note: No significant difference existed between the underlined means. Other differences are significant at the .01 level.

Table 16.12
Analysis of Variance for Tempo Standard Deviations, Fugues

Source	Sum of squares	*df*	Mean square	*F*	*p*
Total	1671.3	71	—	—	—
Fugues	387.3	23	—	—	—
Groups	515.3	2	257.7	15.34	—
Error	772.7	46	16.8	—	—

Table 16.13
Summary of Newman-Keuls Multiple Comparison Procedure for Means of Standard Deviations, Fugues

Editors	Pianists	Harpsichordists
5.4	11.1	11.1

Note: (Obviously) no significant difference existed between the underlined means. Other differences are significant at the .01 level.

Table 16.14
Preludes and Fugues in Which One or More Performance Was Played at Least Twice as Fast or Slow as One or More of the Other Performances

Piece	Fastest version(s)	Slowest version(s)
Prelude 2	Fischer: Martins	Gulda
Prelude 7	Kirkpatrick	Gould
Prelude 10	Kirkpatrick	Martins
Prelude 11	Fischer	Leonhardt
Prelude 12	Fischer	Gould
Prelude 13	Fischer	Gould
Prelude 19	Gulda	Leonhardt
Prelude 22	Leonhardt	Gould
Prelude 23	Richter	Landowska
Prelude 24	Newman	Hamilton
Fugue 14	Newman	Hamilton
Fugue 16	Newman	Landowska
Fugue 17	Gould	Hamilton
Fugue 23	Richter	Landowska
Fugue 24	Gould	Hamilton

> ing example. Compare Malcolm Hamilton's ♩ = 40 with Glenn Gould's ♩ = 84 and with Anthony Newman's ♩ = 132. The present editor would be the last to say that any of these tempos is wrong.
>
> It is well to remember that tempos may vary with factors other than the taste and moods of the individual, including the responsiveness and tonal clarity of a particular instrument, as well as the acoustics and resonance of a room or hall. It was completely in the baroque spirit to leave the choice of tempo to the performer (Palmer, in Bach, 1981, p. 218).

Notwithstanding Palmer's second paragraph in the quotation above, it seems likely that the "tastes and moods" of the individual performers were the primary factors in determining their tempo selections. Recordings were all made in studios, and studios would seem more likely to be similar to each other in acoustical properties than would be concert halls. Also, considerable variability existed among pianists and among harpsichordists. This variability within groups would seem to mitigate against contributing large differences in tempo selections among the performers to differences in specific instruments. Finally, most performers were not consistently slow or fast relative to other performers. It is difficult to explain away what appear to be idiosyncratic personal choices by constants such as acoustics or qualities of instruments.

Palmer's apparent hesitation to consider any of a number of widely fluctuating tempos to be wrong raises the interesting question of whether there is such a thing as a wrong tempo in this music. A judgment of wrongness would have to be based upon subjective decisions (e.g., the piece is played so slowly that it "drags," or is played so rapidly that it cannot be clearly heard). It is likely that the suitability of a given tempo is dependent upon how the piece is played—a performance that emphasizes contrapuntal relationships may be played slower than one which does not, for example. It is nevertheless difficult to attribute differences in musical interpretations as being solely responsible for the large variability in tempos among performances.

One possible reason why such variability in tempo selection by pianists and harpsichordists occurred is that Bach provided very few tempo indications in the *Well-Tempered Clavier.* Without such indications, the instrumentalists may have been freer to choose widely differing tempos than if such indications had been present. However, Bach did include tempo indications for the last prelude and fugue in the *Well-Tempered Clavier,* Book I: these pieces are marked *andante* and *largo,* respectively. As can be seen from Tables 16.2 and 16.3, Bach's tempo indications did not serve to make tempo selections more uniform than they were for the other 23 preludes and fugues.

The differences in tempo selection among editors, pianists, and harpsichordists can be explained by a number of conjectures, none of which can be convincingly demonstrated as a result of this study. Editors were more consistent among themselves and chose the fastest tempos of the three groups. The second fact may explain the first in that the editors' variability may have been restricted by a "ceiling effect": tempos any faster than the ones they advocated may have been patently ridiculous. Their advocacy of faster tempos than those chosen by the performers in this study may have been a consequence of not having to limit their tempos by practical considerations, such as the technical ability to play the music.

Pianists also tended to play slow pieces in the *Well-Tempered Clavier* slower than did harpsichordists and they played fast pieces faster than did harpsichordists. A number of possible explanations can be made for these results. First, the harpsichord has a much quicker decay rate than does the piano. In slow pieces, it may have been more difficult to "bind" melody notes together on the harpsichord than on the piano. A faster tempo on the harpsichord would thus have been called for:

> When someone took me to task for playing the C-sharp major Prelude of Book II too fast, my answer could have been: "Well, just try to make that sound on either the harpsichord or the clavichord at the tempo you suggest!" Yet this prelude could have been brought to sound absolutely marvelous on an instrument that would sustain enough to permit a slow tempo, even though in the literal sense it would have been contrary to what is likely to have been Bach's own treatment of it (Kirkpatrick, 1984, p.46).

In fast pieces, it may have been that the clarity of the harpsichord sound was impaired by percussive jangling, and that a slower tempo than that taken by some pianists was necessary in order for individual notes to be heard clearly. Other possible explanations are that technical limitations in either harpsichords or harpsichordists rendered faster tempos very difficult. It can easily be ascertained from listening to harpsichord recordings of other music, however, that it is indeed possible for harpsichordists to play very rapidly. In view of this, it seems more likely that they chose slower tempos for fast pieces because of personal preferences rather than because of technical constraints. As a result of their training or of other factors, they may have preferred more moderate tempos than did pianists.

This study consisted of a statistical analysis of metronomic data from professionally recorded performances and from recommendations made by editors of the *Well-Tempered Clavier.* Its findings are limited by the following factors:

1. *Selection of Music.* Specifically, the divergence of opinion regarding tempo selection may have been a function of the music being by Bach, the music representing the Baroque era, or the fact that the *Well-Tempered Clavier* contained few tempo indications.
2. *Subjects.* The subjects were professional musicians. It is possible that tempos selected by less accomplished performers would be both slower and more uniform.
3. *Recordings.* The pianists and harpsichordists who each recorded the *Well-Tempered Clavier* presumably had the opportunity to listen to their recordings, modify them, make splices, and so forth. Under live concert conditions, they might well have chosen different tempos.

17 Pitch and Tempo Preferences in Recorded Popular Music

John M. Geringer
Clifford K. Madsen

Summary

This study investigated pitch and tempo preferences within the context of current popular music. Subjects from the fifth grade through college age preferred the original, unaltered version of each excerpt to the alterations of pitch and tempo. This finding is in contrast to previous studies that have indicated preferences for faster tempi and increased pitch levels in recorded symphonic, piano, and literature of other generic styles. Written comments of subjects were related predominantly to tempo changes. Additional study of listener preferences and discrimination of the elements of music across varying styles appears warranted.

Design: Posttest only $N = 500$ Groups: 10 (ten levels of age and training: fifth grade–college)

Statistical Analysis: chi-square, Mann-Whitney *U*, Kruskal-Wallis one-way analysis of variance, Friedman two-way analysis of variance

Independent Variables: Pitch and tempo alterations ($\pm 12\%$) of popular music excerpts

Dependent Variables: Frequency of subjects' preferences for original and altered (pitch and tempo) popular excerpts; written comments concerning liked and disliked versions

Music: Listening, group

* * *

The study of music preference and selection has been of considerable interest to the music therapy and education professions. Many of the long-term subject and training variables have been reviewed by Farnsworth (1969). Thorough and more recent literature reviews regarding the effects of variables, such as familiarity, media exposure, complexity, and generic styles on music preference and attitude, may be found in Wapnick (1976) and Kuhn (1980).

A direct relationship between knowledge of the music art form and music preference has not been demonstrated (Kuhn, 1980). Among the general population, preference and selection of popular rock music appears to increase with age and grade level, but, conversely, the preference for music classics appears to decrease (Greer, 1981). Although college music students agree among themselves extremely well and indicate marked preferences for composers in the formal tradition when verbal measures are used, measures of free-choice music listening indicate inconsistent preferences among this same population (Geringer, 1982).

Investigation of listener preferences regarding the elements of music has been of recent experimental interest. In two studies concerning the interrelationship of intonation and tone quality, it was found that subjects' preferences for sharp and in-tune intonation conditions exerted a stronger influence than preferences regarding tone quality (Geringer & Madsen, 1981; Madsen & Geringer, 1976). Subjects, when indicating tone-quality preferences, were responding actually to pitch variables rather than quality variables. In both these studies, subjects preferred pitch deviations in the direction of sharpness compared to flatness deviations. Geringer (1976) found that subjects listening to recorded orchestral music preferred faster tape speeds relative to the unaltered recordings. These preferences could have resulted from higher pitch levels, faster tempi, brighter timbres, or any combination of these variables. Using recorded piano music, Wapnick (1980b) attempted to isolate pitch, tempo, and timbre effects. Subjects preferred increased tape speed, fast tempo, and bright timbre when these variables were examined independently of the other factors. Preference for fast tempo was stronger for the more familiar music examples. A series of investigations has shown that the music preferences of fifth- and sixth-grade students were influenced strongly by tempo (LeBlanc, 1981; LeBlanc & Cote, 1983; LeBlanc & McCrary, 1983). Subjects in the LeBlanc and McCrary study rated each faster level of tempo higher in preference than slower levels. A strong positive correlation existed between increases of tempo and higher preference ratings.

A number of research studies have been made concerning the perception and performance of pitch and tempo (Geringer & Madsen, 1984). As noted by LeBlanc and McCrary (1983), caution is advised when extrapolating findings from discrimination and performance investigations to studies where subjects' preferences are the primary dependent variable. However, two recent studies are of particular relevance to the present investigation. Geringer and Madsen (1984) investigated pitch and tempo discrimination of musicians and non-musicians using relatively familiar orchestral music as stimuli. Consistent with previous research, subjects identified correctly the examples of decreased-pitch levels more than pitch-increase examples. It was surprising, however, that tempo-increase examples, rather than tempo decreases, were identified more accurately. Additionally, tempo increases exerted the greatest influence on correct discrimination compared to the pitch alterations and the unaltered and decreased tempo examples. A subsequent study (Madsen, Duke, & Geringer, 1984) used familiar band music as stimuli and corroborated the results above with regard to tempo. It was suggested that the accuracy of subjects' discrimination may be strongly influenced by the content and context of each musical example.

The present study was an attempt to extend the general experimental paradigm followed in the above studies of pitch and tempo discrimination to the investigation of pitch and tempo preferences. Using current popular music, excerpts were presented in pairs to 500 subjects from fifth grade through college age. Pitch levels and tempi were independently or in combination increased, decreased, or remained constant relative to unaltered versions. The study was designed to test the preferences of subjects for pitch and/or tempo alterations compared to original, unaltered presentations of current popular music excerpts.

Method

Five hundred subjects participated in the study: 50 subjects each from 10 levels of age and music training. There were 8 groups of 50 subjects representing Grades 5–12, selected randomly from public schools in Austin, Texas, and Tallahassee, Florida. Non-music majors ($n = 50$) and music majors ($n = 50$) randomly selected from the University of Texas at Austin and the Florida State University also served as subjects.

The popular music examples utilized as stimuli in the present study were selected from the top-selling records listed by *Billboard* magazine at the time of the study, local radio station playlists of current popular music, and on the basis of a pilot investigation. The pilot study ($N = 188$) asked junior and senior high school students to list their 10 favorite songs among current popular recordings. Information from these sources was collated and a representative list of 10 current popular songs was determined. A list of the selected songs is presented in Table 17.1. Pilot investigation indicated approximately 30 seconds to be the optimal duration for song excerpts. A panel of music faculty and graduate students selected representative ex-

Table 17.1
Frequency of Preferences across Excerpts

Excerpt	Alteration		Frequency of preference		
	Pitch	Tempo	Original	Altered	No preference
1. "Telephone" (S. Easton)	0	+	387	65	48
2. "Delirious" (Prince)	–	+	448	24	28
3. "Say Say Say" (P. McCartney & M. Jackson)	–	0	428	13	59
4. "Cum on Feel the Noize" (Quiet Riot)	+	0	289	35	176
5. "Total Eclipse of the Heart" (B. Tyler)	+	–	455	11	34
6. "Uptown Girl" (B. Joel)	+	+	451	20	29
7. "All Night Long" (L. Ritchie)	0	–	409	42	49
8. "Beat it" (M. Jackson)	–	–	464	14	22
Total			3331	224	445
	Control excerpts				
			First	Second	No preference
9. "Dr. Heckyll and Mr. Jive" (Men at Work)	0	0	56	65	379
10. "Islands in the Stream" (K. Rogers & D. Parton)	0	0	59	81	360

(+) increase; (–) decrease; (0) no change

cerpts, which ranged in actual length from 26 to 38 seconds in order to provide for completion of musical phrases.

A master tape was recorded with the 10 selections at a constant input voltage. A Lexicon model 1200 audio time compressor/expander was used in conjunction with a Revox B77 variable speed tape recorder to prepare tapes for the experimental conditions. The studio-quality compressor/expander allows the pitch level of recorded material to be raised or lowered without altering the musical tempo during playback on a variable speed tape player. Alternatively, it can alter tempo without affecting pitch level, or it will allow simultaneous tempo and pitch change. The microcomputer-generated digital splicing allows musical material to be altered virtually free from tape noise and distortion artifacts.

Preparation of experimental tapes followed the procedures used in previous studies (Geringer & Madsen, 1984; Madsen et al., 1984). Tapes were prepared so that subjects heard each of the 10 excerpts twice for the purpose of comparison. One member of each pair was the unaltered, original version of each popular excerpt. The other member of each pair had been altered by the compressor/expander in one of the following ways: pitch was increased, decreased, or remained constant, and tempo was increased, decreased, or remained constant. The three possibilities for pitch combined with the three tempo possibilities resulted in nine conditions of pitch/tempo alteration. To provide for additional control, a second condition of no change in either pitch or tempo was incorporated. Conditions of pitch/tempo alteration were randomly assigned to the 10 excerpts. Table 17.1 presents the 10 excerpts and the respective alterations in pitch and tempo.

As in the previous studies cited above, the amount of change for both pitch and tempo increases or decreases was either +12% or −12%. A change in pitch level of 12% corresponds to raising or lowering of pitch level by approximately one whole step. Similarly, a change in tempo of 12% would result in an original tempo of 10 beats per minute presented at an altered tempo of 112 or 88 MM, without concomitant change in pitch level. An aspect of the present study that differs from the two studies given above is that no control was added to prevent subjects from rehearsing pitch levels and/or tempi between members of an excerpt pair. Because the purpose of this study was to investigate preferences for altered musical material, it was not necessary to inhibit memory of pitch or tempi levels.

Subjects were tested in small groups of 8 to 12. Excerpts were presented in counterbalanced orders. The intertrial interval was 15 seconds to allow subjects adequate time to respond. The interval between pair members was 5 seconds. After listening to a given pair of excerpts, subjects were asked to indicate which of the two versions was preferred (by checking on answer sheets "Version 1" or "Version 2") or to indicate no preference (by checking "Like the same"). After all 10 selections were heard, subjects were asked to give written comments regarding the aspects most liked and most disliked about the different versions. It should be noted that alterations of pitch and tempo result in concomitant differences in timbre as well. Although this effect was minimized by the use of studio-quality tape-production equipment, the space provided on the answer sheets also allowed subjects to comment on other perceived changes in addition to the pitch/tempo alterations.

Results

Data for the assessment of pitch and tempo preferences consisted of the frequency with which a particular version of the 10 excerpts was judged by subjects as the preferred version. These data, including the frequency of no preference between versions, are presented in Table 17.1. The eight selections that were altered are shown, as are also the two control trials that were not altered. It can be seen that, across all altered excerpts, subjects preferred the original, unaltered version. Total frequency of preferences for the original pitch/tempo versions was 3,331, with a frequency of no preference between versions of 445, and total preference frequency for altered versions was only 224. The consistency and magnitude of preferences for the unaltered versions across the eight excerpts is apparent, χ^2_r (2, N = 500) = 14.25, $p < .001$.

Preference responses for the two unaltered excerpts are also shown in Table 17.1 (labeled as Excerpts 9 and 10). An analysis of total responses for these two trials intended to serve as controls indicated that subjects marked the no preference category significantly more often than either the first or second presentation of the unaltered excerpts, χ^2 (2, N = 500) = 742, $p < .001$. Although the second presentation of these excerpts was preferred slightly more frequently than the first presentation (even though both were identical presentations), analysis did not indicate significant order effects, χ^2 (1, N = 500) = .30, $p > .50$. Additionally, analysis of the order of presentation across the eight altered trials revealed no significant difference between presentation orders, U (8,8) = 22, $p \geq .164$.

Possible differences among the 10 age and training groups of subjects were examined. The Kruskal-Wallis one-way analysis of variance procedure did not indicate significant differences among the preference categories across the age and training groups, H (9, N = 500) = .17, $p > .50$. These data further confirm the consistency of subjects' preferences for the original, unaltered versions among all age and training levels.

Examination of responses to each of the eight altered excerpts revealed that, across all excerpts, subjects preferred the unaltered versions to the pitch/tempo changes. This finding is somewhat surprising in view of previous research. Subjects also checked the no preference category more frequently than the altered version category for all excerpts except for one selection (Excerpt 1 in Table 17.1). The magnitude of these preferences across categories compared among the eight altered selections was not significantly different, $H\ (7,\ N = 500) = 1.29,\ p > .50$.

Of interest in the present study was the assessment of subjects' preferences regarding alterations of pitch and tempo. Comparisons of preference frequency for only the altered tempi and pitch versions were made to analyze the effects of these changes across excerpts. The conservative methods outlined in Everitt (1977) were followed to partition contingency tables into component parts. Analysis of preferences for altered versions when tempo was changed indicated that subjects preferred significantly the versions where tempo was increased (109) to versions where tempo was decreased (67) across all three conditions of pitch, $\chi^2\ (2,\ N = 500) = 10.02,\ p < .02$. Analysis of preferences for the altered categories when pitch was changed, however, did not reveal a significant difference in preference for pitch increases (66) as opposed to pitch decreases (51) across the tempo conditions, $\chi^2\ (2,\ N = 500) = 1.92,\ p > .30$.

Analysis of preference frequency for the no preference category indicated that subjects responded differentially within this category across the eight altered excerpts, $\chi^2\ (7,\ N = 500) = 317.74,\ p < .001$. Subsequent analysis revealed that for Excerpt 4 subjects indicated the no preference category significantly more frequently than for the other seven altered excerpts. This excerpt was altered by a pitch increase with no change of tempo.

A summary of subjects' written comments regarding the various versions is presented in Table 17.2. It can be seen that subjects across all grade levels asked to comment upon aspects liked and disliked about the version predominantly used tempo-related comments. Tempo comments of subjects (462) were significantly more frequent than comments related to pitch changes (81) or other aspects of the versions (194), $\chi^2\ (2,\ N = 500) = 311.8,\ p < .001$. The most frequent comments in the "Other" category included recognition of the versions as "regular" and familiar, and several comments were related to timbre changes, such as more or less bass.

Discussion

Subjects in this study demonstrated marked preferences for the original, unaltered versions of the recorded popular music excerpts. This preference was consistent across excerpts, pitch and tempo alterations, as well as age and music training levels of subjects. When only the preference responses for the altered versions were considered, subjects indicated significant preferences for faster tempo versions, which is consistent with previous research (LeBlanc, 1981, Wapnick, 1980b). No significant difference occurred in pref-

Table 17.2
Frequency of Comments Concerning Versions Liked and Disliked

Grade	Tempo related	Pitch related	Other
5	52	5	22
6	44	11	6
7	56	3	20
8	50	3	8
9	40	6	15
10	43	8	6
11	43	11	20
12	43	10	17
University students, non-music majors	49	14	34
University students, music majors	42	10	46
Total	462	81	194

erence for pitch-increase examples compared to pitch-decrease versions. Comments written by subjects to indicate overall likes and dislikes were related predominantly to tempo changes as opposed to changes of pitch level. Although not experimentally isolated in the present study, it would appear that tempo exerted the larger influence on preferences compared to the pitch alterations.

Several aspects of this study may serve to illustrate the complexity of listener preferences in musical contexts. The excerpts used as stimuli were selected on the basis of current popularity, that is, they were familiar to the majority of subjects. It seems likely that this degree of familiarity with the unaltered version mitigated against the selection of preferences on the basis of the pitch and/or tempo alterations. Recorded popular music is generally heard in one version only, performed by the same artist or performing group on the same recording, and presented with frequent repetition by media until the song is no longer popular. In contrast, music in the formal tradition is performed by different ensembles, and is heard at different tempi and slightly different pitch levels.

Perhaps these and other similar variations of the elements of art music are judged as being acceptable, and alterations of music elements in current popular music are judged simply as "wrong" by listeners familiar with the original recording. Informal comments written by subjects support this possibility. Indeed, popular music listeners are sometimes disappointed when a "live" performance version does not correspond closely to the recorded version. Further, all the excerpts in the present study contained vocal parts. Subjects' familiarity with the performers' usual vocal timbres and pitch levels also may have influenced preferences. The words themselves may have functioned as discriminative stimuli to enhance identification of the unaltered versions.

As suggested previously, caution is advised when comparing the results of the present study with those of two investigations utilizing a similar experimental routine (Geringer & Madsen, 1984; Madsen et al., 1984). The recorded instrumental music excerpts of those studies differed with respect to performance medium, degree of familiarity, as well as generic style. Additionally, the present study used listener preferences for pitch and tempo alterations as the dependent variable of interest, but the earlier studies assessed listener discrimination of pitch and tempo. The apparent lack of direct corroboration of results with the above studies and other pitch and tempo preference investigations also differing in many of the same aspects (cf. review of literature) should not be unexpected. It was suggested in an earlier study (Madsen et al., 1984) that discrimination may be influenced by the content and context of the individual musical example. It would appear that, with regard to preferences for pitch and tempo alterations of popular music, additional factors such as listener familiarity and/or generic style also exert strong influence. Regardless, subsequent investigation might compare more directly the effects of familiar versus unfamiliar examples, generic styles, and vocal versus instrumental excerpts.

The additional study of listener discrimination and preference in relationship to the elements of music seems important because these conceivably influence music instruction and the performance of music. Further study might attempt to investigate the nature of the relationship between specific knowledge of the music art form, for example, aural discrimination ability, and subsequent music preference and selection. The application of an audio compressor/expander to research in music appears useful in that it allows manipulation of musical elements independently and concomitantly within a musical context.

18 The Effect of Choral Compositional Style on Operant Balance Preference

Janice N. Killian

Summary

This study offers operant data regarding what constitutes an "ideally balanced" choir for various age/experience groups. The study replicates previous findings that indicate an initial perception effect. If how a musical event is perceived initially can reliably affect subsequent preference or performance, the way a musical stimulus is initially heard would seem to be of critical importance in both educational and therapeutic situations.

Design: Statistical $N = 249$ Groups: 6
Statistical Analysis: Friedman two-way analysis of variance
Independent Variables: Selections; (six style periods—homophonic/polyphonic); age/experience (high school, college, and conductor musicians); trials (balanced/imbalanced)
Dependent Variables: Choral balance preference: 0–10 on mixer slide indicating loudness of soprano, alto, tenor, and bass voices
Music: Listening, individual

* * *

Choral balance preference, defined as the relative loudness of soprano, alto, tenor, or bass sections of a choir, has been an issue of interest to choral educators. Little consensus appears to exist in that writers of choral education texts note that balance preferences may include more and heavier male voices (Westminster Choir College: Swan, 1973), more soprano sound (St. Olaf College: Robinson & Winold, 1976), or numerically balanced sections (Roger Wagner Chorale, Robert Shaw Chorale: Robinson & Winold, 1976). Some of the factors thought to affect balance preference include: frequency of pitch sung (Wagner, 1977), complexity of tone (Goodwin, 1980), the particular vowel sung (Roe, 1983), position in the chord (Garretson, 1970), or the style of the selection (Roe, 1983; Robinson & Winold, 1976). Recognizing the differing opinions and the variety of factors that may affect balance preference, choral educators advise novice conductors to rely on "aesthetic judgment" to determine proper balance (Hoffer, 1965).

Recently, data have been gathered to determine what balance is preferred when the subject could control balance. Killian (1985) asked choral conductors and high school choir students to listen to four-voice chorales that were recorded in such a way as to allow subjects to change the loudness of a single voice without altering the other three. Thus, subjects could manipulate the sound to produce their "ideally balanced choir." Subjects heard rhythmically identical chorales (all quarter notes with no passing tones) sung on a neutral syllable to isolate balance preference from stylistic considerations. Subjects heard both equally balanced chorales and chorales in which a single voice was 9–13 db louder than the other three to check for possible initial perception effects. Selected results indicated that subjects preferred significantly less bass relative to other voice parts; subjects could discriminate when a single voice-part was unbalanced (louder than the other three), but the unbalanced voice was adjusted significantly louder relative to balanced trials, indicating an initial perception effect; and no significant difference existed in balance preference between conductors and choir students.

The present study was designed as a continuation of the original with the intention of replicating results under more controlled conditions and of extending data-based information to other factors contributing to balance preference. Several experimental questions were asked: (1) Under more controlled recording conditions, do subjects continue to prefer less bass or were the original findings the result of equipment artifact?; (2) Does balance preference vary with music of different style periods or of different compositional techniques (homophonic vs. polyphonic)?; (3) Because conductors and high school choir students exhibited very few differences in balance preference in the original study, the present experiment was extended to younger subjects and to subjects without musical training to examine the question: Is balance preference affected by age or musical training?; and (4) Is the initial perception effect noted in the original study present across differing styles of music and among differing age/experience groups?

Method

Selection of Excerpts

Music history and theory faculty members at the State University of New York at Buffalo indicated which of several selections could be considered representative of each of six style periods (Renaissance, Baroque, Classical, Romantic, Twentieth Century, and Popular). The four most frequently chosen pieces from each period were then recorded for experimental use. Subsequently, a panel of 30 graduate music students rated the resulting excerpts as to "equal balance between sections" and "general musical accuracy and affect." The two most frequently chosen selections within each style period were then used in the final experiment. The 12 chosen excerpts were:

Renaissance:

1. Josquin des Prez. "Tu pauperum refugium." Meas. 1–8. Davison & Apel, *Historical Anthology of Music: Renaissance* (Cambridge: Harvard University Press, 1964).
2. Palestrina. "Adoramus te." Meas. 1–13. G. Schirmer, Octavo No. 6091.

Baroque:

3. Schütz. "Cantate Domino." Meas. 117–end. G. Schirmer, Octavo No. 8678.
4. J. S. Bach. "O Sacred Head Now Wounded." Meas. 1–8. E. C. Schirmer, Octavo No. 1301.

Classical:

5. Mozart. "Ave Verum Corpus." Meas. 3–18. G. Schirmer, Octavo No. 5471.
6. Mozart. "Laudate Pueri," from *Vesperae solemnes de confessore*. K.V. 339. Meas. 92–114.

Romantic:

7. Brahms. "Wondrous Cool, Thou Woodland Quiet." Meas. 1–12. G. Schirmer, Octavo No. 9335.
8. Mendelssohn. "He Watching Over Israel," from *Elijah*. Meas. 14–29. G. Schirmer, Octavo No. 2498.

Twentieth Century:

9. Hindemith. "A Swan," from *Six Chansons*. Meas. 5–11. Associated Music Publishers, Inc., #A-505.
10. Bartok. "Dancing Song from Poniky," from *Four Slovak Folk Songs*. Entire song. Boosey & Hawkes #17858.

Popular:

11. Schwandt & Andre. Arr. Brent Pierce. "Dream a Little Dream of Me." Meas. 9–16 (repeated). Plymouth Music Company VJS-102.
12. Kenny. Arr. Lojeski. "I Made It Through the Rain." Meas. 18–40. Hal Leonard #08233000.

Recording Procedures

The excerpts were recorded by six singers auditioned from faculty and students at SUNY/Buffalo. Each voice-part (soprano, alto, tenor, bass) was recorded separately with the three male singers singing both tenor and bass and the three women singing both soprano and alto to decrease possible timbre differences between voice parts. Three singers were placed on each part to give the aural impression of a group of singers and yet minimize timbre and pitch variation within sections. All parts were sung on a neutral syllable to eliminate vowel changes as a possible factor in balance preference (Roe, 1983) and to focus subject attention on balance rather than textual subject matter.

All recording was done in a professional recording studio by a professional audio engineer. All excerpts were checked for equal balance while recording, and the master tape was rechecked after final recording. Subsequently, duplicates of the tapes were made in which individual voice-parts were 10 db louder than the other three. All tape dubs were checked for accuracy at the studio using professional calibration equipment.

Subjects

Subjects ($N = 249$) consisted of musicians ($n = 150$) and non-musicians ($n = 99$). Specifically, musicians included high school choir students who were currently enrolled in a high school choir ($n = 76$), university music majors ($n = 41$), and practicing choral conductors with at least one year of conducting experience ($n = 33$). Non-musicians included fifth- and sixth-grade children ($n = 37$), and both high school students ($n = 30$) and undergraduates ($n = 32$) who had never been in a musical organization.

Procedures were explained to individual subjects as they viewed the experimental equipment. The experimental playback equipment consisted of a mixer with four slide controls ranging from 0 (soft) to 10 (loud). The four slides were labeled soprano, alto, tenor, or bass. The mixer was attached to a hidden four-channel tape recorder that played a tape on which each voice part was recorded on a separate channel, which allowed subjects to change the loudness of a single voice without affecting the other three. Instructions included:

> You will hear excerpts of choral music of different styles. The loudness of one voice part (Experimenter points to soprano, alto, tenor, and bass slide controls.) can be changed without affecting the other three. (Experimenter demonstrates.) Your task is to act as a conductor and decide on the balance you prefer for each excerpt. You will have about 30 seconds to manipulate the slides and at the end of that time I will note where you have set the slides to indicate the balance you like the best. Any questions?

Each subject heard 12 excerpts. Between trials, the experimenter noted the final position of each slide and then returned the four slides to a center point (5) to insure independence of trials. Each set of 12 excerpts consisted of six selections played under two conditions: equally balanced; and one voice-part 10 db louder than the other three to discourage the placement of

Table 18.1
Mean Scores of Musicians and Non-musicians: Balanced Trials

	Soprano	Alto	Tenor	Bass
Musicians	5.45	5.26	5.09	4.70
High school	5.04	5.14	4.80	4.52
College	5.84	5.46	5.47	5.08
Conductors	5.45	5.16	4.99	4.48
Non-musicians	5.43	5.33	4.92	5.15
Elementary	4.99	4.65	4.27	4.28
High school	5.57	5.59	5.19	5.30
College	5.71	5.74	5.29	5.87
Total	5.44	5.30	5.00	4.93

all slides in a center position for every trial and to examine possible initial perception effects. Subjects heard either of two sets of 12 excerpts to distribute effects specific to a particular set of selections. Selection order was presented in four different counterbalanced orders in each of the two sets to distribute any order effects and to allow each condition to appear an equal number of times. Thus, each subject heard six selections (one from each style period) in both an equally balanced condition and a condition in which one voice was 10 db louder than the other three in a counterbalanced order. Individual subjects heard each of the 12 trials monaurally through headphones.

Results

General Balance Preference

The first aspect of this investigation concerned general balance preference regardless of style period of the selections. Raw data consisted of a score on each of the 12 trials for each subject. A single score was composed of four numbers (responses in 0.5 increments on the 0–10 scale of the mixer) indicating preference for balance among soprano, alto, tenor, and bass voices.

Individual responses ranged from 0 to 10. Within subject variability for a single trial varied from 0 points (all four responses equal) to 9 points difference between the four voices. Table 18.1 presents the means of balanced trials for musicians and non-musicians and represents the scores of 249 subjects during 2,988 trials.

Table 18.2
Multiple Comparisons of Ranks Indicating Balance Preference: Mean of Balanced Scores Across Twelve Trials

Bass	Tenor	Alto	Soprano
20	21	37	42

Note: Underlines indicate no significant differences at the .05 level.

As in previous research (Killian, 1985), non-parametric statistical techniques were necessary because a linear scale (0–10 on the control slide) was used to measure a non-linear event (decibel differences between each number on the control slide). Thus, ordinal data could be assumed, but intervallic data were questionable. Results should be interpreted as indicating the preferred direction and relative loudness among the four voice-parts rather than as a measurement of the magnitude of differences. No attempt was made to measure exact decibel differences.

The first analysis utilized the Friedman two-way analysis of variance by ranks to analyze what general balance was preferred across all styles (balanced trials only). The results of the 4 (SATB) $\times$ 12 (six age/experience groups by two sets) Friedman was χ_r^2 $(3, N = 249) = 18.70, p < .001$. Subsequent multiple comparison (Hollander & Wolfe, 1973) revealed that significantly less bass and tenor was preferred (Table 18.2). Comparison of musicians' and non-musicians' general preference indicated that both exhib-

Table 18.3
Multiple Comparisons of Ranks Indicating Balance Preference: Musicians versus Non-musicians

Musicians

Bass	Tenor	Alto	Soprano
6	13	19	22

Non-musicians

Tenor	Bass	Alto	Soprano
7	15	18	20

Note: Underlines indicate no significant differences at the .05 level.

ited a differential preference for loudness among the four voice-parts (musicians: χ_r^2 (3, N = 150) = 15.00, $p < .01$; non-musicians: χ_r^2 (3, N = 99) = 9.80, $p < .05$). However, multiple comparisons revealed that musicians preferred significantly less bass than alto or soprano, and non-musicians preferred significantly less tenor than alto or soprano (Table 18.3). Because a difference was manifested between musicians and non-musicians, that division was considered in all subsequent analyses.

Continuing analyses concerned differences between age/experience groups. Among musicians, a significant difference in preference for the four voice-parts was noted for high school musicians, χ_r^2 (3, N = 76) = 20.30, $p < .001$, college musicians, χ_r^2 (3, N = 41) = 22.08, $p < .001$, and conductors, χ_r^2 (3, N = 33) = 26.50, $p < .001$. Subsequent multiple comparisons revealed that the three groups had only slightly different ranking orders. All groups preferred significantly less bass, and usually more soprano was preferred. The exception was high school choir students, who preferred relatively more alto (Table 18.4).

Analyses of non-musicians divided into age/experience groups revealed less consistent results. Elementary non-musicians exhibited a differential preference for loudness among the four voice-parts, χ_r^2 (3, N = 37) = 21.70, $p < .001$, as did college non-musicians, χ_r^2 (3, N = 32) = 12.23, $p < .01$. However, high school non-musicians demonstrated no significant differences in loudness preference for the four voice-parts, χ_r^2 (3, N = 30) = 6.70, $p > .05$. Multiple comparisons allowed consideration of specific differences (Table 18.5). Although differences existed in the statistical significance of the preference for balance, examination of Table 18.5 reveals that elementary and high school students preferred the same rank order (tenor, bass, alto, soprano, ranked from softest to loudest). College non-musicians varied widely from that order and preferred significantly less tenor than soprano or bass. It is noteworthy that college non-musicians chose bass as the loudest voice, but all others (musicians and non-musicians) preferred either bass or tenor as the softest voice.

Balance Preference for Different Compositional Styles

A second research question concerned balance preference in selections from various style periods. Analyses were made of each of the six style periods. As before, musicians and non-musicians were considered separately, and balanced trials only were considered. Musicians exhibited a significantly different preference for loudness among the four voice-parts in Renaissance selections, χ_r^2 (3, N = 150) = 7.82, $p < .05$, in Baroque examples, χ_r^2 (3, N = 150) = 10.94, $p < .02$, in Classical excerpts, χ_r^2 (3, N = 150) = 15.80, $p < .01$, in Romantic excerpts

Table 18.4
Multiple Comparisons of Ranks Indicating Balance Preference: Musicians Across Age Groups

High School Musicians

Bass	Tenor	Soprano	Alto
16	26	35	43

College Musicians

Bass	Alto	Tenor	Soprano
15	28.5	32	44.5

Conductors

Bass	Tenor	Alto	Soprano
13	26	39	42

Note: Underlines indicate no significant differences at the .05 level.

Table 18.5
Multiple Comparisons of Ranks Indicating Balance Preference: Non-musicians Across Age Groups

Elementary Non-musicians

Tenor	Bass	Alto	Soprano
19	21	36	44

High School Non-musicians

Tenor	Bass	Alto	Soprano
22	27	35	36

College Non-musicians

Tenor	Alto	Soprano	Bass
17.5	30	34	38.5

Note: Underlines indicate no significant differences at the .05 level.

Table 18.6
Multiple Comparisons of Ranks Indicating Balance Preference: Musicians Across Style Periods

Musicians: Renaissance

Bass	Soprano	Tenor	Alto
7	16.5	18	18.5

Musicians: Baroque

Bass	Tenor	Alto	Soprano
6	17	18.5	18.5

Musicians: Classical

Bass	Tenor	Alto	Soprano
6	13	18	23

Musicians: Romantic

Bass	Tenor	Soprano	Alto
6	12	20.5	21.5

Musicians: Twentieth Century

Bass	Tenor	Alto	Soprano
6	13	19	22

Musicians: Popular

Bass	Tenor	Alto	Soprano
12	12	15	21

Note: Underlines indicate no significant differences at the .05 level.

χ^2_r (3, N = 150) = 16.25, $p < .01$, and in Twentieth Century selections χ^2_r (3, N = 150) = 15.00, $p < .01$. No significant difference occurred in preference for the soprano, alto, tenor, or bass voices in Popular selections, χ^2_r (3, N = 150) = 5.40, $p > .20$. Multiple comparisons for each style period indicated that, except for Popular style selections, musicians continued to prefer significantly less bass (Table 18.6). The fact that the preference for less bass was not significantly different from other voices for Popular styles would indicate that musicians preferred comparatively more bass on Popular examples than on any other style period.

Unlike musicians, non-musicians often exhibited no significant differences in preference for the loudness of soprano, alto, tenor, or bass voices across the various style periods. No significant difference existed during Renaissance selections, χ_r^2 (3, N = 99) = 3.05, $p > .30$, Baroque excerpts, χ_r^2 (3, N = 99) = 7.20, $p > .05$, Classical examples, χ_r^2 (3, N = 99) = 2.55, $p > .30$, or in Romantic excerpts, χ_r^2 (3, N = 99) = 2.15, $p > .50$. Non-musicians did exhibit a significant difference in balance preference during Twentieth Century examples, χ_r^2 (3, N = 99) = 8.45, $p < .05$, and in Popular selections, χ_r^2 (3, N = 99) = 12.65, $p < .01$. Table 18.7 presents the multiple comparisons for non-musicians across style periods. Non-musicians consistently maintained the same ranking of tenor (softest), bass, alto, to soprano (loudest) throughout all style periods. A very slight and statistically non-significant difference occurred during Renaissance selections. It is not possible to determine from this data whether non-musicians, like musicians, preferred more bass during Popular excerpts, or if they preferred less tenor in Popular selections.

Analyses were made of Set I versus Set II selections to determine if a significant difference existed due to specific sets of selections heard. Results indicated a significant difference among balance preference both for those hearing Set I, χ_r^2 (3, N = 125) = 10.80, $p < .01$, and Set II, χ_r^2 (3, N = 124) = 8.20, $p < .05$. Multiple comparisons (Table 18.8) indicated a similarity in the rankings, with both sets ranking tenor (softest), bass, alto, and soprano (loudest). Thus, for the purposes of further analyses, Sets I and II were considered as equivalent and no further analyses of this factor were made.

Polyphonic versus Homophonic Compositional Style

Another question of experimental interest concerned whether musicians and non-musicians would exhibit differential balance preferences during polyphonic or homophonic compositional styles. Analyses were made only of those selections that were entirely polyphonic or homophonic. Chosen selections included excerpt numbers 3, 6, and 8 (polyphonic) and numbers 2, 4, and 5 (homophonic). Analyses indicated that musicians showed a differential preference both during polyphonic examples, χ_r^2 (3, N = 150) = 17.83, $p < .001$, and during homophonic pieces, χ_r^2 (3, N = 150) = 14.70, $p < .01$. Multiple comparisons indicated very few differences in balance preference between the two compositional styles (Table 18.9).

Table 18.7
Multiple Comparisons of Ranks Indicating Balance Preference: Non-musicians Across Style Periods

Non-musicians: Renaissance

Tenor	Alto	Bass	Soprano
10.5	15.5	16	18

Non-musicians: Baroque

Tenor	Bass	Alto	Soprano
9	13	19	19

Non-musicians: Classical

Tenor	Bass	Alto	Soprano
11	15.5	15.5	18

Non-musicians: Romantic

Tenor	Bass	Alto	Soprano
11	16	16.5	16.5

Non-musicians: Twentieth Century

Tenor	Bass	Alto	Soprano
11	11.5	15	22.5

Non-musicians: Popular

Tenor	Bass	Alto	Soprano
6	14.5	19.5	20

Note: Underlines indicate no significant differences at the .05 level.

Analyses of non-musicians' preference during polyphonic and homophonic excerpts revealed that no significant differences existed in polyphonic examples, χ^2_r (3, N = 99) = 5.67, $p > .10$, or homophonic trials, χ^2_r (3, N = 99) = 1.03, $p > .70$. Multiple comparisons indicated that non-musicians continued the same ranking patterns as had been noted previously (tenor-softest, bass, alto, soprano-loudest). See Table 18.10. Appar-

Table 18.8
Multiple Comparisons of Ranks Indicating Balance Preference: Set I versus Set II

Set I

Tenor	Bass	Alto	Soprano
10	10	18	22

Set II

Tenor	Bass	Alto	Soprano
10	11	19	20

Note: Underlines indicate no significant differences at the .05 level.

ently, compositional style made little significant difference in balance preference for either musicians or non-musicians.

Unbalanced Trials

The experiment included trials in which a single voice was 10 db louder than the other three in order to test whether subjects could discriminate when a voice was "too loud" and to test whether the balance initially heard

Table 18.9
Multiple Comparisons of Ranks Indicating Balance Preference: Musicians, Polyphonic versus Homophonic Style

Musicians: Polyphonic

Bass	Tenor	Alto	Soprano
9	23	28.5	29.5

Musicians: Homophonic

Bass	Tenor	Alto	Soprano
10	25	25.5	29.5

Note: Underlines indicate no significant differences at the .05 level.

Table 18.10

Multiple Comparisons of Ranks Indicating Balance Preference: Non-musicians, Polyphonic versus Homophonic Style

Non-musicians: Polyphonic

Tenor	Bass	Alto	Soprano
17	19	26	28

Non-musicians: Homophonic

Tenor	Bass	Alto	Soprano
19.5	22.5	23	25

Note: Underlines indicate no significant differences at the .05 level.

affected subsequent balance preference. If the subject discriminated that a voice was unbalanced, the results should indicate that the "too loud" voice was softest in the balance preference. Among musicians, no significant differences occurred in balance preference when soprano was unbalanced, χ_r^2 (3, N = 150) = 6.35, $p > .05$. However, a significant difference in preference for loudness among the four voice-parts was noted when the alto was unbalanced, χ_r^2 (3, N = 150) = 16.40, $p < .001$, tenor was unbalanced, χ_r^2 (3, N = 150) = 17.00, $p < .001$, or when bass was unbalanced, χ_r^2 (3, N = 150) = 18.00, $p < .001$. Table 18.11 presents multiple comparisons for musicians during unbalanced trials and also includes musicians' balanced trial preference for comparison purposes. It is apparent that musicians discriminated when a voice was unbalanced when results are compared with balanced results.

Analyses of the unbalanced trials among non-musicians indicated that they showed no significant differences in balance preference among the four voice-parts when soprano was the unbalanced voice, χ_r^2 (3, N = 99) = 3.00, $p > .30$. However, significant differences were apparent when alto was unbalanced, χ_r^2 (3, N = 99) = 9.80, $p < .05$, tenor was unbalanced, χ_r^2 (3, N = 99) = 11.40, $p < .01$, or bass was unbalanced, χ_r^2 (3, N = 99) = 12.15, $p < .01$. Examination of the multiple comparisons (Table 18.12) revealed that, unlike musicians, who consistently ranked the unbalanced voice as the softest, non-musicians tended to be less consistent. Perhaps the tendency to prefer more soprano and bass than musicians superseded the tendency to decrease the unbalanced voice. Perhaps non-musicians could not identify which voice was unbalanced as quickly as musicians and thus produced more variability in results.

Table 18.11
Multiple Comparisons of Ranks Indicating Balance Preference: Musicians, Unbalanced Trials

Musicians: Soprano Unbalanced			
Soprano	Bass	Alto	Tenor
9.5	13	18	19.5

Musicians: Alto Unbalanced			
Alto	Bass	Tenor	Soprano
6	14	16	24

Musicians: Tenor Unbalanced			
Tenor	Bass	Alto	Soprano
6	13	17	24

Musicians: Bass Unbalanced			
Bass	Tenor	Alto	Soprano
6	12	18	24

Musicians: Balanced Trials			
Bass	Tenor	Alto	Soprano
6	13	19	22

Note: Underlines indicate no significant differences at the .05 level.

Unbalanced Trials (Adjusted)

The experiment was designed to determine whether the way subjects first heard an example affected subsequent preference or to examine what has been termed an "initial perception effect" (Geringer, 1976). To examine the possibility of this effect, balanced and unbalanced trials were compared. It should be remembered that unbalanced trials contained one voice that was 10 db louder than the other three. If there was an initial perception effect, subjects would *not* adjust the loudness of the "too loud" voice to the same

Table 18.12

Multiple Comparisons of Ranks Indicating Balance Preference: Non-musicians, Unbalanced Trials

Non-musicians: Soprano Unbalanced

Alto	Soprano	Tenor	Bass
11	14	17	18

Non-musicians: Alto Unbalanced

Tenor	Alto	Bass	Soprano
8	13	18	21

Non-musicians: Tenor Unbalanced

Alto	Tenor	Bass	Soprano
10	13	13	24

Non-musicians: Bass Unbalanced

Tenor	Alto	Bass	Soprano
9	13.5	13.5	24

Non-musicians: Balanced Trials

Tenor	Bass	Alto	Soprano
7	15	18	20

Note: Underlines indicate no significant differences at the .05 level.

extent as they would that same excerpt played in an equally balanced condition. To facilitate comparisons between balanced and unbalanced trials, the raw score for each unbalanced voice was increased by 2.5, the distance on the control slide that subjects would decrease the loudness if the unbalanced voice were to be "rebalanced." Any discrepancies between adjusted trials and balanced trials could be considered to be an initial perception effect.

Musicians indicated the following preferences across adjusted unbalanced trials: Soprano Unbalanced (adjusted), χ^2_r (3, N = 150) = 12.60, $p < .01$; Alto Unbalanced (adjusted), χ^2_r (3, N = 150) = 16.40,

Table 18.13
Multiple Comparisons of Ranks Indicating Balance Preference: Musicians, Adjusted Unbalanced Trials

Musicians: Soprano Unbalanced (Adjusted)

Bass	Alto	Tenor	Soprano
9	12	15	24

Musicians: Alto Unbalanced (Adjusted)

Bass	Tenor	Soprano	Alto
8	10	18	24

Musicians: Tenor Unbalanced (Adjusted)

Bass	Alto	Soprano	Tenor
7	11	18	24

Musicians: Bass Unbalanced (Adjusted)

Tenor	Alto	Soprano	Bass
6	12	18	24

Musicians: Balanced Trials

Bass	Tenor	Alto	Soprano
6	13	19	22

Note: Underlines indicate no significant differences at the .05 level.

$p < .001$; Tenor Unbalanced (adjusted), χ_r^2 (3, N = 150) = 17.00, $p < .001$; and Bass Unbalanced (adjusted), χ_r^2 (3, N = 150) = 18.00, $p < .001$. Multiple comparisons (Table 18.13) indicated that no unbalanced trials were perceived similarly to balanced trials. All unbalanced adjusted voices were significantly louder than surrounding voices, indicating that musicians tended to adjust the unbalanced voice in the direction in which it was originally presented (louder). Thus, there was a distinct initial perception effect.

Table 18.14
Multiple Comparisons of Ranks Indicating Balance Preference: Non-musicians, Adjusted Unbalanced Trials

Non-musicians: Soprano Unbalanced (Adjusted)

Alto	Tenor	Bass	Soprano
7	13	16	24

Non-musicians: Alto Unbalanced (Adjusted)

Tenor	Bass	Soprano	Alto
7	13	16	24

Non-musicians: Tenor Unbalanced (Adjusted)

Alto	Bass	Soprano	Tenor
8	10	18	24

Non-musicians: Bass Unbalanced (Adjusted)

Tenor	Alto	Soprano	Bass
8	10	18	24

Non-musicians: Balanced Trials

Tenor	Bass	Alto	Soprano
7	15	18	20

Note: Underlines indicate no significant differences at the .05 level.

Non-musicians indicated significant differences in balance preference among the four voice-parts during adjusted unbalanced trials as follows: Unbalanced Soprano (adjusted), χ^2_r (3, N = 99) = 15.00, $p < .01$; Unbalanced Alto (adjusted), χ^2_r (3, N = 99) = 15.00, $p < .01$; Unbalanced Tenor (adjusted), χ^2_r (3, N = 99) = 16.40, $p < .001$; and Unbalanced Bass (adjusted), χ^2_r (3, N = 99) = 16.40, $p < .001$. Multiple comparisons (Table 18.14) indicated that the adjusted voices were perceived as significantly louder in each case, indicating that non-musicians as well as musicians seem to be affected by the loudness at which a sound was originally presented.

Discussion

The present study was designed to replicate experiments involving preference for vocal balance and to extend results to the consideration of music of differing style periods and compositional styles as well as to subjects of varying ages and musical experience. Results may be summarized as follows:

1. Consistent with previous research, subjects preferred significantly more soprano and alto and significantly less bass and tenor.
2. A consistent difference existed in balance preference between musicians and non-musicians regardless of age. Specifically, musicians preferred significantly less bass on all trials, and non-musicians generally preferred significantly less tenor. Results were not as consistent for non-musicians as for musicians.
3. Style of music appeared to make little difference in balance preference. The only exception was for musicians who preferred relatively more bass on Popular style selections than for other styles.
4. There appeared to be no significant differences in balance preference for homophonic versus polyphonic compositional styles.
5. Musicians discriminated when a voice was unbalanced (10 db too loud); non-musicians were less consistent in their discriminations in this regard.
6. A distinct initial perception effect was present for both musicians and non-musicians.

Results of the present investigation replicate the findings previously noted by Killian (1985) in that musicians consistently preferred less bass. Balance preference would also seem to be quite consistent across differing style periods and across differing compositional techniques. Factors that affect balance preference and when those preferences are formed would seem to be areas of future research. Choral educators might conclude that fewer male voices may be needed to balance a choir regardless of the style of music being performed. The only exception is in the area of Popular music, in which more bass was preferred.

Many unanswered questions arise. Is the fact that non-musicians consistently preferred more bass than musicians due to the influence of Popular music, or of the recording equipment available that allows bass to be increased, or a difference in how musicians and non-musicians perceive choral music? Many more variables could be operating.

Choral experience appears to affect balance preference. Are other musical variables similarly affected? Were differing preferences between musicians and non-musicians due to differing opinions, or were results due to a response time variable? That is, musicians could identify which voice was too loud and adjust it, but non-musicians often did not in the time allotted. Do non-musicians, who are not as familiar with four-part music, need more time to hear what musicians can hear quickly? Or does choral experience change balance preference?

Both musicians and non-musicians preferred louder female than male voices. Is this result attributable to acoustical differences in the perception of high and low pitches or an indication of preference for high pitches in choral music?

Present results were consistent with previous research of pitch preference (Geringer, 1976) as well as balance preference (Killian, 1985), indicating the presence of an initial perception effect. What other perceptual qualities are subject to this effect and how it might be utilized for educational/therapeutic purposes would appear to be areas for continued experimental research.

This project was funded by the Research Development Fund of the State University of New York (SUNY) at Buffalo. The author is grateful to the SUNY/Buffalo Electronic Music Studio and the Department of Industrial Engineering for the loan of equipment, and to Lawrence Timm, graduate assistant for the project.

19 Expressed Opinions of Composers, Musical Training, Recording Ownership, and Their Interrelationship

Harry E. Price
Cornelia Yarbrough

Summary

This study made four comparisons: musicians' versus non-musicians' opinions of composers; verbally expressed opinions and recording ownership; verbally expressed opinions and musical training; and reported and actual recording ownership. Different calculations of the same data emphasize differences in methods of summarization. Verbal opinions are moderately but significantly related to behaviors. Reported recording ownership is highly correlated to actual recording ownership. Non-musicians list and prefer fewer formal traditional composers.

Design: Statistical $N = 453$ Groups: 2
Statistical Analysis: Pearson product-moment correlation
Independent Variables: College musicians versus college non-musicians, training
Dependent Variables: Composer rankings, recording ownership, frequency of composer mention

* * *

Musical taste has been an ongoing area of investigation since the 1930s. The primary methods employed to investigate opinions through the late 1960s have been self-report measures, including rating scales, summated ratings, and ranked preferences. With some exceptions, the late 1960s saw the advent of the use of behavioral measures in the form of direct observation, listening time as well as choice, and other devices that allowed direct manipulation of the musical elements of a composition (Kuhn, 1980; Wapnick, 1976).

There is a relationship between self-reported measures and behavioral measures, but it is moderate (Fishbein, 1967; Geringer, 1977, 1982; Greer, 1981; Kuhn, Shehan, & Sims, 1980; Morgan & Lindsley, 1966; Pessemier, 1960; Wapnick, 1976; Yarbrough & Price, 1982). This would indicate that these two types of measures, though related, assess different aspects of musical taste or different variables that are in some way related.

The age of an individual does appear to be related to the response on both self-reported and behavioral measures of musical preferences for differing styles of music. It appears that the preference for popular/rock music increases and preference for formal-tradition music decreases with the age of individuals who have little or no musical training (Greer, Dorow, & Hanser, 1973; Greer, Dorow, & Randall, 1974). However, the opposite was found to be true by Baumann (1960), Geringer and McManus (1979), and a series of articles in the *Music Journal* in 1951–52.

In reviewing the extant literature on composer preference, Farnsworth (1969) found that with increased age and training respondents became more alike and also their judgments more closely approximated those of musicologists. However, other research indicates that "liking both classic and modern music shows an inverse relationship with age," and that training does have a positive relationship with reactions to modern music (Rubin-Rabson, 1940). The conflict in these findings may be due in part to a lack of control for musical training in the Rubin-Rabson study.

Kelly (1961) did find an "increase in preference of classical music and decrease in that of popular music from the lower to the higher grades," but also discovered a strong relationship between an increase of musical training and higher grade level. Keston and Pinto (1955), using statistical manipulation in an effort to isolate training from age, found that training and not age was an important factor in influencing musical preference.

A study that investigated the relationship of musical training, in the form of high school music experiences, to record ownership, contended that a larger percentage of college students who had high school music experience owned records than did those with no high school music background (Birch, 1962). Additionally, significantly more students owned serious music recordings if they had at least three years of high school music experience.

A clear preference for composers in the formal tradition has been indicated by college music students, and college non-music as well as younger students prefer current popular composers (Geringer, 1982; Geringer & McManus, 1979). Some of these music students showed a significant relationship among the frequency of mention, average rank-order, number of concerts reported to have attended, and the reported number of records owned of the music of composers, but non-music majors and younger students did not (Geringer & McManus, 1979).

In research that compared actual listening behavior with expressed opinions, Geringer (1982) compared responses on a free-recall survey to music selection on an operant music listening recorder. Both elementary and college non-music students listened to popular composers more than the traditional composers, and music majors had the opposite response. This showed a relationship of verbal opinion to listening behavior, but the agreement was moderate, which was consistent with previous research.

The current study investigated the relationships among verbal opinion, training, and record ownership. This follows the line of research by Geringer (1982) and is in keeping with the recommendations by Geringer and McManus (1979):

> The music educator concerned with assessing individual taste and preference might consider techniques to reduce such verbal-report versus behavior discrepancies. Further information regarding music behavior could be achieved by systematic observation in performance and functional contexts, such as the individual's actual concert attendance, or counting the number of recordings owned by individuals (p. 76).

The current study investigated expressed opinions regarding preferences of college music and non-music majors for specific composers. Additionally, the relationship of these opinions to the number of recordings owned and years of musical training was investigated.

Method

Some 453 students from two universities (Virginia Polytechnic Institute and State University, and Syracuse University) responded to a free-recall survey of musical taste for composers. The respondents were music majors (education, performance, composition, and industry) who were enrolled in undergraduate as well as graduate music courses ($n = 116$) and non-music majors who were enrolled in music appreciation and music fundamentals for elementary education majors classes ($n = 337$).

A survey was administered by the experimenters early in the term during regularly scheduled classes. Brief instructions were given, in addition to those on the form, which emphasized that only those who compose music were to be listed and not those who only perform and do not compose. The survey asked for a variety of demographic data; expression of willingness to participate in the second half of the project; and a list of 10 favorite composers, their ranks, number of recordings featuring their music, and the number of live performances the students had attended in which the music of each composer had been performed. Subjects were permitted to use the name of a group when they did not know the composer for the group. Approximately 15 minutes were required to complete the form.

After the surveys were completed, random samples of non-music majors ($n = 124$) and music majors ($n = 66$) who indicated an "interest in participating in the second half of our project" were selected for further investigation. These subjects were interviewed in their domiciles using a form that was completed based upon the verbal rankings of their 10 favorite composers. The interview included counting the number of recordings that contained a composition by a preferred composer as well as the total number of formal and popular tradition recordings owned by the subject.

Results

The purpose of this study was twofold: to assess preference for composers; and investigate recording collections in light of these preferences. The first part assessed the preferences for composers as verbally expressed by college music and non-music majors in the absence of any music stimuli. The second part involved taking a sample of these students and analyzing their collections of recordings in light of their verbally expressed preferences for composers.

Table 19.1 summarizes the frequency with which composers were mentioned by all the students (non-music and music majors). The non-music majors mentioned fewer composers of the formal tradition in the 22 most-mentioned composers than did the music majors. The order of the 6 formal tradition composers mentioned by the non-music majors is exactly the same as that reported by Geringer and McManus (1979), and 4 of the 6 were among the top 10. Although there was a consistency of response when compared with previous research for the ranking of composers of the formal tradition, only 5 of the composers in the popular tradition were the same and these were in a different order.

The percentage of formal tradition composers who were mentioned by subjects is related to the number of years of musical training reported. The data in Table 19.2 clearly indicate a linear relationship between these two variables. The correlations for non-music majors and music majors are $R = .2936$ ($p < .0001$) and $R = .3764$ ($p < .0001$), respectively. These relationships are moderate.

Samples of non-music majors ($n = 124$) and music majors ($n = 66$) were randomly selected for further investigation. Each subject's recording collection was analyzed for the number of recordings that contained a com-

Table 19.1
Frequency of Composers Mentioned

Non-music Majors (N = 337)	Music Majors (N = 116)
180 Beethoven	49 Beethoven
156 Bach	43 Bach
128 Taylor	31 Mozart
122 Beatles	26 Debussy
100 Fogelberg	24 Copland
95 Mozart	23 Beatles
94 Joel	22 Chopin
86 Manilow	Brahms
85 Stones	21 Rachmaninoff
81 Tchaikovsky	18 Mangione
78 Springsteen	16 Tchaikovsky
67 Browne	13 Fogelberg
64 Chopin	Joel
62 Earth, Wind, & Fire	Schubert
61 Handel	12 Taylor
54 Styx	11 Chicago
Young	10 Gershwin
51 Eagles	Haydn
49 Cross	Mitchell
45 Journey	Ravel
44 Commodores	Schumann
43 Benson	Vivaldi

Table 19.2
Mean Percentage of Formal Composers Mentioned by Years of Musical Training

Years Training	Non-music Majors	Music Majors
≤ 3	9.16 N = 137	18.18 N = 11
4–6	12.40 N = 72	36.08 N = 19
7–9	18.25 N = 78	40.38 N = 26
> 9	30.60 N = 50	54.41 N = 60

position by one of the verbally expressed 10 favorite composers. The frequency of mention, number of recordings reportedly owned of composers, and number of recordings actually owned were compared for these samples by means of a Pearson product-moment correlation analysis (see Table 19.3). These analyses yielded levels of relationship that were all less than $p = .0001$. Although they were significant, the comparisons of frequency of composer mention resulted in moderate relationships with the number of recordings reportedly owned and number of recordings actually owned. These data also seem to indicate a greater disparity between verbal responses and behavioral measures for non-music majors than for music majors. However, the relationship of the number of recordings reported to those actually owned was very strong for both groups.

The relationships among years of musical training, percentages of formal composers mentioned, and recordings owned of a formal tradition were also

Table 19.3
Correlations of Composer Frequency of Mention, Recordings Reportedly Owned, and Recordings Actually Owned

	Non-music Majors		Music Majors	
	Reported	Actual	Reported	Actual
Frequency	.38174	.39258	.79123	.78548
Reported		.92702		.96796

analyzed using Pearson product-moment correlation analyses. For both groups, the relationship of percentages of formal tradition composers mentioned to recordings owned was found to be significant ($p < .001$) and moderate ($R = .7630$ for non-music and $R = .6421$ for music majors). The relationships for training to the percentage of formal composers mentioned by the non-music students ($R = .3188$, $p < .001$) and to the composers mentioned ($R = .2830$, $p < .05$) and recordings owned ($R = .2774$, $p < .05$) by music students were significant but minimal. However, the relationship of training to recording ownership for non-music majors was not significant ($R = .1274$).

In examining the results, one might analyze the data in several ways, depending on the research focus. Tables 19.4 and 19.5 are included as comparisons of different approaches to dealing with the data for the interviewed non-music and music majors, respectively, with all measures listed in descending order. A score was calculated for each of the subjects' preferred composers by giving 10 points to the most preferred, 9 points to the second most preferred, to 1 point for the tenth most-preferred composer listed; then these scores were summed across all the subjects in each sample for each composer to arrive at a total score, which is found in the first column. The total score is included to try and assess an overall ranking that includes both magnitude and frequency of composer mention. The next column summarizes the total frequency with which a composer was mentioned. The third column is a listing of the mean scores, which were calculated by dividing the total score by the frequency of mention for each composer. This yields a measure of the average strength of the rankings. For example, if only five people mentioned J. S. Bach, but all designated him as the most preferred, the mean score would be 10 (score 50/frequency 5), thus indicating that those who do prefer Bach also feel strongly in favor. This mean score is reported only for those 19 composers mentioned by 10 or more interviewed non-music majors, and for the 22 composers with the highest mean scores who were mentioned by five or more interviewed music majors. The last two columns of Tables 19.4 and 19.5 list the total number of recordings reportedly and actually owned of the composers' music by the interviewed music and non-music majors.

The composers listed in each column of Tables 19.4 and 19.5 are in rank-order based upon the value of the number for that variable (total score, frequency of mention, mean score, recordings reportedly owned, and recordings actually owned). There is considerable inconsistency among the five sets of rankings. However, upon closer examination of Tables 19.4 and 19.5, the discrepancies among the five rankings appear greater for the non-music majors than for the music majors. This would be an indication that the latter gave more consistent responses for the frequency of composer mention and

Table 19.4
Comparison of Measures of Opinion and Preference for Interviewed Non-music Majors, N = *124*

Score	Frequency	Mean Score	Reported	Actual
205 Taylor	32 Taylor	8.31 Young	133 Bach	75 Beatles
164 Beatles	26 Bach	7.17 Ritchie	121 Mozart	69 Bach
148 Fogelberg	24 Beethoven	7.13 Beatles	104 Beethoven	64 Beethoven
143 Beethoven	Fogelberg	7.12 Manilow	81 Beatles	47 Mozart
142 Browne	23 Beatles	6.76 Browne	62 Taylor	45 Browne
139 Bach	21 Browne	6.75 Joel	59 Tchaikovsky	Tchaikovsky
135 Joel	20 Joel	6.73 Benatar	55 Browne	43 Springsteen
121 Manilow	18 Springsteen	6.70 Morrison	54 Fogelberg	42 Fogelberg
113 Springsteen	Tchaikovsky	6.58 Cross	52 Joel	Taylor
108 Tchaikovsky	17 Manilow	6.46 Stones	40 Springsteen	41 Joel
Young	13 Stones	6.41 Taylor	37 Yes	39 Stones
86 Ritchie	Young	6.40 Fleetwood Mac	33 Stones	31 Mac Davis
84 Stones	12 Cross	6.28 Springsteen	32 Rachmaninoff	29 E. W. & F.
79 Cross	Ritchie	6.17 Fogelberg	31 Handel	Yes
74 Benatar	Mozart	6.00 Tchaikovsky	Manilow	28 Young
67 Morrison	11 Ferguson	5.96 Beethoven	30 Ferguson	25 Led Zeppelin
64 Fleetwood Mac	10 E. W. & F.	5.35 Bach	Led Zeppelin	24 Ferguson
Yes	Fleetwood Mac	5.00 Mozart	29 Young	23 Ritchie
63 E. W. & F.	Morrison	4.00 Ferguson	28 Morrison	20 Anderson
60 Mozart			Ritchie	Eagles

Table 19.5
Comparison of Measures of Opinion and Preference for Interviewed Music Majors, N = *66*

Score	Frequency	Mean Score	Reported	Actual
202 Beethoven	28 Beethoven	7.21 Beethoven	133 Beethoven	155 Beethoven
144 Bach	25 Bach	7.20 Spyrogyra	68 Beatles	73 Bach
86 Brahms	19 Copland	7.00 Led Zeppelin	59 Bach	48 Beatles
Copland	16 Brahms	6.86 Haydn	39 Copland	36 Taylor
84 Beatles	15 Mozart	6.67 Chicago	36 Chicago	34 Mozart
75 Mozart	13 Beatles	6.46 Beatles	Taylor	31 Brahms
66 Tchaikovsky	12 Debussy	6.43 Mitchell	28 Chopin	30 Chicago
59 Debussy	Tchaikovsky	6.25 Chopin	Tchaikovsky	28 Copland
58 Rachmaninoff	10 Mangione	6.14 Taylor	27 Mozart	Tchaikovsky
53 Gershwin	Rachmaninoff	6.00 Fogelberg	25 Mangione	27 Fogelberg
50 Chopin	9 Gershwin	5.89 Gershwin	24 Ives	26 Mitchell
48 Fogelberg	8 Chopin	5.86 Joel	23 Fogelberg	Stravinsky
Haydn	Fogelberg	5.80 Rachmaninoff	22 Mitchell	24 Chopin
46 Mangione	Stravinsky	5.76 Bach	Stravinsky	Yes
45 Mitchell	7 Haydn	5.50 Tchaikovsky	21 Brahms	22 Led Zeppelin
43 Taylor	Joel	5.38 Brahms	20 Joel	20 Joel
41 Joel	Mitchell	5.00 Mozart	Led Zeppelin	19 Ives
40 Chicago	Ravel	4.92 Debussy	19 Hendrix	18 Rachmaninoff
36 Spyrogyra	Taylor	4.60 Mangione	18 Debussy	17 Genesis
35 Led Zeppelin	6 Chicago	4.53 Copland	Genesis	Hendrix
	Hendrix	4.43 Ravel	Vivaldi	Mangione
	Vivaldi			

ranking, and demonstrated a stronger relationship between verbal responses and behaviors than did non-music majors.

Discussion

This study investigated the opinions of college music and non-music majors regarding favorite composers as verbally expressed in the absence of music stimuli. The relationships of these opinions to the number of years of musical training and number and type of recordings owned by these students were also examined. Finally, several methods of assessing the verbally expressed opinions were compared to the number of recordings reportedly and actually owned, as well as to each other.

It was found that non-music majors indicated a preference for fewer composers of a formal tradition than did music majors. However, the order of preference for these composers by non-music majors replicates Geringer and McManus (1979). As has been previously reported in other research, this study also discovered that musical training was related to the verbally expressed preferences for composers of a formal tradition, but, though these relationships were significant, they were moderate.

When the recording collections of a sample of these subjects were assessed, it was found that the frequencies of composer-mention bore significant but moderate correlations to the ownership of corresponding recordings, and the percentage of recordings owned and composers mentioned of a formal tradition were significantly and more strongly related. However, the correlations of the percentages of formal tradition recordings owned and years of musical training were only significant for music majors and not for non-music majors, and this relationship was moderate. These results for non-music majors do not replicate those of Birch (1962).

The relationship of actual and reported recording ownership was also significant, but this was much stronger than other comparisons. Although discrepancies existed between the resultant rankings using these two measures, the overall results were quite similar. This comparison resulted in the highest correlation of all those in this study. This may have been because it compared an assessment of a concrete behavior to the actual behavior, versus comparisons of free verbal responses to behaviors or assessments of behaviors.

The results of this study replicate those of previous research that investigated the relationships of self-reported and behavioral measures. Although the frequency of composer-mention and recordings owned were significantly correlated, the relationship was moderate.

Many factors other than musical training can affect the results of verbally expressed preferences for composers in a study such as this. The survey was administered within a few months of a Taylor concert on one of the two campuses. This clearly could have affected the reported preference for this composer, as well as the number of recordings by this composer that the students owned. The non-music majors completed this survey in classes that they knew focused primarily on music of the formal tradition, and consequently this may have caused a bias in their responses.

The ownership of recordings is obviously affected by the financial situation of an individual and, in this instance, little by musical training. However, regardless of the number of recordings an individual owns, this person has made choices to spend the money available on certain recordings rather than others. This measure would clearly be in agreement with the definition of preference presented by Radocy and Boyle (1979): "an expressed choice of one musical work or style over other available works or styles." In this instance, the expression is through the purchase of some recordings over others. The choice is a concrete indication of preference, regardless of whether an individual can purchase 100 recordings or 2. Consequently, one might assume that, if a person clearly preferred music of a formal tradition or certain composers, the proportion of this type of recording or the proportion of composers on the recordings owned would be an indicator of preference.

Whether one uses a total score, frequency count, mean score, or recording count is a decision that must be based upon the research question because each one may answer a different question. Total score, frequency count, and mean score yield different types of data, but they may always be, at least in part, a function of eminence and/or famousness. Names such as Bach and Beethoven seem to be readily on the lips of many people, but one wonders how many of them are familiar with the music. This study did not present any musical stimuli, and a discrepancy exists among the rankings by frequency count, total score, and mean score. Bach and Beethoven are the most frequently mentioned composers after Taylor and were the composers who received the fourth and sixth highest total scores. Even though total score yields some assessment of magnitude, it is also a function of frequency because it is a multiplier. However, the mean score yields different information, and in this case the resultant rankings are different. Although a mean score eliminates the effect of the frequency of mention, it indicates the strength of preference for those people who included these composers in their top 10. In this study, Beethoven and Bach were ranked 16th and 17th respectively, based on the mean score, out of the 19 composers who were mentioned (frequency count) by a minimum of 10 people. When all three of these rankings by the non-music majors are taken in combination, it might be concluded that the Beatles (including responses of "Lennon/McCartney" and "Beatles") are the most famous and preferred overall because they are ranked no lower than fifth in any of the three rankings.

Just as these measures yield related but different results, so do the measures of recordings reportedly and actually owned. However, although the rankings of these two measures are not exactly the same, they do have a strong overall relationship, and one needs to consider the expenditures of time and effort necessary to collect data directly regarding the recording collections owned by the subjects.

The arguments presented here are not intended to favor one type of measure or data summary over another. It is suggested that the researcher consider what type of information will result in the appropriate answer to a research question for this type of research. Is the focus on how many people know of or mention a composer? If so, a frequency count may be most appropriate. Is it to assess the number of times a composer is mentioned in combination with the relative ranking? Then, a total score might be considered. Is it to assess how strongly individuals feel about a composer without regard for how many people this value represents? In this case, one might use a mean score. If there is concern about these measures because they do not evaluate actual events that indicate composer preferences, then one might ask for summaries of recording collections, and, when possible, one could directly examine the recording collections for assessment. Other direct measures that might be used are concert attendance, music listening time and choice, and familiarity with the music under investigation.

These are not new or radical concepts. The results of the comparisons in this study confirm the fact that careful attention needs to be paid to these issues prior to a choice of measurement instruments and data analyses. Whatever choice is made, one needs to attend to their specific meaning.

20 Programmatic Research in Music: Perception and Performance of Intonation

John M. Geringer
Clifford K. Madsen

Summary

This paper represents not a review of literature, but an attempt to illustrate a continuing research effort intended to be applicable to various aspects of musical endeavor. Findings are presented that pertain to the perception and the performance of intonation in both experimental and applied settings.

Much is said concerning the need for extended long-term investigation as opposed to individual "one-shot" experimentation. This series of studies represents one attempt at progressive structuring. Presented in abstract form, the presentation is intended to provide an example of a developing model for continuing research.

Design: Statistical, pre-post, posttest only, varies with study
N = 40–500, varies with study Groups: 1–10, varies with study
Statistical Analysis: several, varies with study
Reliability: Varies with study
Independent Variables: Age, training, scale direction, performance mode (vocal and instrumental), practice sessions, instruction, reinforcement, modulated frequency, verbal feedback, tuning tones, tone quality, tuned and mistuned accompaniment, pitch alterations, modulated tempo, generic styles
Dependent Variables: Cent deviation, direction of deviation (sharpness and flatness), choice of reinforcement, pitch discrimination, discrimination time, tuning responses, vocal pitch-matching, tone quality preferences, intonation preferences, tone-quality discrimination, listening time, adjustment of tape speeds, tempo discrimination
Music: Performance, listening, individual, group

* * *

Perhaps one of the most important areas of study for any musician concerns playing or singing "in tune." Aural discrimination abilities and actual performance practices demand continued consideration. Research investigations clearly demonstrate a need for the pursuit of careful and controlled inquiry in these aspects.

Thus, improving musical performance has merited the serious study of music teachers and researchers for years. Clearly, much inquiry is needed in the attempt to reach valid conclusions relevant to a phenomenon as complex as musical experience. It seems, however, that continuing and systematic research efforts are needed to yield those benefits that might accrue from long-term systematic research. Much is said concerning the necessity of such inquiry, and this series represents one line of progressive study.

Following is a brief résumé of some of the important findings of investigations conducted over more than 25 years. This summary is not intended as a review of literature concerning intonation, nor should it be regarded as the conclusion of this continuing series of investigations. It does, however, represent one line of programmatic research effort intended to be applicable to various aspects of musical endeavor. Findings are presented that pertain to the perception and the performance of intonation both in experimental and applied settings. Other aspects of music behavior are discussed in relationship to intonation, such as instructional techniques, the use of reinforcement, tone quality, tempo, and the nature of the relationship between perception and performance.

It should be emphasized that each experiment is a very complicated process, and generalizations drawn from such research can be extremely misleading unless the original experiments are studied in detail. Also, extensive literature from additional sources served to influence, modify, and more specifically focus subsequent endeavors, though not reported here. Regardless, it is hoped that analysis and synthesis of such collective findings will provide the music profession with one example of long-term investigations and, thereby, more information toward the goal of improving the teaching of music.

Performance

Experiment 1

Experience in rehearsal settings and the applied studio led to an initial, exploratory study of the intonation of instrumentalists and vocalists in the performance of ascending and descending scales. Performances were tape-recorded and analyzed with a chromatic stroboscope according to cent (one-hundredth of an equal-tempered semitone) deviations. Striking differences occurred between ascending and descending performances. The ascending scalar patterns were performed with much greater deviation than the descending patterns. Clearly, the area of intonational performance practice warranted more extensive investigation.

Experiment 2

The second study involved vocal performances of ascending and descending major scales. Subjects were chosen from five categories of age and musical training: elementary school, high school, and undergraduate voice, piano, and violin majors. Consistent with the initial study, subjects were almost four times more accurate when descending rather than ascending the same scale. Students who had formal music training performed with greater pitch acuity and with less variability than untrained ones.

Experiment 3

To further refine the understanding of performed intonational deviation, the third study was designed to investigate the direction of deviation (sharpness and flatness). Subjects were from the same age and training groups as in the second experiment. Grade school and high school students major scale vocal performances tended to be flat relative to those of college voice, piano, and violin majors. Among college students, voice majors' performances were very sharp compared to piano and violin majors. Practice sessions tended to further sharpen solo vocal performance, particularly for ascending patterns. No consistent differences existed in sharpness or flatness regarding scale degrees, that is, progressive sharpening or flattening as students performed through a scale did not occur.

Experiment 4

The short practice sessions in the above study were intended to improve intonation, but surprisingly had the effect of further sharpening vocal performance. The next study compared various teaching procedures in an attempt to improve scale singing. Sixth graders received five sessions of instruction and practice following a pretest. Four instructional groups of students practiced only ascending scales, only descending scales, both ascending and descending scales, or sang songs (control group). Analyses of subsequent intonation performances indicated that all groups improved significantly, and differences between instruction groups were not significant. Sixth graders receiving reinforcement did not perform differently from the nonreinforcement groups. "Uncertain singers" within the study improved the most with the descending practice.

Experiment 5

The previous study indicated no difference between the reinforcement and non-reinforcement groups with respect to intonational improvement. It was speculated that music may constitute its own reward, and a follow-up study was designed to investigate the effects of using music itself as a reinforcer for intonational improvement. Half of a sixth-grade group were assigned to a reward group (following daily ascending and descending scalar practice) and received tokens for improved performance of scales during practice. The other students were assigned to a control group, receiving tokens but no instruction. Results were not surprising. Students receiving instruction with reinforcement improved intonation significantly, and control subjects did not. Subjects given tokens without instruction or practice spent more on "soul music" than on candy or sixth-grade basal series music, and the instruction group selected candy predominantly. Apparently, participation in a music activity lessened the amount of additional music chosen as reward.

Perception and Performance

Experiment 6

The second and third studies presented above revealed tendencies toward increased sharpness in almost direct proportion to academic training. Although they were not designed to ascertain reasons for an intonational difference with respect to scale direction, inferences drawn from the data in each study indicated that perhaps both perceptual and neuromuscular responses were involved. Further inquiry regarding the underlying perceptual processes was warranted, particularly across age and levels of music experience. Therefore, the next experiment of this series was structured to explore the ability of 200 subjects, from first grade through school of music faculty, to distinguish whether a slowly changing stimulus tone becomes increasingly sharp, increasingly flat, or remains constant. Stimulus tones deviated 2 cents per second for 25 seconds. Design of the study enabled analysis relevant to direction of perceived pitch change and amount of time needed to make that discrimination. It was found that pitch-perception ability increases in direct proportion to music training and age, with older subjects developing greater discrimination of flatness as opposed to sharpness. Younger subjects were incorrect more often and perceived more changes as being sharp, and older subjects perceived more tones as going flat. Perceptions of pitch changes were more accurate during the first 5 seconds of change, with flattened pitches more easily perceived than sharpened pitches.

Experiment 7

At this point, there was evidence of consistency in the perception and performance of intonation. Both appear to be less accurate in the direction of sharpness compared to the flatness direction, particularly among trained musicians. The focus of the next several studies was to compare more directly the performance and perception of intonation. The initial comparison was made between groups of college music majors performing ascending scale patterns on their own instrument or voice, with subjects listening to their own intonational performances and making desired adjustments on a tunable tape recorder. It was reasoned that the performers attempted to attain accurate intonation using their instrument as well as their perceptual and neuromuscular skills, whereas the latter perception group had only their perceptual skills as a frame of reference. Results indicated a tendency toward sharp intonation throughout the study. The perception of intonation was less accurate and produced sharper responses than the performance conditions. Subjects given verbal feedback to reduce sharpness was not effective on subsequent performance or perception assessments. Thus, there was little indication in this (and other studies) that verbal feedback alone improves intonation, making the implication in applied settings considerable. The need for the development of effective feedback techniques that are not economically or musically restrictive is apparent for both individual and group performance settings.

Experiment 8

A subsequent study examined the relationship between pitch discrimination and vocal pitch-matching abilities of young children. Preschool and fourth-grade children were given a pitch discrimination test and grouped according to ability. Although a difference in pitch-matching abilities was apparent between the age groups, no significant difference existed between the ability groups. Thus, consistency between discrimination scores and pitch-matching abilities was low, except for the high ability group of fourth graders who showed a moderate consistency. It is possible that long-term maturation and musical training are necessary to develop a relationship between pitch discrimination and pitch performance.

Experiment 9

Another study was designed to investigate the tuning performance versus tuning perception of string instrumentalists. High school, college, and professional string players were asked to tune to one of three tape-recorded oboe tones. Tones were 25 cents sharp, 15 cents flat, or in tune relative to A = 440 Hz. Subjects also were asked to make verbal judgments regarding the intonation of the tuning tone. Generally, tuning performances were sharp relative to A = 440 Hz regardless of the tuning tone presented, particularly for the college/professional group. Subjects made more "flat" than "sharp" or "in tune" verbal judgments. The relationship between tuning performance and perception was assessed through a comparison of the verbal response and actual performance; for example, if a subject judged the given tuning tone to be "flat," then tuning above the pitch indicated consistency. Although the college/professional subjects exhibited a higher correspondence than the high school students, the percentages revealed a somewhat limited association between perceptual judgments and performances. Many music educators regard the process of aural perception as a fundamental component of both music performance and music listening. Clearly, continued inquiry within musical contexts seems advisable to further describe this important relationship.

Intonation and Tone Quality

Experiment 10

Although good intonaton is recognized as a fundamental skill, most musicians would suggest that good tone quality is also necessary to excellence in musical performance. The question as to the relationship between tone quality and intonation is indeed relevant to the applied teacher. This study assessed differences in college music students' preferences for trumpet tone quality versus intonation. Initial testing verified that all subjects could discriminate good from bad trumpet tone quality in an unaccompanied context. However, when the trumpet was accompanied by purposely mistuned (25 cents flat or 50 cents sharp) or in-tune accompaniment, preference for good versus bad tone quality was not significantly different. Additionally, despite the cent discrepancy between the sharp and flat conditions, subjects preferred the sharp and in-tune accompaniments more than flat accompaniment. Subjects consistently evidenced preferences due to intonation rather than tone-quality variables.

Experiment 11

Another study was designed to yield additional information regarding musical discrimination of intonation versus tone quality. Melodies were recorded as flute and oboe duets. Performance conditions varied in tone quality (good/bad) and intonation (sharp/in tune). Subjects, who listened to each duet and responded by indicating performance errors in intonation and/or tone quality, discriminated between correct and incorrect performances, though music majors were more accurate than non-music majors. As in previous intonation studies, subjects perceived more "wrong" performances as flat rather than sharp. Apparently, they were able to identify correctly performances that contained intonation or quality errors, but were not usually able to determine correctly the specific cause of the problem. Subjects generally failed to respond to good versus bad quality in musical context.

Experiment 12

An additional experiment combined aspects of the two above studies. Music and non-music majors listened individually to 15 examples of flute/oboe duet pairs varying in intonation and tone quality. Examples were presented via a special listening device so that subjects were able to alternate listening between the two performances, thus allowing direct comparisons. Data consisted of time spent listening to each pair member and verbal preferences for the better performance of a pair. As above, both groups of subjects discriminated between correct and incorrect performances. Music majors verbalized preference for in-tune performance over either mistuning (oboe sharp or flute sharp), though listening time was not different. Both groups of subjects chose both instruments' good quality and oboe bad quality over any performance with flute bad quality. As in previous experimentation, in most all instances subjects preferred good intonation over tone-quality variables with the possible exception of bad flute tone quality.

Experiment 13

The next experiment was designed to investigate yet another aspect in the flute/oboe comparisons by adding a procedural variable first introduced by Geringer whereby subjects could "tune" (via a variable speed switch) performances, making them either faster (sharper) or slower (flatter). Subjects did turn up the speed and perceived these tunings to have had the effect of making the performances better.

Pitch and Tempo

Experiment 14

Knowledge of performer and listener discrimination abilities and preferences with respect to other elements of music may also influence music instruction and performance. Another related series of experiments is continuing that investigates the relationship of pitch and tempo within musical contexts. In the initial study, music majors listened individually to 10 excerpts of relatively well-known orchestral selections. By manipulating a dial, subjects could increase or decrease the playback speed of a variable speed tape recorder. Subjects preferred predominantly faster tape speeds relative to the unaltered recordings. This result could have occurred because of preference for higher pitch levels, faster tempi, brighter timbres, or any combination of these variables.

Experiments 15 and 16

More recent study (using an audio time compressor/expander) has isolated the effects of pitch and tempo. In a study of pitch and tempo discrimination using orchestral music, subjects identified correctly the examples of decreased-pitch levels more than pitch-increase examples. Tempo increases, however, rather than examples of tempo decreases, were identified more accurately. Moreover, tempo increases exerted the greatest influence on correct discrimination compared to the pitch alterations and decreased-tempo examples. A subsequent study used familiar band music examples and also indicated that tempo increases exerted larger influences than pitch changes on listener discrimination abilities. Continued study might view additional factors, such as the effects of generic styles, listener familiarity, and the content and context of the individual music example on the performance and perception of pitch and tempo.

Continuing Inquiry

The foregoing experiments represent a long-term involvement toward the ultimate goal of improving music teaching. Relevant individual aspects of music learning ought to be investigated with extreme care. All experimental variables must be diligently pursued, with replication attempted not only by those disinterested and personally uninvolved, but also by those possessed with a desire to *refute*, in order that subsequent analysis not be cloaked in the respectability of unintentional bias. If inquiry concerning the practical effects of methodology follows such a firm basis regarding the underlying perceptual phenomena involved, the music profession will perhaps have more information upon which to proceed.

Experimental research in music, however well controlled, should be viewed as only one mode of inquiry with which to pursue increased teaching effectiveness. It is inadvisable that any one study or mode of inquiry be accepted as final evidence; continuing analysis and synthesis should provide support or refutation for aspects of individual studies that appear consistent. With these due cautions, it is hoped that information gained from any continuing line of research will find application by music teachers to produce successful and rewarding musical experiences.

EXPERIMENTS

Experiment 1
Madsen, C. K. (1962). A study of directional harmonic scale solo performances. *Utah Music Educator, 7,* 13–15.
Experiment 2
Madsen, C. K. (1966). The effect of scale direction on pitch acuity in solo vocal performance. *Journal of Research in Music Education, 14,* 266–275.
Experiment 3
Madsen, C. K. (1974). Sharpness and flatness in scalar vocal performance. *Sciences de l'Art-Scientific Aesthetics, 9,* 91–97.
Experiment 4
Madsen, C. K., Wolfe, D. E., & Madsen, C. H. (1969). The effect of reinforcement and directional scalar methodology on intonational improvement. *Council for Research in Music Education, 18,* 22–23.
Experiment 5
Madsen, C. K., & Madsen, C. H. (1972). Selection of music listening or candy as a function of contingent versus noncontingent reinforcement and scale singing. *Journal of Music Therapy, 9,* 190–198.
Experiment 6
Madsen, C. K., Edmonson, F. A., & Madsen, C. H. (1969). Modulated frequency discrimination in relationship to age and musical training. *Journal of the Acoustical Society of America, 46,* 1468–1472.

Experiment 7
Geringer, J. M. (1978). Intonational performance and perception of ascending scales. *Journal of Research in Music Education, 26,* 32–40.
Experiment 8
Geringer, J. M. (1983). The relationship of pitch-matching and pitch-discrimination abilities of preschool and fourth-grade students. *Journal of Research in Music Education, 31,* 93–99.
Experiment 9
Geringer, J. M., & Witt, A. C. (1985). An investigation of tuning performance and perception of string instrumentalists. *Council for Research in Music Education, 85,* 90–101.
Experiment 10
Madsen, C. K., & Geringer, J. M. (1976). Preferences for trumpet tone quality versus intonation. *Bulletin of the Council for Research in Music Education, 46,* 13–22.
Experiment 11
Madsen, C. K., & Geringer, J. M. (1981). Discrimination between tone quality and intonation in unaccompanied flute/oboe duets. *Journal of Research in Music Education, 29,* 305–313.
Experiment 12
Geringer, J. M., & Madsen, C. K. (1981). Verbal and operant discrimination/preference for tone quality and intonation. *Psychology of Music, 9,* 26–30.
Experiment 13
Madsen, C. K., & Flowers, P. J. (1981/1982). Effect of tuning in an attempt to compensate for pitch/quality errors in flute/oboe duets. *Contributions to Music Education, 9,* 1–7.
Experiment 14
Geringer, J. M. (1976). Tuning preferences in recorded orchestral music. *Journal of Research in Music Education, 24,* 169–176.
Experiment 15
Geringer, J. M., & Madsen, C. K. (1984). Pitch and tempo discrimination in recorded orchestral music among musicians and nonmusicians. *Journal of Research in Music Education, 32(3),* 195–204.
Experiment 16
Madsen, C. K., Duke, R. A., & Geringer, J. M. (1984). Pitch and tempo discrimination in recorded band music among wind and percussion musicians. *Journal of Band Research, 20,* 20–29.

Experiments 17 and 18 have been completed. Some of these data, as well as their "spinoffs," appear in the present volume.

Experiments 19 and 20 are in the planning stage—to be continued.

Part V
Applications of Research: New Horizons

What will the future bring? The world is changing so quickly that constant updating is standard operating procedure. In music education, even as we reassess children's music, teacher education, or preference and perception, new areas of exploration are opening. Each of the papers in Part V deals with a unique aspect of music behavior in the late twentieth century.

In everyday conversation and behavior, traditional assumptions about music's uses and effects have been repeated so frequently and with such conviction that they are rarely questioned. Oft-repeated assertions—such as "Music is always a creative art," or "Music aids learning," or "Background music is an environmental enhancement"—have been used to justify everything from music education programs to taped music in supermarkets. If asked, many musicians and non-musicians probably would agree that these statements are true. It is assumed, because it has been said so often, that music is all these things and more. The researchers whose work appears in this section have dared to explore, to question seemingly plausible assumptions, and to open new territory for the study of music behavior.

Is listening to a recording creative? Is performing a sonata creative, or is composition the only mode of musical creativity? Is a single member of a large ensemble performing a piece from the standard literature engaged in a creative experience simply because it is a musical experience? Is creativity a way of approaching musical tasks, rather than a particular criterion for a product? Can creative thinking be identified and expanded? Although creativity is as old as the arts, the controlled study of the cognitive processes is, indeed, a new horizon.

Innovations in electronic technology are revolutionizing almost every human endeavor. Will the multisensory capabilities of the new computers en-able us to teach more efficiently? Can the increasingly precise machines for measuring cortical activity tap the inner experience of music listeners and assess just what is happening? For music educators, sorting out the useful applications of modern electronics from all the gadgets and gimmicks available is, obviously, a new horizon.

Can a musical context aid learning a non-musical skill? Does background music help or hinder the accomplishment of academic tasks? What factors influence the efficacy of music as a teaching tool? When, if ever, is music contraindicated? Folk wisdom says that music is an asset in learning; students say they need background music to do their homework. Assessing music's ability to contribute to or detract from the learning of non-musical material is, undoubtedly, a new horizon.

The common characteristic of the studies that follow is the application of a scientific approach to difficult questions. When no one has laid groundwork, a researcher's challenge to be objective is doubly critical. Relying on data, rather than traditional lore, takes on new importance.

It requires a certain courage to strike off in a new direction, to blaze a trail, to try something no one else has tried. Onlookers find it easy to criticize. Results may well prove to be disappointing. Nevertheless, new knowledge, which does not come cheap, demands this courage. Using a data-based approach to attack ancient questions, find new uses for technology, or test folk wisdom is the challenge the writers who follow have accepted.

21 Refinement of a Measure of Creative Thinking in Music

Peter R. Webster

Summary

This study provides additional data to support the reliability and validity of a measure of creative thinking in music. It extends and replicates other research and indicates that the music creativity measure proposed, indeed, assesses aspects not found in teacher ratings or a music aptitude test.

Design: Test development $N = 32$ Groups: 1
Statistical Analysis: Pearson product-moment correlation, Cronbach alpha, factor analysis, *t*, ANOVA
Independent Variables: Creativity of young children aged six to nine; teacher ratings and relationship of creativity and music aptitude; revised measure of music creativity; teacher rating scale; Gordon Primary Measure of Musical Audiation
Music: Performance, individual

* * *

In the closing pages of *Invented Worlds: The Psychology of the Arts,* Winner (1982, pp. 385–386) suggests that cognitive psychologists have focused largely on the question of perception rather than production in the study of artistic behavior. The issue of how art works are produced has received much less attention. A study of the most recent literature in music education, the psychology of music, and psychoacoustics will reveal this tendency toward the study of the "receiver" rather than the "producer." Rigorous and controlled empirical study of the perception of music is a relatively attractive approach, particularly for those who subscribe to the current line of thought regarding information-processing theory in psychological research.

There is little doubt that such research is needed and that it is a welcome addition to our understanding of man. At the same time, it is dangerous to ignore the questions that surround the producers of art only because of difficulties in research design or quantification. One would hope that rigorous and controlled research might be done with these questions, as well, in order to accompany and make more rich the data on perception. How does man create? Are there patterns of behavior common to all? Is the process of creation different for adults than for children? Can you teach creative thinking?

In terms of music, these questions—and others like them—have been asked for generations. A rather large body of speculative literature exists, but little empirical evidence of the type that contemporary cognitive science would view as meaningful is available.

Some rather clear signs indicate that this is changing. Interest within the research communities in the study of creative thinking is growing, as evidenced by such groups as Project Zero at Harvard University and the recent Ann Arbor Symposium on Creativity and Motivation, sponsored in part by the Music Educators National Conference. This interest is supported by or is a result of: philosophical endorsement of naturalistic data collection techniques; advances in cognitive science research techniques, including protocol analysis, videotaping, and computer-aided data collection; and a more daring and creative resolve on the part of the researcher, a willingness to take the risks associated with difficult and supposedly "unmeasurable" tasks.

Approaches to the study of creative behavior in music are detailed by this author in a number of other writings. Of main importance to the present study is the aspect of the empirical approach that deals with the direct observation of the creative process/product in a musical context. Research in this subcategory might be best viewed in terms of how composition, analysis, and improvisation behaviors interact with process and product. It is possible to place both composition and analysis (written and listening) in terms of musical process and musical product. Because of its singular nature, improvisation is seen as residing in both process *and* product.

Surprisingly, we have little organized study of student composition from the standpoint of the finished product. This may be a function of the music teacher's lack of emphasis on original composition in the classroom or perhaps a reluctance by researchers to face the difficult problems of analysis in this area. Webster (1977) asked high school music students to complete a set of composition tasks that were evaluated with factors borrowed from the general creativity literature but defined in musical terms. Results suggested that musical achievement was the most strongly related variable to creative behavior in high school students and was the best single predictor. Cognitive intelligence, grade level, age, and gender played minimal roles in terms of relationship. More recently, Kratus (1985) used a portable Casio keyboard to engage grade school children in composition of original songs. Results demonstrated specific developmental patterns across different ages, many of which suggest a desire to conform to traditional patterns of tonal music. Of equal importance was the fact that the methodology used to gather and study these songs is reliable, practical, and shows great promise for the future.

In terms of creative analysis from the product side, the study by Pfeil (1972) is noteworthy. His measure of creative listening analysis, designed for college level non-music majors, is itself a model of creative thinking and is quite applicable to younger subjects. Although the study yielded little data, the use of graphic patterns to stimulate musical imagination in a measurement context is noteworthy. The approach deserves more study and refinement, especially if merged with the creative listening approaches outlined by Feinberg (1973).

The organized study of the compositional process has received little attention, especially in younger subjects. Bamberger's study (1974), using compositional tasks that are monitored by computer, offers a fascinating angle on this aspect of musical behavior. In such a context, the computer can be used both as an aid to composition and as a recording device for discovering patterns of thought. Although her study did not yield conclusive evidence, it remains as an excellent candidate for future replication and extension using modern microprocessors.

Improvisation activities have received the most attention by researchers whose goal it has been to measure creative behavior. The pioneer work of Pond (Moorhead & Pond, 1941–44; Pond, 1981) and the more recent research by Flohr (1979) are examples of naturalistic observation that emphasizes process. Developmental patterns are noted in this research, and the tentative findings help establish hypotheses of musical thinking and behavior.

Other researchers interested in improvisation have taken a more product-oriented approach, including the work of Vaughan (1971), Webster (1977, 1983), and Gorder (1976). It is in this tradition that the present study most directly falls. Children are presented with simple musical tasks and asked to improvise while the researcher records the sounds on audio- or videotape. A carefully defined set of criteria are then used to evaluate these improvisations, basing judgments on musical and psychological constructs. Results from these studies have demonstrated modest levels of reliability and validity and some tentative conclusions about relationships with other variables. A need exists for more refined tasks and evaluation schemes, tighter statistical evidence, and replicated results. This study is based on those needs.

This paper presents the results of the second in a series of studies devoted to the refinement of a measure of musical thinking in young children. The first study was completed in 1980 and was published as part of the proceedings of the second Bowling Green State University Symposium on Music Teaching and Research (Webster, 1983). The purpose of this second study is conceived in three parts: to refine aspects of the measure, including the underlying factors, scoring procedures, and task items; to use this refined measure to replicate questions of relationship and mean differences determined in the first study; and to study, for the first time, the relationship between scores on this refined measure and those from an established, traditional music aptitude test.

Background: The First Study

Through a carefully organized period of field testing and content analysis, an 18-task measure was constructed that employed several different musical tasks and sound sources. Tasks were evaluated using 10 component factors that were defined before evaluation. The measure was administered individually and recorded on videotape for analysis. Of the 10 factors, 7 were scored objectively by one judge, and 3 factors were aesthetic judgments made by two independent referees who were familiar with the established criteria for the factors involved. In addition to divergent musical factors, factors of convergent musical behavior and factors of verbal creative thinking were defined.

The measure was administered to 42 randomly selected children ranging in age from 6 to 9 years. The sample was drawn from two different school settings and was balanced with respect to gender and grade level. Data relating to school behavior as well as achievement and various musical skills were collected from classroom and music teachers in each school. Three questions were posed:

1. To what extent were the 10 factors viable in terms of frequency distribution, shape, and intercorrelation?
2. To what extent were the 10 factors related to aspects of classroom behavior (general classroom and music clasroom) and variables of grade, age, and gender?
3. Were there significant differences between means on the 10 factors when compared across grade level, gender, and school setting?

The detailed results of this first study will not be completely reviewed here (see Webster, 1983). However, findings that are particularly important for the present study are summarized below:

1. A number of the factors were found to have satisfactory shape and discrimination, but the large number of significant intercorrelations between these factors suggested the feasibility of factor and/or task reduction.
2. The relationships between the factors and classroom teacher ratings on such items as motivation, ability to imagine and adapt, confidence, originality of ideas, and quickness of response showed little or no relationship to creative behavior in music. Assuming valid measurement, this suggests the uniqueness of this musical behavior.
3. A study of the means of the factors suggested a tendency for second- and third-grade children to score closely together, with the larger gap occurring between these two groups and the first graders. The musical originality factor was statistically significant across grades; the greatest gap existed between the first and second grades. In terms of gender, no real pattern of difference was demonstrated except that the musical extensiveness factor was significantly in favor of the males.

Method

Measure Refinement

The first step in the refinement process was to restructure the measure in terms of the tasks themselves and the scoring strategy. Rationale for this work came from two sources: a decision to eliminate the verbal and the convergent music factors (and their associated tasks) that were included in the first measure; and statistical evidence provided by a factor analysis and a Cronbach alpha analysis of internal task reliability.

Task revision was clearly necessary because of the length of the scoring process and the unfocused nature of the original instrument. The divergent musical factors were chosen as the only factors for the new instrument, and the musical tasks that related directly to these factors were retained for study. All other factors and related tasks were deleted. The divergent factor associated with spontaneity was also deleted because initial experience with this showed a complete lack of discrimination ability.

The four divergent factors of creative musical thinking were evaluated by a principal components factor analysis. The goal was to determine if any further factors could be eliminated. Another statistical strategy was also used to evaluate each musical task's contribution to the reliability of the various factors using the Cronbach alpha.

Finally, to improve both the statistical qualities of the instrument and its content validity, a rethinking of the nature of each scoring factor was also accomplished. A panel of music educators carefully reviewed the definition of factors, the scoring process, and the content of the tasks and suggested revisions. The panel also recommended changes in instrument choice, wording of the directions, and physical layout of the equipment.

Questions of Relationship and Mean Difference

The second purpose of this study was to attempt a replication of the statistical findings of the first study using the revised measure. Of particular interest were the relationships between factors of creative behavior in music and ratings by classroom teachers because such data was seen as helpful in establishing inverse validity. To accomplish this, a new sample of children was drawn and new data collected.

The Sample

Based on a desire to obtain meaningful data that could be generalized to as large a population as possible, several initial decisions were made about the nature of the desired sample:

School Setting. The school chosen served a middle to upper middle-class, suburban community on the east side of Cleveland. The student population was mixed with respect to race and religion, and the final random sample reflected this mix.

Random Selection. To control for selection bias, children were chosen randomly for participation in the study. Those who had prior musical training in the form of private lessons or special lessons in music theory or musical enrichment were systematically eliminated from the final population pool. Final selection ($n = 32$) was made from a pool of 93 children.

Grade Level. The sample was limited to nearly equal numbers of children from the entire first, second, and third grades (ages 6–9).

Gender. Care was taken to balance the sample with respect to gender. In addition to making a more representative sample, this also allowed for the proper comparison of group means.

Table 21.1
Sample Broken Down by Grade and Gender

	1st		2nd		3rd	
	M	F	M	F	M	F
	5	6	6	5	4	6
Totals	11		11		10	
Grand total: 32						

Table 21.1 displays the breakdown of the numbers of children in the sample by grade and gender.

Data Collection

The revised measure was administered to children individually in the school auditorium. They were excused from their regular classroom activities for the 25-minute testing period. No attempt was made to control for the time of day for each testing. Great care was taken to ensure that the child felt at ease during the session. This was accomplished, in part, by the measure itself, which begins with warm-up activities that familiarize the child with the musical instruments and the simple techniques needed to play them. The evaluated tasks that follow are presented in a game-like fashion, allowing the child to respond freely.

In addition to the data generated by this measure, a 14-item rating scale dealing with student behavior characteristics was completed by each child's classroom teacher. This rating scale, identical with the instrument used in the first study (Webster, 1983), dealt with such items as attention span, school conduct, school achievement, originality of ideas, and quickness of response.

Relationship to Music Aptitude

The third purpose of the present study was to investigate possible relationships between the revised measure and scores on a measure of musical aptitude. It was important to determine if the abilities measured by the creative behavior measure were the same as those tapped by traditional aptitude tests, which typically require discrimination of tonal and rhythm patterns. It was reasoned that if this were the case, large correlations would be found. This would throw into question just how unique and meaningful the creative thinking measurement was.

The Gordon (1979) Primary Measure of Musical Audiation (PMMA) was administered to the children during regular class time. Part 1, the Tonal Test, was given a week prior to administration of the creative behavior measure. This was done to familiarize the children with the test administrator and his presence in the school. Part 2, the Rhythm Test, was given after a 3-week period. The test was administered as specified in the manual.

Statistical Procedures

All data were submitted to various subroutines of the Statistical Package for the Social Sciences (SPSS), Version 9 (Hull & Nie, 1981). The .05 level of significance was used as the decision rule.

Results

Measure Refinement

Musical data from the first measure were studied by factor analysis to determine the feasibility of factor reduction. In brief, the four musical factors at issue were: Musical Extensiveness (ME), the actual clock time (in seconds) involved in a musical response; Musical Flexibility (MF), the extent to which a child can freely move from one extreme to another with one of the three musical parameters: low to high, soft to loud, fast to slow; Musical Originality (MO), the extent to which the child manipulates musical phenomena in a unique fashion; and Musical Syntax (MS), the extent to which the child manipulates musical phenomena in a logical and inherently musical manner, with attention to the shaping of the whole response and not just a single part. The first two factors are measured behaviorally by studying the audio- and videotapes. MO and MS, on the other hand, are evaluated subjectively by judges using rating scales. Strong intercorrelations of these factors in the first measure lead to the hypothesis that some of these factors might be reduced without seriously weakening the measure.

Table 21.2 gives the factor matrix using a principal factor method with no interactions. It can be seen that each factor contributes to one of two global factors. On the basis of this evidence, it was concluded that any factor elimination would be unwise. These four factors were retained as the basis for the revised measure. (One plausible interpretation of the global factors

Table 21.2
Factor Matrix Loadings, Musical Factors

	Factor 1	Factor 2
ME (Extensiveness)	0.817	0.279
MF (Flexibility)	−0.383	0.569
MO (Originality)	0.172	−0.778
MS (Syntax)	0.814	−0.221

would be that ME, with loadings on the extensiveness and syntax factors, represents the rational side of creative thinking. MF, with its loadings on flexibility and originality, might represent the more fanciful.)

Another approach to revision was to study each individual task's contribution to the stability of each factor. The tasks from the first measure that contributed to each of the four factors were studied using the Cronbach alpha procedure. The results are displayed in Table 21.3.

It was concluded that MF was in need of special attention in terms of task redefinition. A careful study of the scoring procedures by the panel of music educators revealed a possible flaw in the way points were awarded for flexibility, a problem that was subsequently corrected in the revised measure.

Table 21.3 also gives the Cronbach alpha assessed after the administration of the revised measure to the new sample. Results indicate that changes in ME and MF resulted in marked improvement of reliability, but some ground was lost in MO and MS factors.

Final adjustments were made in the measure upon the recommendation

Table 21.3
Cronbach Alpha Data for Factors

	1st Version		2nd Version	
Factor	No. of tasks	Standardized alpha	No. of tasks	Standardized alpha
ME	8	.74	7	.80
MF	11	.45	10	.78
MO	3	.72	5	.66
MS	3	.55	3	.51

of the content validity panel of music educators. Additional suggestions included the following: feature the three principal instruments (piano, voice, and temple blocks) more systematically as the child explores sound; tie the tasks more closely to the exploration of the three music parameters used in the measure (low to high, soft to loud, fast to slow); and give the child more time with each instrument.

The New Measure

Figure 21.1 briefly summarizes the revised measure that was the product of these refinements. The interested reader should compare the measure as it was first proposed (Webster, 1983, pp. 105–107) with the current version as outlined in Figures 21.1 and 21.2 in order to achieve a complete picture of the changes made. The title "Measure of Creative Thinking in Music–Version II (MCTM–II)" was given to this new version. Figure 21.2 displays the scoring summary in order to demonstrate which tasks contribute to the factors.

MCTM-II consists of a series of 10 scored tasks, divided into three parts: exploration, application, and synthesis. The exploration section is designed to help the children become familiar with the instruments used and how they are arranged. The musical parameters of "high/low," "fast/slow," and "loud/soft" are explored in this section, as well as throughout the measure.

The application tasks ask the children to engage in more challenging activities with the instruments and focus on the creation of music using each of the instruments singly. In the synthesis section, the children are encouraged to use multiple instruments in tasks whose settings are the least structured.

The activities are intended for children in first through third grade, and the measure takes about 25 minutes to administer. All responses are recorded on videotape for future analysis. In terms of scoring, objective observation of the tapes for ME and MF is required. MO and MS are evaluated with 5-point rating scales. Total scores for each factor are entered on the bottom, summary line. If a grand total is required, conversion to standard scores is necessary for each factor and an equally weighted average of all four factors is recommended.

Questions of Relationship and Mean Difference

Table 21.4 displays the correlations between the rating items on the classroom teacher's rating scale of student behavior and the MCTM-II factors.

Figure 21.1
MCTM Activity Summary

MCTM–II

Equipment needed:
1. Set of temple blocks
2. Microphone connected to an amplifier with echo
3. Nerf ball
4. Piano
5. Set of colored line drawings
6. 3 pieces of blank paper
7. Cassette tape recorder/video tape recorder

Section	Factor	Instrument	Task
Warm-up	Not scored	All	Freely experiment with the sounds of all instruments
Part I: Exploration			
1 a–c Rain bucket	MF	Temple blocks	Sound of rain falling into a bucket (slow/fast)
2 a–b Elevator	MF	Nerf ball/piano	Sound of voice on an elevator (low/high)
3 a–c Truck	MF	Voice in mic	Truck coming toward you (soft/loud)
Part II: Application			
4 a–d Robot	ME, MF, MO	Voice in mic	Robot singing in a shower
5 a–b Talking blocks	ME, MF, MO	Temple blocks	Stimulus-response back and forth
6 a–c Frog	ME, MF, MO, MS	Nerf ball/piano	Frog music
Part III: Synthesis			
7 a–d Space story	ME, MF, MO, MS	All inst.	Sound story based on trip into outer space
8 Free composition	ME, MF, MO, MS	All inst.	Compose your own piece with a beginning, middle, and end

Note: Guidelines for MCTM–II, including the complete text for administering the measure, a set of scoring sheets, and suggested criteria, are available from the author. A small fee is required, to cover photocopying and mailing costs, and an agreement form must be signed. Sample videotapes are also available.

Figure 21.2
MCTM Scoring Summary

MEASURE OF CREATIVE THINKING IN MUSIC
Scoring Summary

Child's Name______________________ Classroom Teacher________ Room______

School______________________ Music Teacher______________________

Age in Months________ Gender________ Grade Level________

Task	Musical Extensiveness	Musical Flexibility	Musical Originality	Musical Syntax
Part I				
1c Rain Bucket (Temple Blocks)		________		
2c Elevator Music (Nerf Ball/Piano)		________		
3c Truck Music (Voice/Microphone)		________		
Part II				
4d Robot Song (Voice/Microphone)	________	________	________	
5a Talking Blocks Responses (Temple Blocks)	________	________		
5b Talking Blocks Stimuli (Temple Blocks)	________	________	________	
6c Frog Music (Nerf Ball/Piano)	________	________	________	________
Part III				
7a Space Pictures (All instruments)	________	________		
7b Space Voyage (All instruments)	________	________	________	________
8 Free Composition (All instruments)	________	________	________	________
Totals	________	________	________	________

Table 21.4
Coefficients of Correlation between Classroom Teacher Ratings and Factors of MCTM-II, n = *32*

Items	ME	MF	MO	MS	ZT
Attention span	.05	.00	.06	.26	.11
Handling of stress	.00	−.06	.11	.20	−.07
Motivation	.00	−.09	−.07	.23	−.02
School achievement	.01	−.02	.02	.30	.09
Conduct	.05	.12	.16	.27	.18
Ability to imagine	.14	.34	.17	.23	.26
Ability to adapt	−.11	−.02	−.02	.07	−.03
Confidence	.09	.18	.25	.38*	.27
Self-esteem	.15	.15	.21	.35*	.25
Peer respect	−.07	.07	.19	.41*	.18
Shyness	−.13	−.25	−.39*	−.44**	−.36*
Aggression for work	.00	−.02	.12	.16	.08
Original ideas	.11	.46**	.23	.38*	.35*
Quickness of response	.00	.22	.11	.38*	.21

*$p < .05$
**$p < .01$

Assuming accurate measurement, it might be concluded that MCTM-II is measuring characteristics unrelated to the teacher ratings—at least for the most part. The higher ratings for such items as confidence, self-esteem, peer respect, shyness (negatively related), originality of ideas, and quickness of thought are quite consistent with the literature on creative thinking. Similar results were also seen in the first study. Such findings offer some evidence of the validity of the measure, but in an inverse sense.

Table 21.5 reveals no significant differences across grade and gender for any of the factors. The grouping of second and third graders that was noted in the first study is not seen here. It should be clear from these findings that conclusions about developmental patterns are hardly possible. The same is true for gender differences.

Table 21.5
Mean Comparisons across Grade and Gender

	Grade				Gender		
	1st	2nd	3rd	*F*	M	F	*t*
ME	205.8	183.9	241.7	.44	228.7	192.5	.73
MF	23.5	25.8	28.3	.72	27.1	24.6	.74
MO	7.5	7.8	8.7	.33	8.3	7.7	.53
MS	3.4	3.6	3.3	.07	3.3	3.6	−.41
ZT	−.1	−.04	.16	.29	.08	−.07	.47

Relationship to Music Aptitude

An important aspect of this study was the question about relationship between MCTM-II scores and the PMMA of Gordon (1979). Table 21.6 displays these results. Correlations range from .00 to .24, all non-significant. Although this is a hopeful indication of the establishment of a valid measure (again, in an inverse sense), caution must be exercised because of the small sample size. Certainly, any further study should investigate this issue closely.

A Final Word

This is the second in a series of studies devoted to the refinement of a measure of creative thinking in music. Much remains to be done before this measure can assume any professional posture of note. By combining the re-

Table 21.6
Coefficients of Correlation between Scores on the PMMA and the MCTM-II, n = 32

	Factors				
	ME	MF	MO	MS	ZT
Rhythm test	.24	.14	.02	.00	.12
Tonal test	.00	.15	.23	.18	.17

sults of the first study together with the findings of this work, a start has been made toward respectability. Two panels of musicians have contributed to the content validity of the measure. Construct validity has been supported by some factor analysis data and by the use of widely endorsed psychological factors that are defined in musical terms. There is some empirical validity data in the form of music teacher ratings (Webster, 1983) as well as a good deal of inverse relationship with general classroom teacher ratings and traditional music aptitude.

In terms of reliability, there is evidence of acceptable interjudge reliability for the MO and MS factors (.57 and .72 in earlier studies and .78 and .67 in later work). Cronbach alpha data indicates improving levels of internal task reliability. No studies have been made of test-retest reliability, nor of predictive validity.

Perhaps a more pressing question is the measure's practicality. It requires a good deal of time to administer and certainly to score. Will professionals be interested in investing the time required? Probably not. Can the measure be shortened further or made less complicated without endangering its quality? Perhaps so. Research will continue, particularly for those of us who are convinced that such study reveals a vital part of the musical mind that has been all but ignored.

This study was supported in part by the Charles Rieley Armington Research Program on Values in Children, at Case Western Reserve University.

22 The Effects of Visual versus Verbal Instruction on Beginning Guitar Students' Tuning Accuracy

Peggy A. Codding

Summary

Beginning guitar students frequently demonstrate difficulties in tuning which suggest that related abilities and concepts may be too complex and/or too abstract to master without intensive individual training. Data indicate that when visual or verbal feedback immediately follow student pitch-matching responses, intonation is relatively accurate. Withdrawal of visual cues substantially lessens tuning accuracy, and the presentation, then deletion, of verbal cues results in a consistent increase in intonational precision.

Music educators might consider a variety of methods to teach tuning to novice musicians. Techniques utilized may include visual and verbal training procedures, adapted for individual students, which are introduced and then faded to stimulate internalization of tuning abilities.

Design: Pretest–posttest control group $N = 68$ Groups: 3
Statistical Analysis: ANOVA with repeated measures
Independent Variables: Visual and verbal instruction
Dependent Variables: Guitar tuning accuracy (absolute cent deviation scores)
Music: Listening, performance

* * *

Accuracy in tuning the guitar is essential to aesthetically pleasing musical performance. For beginning guitarists, learning to tune the instrument can be more challenging than mastering functional playing skills. Tuning accuracy seems to be a product of successful synthesis of complex aural, academic, and psychomotor skills, including the abilities to discriminate and to match pitch, to manipulate tuning pegs while plucking strings, and to evaluate an achieved pitch relative to a unison pitch. Beginning students frequently demonstrate difficulties in tuning which suggest that related concepts and abilities may be too abstract and/or too complex to master without intensive individual training.

Studies to assess aural discrimination and pitch-matching skills include those of Pedersen and Pedersen (1970) and Kantorski (1983). Pedersen and Pedersen examined the relationship between pitch-discrimination and pitch-matching skills among sixth-grade students relevant to single pitches, melodic intervals, and three-pitch sequences. A moderate correlation was found to exist between pitch-discrimination and vocal pitch-matching ability. Kantorski investigated the relationship between vocal and instrumental pitch-matching abilities among fourth- and sixth-grade students. Kantorski determined that pitch-matching success at either a vocal or an instrumental task did not necessarily guarantee successful demonstration of the related skill. Porter (1977) found that students trained to match pitch instrumentally were more accurate in matching instrumental pitches than were students trained vocally in completing a similar vocal pitch-matching task. Yank (1975) and Porter (1977) indicated that an inability to match pitch is not the result of inaccurate pitch perception. The literature suggests that pitch-discrimination and pitch-matching skills can be learned and may be acquired through instruction. Procedures that combine presentation of instruction with contingent reinforcement of pitch-matching approximations have been successful in improving tonal accuracy (Porter, 1977; Fullard, 1977).

Remediation of the pitch-matching skills of uncertain singers (Dennis, 1977; Geringer, 1983; Pedersen & Pedersen, 1970; Welch, 1984; Yank, 1975) and instrumentalists (Lader, 1977; Salzberg, 1977; Duke & Prickett, 1982; Flohr, 1982; Fullard, 1977) is well documented in music education research. Procedures utilized to develop accurate pitch production have been diverse and have been applied with varied results.

Computer-assisted instruction (CAI) has been used to supplement or substitute for traditional classroom methods in many educational settings, often with encouraging results. Conklin (1983) and Pagliaro (1983) utilized CAI in the training of surgical nurses and pharmacologists, respectively, and reported that students using this technique achieved established competencies to levels that equaled or exceeded the learning of students using other methods. Lavin (1980) determined that students using CAI as test practice for sociology exams received higher scores on subsequent tests than did those who chose not to practice with a computer.

Computer applications in music have been demonstrated by Arenson

(1982), Canelos, Murphy, Blombach, & Heck (1980), and Hofstetter (1981). Arenson (1982) utilized CAI in a competency-based education program to teach music fundamentals to non-music majors. A comparison of pre- and posttest scores of students using CAI and those completing more traditional homework assignments for drill-and-practice resulted in substantially higher skill acquisition by the computer group. Canelos et al. (1980) incorporated the use of CAI in teaching music intervals to beginning music majors. CAI subjects demonstrated significant improvement over programmed instruction and self-practice subjects. Hofstetter (1981) described the use of GUIDO® to teach and complete research in aural training skills. Furman (1984) and Hasselbring and Duffus (1981) demonstrated applications of computers in music research in which computer systems were used to assist in the analysis of music and non-music behavior in music therapy clinics and classrooms.

The computer has been a useful tool in developing instructor-researcher identified skills across the educational spectrum. Although computers have most frequently been used by individuals of average to gifted intellectual ability, recent applications of CAI have included remedial instruction and use with handicapped populations (Jamison & Lovatt, 1983; McDermott & Watkins, 1983).

This study was designed to investigate the effects of computer-based visual versus verbal instruction on beginning guitar students' tuning accuracy. Subjects in the study were students identified as "uncertain tuners" who had demonstrated gross tuning error.

Method

Sixty-eight students who were enrolled in 14 sections of a beginning guitar class served as subjects. All of them were college undergraduates completing degrees in fields other than music. Demographic information collected at the onset of experimentation indicated no substantial differences in prior musical training among the subjects.

A pretest that required the student to tune a guitar by matching each of six mistuned strings to a specified prerecorded reference pitch was the basis for inclusion in the study and random assignment to one of three treatment conditions: visual, verbal, and contact control groups.

Equipment and Materials

Equipment used may be defined categorically into computer hardware and software (three programs), audio equipment, stimulus tape, and musical instruments. Computer hardware was comprised of the Republic VII, S-100 Bus Microcomputer System and the Digital Pitch Extractor developed at the Computer-Based Education Research Laboratory (CERL), University of Illinois, at Champaign/Urbana.

The Digital Pitch Extractor was built as a PLATO® peripheral device. This equipment was interfaced to the Republic VII microcomputer through the PLATO® parallel channel emulator built at the Center for Music Research (CMR), The Florida State University. Computer hardware was interfaced to a console, a graphics monitor, and audio equipment. The soundproof booth used for experimentation contained a guitar with a contact microphone, two speaking microphones, speakers, and an intercom device. A chair was provided for use by the student.

The equipment was designed to function in program one as follows. As a student played a guitar string, the sound was received by a contact microphone, which in turn fed the signal to the pitch extractor, which sampled played frequencies. A microcomputer received this frequency information from the pitch extractor and displayed the student's cent deviation (score) from a simultaneously presented but not computer-recorded reference pitch on a console visible to the researcher. The reference pitch was defined as the tape-generated stimulus tone to be matched by the student. The microcomputer sampled the student-generated pitch approximately 12 times per second, and converted stimuli to digits, reliable to plus or minus 1.5 cents, prior to presenting the visual display. During treatment, pitch error information could be viewed by the student on a color graphics monitor as an arrow moving up and down reflecting pitch deviation and/or changing color indicating pitch deviation above or below two semitones. This sequence of presentation was utilized in the visual treatment condition only.

By choice, pitch deviation information for an entire trial could also be displayed on the monitor. A graph of tuning accuracy for each of six strings across a given trial was used as a means of providing the student with feedback regarding tuning accuracy. This was done at established points in the experimental procedure.

For this program, volume information from the pitch extractor was used to avoid picking up a low signal-to-noise signal. This and the subsequent two programs were written in computer language "C."

A second computer program was developed to allow retrieval of a desired pitch from a sample of pitches. For this study, the program allowed the experimenter to choose the pitch representing the students' final deviation relative to the reference tone from among all frequencies generated by a given string. The program was designed so that the final pitch on an individual graph, for example, the string-six posttest trial 1, could be marked by a movable, manually manipulated cursor, read by the pitch extractor, and converted to a single cent-deviation score. This process ensured a relatively accurate picture of the subject's tuning skill for each of six strings at the end of a tuning trial. The program was written to allow any pitch in the 34-second trial to be marked and recorded for further experimental analysis.

A third program was written to allow basic summation of data recorded using the previously described software. This provided a method for generating various raw data totals, including absolute cent deviation per subject and per group across six strings for four to six trials and group averages of absolute, sharp, and flat deviations. Other capabilities were designed for use in subsequent research. Components were designed to allow verbal contact between subject and researcher, presentation of stimulus pitch to the subject, and cassette recording of auditory activity in the booth.

Reference pitches and vocal cues for use in pre- and posttests and both treatments were generated by a Moog synthesizer using a sawtooth wave form and recorded on reel-to-reel tape. These sounds approximated guitar timbre, but were used in place of guitar. Guitar-generated pitches have been observed to decay too rapidly to promote aural pitch-matching skills among beginning guitar students (Codding, 1983). The machine-generated pitch was a sustained reference tone containing an initial attack and a second attack after four seconds of pitch presentation.

Instructional materials used during pretest included two identical "String and Color Guides," consisting of six differently colored and numbered horizontal lines denoting string names with color reference. The highest and lowest pitched strings were marked accordingly to encourage auditory referencing of pitches. One chart was introduced in pretest preparation. A second chart was posted in the soundproof booth for quick visual-with-auditory referencing during tuning trials.

Procedure and Design

Student participation in the tuning project was introduced as a course requirement of the beginning guitar class. Students were informed that tuning tasks would not be graded, but that participation would be noted by instructors and considered as extra effort in the assignment of final course grades. The importance of accurate tuning was stressed in class and modeled by the instructors.

Prior to the beginning of the guitar course, eight class guitar instructors were informed that some students in their sections would receive individualized tuning instruction outside of class. The students were to be informed as to the coming task during course orientation. During the fourth week of class, a majority of non-music majors randomly selected from 14 class sections were scheduled to be pretested.

All pre- and posttest as well as treatment procedures took place in a laboratory designed for experimentation. Before each battery of subject trials, equipment was checked for proper functioning, and the output signal (1 kHz) was aligned at point zero on the OVU meter of the reel-to-reel tape recorder to prevent signal distortion.

Pretest

Sixty-eight students completed pretest procedures during week five of the course as part of the Pretest–Posttest Control Group Design. The pretest sequence included pretest preparation and completion of two within-booth tuning trials. The pretest preparation phase was to teach the student concepts and procedures necessary to complete the tuning trials. Pretest preparation procedures with each individual student were completed by a trained research assistant just prior to the initial trial. Only demographic data were recorded during this period. Two pretest tuning trials were completed in the soundproof booth following preparation. For this procedure, the student held a guitar, listened momentarily to a continuous 34-second taped stimulus tone through both booth speakers, and then plucked the identified string with slow repetitions using a flat pick. Slow repeated strokes and use of the pick were necessary to provide a continuous signal strong enough to be read by the pitch extractor. The student was instructed to begin plucking the string approximately 5 seconds after the reference tone began and to stop plucking when the reference tone stopped. This procedure was followed for each of six strings across two tuning trials. Order of string presentation was designed to approximate commonly used classroom tuning procedures, and was, therefore, strings 6 (low) to 1 (high). Trials 1 and 2 were separated by a period of silence approximating 30 seconds. The pretest concluded after two 5-minute tuning trials.

Guitar strings were mistuned by the researcher using a portable stroboscope prior to trial 1 only. Strings 6, 4, and 2 were tuned one half step below standard "E" tuning pitches, and strings 5, 3, and 1 were mistuned higher by half a step. Strings were not mistuned again for trial 2; rather, each student was instructed to begin tuning from the final pitch achieved in the previous trial. The purpose of a second trial was to provide the student with two opportunities to tune the guitar as accurately as possible by completion of the pretest.

Following the completion of the pretest procedures, students selected for inclusion in the study (the 57 least accurate tuners), were randomly assigned to one of three treatment conditions. Eleven students who demonstrated only moderate tuning inaccuracies were excluded from further participation in the study because their scores placed them outside the accuracy parameters of the desired subject population. Prior to implementation of treatment, a one-way analysis of variance was computed on absolute cent deviation scores of groups to determine that groups were not biased regarding tuning ability. Completion of treatment and posttest procedures occurred during weeks nine, ten, and eleven of the course.

Treatment I: Visual Condition

Students receiving these instructional procedures ($n = 19$) completed training and posttest procedures during one individual tuning session. Treatment I consisted of pre-booth preparation and computer-assisted instruction. The research assistant prepared each student for within-booth procedures using guitars and simulated computer-graphics models. This 10-minute procedure was accomplished just prior to entry into the soundproof booth. Following completion of treatment preparation procedures, the individual student was placed in the soundproof booth to begin one of two tuning trials. Trial 1 procedures were identical to those for pretest Trial 1. Following this trial, graphs of tuning accuracy across all six strings were displayed on the graphics monitor. The student, having been trained to interpret the tuning graphs, was instructed to study the graphs and then indicate readiness to continue treatment. The guitar was mistuned following Trial 1.

During Trial 2, the student utilized the color graphics program, that is, visual alignment, with the simultaneously presented stimulus pitch to tune the instrument. For Trial 2, the guitar was mistuned to random pitches of approximately one half step deviation from the reference pitch. Following this trial, a second graphic display of the six string graphs appeared on the monitor. The student was again instructed to study the graphs before continuation of the session. Students in the visual condition received no verbal instruction during treatment.

Between treatment and posttest procedures, the student was released from the booth and seated for a period of approximately 3 minutes. Once the guitar was mistuned, the student was reseated in the booth, given a brief review of posttest procedures, and posttested for tuning accuracy.

Treatment II: Verbal Condition

Students receiving these instructional procedures ($n = 19$) completed training and posttest procedures during one individual tuning session.

Treatment II consisted of pre-booth preparation and a within-booth verbal instruction phase. Trial 1 procedures were identical to pretest and visual treatment activities except that an experienced guitar instructor was present in the booth. The instructor was seated to allow observation of the color graphics monitor, but the student was unable to view the screen. Prior to starting the test tape of reference pitches, the student was informed that no eye contact from the instructor would be given during individual string trials, but that, following the tuning of all six strings, the instructor would provide specific instruction to assist the student in tuning during the subsequent trial.

During Trial 1 the instructor passively observed the student for technique and tuning accuracy. Following the trial, the student was informed concerning which of the demonstrated tuning techniques increased accuracy and concerning the accuracy accomplished for each string. Additionally, the student was instructed to make one or two specific adjustments in tuning technique. Feedback concerning tuning accuracy was verbally stated by the instructor and consistent with information presented in posttrial graphs observed by the instructor, but not by the student, in this condition. The guitar was mistuned following Trial 1.

Trial 2 procedures were identical to those of Trial 1 except that the student received verbal instruction following the tuning of each string, as well as at the conclusion of the trial. Students in the verbal condition received no primary contact with the computer during treatment.

The student was released from the booth and was seated for approximately 3 minutes following treatment procedures. During this time, the guitar was mistuned as described in the pretest procedures, after which the student reentered the booth for completion of the posttest.

Treatment III: Contact Control Condition

Students in this condition ($n = 19$) were pre- and posttested for tuning accuracy. These students received instruction inclusive to the guitar class, but participated in no additional tuning activity.

Posttest

Fifty-seven students completed posttest procedures during weeks nine, ten, and eleven of the guitar course. Posttest procedures were identical to pretest procedures, but, following the posttest, all students reviewed trial graphs with the instructor. Students were instructed to utilize any useful techniques to tune the guitar during pre- and posttest trials.

Results

Measured pre- and posttest frequencies were converted to cents for the purpose of comparison. Data points were absolute cent deviation totals of subjects for a maximum of six tuning trials, including pre- and posttest Trials 1–2 and 5–6, respectively, and treatment Trials 3–4. Results of Trials 2, 4, and 6 were selected for inclusion in the study.

Comparison of gain scores for each pre- and posttest tuning trial-by-groups, using an analysis of variance with repeated measures (see Table 22.1), indicated no significant differences among the groups, possibly due to large amounts of subject variability. The eta-square coefficients indicated that the error terms accounted for 91% to 92% of both the between-group and within-group variance. As shown in Table 22.2, comparison of the two treatment groups across pretest, treatment, and posttest trials (Trials 2, 4, and 6) resulted in a significant main effect for treatments. This difference, however, is subsumed under the significant groups-by-trials interaction. Large proportions of error variance were again evident.

As can be seen in Figure 22.1, both treatment conditions seemed to have an effect in improving mean deviation scores from pre- to posttest. Mean scores across final pretest, treatment, and posttest trials suggest a consistent increase in tuning accuracy by students in the verbal instruction group. Mean scores across these same trials for students receiving visual instruction indicate a substantial improvement in tuning accuracy from pretest to treatment Trial 2, then a decrease in accuracy from treatment to posttest.

Although students in the verbal condition tuned with less accuracy during treatment, mean scores indicate that this group was more accurate than the visual group in the final posttest trial. Results suggest that visual instruction was more effective than verbal instruction in effecting immediate increases in tuning accuracy, but was less effective once the treatment procedures were withdrawn.

Discussion

This study was designed to test the effects of computer-based visual versus verbal instruction on the ability of novice musicians to tune six guitar strings to a unison, considering magnitude but not the direction of the tuning error. Instructional techniques were devised for use by students demonstrating gross tuning error or major inconsistencies in tuning accuracy; therefore, students exhibiting only moderate tuning difficulties were excluded from the study following administration of the pretest. Fifty-seven of the sixty-eight pretested subjects completed the six tuning trials. The

Table 22.1
Summary Table: Repeated Measures ANOVA, Comparing Gain Scores for Each Pre-Posttest Tuning Trial by Groups

Source	*df*	Sum of squares	Mean square	*F*	η^2
Between	56	15158955.96			.8990/Total
Groups	2	1313132.96	656566.50	2.56	.0870/Between
Error	54	13845823.00	256404.10		.9130/Between
Within	57	1730884.00			.0940/Total
Trials	1	990.31	990.31	.03	.0006/Within
Groups × trials	2	134679.00	67339.50	2.28	.0780/Within
Error	54	1595214.70	29541.01		.9220/Within
Total	113	16889840.06			

Table 22.2
Summary Table: Repeated Measures ANOVA, Comparing the Two Treatment Groups across Pretest, Treatment, and Posttest Tuning Trials

Source	*df*	Sum of squares	Mean square	*F*	η^2
Between	37	6680313.98			.46/Total
Groups	1	60352.00			.01/Between
Error	36	6619960.98	60352.0	.33	.99/Between
Within	76	7853684.01			.54/Total
Trials	2	2517073.31	1258536.7	19.51*	.32/Within
Groups × trials	2	693199.70	346599.8	5.37*	.09/Within
Error	72	4643411.00	64491.8		.59/Within
Total	113	14533997.99			

$^*p < .05$

Figure 22.1
Treatment-by-Trial 2 Interaction by Means

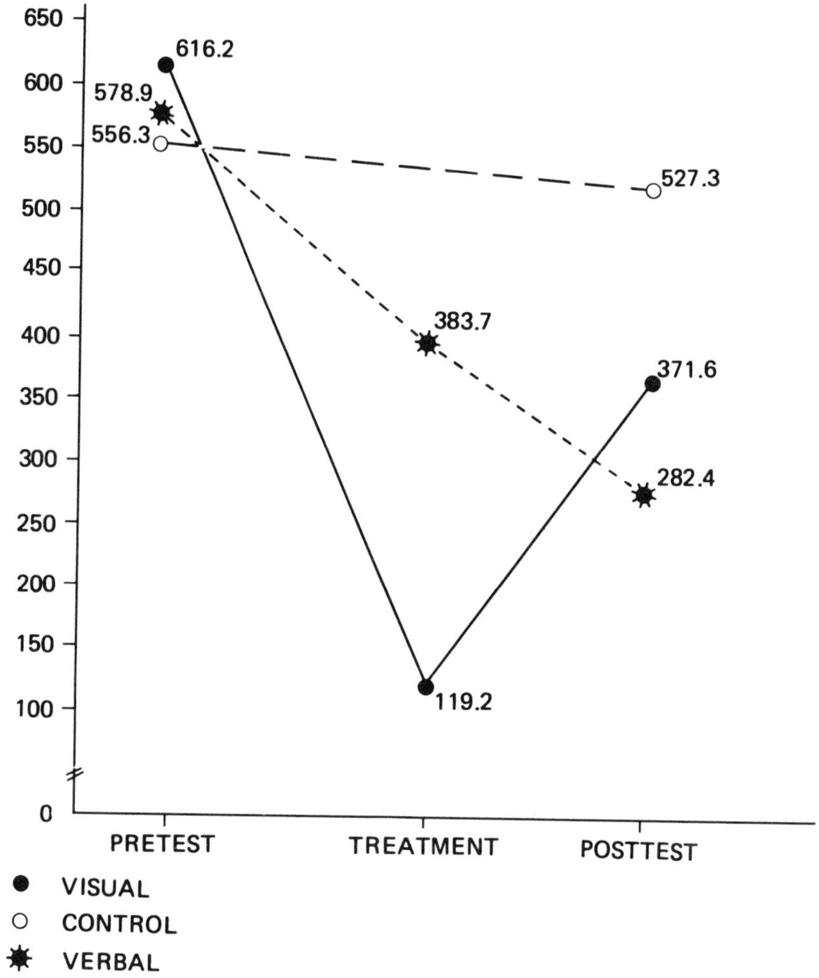

analysis examined the effects of the treatments on subjects with demonstrated difficulty in tuning to the degree that absolute scores would seem to place them near the center or to the left of the learning (tuning) curve.

To give perspective to study results, it must be emphasized that the units of measurement used for comparison were extremely small. One cent is equal to one-hundredth of an equal tempered semitone in pitch. Conversion of cents to semitones indicated that the mean scores of both groups across six strings for the pretest were between 5.5 and 6.5 semitones, decreasing during treatment to between 1 and 4 semitones, and in the posttest to between 2.5 and 4 semitones from reference pitches. Posttest means suggest that consequential tuning error continued to exist following treatment procedures, but both groups demonstrated significant and substantial improvement in tuning accuracy as a result of the study. Treatment conditions were devised to bring students consistently closer to matching individual unison pitches, and to provide approximation of "in-tune" chordal playing. The development of more exact tuning capabilities by beginning guitarists was beyond the scope of this study.

Of particular interest was the difference in mean cent deviation scores between groups and across trials. It would appear that "transfer" of learning occurred from treatment to posttest trials only in the verbal condition. "Transfer" is defined as one's ability to generalize possibilities to other subjects or situations. In the visual condition, when visual and auditory cues were paired in presentation, students tuned with relative accuracy. Withdrawal of the visual instruction cues from the tuning exercise resulted in substantially less accurate tuning abilities. Future research might include an investigation into visual and auditory instructional techniques that promote internalization of tuning skills by introducing, then fading to extinction any initially useful, but ultimately extraneous, tuning procedures.

23 Music as an Intonational Cue for Bilingual Language Acquisition

Myra J. Staum

Summary

By pairing melodies with sentences according to the rhythmic patterns and intonational contours of the English language, foreign students may be able to learn the proper non-linguistic elements of speech necessary for communication. In this study, music paired with speech significantly increased accuracy in verbal inflection.

Results of this study may be applied to foreign language teaching and to the hearing impaired in any classroom setting, extending the procedures to encompass the pairing of rhythmic patterns to increase accuracy in stress, duration, and timing of speech.

Design: Statistical, pre-post $N = 30$ Groups: 1
Statistical Analysis: one-way ANOVA
Reliability: Two replications in two different universities; 100% listener reliability
Independent Variables: Sentences paired with music; sentences spoken without music
Dependent Variable: Degree of improvement in verbal intonation of sentences as measured by pre- and posttest semitone difference
Music: Listening, individual, group

* * *

During the 20th century, our country has witnessed an enormous population shift characterized by an influx of foreigners and the growth of bilingual communities. One of the primary concerns is in teaching these individuals the English language and in finding innovative techniques to foster attention to the fine discriminations necessary for mastering this skill.

Bilingual individuals have a unique set of problems related to the perception, production, and memorization of an additional language. Keeping the phonological and syntactic systems of two languages separate plus the many thousands of words is a fatiguing and complex process.

One of the most noticeable areas of bilingual language acquisition that, if incorrect, affects the whole character, emotion, and meaning of communication, is prosody. Prosody is an expressive, rather than formal, linguistic property of speech. Prosodic elements are a function of the tonal patterns in the voice pitch, the variations in syllable stresses, and the duration and timing of rhythmic patterns. More specifically, prosody is a function of the periodicity, amplitude, spectral character, and duration of the output of the larynx (Lieberman, 1976; Miller, 1984). Although every sentence, word, and syllable is given some pitch and temporal pattern when it is spoken, prosodic rules differ in each language. Not infrequently, the confusion and difficulty in understanding a foreigner is a result of distorted prosody.

Historically, music has played an important role in the speech development of language impaired individuals (Galloway, 1975; Solomon, 1980). A number of studies have used music as a paired auditory stimulus in testing various aspects of language discrimination or retention. Most of these have consisted of isolated syllables, nonsense syllables, or digits (Austen, 1977; Baugh & Baugh, 1965; Jellison, 1976; Sims, 1980). Some studies have included single-word pairs or serially ordered words (Jellison & Miller, 1982; Madsen, Madsen, & Michel, 1975; Shehan, 1981). Others have incorporated phrases and sentences for language development (Cartwright & Huckaby, 1972) and for discrimination of prereading and grammatical concepts (Staum, 1979). Although this body of research reports variable degrees of effectiveness in language retention and discrimination, almost all the studies infer a strong reinforcing value in using musical stimulus when compared with spoken stimuli.

Music used for foreign language teaching or for foreigners learning English appears to be quite rare from the paucity of research in this area. It seems limited to the singing of songs primarily for entertainment and cultural education. It is acknowledged in the literature, however, that music and song could be useful in reinforcing the practice of vocabulary, sentence patterns, idioms, pronunciation, stress, and rhythm of speech (Rees, 1977). It is hypothesized that teachers rarely use this medium for foreign language training because song lyrics differ from spoken language in their use of unusual word order, false rhymes, and archaic-type words (Rees, 1977).

In some foreign countries, particularly those in which tonal languages are prominent, song and chant are sometimes used to aid students in reciting their lessons. In Thailand, the public school system actively engages in songs in order to practice the pitch or tonal aspects of the language (List, 1972). Only one program is reported to teach English as a second language through the analysis of a song's melody and rhythm primarily to improve comprehension (Sheeder, 1976).

Because phoneticians are concerned primarily with analyzing the linguistic aspects of speech and less with the prosodic elements of language, it is not surprising that educational methods also deemphasize these musical features. Techniques for instruction in prosody are greatly overlooked in the research literature except as they relate to the speech of hearing impaired individuals (Darrow, 1984; Lehiste, 1970).

The purpose of this study was to determine whether music paired with English sentences would affect the intonational speech patterns of foreign subjects studying English as a second language as compared to sentences presented without music, and whether generalization to unfamiliar sentences with the same linguistic structure would occur.

Method

Subjects

Subjects were 43 foreign students who were enrolled in the Intensive English programs of two universities. All were first- or second-year students and were selected on the basis of their enrollment in conversational language lab classes. Six different classes were utilized for the study. Native languages among the subjects included: Indonesian, Spanish, Arabic, Somali, Japanese, Turkish, Portuguese, Malayan, Chinese, Korean, and Hindi.

Experimental Materials

Three audiotapes were developed for this study, including both spoken and sung sentences. Sentences were constructed in four areas frequently considered problematic in prosody by teachers of English as a Second Language (ESL). These areas were: yes/no questions, prepositional phrases with object pronoun, alternative sentences, and informational questions. The sentences used for each tape are shown in Table 23.1. Sentences were constructed to be equal in progressive syllabic length for each day's practice, and all were considered equivalent in phonemic difficulty and intonation by four ESL teachers. Because the sentences were equivalent, the yes/no and alternative sentences were randomly selected to be paired with mu-

Table 23.1
Verbal Stimuli

Set I	
Both of them need washing.	
The girl with him is pretty.	
The papers of ours are missing.	
The sunset behind us is beautiful.	
May I read yet?	No.
Are they watching him?	Of course.
Could you sing it for me?	Maybe soon.
Do they have some ice cream cones?	I think they do.
Why are you here?	Because.
What's the assignment?	I don't know.
Whose coat is on the floor?	It's Marjorie's.
Who's the desperate lady?	It's Mrs. Jones.
Do you want juice or water?	
Is it usual or peculiar?	
Could we go to the park or to the beach house?	
Are you an interesting man or a boring person?	
Set II	
May we go there?	Yes.
Are you ready yet?	Not yet.
Should rabbits run a lot?	Yes, they should.
Are you getting closer now?	Well yes, I am.
Most of them are authors.	
She frowned at us in anger.	
He talked to himself in the shower.	
The advantage of it is obvious.	
Should we play cards or tennis?	
Is Jessie senile or just sleepy?	
Are they polygamous or monogamous?	
Would you like to scuba dive or read some poetry?	
When's the party?	Tonight.
Where's the battery?	In the car.
How comfortable is it?	It's quite soft.
Why'd you come to this college?	To study physics.
Set III	
What's his message?	"I love you."
Whose library card?	The professor's.

When did the mayor come?	Yesterday, I think.
Why is your temperature high?	I sat in the hot tub.
Do you read books or papers?	
Will you drink coffee or some soda?	
Is it a rare flower or a common one?	
Should we hear a symphony or listen to records?	
Some of you can write well.	
The gift from him seemed perfect.	
Our perception of him is changing.	
That creation of his is amazing.	
Would it matter?	No.
Could you help the girl?	I'll try.
Can we go already?	No, not now.
Could it be Mary I love?	I'd like to know.

sic, and the prepositional phrase with pronoun object and informational sentences were selected to be presented without music.

A female vocalist served as the voice stimulus on the tape. Spoken sentences were read seven times each at three tempi: slow (MM 60 = strong stress points), medium (MM = 76), and fast (MM = 88), for a total of twenty-one repetitions per sentence. The progressive tempi were structured to provide a successive approximation to normal speech fluency, while allowing students an opportunity to internalize the pronunciation of each sentence.

Spoken sentences were read with a predetermined inflectional and stress pattern considered by the ESL teachers to be normal to a native American. Because content, emotion, and meaning are directly related to prosody in English (Chomsky & Halle, 1968), this intonational choice did not infer that it was the "correct" melodic contour, simply a more common one. Sung sentences were sung along a normal melodic contour closely approximating the intervallic distances and contour of each sentence. To compose the melodic selections, four ESL teachers were independently taped reading the yes/no and alternative sentences. Each syllable in relationship to the next syllable was analyzed for its intervallic distance, and melodic phrases were composed to parallel these intervals. Melodies were also determined by having a pilot sample of nine subjects sing a scale from their lowest to highest vocal pitch in order to determine a comfortable singing range. Because research suggests that the typical median frequency range for speaking is between 134–146 Hz for men and 199–295 Hz for women (Lehiste, 1970), these factors were considered in composing the musical material. Songs were sung

Figure 23.1
Yes/No Sentences

Set 1:1 May I read yet? No.
Set 2:1 May we go there? Yes.
Set 3:1 Would it matter? No.

Set 1:2 Are they watching him? Of course.
Set 2:2 Are you ready yet? Not yet.
Set 3:2 Could you help the girl? I'll try.

Set 1:3 Could you sing it for me? Maybe soon.

Set 2:3 Should rabbits run a lot? Yes, they should.

Set 3:3 Can we go already? No, not now.

Set 1:4 Do they have some ice cream cones? I think they do.
Set 2:4 Are you getting closer now? Well, yes I am.

Set 3:4 Could it be Mary I love? I'd like to know.

on a master tape with a simple piano accompaniment. Each of the three different tape sets was composed of four sung yes/no sentences, four spoken prepositional phrases, four sung alternative sentences, and four spoken informational sentences. Figure 23.1 depicts the notation for the sung yes/no sentences, and Figure 23.2 shows that for the sung alternative sentences.

Pre/posttesting

Subjects were pre- and posttested individually the day before and after the 9-day experimental period by reading sentences into a tape recorder. Pre- and posttest stimuli consisted of one sentence from each of the four experimental verbal areas plus four new or transfer sentences of equivalent structure and difficulty (see Table 23.2). In addition, during the posttest, the yes/no phrase "Should rabbits run a lot? Yes, they should," which was sung during the experimental procedure, was presented again in its musical

Figure 23.2
Alternative Sentences

Set 1:1 Do you want juice or water?
Set 2:1 Should we play cards or tennis?
Set 3:1 Do you read books or papers?

Set 1:2 Is it usual or peculiar?

Set 2:2 Is Jessie senile or just sleepy?

Set 3:2 Will you drink coffee or some soda?

Set 1:3 Could we go to the park or to the beach house?

Set 2:3 Are they polygamous or monogamous?

Set 3:3 Is it a rare flower or a common one?

Set 1:4 Are you an interesting man or a boring person?

Set 2:4 Would you like to scuba dive or read some poetry?

Set 3:4 Should we hear a symphony or listen to records?

form. Subjects were asked to listen one time, sing three times, then read the sentence immediately. The read sentence was then taped for analysis in order to ascertain whether or not the recency of repeating sung phrases affected intonational performance.

Procedures

Fifteen-minute language lab sessions were conducted for a period of 9 days. During this time, a tape (either Set I, II, or III) was placed on the

Table 23.2
Pre/Post Test Sentences for Analysis

Yes/No Sentences (music)	
Lab:	Should rabbits run a lot? Yes, they should.
Transfer:	Will you marry me, John? Heavens, no!
Prepositional Phrases with Object Pronoun (non-music)	
Lab:	He talked to himself in the shower.
Transfer:	The rest of it looked delicious.
Alternative Sentences (music)	
Lab:	Are they polygamous or monogamous?
Transfer:	Can we play with Joe's friend or someone else's?
Informational Sentences (non-music)	
Lab:	How comfortable is it? It's quite soft.
Transfer:	How's dinner? Tasty.

master control system while subjects listened through earphones into their individual laboratory booths. Subjects received printed sentences each day according to the set they were to practice. Set I was presented on days 1, 4, and 7; Set II on days 2, 5, and 8; and Set III on days 3, 6 and 9. Therefore, each set was practiced three times during the 9-day period.

When the tape was turned on, subjects were directed to listen carefully while looking at their papers and to maintain a rhythmic pulse with their hands. They were also directed to "listen only" to the phrase three times, then repeat the phrase four times, twice alone and twice with the taped speaker/singer. At the end of the session, students returned the printed page to the experimenter and continued with their usual laboratory exercises.

Analysis

For the purpose of this study, speech utterances were analyzed by listening to each subject's tape and by matching the pitch to a piano. Each phrase was analyzed for its lowest and highest inflectional point on the vowel sound embedded within the predetermined syllable. Inasmuch as vowel sounds vary in inflection, if a clear, general pitch was not perceived, then the highest tone of that vowel sound was analyzed. Because of the imprecision of this method as compared to mechanical and computerized speech analyzers, in-

Table 23.3
Mean Semitone Difference in High/Low Inflectional Points

	Pre		Post		Post	Normal
	Lab	Transfer	Lab	Transfer	Sung/Read	Speech
Alternative (music)	1.26	.40	5.23	2.28		9
Yes/No (music)	−1.53	−1.80	−2.96	−1.53	−4.66	−9
Informational (non-music)	2.06	2.46	3.46	1.30		−9
Prepositional (non-music)	5.50	5.43	7.10	5.03		9

dependent observer reliability was obtained for all subjects and for all trials of the pre- and posttests. Both observers listened to the tapes independently as many times as necessary in order to determine a predominant pitch. Pitches were then matched to a piano, and the note and octave documented. Subjects' tapes were eliminated if 100% observer reliability was not obtained on all trials of the pre- and posttests.

Results

Analyses of improvement between pre- and posttests were made on lab and transfer sentences. When the pitches of the highest and lowest inflectional points were determined, they were assigned an appropriate semitone count above C_0 (Young, 1976). Therefore, C_3 was assigned a semitone count of 36 because there are 36 half steps above C_0. The lowest and highest inflectional points were subtracted and a difference score determined. Mean difference scores were then compared across all conditions in relationship to native English intonation (see Table 23.3).

Next, a comparison of music and non-music lab and transfer sentences was made over pre- and posttests. Gain scores were calculated by determining the degree of change between pre- and posttest difference scores in relationship to the correct inflectional contour. Therefore, a pretest score of −5 and a posttest score of 4 yielded +9 if the actual English contour was falling (falling difference = a positive number) or would yield a score of −9 if the actual sentence contour was falling but the subject intoned in a rising, thereby erroneous, direction.

An analysis of variance of average gain scores among pre- and posttest

Table 23.4
Inflectional Gain Scores from Pre- to Posttest

	Music		Non-music	
	Lab	Transfer	Lab	Transfer
Score	160	48	0	21
M	5.33	1.60	0	.70
n	30	30	30	30

Note: $F(3,116) = 3.028$, $p < .05$.

sentences presented with and without music yielded a significant difference, $F(3, 116) = 3.028$, $p < .05$ (see Table 23.4). A Newman-Keuls comparison further indicated that sentences presented with music in the laboratory improved in an accurate intonational contour as compared to transfer sentences of the same linguistic structure, or to either lab or transfer sentences presented without music, as shown in Table 23.5.

A cursory look at Table 23.3 indicates that all prepositional phrases with object pronoun were the most correctly intoned sentences in relationship to native English speech. The highest total amount of change in the correct contour occurred with alternative sentences (15.21), then prepositional sentences (6.28), then yes/no sentences (4.56). Informational sentences yielded a total change (6.88) in the inverse direction.

The sentence "Should rabbits run a lot? Yes, they should," which subjects sang and then read immediately during the posttest, demonstrated an average gain of 1.70 semitones when read immediately after being sung when compared to the identical sentence in the posttest. A mean increase of 3.13 semitones in this sentence was evident when compared to the same pretest sentence. Further observations indicate that no conditions ever reached native English intonation, though the contours of all except the informational sentences were intoned in the correct directional contour.

Table 23.5
Newman-Keuls Comparison of Mean Gain Scores

Music		Non-music	
Lab	Transfer	Lab	Transfer
5.33*	1.60	0	.70

*$p < .05$.

Discussion

The purpose of this study was to determine the effect of music as an intonational cue in improving speech prosody among bilingual foreign students. Results indicated that gains were achieved when sentences were paired with music in the language lab but not when generalized to new verbal stimuli with an identical linguistic structure.

That generalization was not achieved is not uncommon in learning and would indicate a need to direct training toward the transfer of concepts. This particular study might have integrated this generalization process by following each daily training session with a number of transfer sentences to be matched with the practiced intonational pattern.

Gains observed in the music conditions are of particular interest. Alternative sentences resulted in the greatest improvement even when compared to the sung yes/no sentences. It would seem that, though both the linguistic and intonational content of all verbal stimuli were identical, differences in the content and meaning of each sentence were sufficient to have contributed to the inconsistencies in inflection. It would be suggested that a replication involving identical verbal stimuli be conducted to further control this factor.

The analysis of intonational features is also an area of consideration. A number of speech analysis tools exist for analyzing prosodic features, including a kymograph, oscilloscope and oscillograph, spectrograph, computerized melodic analyzer (Leon & Martin, 1972), and Vocoder (Borst & Cooper, 1957; Hadding-Koch & Studdert-Kennedy, 1964). Most have been concerned with producing a picture from which the phonetician visualizes one or more aspects of human speech: the melodic contour (fundamental frequency), breath groups and pauses, and stress points (amplitude). Some of the more sophisticated measures (melodic analyzer and Vocoder) are able to extract the fundamental frequency from the speech signal and to display a clear melodic contour simultaneously with an individual's input (Weltens & deBot, 1984). Although the analysis of speech according to musical intervals is considered more applicable for tonal languages than for non-tonal languages such as English (Lehiste & Peterson, 1961) and is generally less reliable for the precision of speech analysis, this method existed prior to the development of sophisticated instrumentation (Jones, 1909). Furthermore, it is believed that one can hear and discriminate sufficiently well without spectrographic analysis. Lehiste (1970) reported that for frequencies below 1000 Hz, two to three cycles must be heard for accurate perception. To perceive a predominant pitch, the sound would need to be audible for 2 to 10 milliseconds. This would explain the relative ease in this study in detecting longer vowel sounds as in the word "soft" and equal difficulty in understanding the final syllable of the word "else's." This factor might have contributed to the elimination of thirteen tapes that did not yield 100% observer reliability. It is suggested that further study comparing music's effect as an intonational cue be analyzed stroboscopically.

In many cultures, the tonalities or rhythms of their languages are indicative of feeling states or attitudes. In Hungarian, for instance, words depicting joy and tenderness are always pitched higher. In French, the lengthening of stressed syllables indicates happiness; and in most other languages, including English, intonation is reflective in great part of the emotion and meaning of the sentence (Fonagy & Magdics, 1972). Any analysis of speech intonation, then, is difficult at best because not only is there a tremendous range of phonetic manifestations, but, in addition, intonation varies according to the contextual and emotional state of the speaker. In this study, the emphasis was not on the correctness or incorrectness of intonation, but simply the power of a musical stimulus to create any effect on the speaker's intonational pattern, preferably in the direction desired. To this degree, because of the limited training time, music did produce an observable effect.

Future study in utilizing music as an auditory cue for foreign and English language learning might focus on other prosodic elements as well. Inasmuch as English is a stress-timed language where progressively more unstressed syllables scramble to accommodate a basic beat (Woods, 1979b), a paired rhythmic structure might facilitate appropriate rhythmic fluency. Distortions in the durations of vowels might also benefit from training with rhythmic cues. Certainly, that which is learned about structuring foreign and English prosodic features would also be applicable in areas concerned with the naturalness of artificially induced computer speech, for speech training and therapy for the hearing and language impaired or text-to-speech for the blind. Because of the complexities inherent in linguistics and language learning, continued research in this area is warranted in order to understand the components necessary for improving speech prosody.

24 The Effect of Guided Listening Information and Music on the Alpha Brainwave Production of Musicians and Non-musicians

Michael J. Wagner
Bernard J. Harding

Summary

The study attempts to isolate distinctive features of the music listening experience by measuring the physiological parameters with the electroencephalograph (EEG). Statistically significant differences between left and right brain hemispheres and between males and females were isolated. Difference in alpha brainwave content usually found between musicians and non-musicians was not evident in this study; it is speculated that eyes open versus eyes closed may have accounted for this difference. No statistical significances were found between the alpha content of the population who received "Guided Listening Information" and those who received silence.

Design: Statistical/behavioral
Statistical Analysis: ANOVA
Graphic Analysis: Analog
Independent Variables: Musician/non-musician, left/right brain, male/female; program notes/no program notes, baseline and five music examples
Dependent Variables: Percent of alpha brainwave activity
Music: Listening, individual

* * *

Since the inception of psychology as a science dealing with investigation of "the mind," confusion has existed over what role the brain plays in this most abstract attribute of the human condition. By labeling physiological experience as different and apart from psychological experience, we have created a chasm between the two that causes mankind to confuse, veil, and ignore the relationship and interrelatedness of one to the other. Deikman (1973, p. 68) states that the human being is an organization of components having biological and psychological dimensions:

> Discussions of states of consciousness usually do not integrate . . . physiological and psychological variables. . . . Psychological and physiological variations are viewed as manifestations of two basic organismic states or modes that are coordinated to a particular function. . . . These components are: . . . an "action" mode and a "receptive" mode. The action mode is a state organized to manipulate the environment. The striate muscle system and the sympathetic nervous system are the dominant physiological agencies. The EEG shows beta waves and baseline muscle tension is increased. The principal psychological manifestations of this state are focal attention, object-based logic, heightened boundary perception, and the dominance of formal characteristics over the sensory; shapes and meanings have a preference over colors and textures. The action mode is a state of striving, oriented toward achieving personal goals that range from nutrition to defense to obtaining social rewards, plus a variety of symbolic and sensual pleasures, as well as the avoidance of a comparable variety of pain.

The electroencephalographic impulses that have been studied and compared for the past twelve years are the combined synaptic discharges of the temporal and occipital lobes. They do not represent thought processes, but the reflections of these processes. One would look there, in the brain, for clues rather than in the heart or the viscera, where it was thought throughout much of human history that the soul of man reposed. Yet, the clues that are studied are extremely difficult to understand because so much information is contained in even 1 second of a human EEG. It is possible that all this information, which we collect in the guise of pen deflections on a roll of chart paper, is only the reflection of a reflection—distorted shadows of how human thought and information processing really function.

Some evidence exists that this view might be shared throughout the scientific community. Fewer research studies report cortical activity, and the number of manufacturers of instrumentation continue to diminish. *Psychological Abstracts*, during the last 3 years, has indexed fewer and fewer research reports using feedback encephalographs as dependent measures.

In the area of brainwaves and biofeedback, research findings conflict with each other at every turn. Electroencephalographic studies dealing with "eyes open" or "eyes closed," handedness, sex of the subject, and especially brain-hemisphere dominance all present conflicting conclusions in the literature. Brainwave and biofeedback history, current research reports, and diversified opinions as they relate to music and music learning have been quite recently reviewed by Wagner and Altman (1984).

The present investigation attempts to pursue one small, but important, area: trying to understand the brain processes relating to music listening. The research in this report is one study in a stepwise process by which we continue to try to isolate those areas of human function that seem to contribute to the learning, recognizing, remembering, and valuing of music and the process by which it is learned. These answers are sought in an effort to understand music information processing, enhance personal enjoyment of music, and improve the pedagogical practices of our profession.

Repeating the process called music listening seems to evoke electrical activity in the temporal/occipital areas of the right hemisphere cerebral cortex. When music is present and subjects attend to it, the brain's activity changes either to accommodate the incoming aural sensory signals, or as a function of them. Musicians (those who regularly spend time attending to music) have produced more alpha brainwave content (8–12 Hz), and non-musicians (those who do not attend often to music) seem to block the alpha production in that cerebral area. This difference between these two groups is referred to as learning. It is suspected that teaching the latter group to produce a higher percentage of alpha brainwaves, similar to that of the former, would increase the likelihood of accommodation to or learning the music. In this study, an attempt has been made to isolate the issue of verbalizing about music from that of listening to it.

Method

Subjects

Thirty-two adult musician subjects and thirty-two adult non-musician subjects participated in the study. Their ages ranged from 18 to 54 years. Each participant was placed into one of four categories ($n = 16$): female musician, female non-musician, male musician, and male non-musician. For the purposes of this investigation, a musician was defined as a person who has studied music for at least 3 years and has done so within the last 3 years. A non-musician was defined as someone who had studied music for less than 3 years and had not studied within the last 3 years (Wagner, 1975; Wagner & Menzel, 1978).

Procedure and Protocol

When subjects entered the experimental environment, the laboratory, each was seated in a reclining easy chair and asked to read and fill out an information and permission form. These documents also explained to participants that they would be listening to some music excerpts while their brainwaves were being recorded. Subjects were also given a short briefing, by the experimenter, on electroencephalographic (EEG) procedures. This included information pertaining to the electrodes that would be placed on the scalp, data concerning the physical composition of the electrodes and the electrolyte solution, plus a description of the battery-operated electroencephalographs. Subjects were then asked to refrain from closing their eyes while listening and to listen to the music as they normally would: with their eyes open.

Electrodes were attached according to the ten/twenty system over the right hemisphere, at points T-4 and O-2; and over the left hemisphere, at points T-3 and O-1. A lightweight stereo headset was then positioned over the subject's ears. The laboratory's fluorescent lights were then turned out, and low-level, indirect lighting was introduced and maintained throughout the experimental period. Immediately before the start of the tape, subjects' EEGs were monitored for approximately 2 minutes (100 millimeters of tracing on the chart recorder) in order to create a feeling of general relaxation and to establish a physiological baseline for each subject.

Equipment

Audio recordings for this investigation were made on high-quality metal cassette recording tape. Each of the two tapes (one containing program notes, or Guided Listening Information, along with the music, and one with silence in the place of the program notes) was 21 minutes in length. They were produced and played back upon a Panasonic stereo cassette deck (Model #RS 260 US). Other playback equipment included a Panasonic stereo amplifier (Model #7828) and Yamaha YHL-005 stereo headphones. EEGs of subjects were monitored using two Autogen Model 120A electroencephalographs. Data were recorded on a Dash IV chart recorder, manufactured by the Astro-Med division of ATLAN-TOL Industries.

As the tape began, each subject was asked if the music could be heard and if it was loud enough or too loud. No other communication occurred between the subjects and the experimenter after the tape had begun.

Music Examples

Subjects were asked to listen to five music excerpts, each having a duration of 3 minutes. Brainwave (EEG) activity was recorded from both the left and right hemispheres. The same music excerpts were played for each participant and in the same order. There were 32 randomly selected subjects (8 from each of the groups) who received 1 minute of silence between music excerpts, and 32 subjects (the remaining 8 from each of the groups) who received Guided Listening Information between music excerpts.

Excerpts were from Ives's "The Unanswered Question"; Chopin's "Ballade in F Major"; Lewin-Richter's "Study No. 1"; Massenet's "Le Cid"; and Saint-Saens's *Symphony no. 3* (2nd movement).

The Guided Listening Information presented to subjects assigned to that experimental group was as follows:

The Unanswered Question—Ives

The piece you are about to hear is "The Unanswered Question," by Charles Ives.

Against the tapestry of deep space, played in this mini-scenario by the String section using mutes, a musical question is asked . . . by a trumpet. The question must deal with "the meaning of life," or some metaphysical issue, because the Muses who guard such wisdom at first try to ignore the question. A simple "Go away" kind of statement is made by a small woodwind ensemble.

The Question returns. This time, however, the discerning listener will notice that the last note of the Question changes. The Muses, after another hesitation, answer a bit more brusquely! Again the Question returns, this time with the original ending note and again the Muses are reviled and, maybe, a bit disgusted. All in all, the "question" is asked seven times.

See if you can put yourself in that metaphysical twilight zone where questions and answers are in the language of musical sound, and where space abounds . . . and goes on forever.

Ballade in F Major—Chopin

Once upon a time, there was a lady who lived in a lake. This beautiful woman fell in love with a young and very handsome man who frequently came to the lake to sit upon the shore and enjoy the peacefulness that it brought to him.

The lady of the lake however, was determined to lure her unsuspecting lover into the lake so that he could live there with her forever.

This piano composition begins with a description of the tranquil state of the lake, the beauty of the water, and the deep adoration which the lady of the lake feels for the object of her affection. After the description of peace and tranquility, listen for the turbulence of the water as her lover is lured closer and closer to its edge, whirlpools, and deadly depths. Ultimately, the young man is taken beneath the water to live forever, and the lake returns to its lovely tranquil state.

Study no. 1—Lewin-Richter

You are about to be bombarded with sound. Cast all your preconceived notions about traditional music aside, and let this piece of electronic music take you . . . and change the way you normally listen. Electronic music simply undertakes to express by different means human situations, ideas, and emotions.

In this piece, the composer's intentions were two-fold. First he wanted to obtain instrument-like sounds, such as the bell-like sonorities of the opening, and later, a vast range of percussive and plucking sounds. Then, he wanted to create tensions and relaxations achieved through complex rhythms, increased densities of tone color, and other similar effects.

These effects occur when a high degree of intensity is diluted by the introduction of richer and more familiar sounds. Traditional melodies, rhythms and harmonies simply are not anywhere to be found in this selection.

Le Cid—Massenet

Music for the dance enjoys a unique place in the world of art. At its best, such music pulsates with rhythmic vitality, glows with the brightest colors, and exudes the spirit of gracefulness. Moreover, it warms the heart and enchants the imagination. Spain particularly, with its past steeped in both pagan and Christian cultures, has produced dance music of such vitality that composers of other nationalities have even imitated its sound.

Jules Massenet, a Frenchman, wrote an opera, *Le Cid*, based on a play about the Spanish war against the invading Moors during the twelfth century. This opera contains a set of colorful dances from three of the provinces of Spain. The dance you will hear now is from the province of Castile. It contains sonorities and instruments which bring to mind swirling Spanish skirts, castanets, tambourines, and the clicking of high Spanish heels on the dance floor.

Symphony no. 3—Saint-Saens

Camille Saint-Saens, a French composer, wrote five symphonies in his lifetime, but allowed only three of them to be published. You are about to hear the second movement of the last of these. Its first performance was in 1886, at the very height of the Romantic age of music history.

The forces used in this instrumental work are of particular interest because in addition to the usual orchestral contingent, he uses a triple woodwind group, an organ throughout, and, in the finale, a piano with two players.

The second movement is marked "poco adagio," or "very slowly." It opens with the organ sustaining a very low tone and continues with the introduction of the string section to become one of music's most introspective examples. On the musical level, the movement is so slow that the metric pulse seems almost suspended, while the melody simply exists to be beautiful! On an emotional level, it is a wonderful companion to quiet solitude.

Results

The total number of millimeters of chart paper for each category of brainwave was carefully measured for each of the experimental periods. By dividing the number of millimeters that were recorded in the alpha brainwave category by the total number of millimeters of chart paper for that portion of the experiment, a percentage of alpha content was computed for each subject. The percent of alpha brainwave content was the dependent measure for this investigation.

Independent measures investigated were: left brain hemisphere vs. right brain hemisphere; musician vs. non-musician; male vs. female; and program notes vs. silence.

Three-way analysis of variance was employed to determine if significant differences existed between the means of the independent variables. All main effects and interactions whose significance level is .08 or smaller are listed in Table 24.1, as is the distance they deviate from the mean for that cell.

It can be noted that male subjects consistently produced more alpha brainwaves in both hemispheres than did female subjects.

Table 24.2 shows, in temporal order, the means of the percentage of alpha brainwave content under each condition for each experimental group.

It was decided that, because of the complexity of the data, means for each variable should be displayed graphically. Figure 24.1 illustrates the left brain relationship of musician/non-musician with whether the subject received program notes (Guided Listening Information) or silence.

Figure 24.2 illustrates the same two variables, but graphs alpha production in the right brain.

Figure 24.3 displays the relationship of brain hemisphere alpha content with whether or not the subject is a musician. It is clear that the brain's right hemisphere in subjects of both groups produces between 10% and 20% more alpha brainwaves than the left hemisphere.

Figures 24.4 through 24.6 isolate temporally the means of each variable for the left and right hemisphere.

Discussion

No significant differences were found in the alpha brainwave content between those who received program notes and those who did not. Thus, the processing of information about music is not reflected in alpha brainwave content. Figure 24.4 shows that the presence of program notes does not significantly change the brainwave content of any experimental population, though it can be seen in Figures 24.1 and 24.2 that at times almost 10% more alpha brainwave content is in the EEGs of musicians who received program notes than in those of the non-musicians who received silence between music excerpts.

The large differences in alpha production in these data are attributable

Table 24.1
3-Way Anova Summary: Significant Male/Female Differences in Left and Right Brain under Each Discrete Aural Condition and Each Music Condition

Variable	*F*	Significance Level	Deviation from Mean
Right brain			−3.81 F
Music 1	3.18	.08	3.93 M
Left brain			−4.36 F
Music 2	3.25	.08	4.50 M
Right brain			−4.13 F
Aural condition 3	3.21	.08	4.26 M
Interaction effect			
Sex × pgm nts/silence	6.01	.02	
Right brain			−4.91 F
Music 3	4.82	.03	5.07 M
Right brain			−4.18 F
Aural condition 4	4.13	.05	4.31 M
Interaction effect			
Sex × mus/non-mus	3.70	.06	
Interaction effect			
Sex × pgm nts/silence	9.90	.003	
Left brain			−4.95 F
Music 4	4.34	.04	5.10 M
Right brain			−4.08 F
Music 4	3.61	.06	4.21 M
Interaction effect			
Sex × mus/non-mus	6.66	.01	
Right brain			−4.68 F
Aural condition 5	5.31	.03	4.82 M
Interaction effect			
Sex × mus/non-mus	5.74	.02	
Interaction effect			
Sex × pgm nts/silence	4.44	.04	
Left brain			−6.94 F
Music 5	8.69	.005	7.15 M
Right brain			−4.10 F
Music 5	3.46	.07	4.23 M

Table 24.2

Means of Each Group Expressed as Percentage of Alpha Brainwave Content, Left vs. Right Hemisphere

Musician — Program Notes ($n = 16$)

	Baseline		Aural cond 1		Music 1		Aural cond 2		Music 2		Aural cond 3		Music 3		Aural cond 4		Music 4		Aural cond 5		Music 5	
	L	R	L	R	L	R	L	R	L	R	L	R	L	R	L	R	L	R	L	R	L	R
F	20.9	25.8	21.0	25.8	26.0	25.4	21.1	33.5	22.5	33.6	22.6	26.9	21.4	29.6	20.4	28.5	21.1	36.4	21.9	32.5	19.8	34.9
M	21.5	38.1	18.9	35.9	27.3	37.1	32.8	39.4	26.3	36.0	31.4	48.0	29.6	41.0	31.4	42.4	33.1	38.1	36.5	40.8	33.1	40.6

Musician — Silence ($n = 16$)

	Baseline		Aural cond 1		Music 1		Aural cond 2		Music 2		Aural cond 3		Music 3		Aural cond 4		Music 4		Aural cond 5		Music 5	
	L	R	L	R	L	R	L	R	L	R	L	R	L	R	L	R	L	R	L	R	L	R
F	13.6	29.6	18.8	38.5	11.8	30.3	18.6	37.6	16.9	32.5	20.8	39.8	15.6	30.3	24.3	30.4	22.1	30.3	20.9	32.1	19.9	36.0
M	15.0	35.4	15.9	35.5	19.5	27.4	14.3	26.3	24.4	24.0	27.1	25.8	25.3	23.6	23.6	21.8	27.1	22.6	19.0	23.1	33.4	28.4

Table 24.2, *con't*
Means of Each Group Expressed as Percentage of Alpha Brainwave Content, Left vs. Right Hemisphere

Non-musician — Program Notes
(n = 16)

	Baseline		Aural cond 1		Music 1		Aural cond 2		Music 2		Aural cond 3		Music 3		Aural cond 4		Music 4		Aural cond 5		Music 5	
	L	R	L	R	L	R	L	R	L	R	L	R	L	R	L	R	L	R	L	R	L	R
F	18.0	35.5	21.4	31.5	15.8	23.8	15.1	24.7	13.6	21.8	13.1	22.4	12.9	21.4	12.0	14.9	11.3	17.6	14.9	16.3	8.8	19.5
M	22.1	36.9	24.8	35.9	29.8	40.3	30.5	40.1	29.9	41.3	28.4	41.0	26.8	42.1	25.9	44.6	31.6	43.4	23.6	44.1	33.0	43.9

Non-musician — Silence
(n = 16)

	Baseline		Aural cond 1		Music 1		Aural cond 2		Music 2		Aural cond 3		Music 3		Aural cond 4		Music 4		Aural cond 5		Music 5	
	L	R	L	R	L	R	L	R	L	R	L	R	L	R	L	R	L	R	L	R	L	R
F	25.0	29.3	24.3	41.1	22.0	34.9	21.0	37.9	15.6	36.8	26.6	32.4	24.8	31.3	19.0	37.3	18.3	31.8	20.8	30.3	17.3	31.5
M	21.5	30.5	25.3	32.1	20.8	37.0	19.8	36.1	21.5	36.6	25.6	37.6	27.5	42.3	23.4	36.8	18.9	41.5	22.4	37.6	22.5	38.6

Figure 24.1

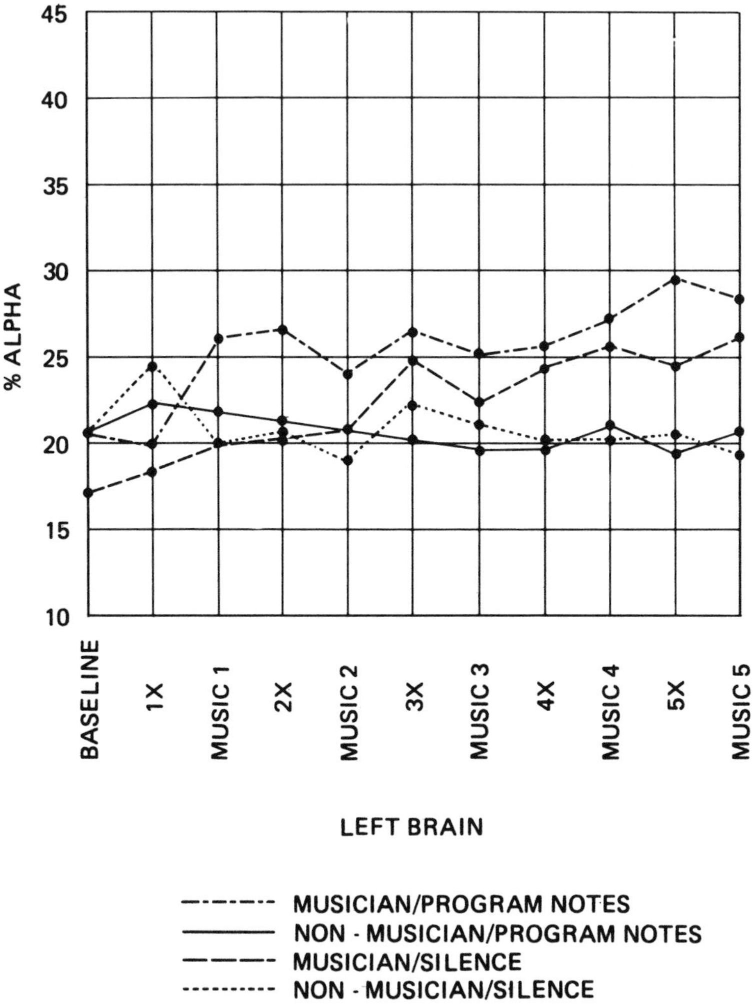
45
40
35
30
25
20
15
10
% ALPHA
BASELINE
1X
MUSIC 1
2X
MUSIC 2
3X
MUSIC 3
4X
MUSIC 4
5X
MUSIC 5
LEFT BRAIN
MUSICIAN/PROGRAM NOTES
NON - MUSICIAN/PROGRAM NOTES
MUSICIAN/SILENCE
NON - MUSICIAN/SILENCE

Figure 24.2

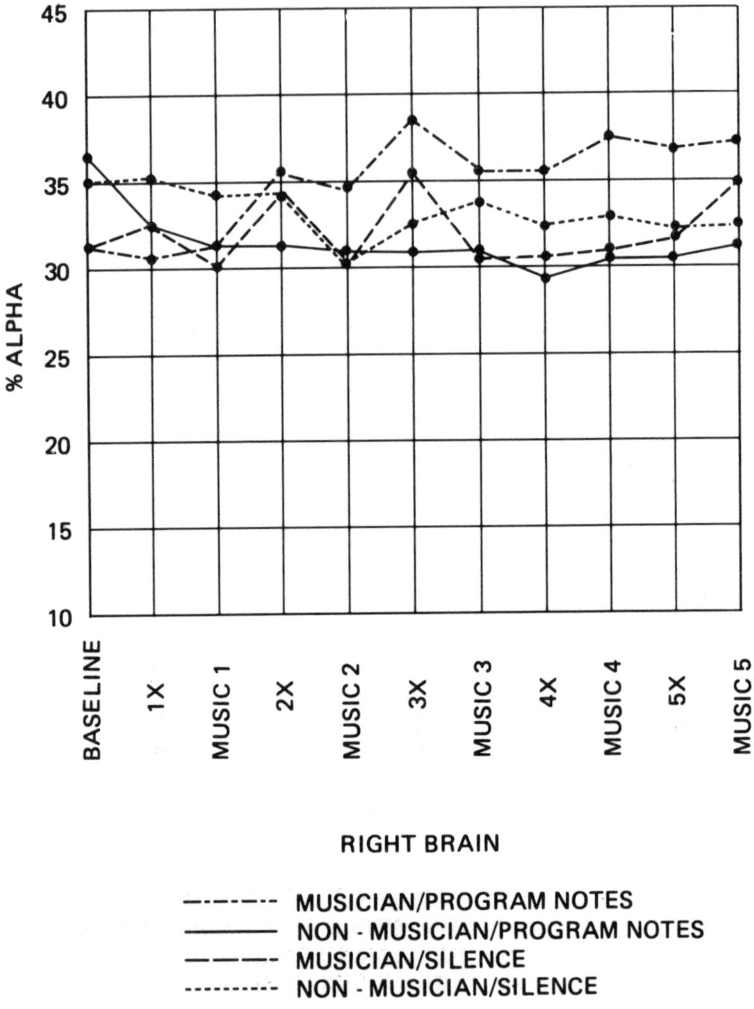
45
40
35
30
25
20
15
10
% ALPHA
BASELINE
1X
MUSIC 1
2X
MUSIC 2
3X
MUSIC 3
4X
MUSIC 4
5X
MUSIC 5
RIGHT BRAIN
MUSICIAN/PROGRAM NOTES
NON - MUSICIAN/PROGRAM NOTES
MUSICIAN/SILENCE
NON - MUSICIAN/SILENCE

Figure 24.3

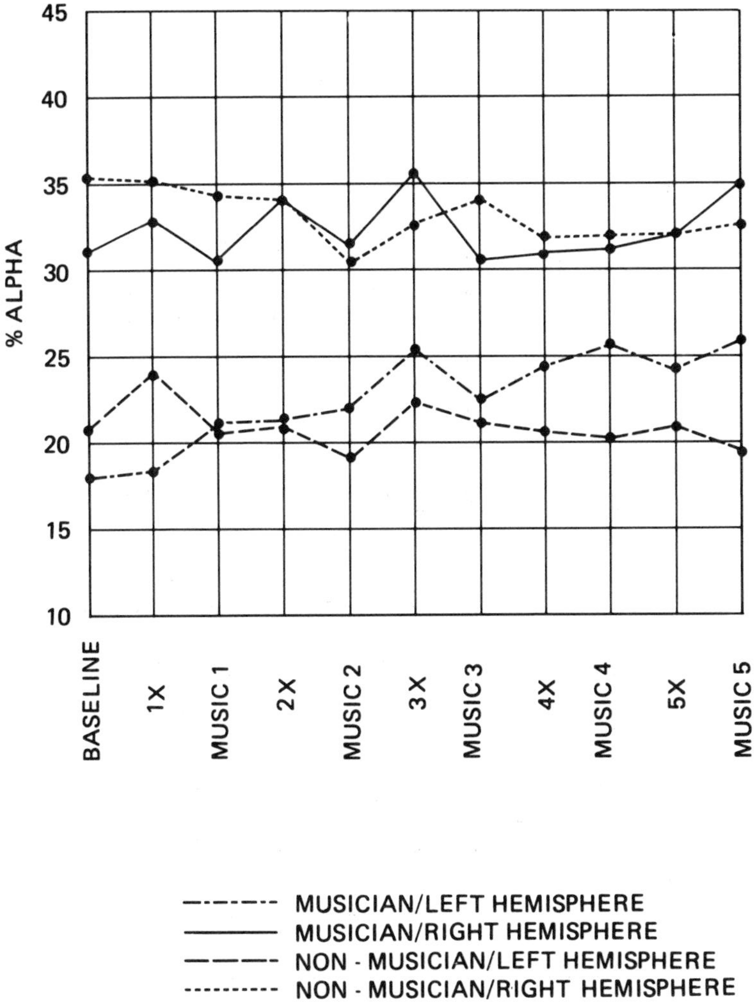
45
40
35
30
25
20
15
10
% ALPHA
BASELINE
1X
MUSIC 1
2X
MUSIC 2
3X
MUSIC 3
4X
MUSIC 4
5X
MUSIC 5
MUSICIAN/LEFT HEMISPHERE
MUSICIAN/RIGHT HEMISPHERE
NON - MUSICIAN/LEFT HEMISPHERE
NON - MUSICIAN/RIGHT HEMISPHERE

Figure 24.4

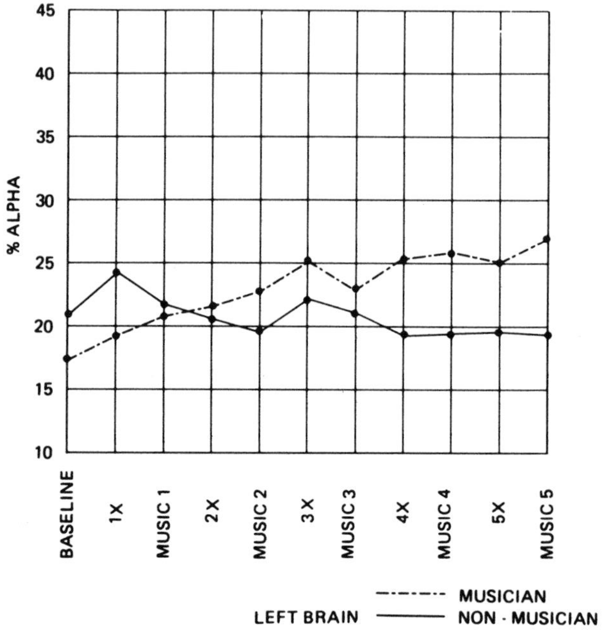
45
40
35
30
25
20
15
10
% ALPHA
BASELINE
1X
MUSIC 1
2X
MUSIC 2
3X
MUSIC 3
4X
MUSIC 4
5X
MUSIC 5
MUSICIAN
LEFT BRAIN
NON - MUSICIAN

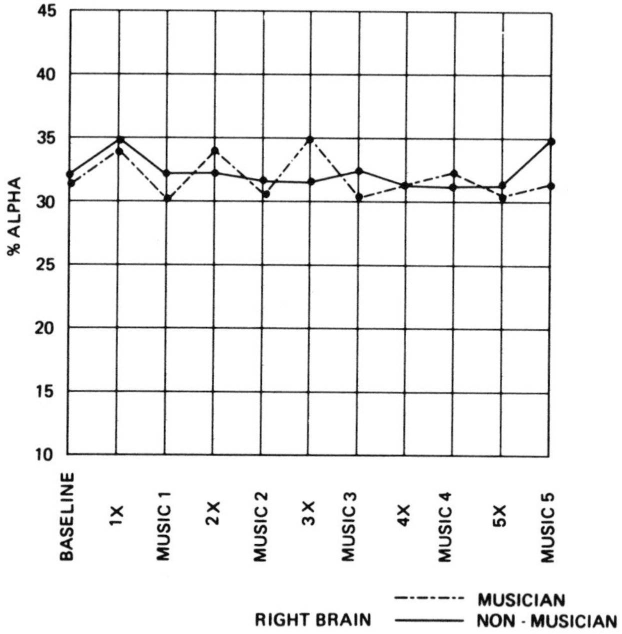
45
40
35
30
25
20
15
10
% ALPHA
BASELINE
1X
MUSIC 1
2X
MUSIC 2
3X
MUSIC 3
4X
MUSIC 4
5X
MUSIC 5
MUSICIAN
RIGHT BRAIN
NON - MUSICIAN

Figure 24.5

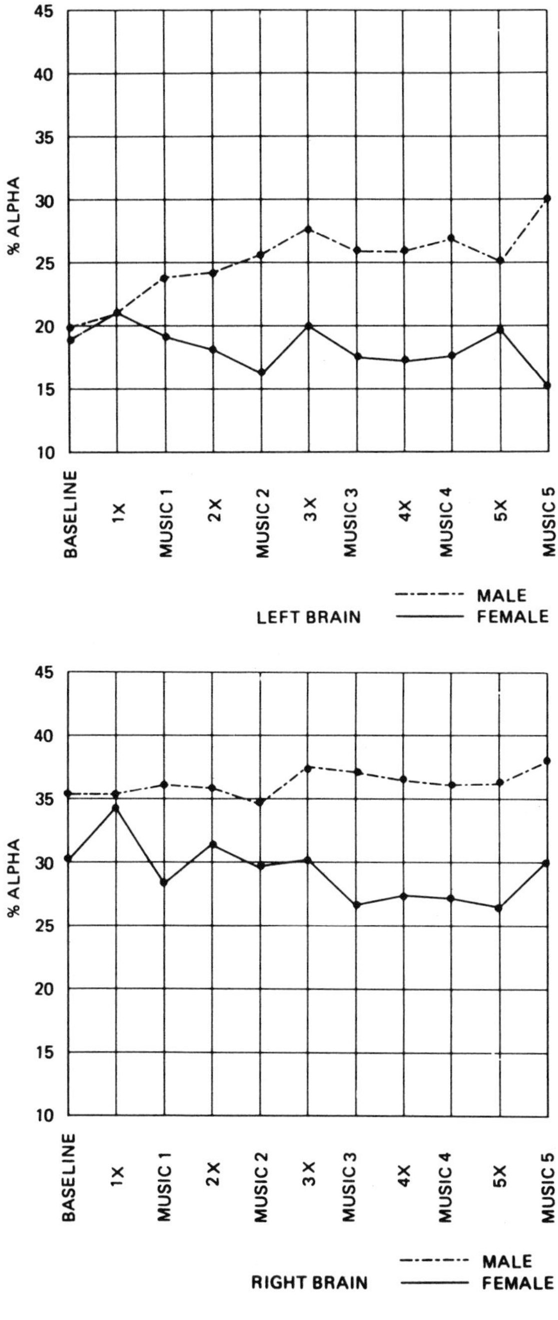
45
40
35
30
25
20
15
10
% ALPHA
BASELINE
1X
MUSIC 1
2X
MUSIC 2
3X
MUSIC 3
4X
MUSIC 4
5X
MUSIC 5
MALE
FEMALE
LEFT BRAIN
45
40
35
30
25
20
15
10
% ALPHA
BASELINE
1X
MUSIC 1
2X
MUSIC 2
3X
MUSIC 3
4X
MUSIC 4
5X
MUSIC 5
MALE
FEMALE
RIGHT BRAIN

Figure 24.6

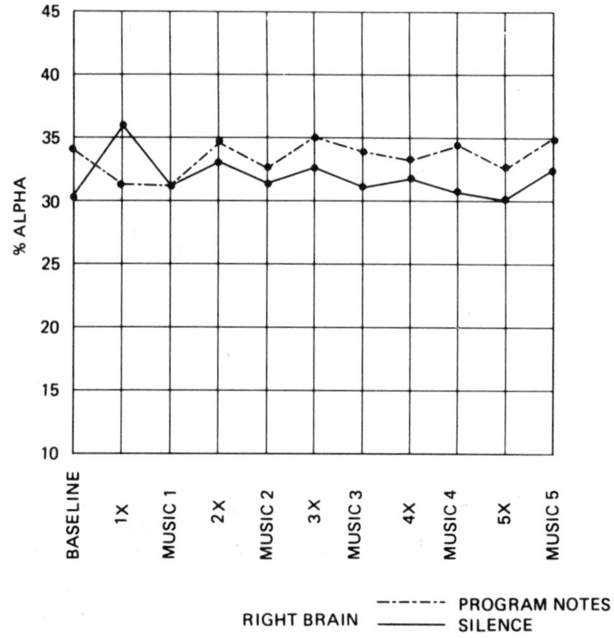
45
40
35
30
25
20
15
10
% ALPHA
BASELINE
1X
MUSIC 1
2X
MUSIC 2
3X
MUSIC 3
4X
MUSIC 4
5X
MUSIC 5
PROGRAM NOTES
RIGHT BRAIN
SILENCE

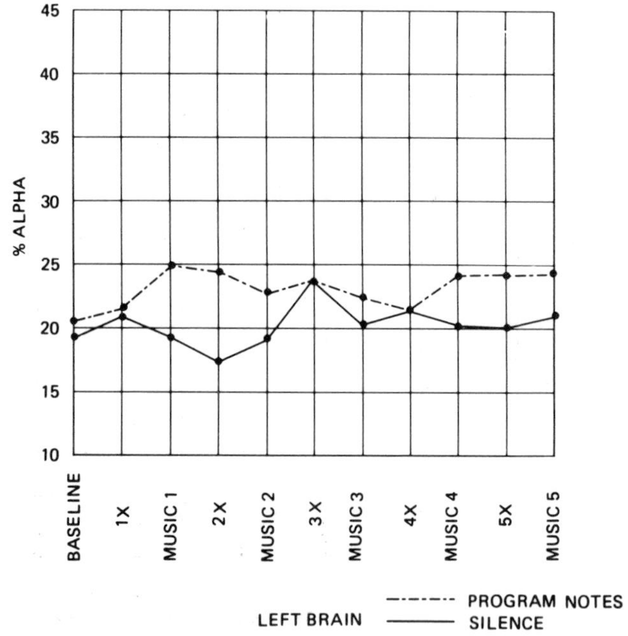
45
40
35
30
25
20
15
10
% ALPHA
BASELINE
1X
MUSIC 1
2X
MUSIC 2
3X
MUSIC 3
4X
MUSIC 4
5X
MUSIC 5
PROGRAM NOTES
LEFT BRAIN
SILENCE

to the male/female variable and to right/left hemisphere differences. Ray, Morell, Frediani, & Tucker (1976) have reported these same differences and state that, though males and females process the same information, they do so with different patterns of brain activity. The six significant interaction effects listed in Table 24.1 are all related to the sex variable. A careful perusal of Figure 24.4 shows that alpha content of males and females grows more disparate as the experimental period continues. This trend seems to affect both hemispheres. Reasons for this trend are unclear, but may be due to the way that males and females process information.

The traditionally higher alpha production of the musician population over non-musicians is not present in this study, as can be seen in Figure 24.4. The differences in alpha production reported in previous research (Wagner, 1975; Wagner & Menzel, 1978) are possibly attributable to whether subjects' eyes remained open or were closed. In the earlier studies, subjects were told to keep them gently closed. The present research is the first investigation in which they have been instructed to keep them open. The experimental decision to have them do so was made during the early planning stages of this project. Questions now raised by the lack of differences in alpha brainwave production between the musician and non-musician populations remain unanswered until further investigation can be completed. If differences are found between eyes open and eyes closed for musicians and non-musicians while listening to music, this will provide evidence why the 32 musician subjects in this study produced alpha brainwaves that were not significantly different from the 32 non-musician subjects.

Figure 24.3 illustrates the disparity between the brain's hemispheres with regard to alpha brainwave content. The right hemisphere produces up to 15% more alpha than the left regardless of a subject's musical training.

Some mention should be made about the musician and non-musician populations in this study. Some of the subjects defined as musicians for this investigation were quite insensitive to music and performed poorly. And, of course, some subjects were consummate musicians who were extremely sensitive to music. Conversely, a portion of those who were defined as non-musicians in this study were far more sensitive to things musical than many in the musician population. It may be assumed that a bell-shaped curve exists with regard to musicality in each of these two experimental groups. How much overlap exists between the two is an area of some concern. Perhaps future research should take special care to define an archetypical musician population containing only the finest, most sensitive musicians and non-musicians whose contact with music is as close to nonexistent as possible in our society. If this kind of dichotomous population can be delimited and tested, new understanding can possibly be brought to already extant data.

Regardless of hemispheric origin, a high percentage of alpha brainwaves is often associated with an increased theta wave content. A high percentage of beta waves is associated with a decreased theta content. It should not be assumed that the remaining percentage of any given alpha content is solely beta production. Indeed, the higher the alpha content for any subject, the higher the theta brainwave content in both hemispheres.

The degree of confusion in interpretation might best be highlighted by a possibly apocryphal story told about the late Albert Einstein. It seems that a team of researchers at Princeton University were recording his EEG. They watched a rather high content of alpha brainwaves, which usually indicates the brain's "idling activity" or "relaxed wakefulness." Generally, alpha activity is "blocked" by beta brainwaves when the brain is aroused with intense activity.

When the researchers started recording the EEG, Einstein was working through and solving quadratic equations "in his head." Yet the EEG revealed that his alpha brainwave content was very high. Suddenly, the alpha content disappeared and was replaced with only beta activity. Alarmed, the researchers rushed to his side and asked what the matter was. "I hear it raining outside," replied the world's greatest scientist, "And I've left my rubbers at home!"

It should be remembered that Albert Einstein was a fine musician.

25 Background Music: Competition for Focus of Attention

Clifford K. Madsen

Summary

These studies question the concept of "background music" in relationship to situations that require a person to concentrate. Data indicate that, though a person can go back and forth from one task to another much like a computer "timeshares," simultaneous input or the ability to concentrate on *both* tasks may not be possible.

All aspects concerning background music need to be carefully examined in order to determine precise effects. This type of music may actually be detrimental to what is perceived as the primary task (i.e., when a person phases music out of awareness in order to concentrate on a more important task). Also, music listening skills (e.g., aural discriminations) might suffer from repeated situations where music is not "listened to" with a high degree of concentration, thus diminishing the enjoyment of music listening.

Design: Two experiments: (1) posttest only with (2) partial replication
N = 300; 50 Groups: 6; 1
Statistical Analysis: Mean test scores with standard deviations
Independent Variables: Music listening, reading task
Dependent Variables: Music test scores, reading test scores
Music: Listening

* * *

It appears axiomatic that an important purpose for music performance is that it have an attentive audience. The history of music education represents an extended chronicle of providing experiences in both performing and attending to music. Yet, though attention to music remains as a paramount educational goal, music as background also seems in great evidence. Perhaps because of its unobtrusive acoustical properties, music has come into the general environment with relative ease. Also, its pairing with television, movies, dancing, and other activities provides a situation where it often takes a subservient role to other "messages." Such is the case in advertisements and perhaps even in the total impact or perceived "gestalt" as in the case with dance and drama.

Although it is not necessary to excise music from its many useful and aesthetically supportive roles, it appears questionable to not differentiate attentive music listening from other aural experiences where one obviously does not even discriminate whether or not the music is "off" or "on" (Madsen & Madsen, 1978).

Rationale for explaining the varied and often contradictory findings of research in the general area of background music has been discussed by Wolfe (1983, p. 191):

> Within the past several decades, a number of studies have appeared in professional literature concerning the effects of background music on human performance. These studies have reported inconsistent results, with some researchers concluding that music can enhance performance, others stating that music seems to interfere with various tasks, and still others claiming that music has no effect on performance behavior. A close examination of many of these publications reveals studies that have used numerous and varied independent and dependent measures that may have contributed to the differences in research conclusions and interpretations.

Some recent research reports have dealt with an aspect of background music that appears outside those variables usually investigated. This aspect concerns competition for attention. The thrust of this specific research presupposes that concentration on a task might preclude even peripheral awareness of competing tasks at the exact same instant in time. Thus, when music becomes a competing factor in relation to another task, the music may be phased out of awareness (ignored) in order that the person can attend to the primary task. (Geringer & Nelson, 1979; Greenwald, 1978; Madsen & Wolfe, 1979; Wolfe, 1980, 1982). Thus, this research suggests that a person is capable of attending to only one primary task at a time, though one can go back and forth very quickly perhaps as a computer is capable of split-second "timesharing." This line of research does not attempt to argue against the affective results associated with background music (Friedrich, 1984), to suggest that environmental music might not be useful in promoting better work environments (Uhrbrock, 1961), financial gain (Milliman, 1982), socialization (Stratton & Zalanowski, 1984), or even in providing distracting "clutter" for those persons who either prefer or sometimes find themselves in situations where music actually provides momentary release from the intensity of high-magnitude attentiveness or long periods of concentration. This research does not question arguments reported by some investigators that ambient music somehow finds its way into the body and elicits changes (Lozanov, 1979), though there do appear to be problems concerning fully operationalized replication, as discussed by Wagner and Tilney (1983).

The thrust of the current line of research is to test the perception and performance of listeners in regard to their attentive listening versus their attention to other tasks when both are presented simultaneously and subjects are asked to attend to both. The inherent difficulty in structuring such a situation is to provide a musical task that demands concentration and is capable of being measured as well as to provide another competing task that also can be measured. To accomplish both tasks, a tape recording consisting of musical examples and narration was presented simultaneously with a reading comprehension task simulating the Graduate Record Examination (GRE). Two multiple-choice tests, respectively, covering each task were also administered simultaneously to assess the relative gains attributable to either task.

Thus, the current investigation(s) were designed to test the ability of subjects to actually attempt two simultaneous tasks: take a test covering a music listening presentation; and take a reading comprehension test.

Experiment 1

Method

Three hundred undergraduates and graduates served as subjects. Subjects were randomly assigned to one of six groups: (1) reading comprehension test; (2) music listening test; (3) simultaneous reading comprehension and music listening tests; (4) reading comprehension test with musical examples from music listening test as background; (5) music listening test without musical examples (script only); and (6) reading comprehension test with varied background music chosen by the experimenter and different for each student.

On entering the testing room, individual subjects were given a test booklet(s) and instructed to read the cover page, which contained a short description of the task(s). Subjects in the reading comprehension groups (1, 4, and 6) were instructed as follows:

> Reading Comprehension: Simulated preparation for the Graduate Record Examination (GRE)

On the following pages, reading exercises are provided. Each consists of passages and 50 questions on these passages. Remember to try to answer each question intelligently and correctly. You must be thoughtful; you must go back to the text in order to find a justification for whatever answer you choose. You will be allowed 40 minutes for this task.

Subjects in the music listening test (Group 2) were instructed as follows:

This tape recorder presentation concerns "Technology—The Leader of Jazz and Pop." This 40-minute presentation concerns changes in musical style attributable to scientific advances tracing 100 years of science and sound. Please complete the 25 multiple-choice test questions as you listen to the narration and music examples.

Subjects in the simultaneous reading comprehension *and* music listening group (3) were instructed as follows:

This is an experiment having to do with concentration and attention. You have two tasks to complete *simultaneously.* One task has to do with the material that you will hear via the tape recorder. This tape recorder presentation concerns "Technology—The Leader of Jazz and Pop." This 40-minute presentation concerns changes in musical style attributable to scientific advances tracing 100 years of science and sound. Please complete as many of the 25 multiple-choice test questions as you can as you listen to the narration and music examples.

The second task is to read the selections from the reading material on the following pages. Each consists of passages and 50 questions on these passages. Remember to try to answer each question intelligently and correctly. You must be thoughtful; you must go back to the test in order to find a justification for whatever answer you choose.

Remember that you should work on each of these tasks concurrently—going back and forth with as much accuracy as possible. You will be allowed 40 minutes for completion of both tasks.

Subjects in the music listening test without musical examples (script only) were instructed as follows:

This narration (script) concerns changes in musical style attributable to scientific advances tracing 100 years of science and sound. Please complete the 25 multiple-choice test questions as you read through the script. You will be allowed 40 minutes for this task.

Following the timed experimental testing period, booklets were immediately collected, and then the subjects in Groups 3, 4, and 6 were given a questionnaire to complete. The questionnaire asked:

1. Do you usually study with music? Yes/No
2. If yes, what type of music?
3. Did you recognize any of the selections played? Yes/No
4. If yes, please list.
5. Did the musical selections interfere with your reading? Yes/No
6. If yes, what aspects of the music seemed to interfere the most?

Group 6 was comprised equally of subjects responding "yes" and subjects responding "No" to the first question. The simulated GRE reading comprehension task was taken from Barron's *How to Prepare for the GRE* (Brownstein & Weiner, 1982). The music listening task consisted of "Technology—The Leader of Jazz and Pop" (Wagner, 1978), presented via tape recorder. A 25-item multiple-choice test was developed from the script (narration) *and* the musical examples (reliability .82 Spearman-Brown corrected). The musical examples used for the technology tape (Groups 2 and 3) and presented as background music (Group 4) covered a wide range of styles and performing media and are presented in table 25.1. All aural stimuli were presented at dBA = 75.

Results

Results are presented in table 25.2. It is seen that the mean score for subjects in Group 1 (reading only) is 31.74. The means for comparable groups with background music, Group 4 and Group 6, are 31.04 and 31.78, respectively. The small differences across these scores would indicate that there is almost no difference among those subjects who took the reading test with music compared to those who did not.

The scores for the music test including musical examples with narration was M = 18.94 (Group 2), and the mean for the group who received only the written narrative was 9.18 (Group 5), indicating that the music examples did contribute to increased scores on the multiple-choice music test. Total scores for Group 6 were almost identical to Group 4 scores, though it should be remembered that Group 6 was equally comprised of subjects who *usually* study to music (n = 25) versus those who *never* study to music (n = 25). A difference in scores between those who usually study with music compared to those who never study with music (33.92 vs. 29.64) indicates that music might be more distracting to those subjects who never study to music.

Table 25.1
Discography and Bibliography (in order of presentation)

"Enoch Light Presents Urbie Green and Twenty-One Trombones," "Stardust," Project 3, PR 50145D

Eastman Wind Ensemble, "Music of the Civil War," "Dixie," Mercury Records

"Anthology of the Banjo," Erik Darling, "Banjo Tune," Everest Tradition, 2077

Limelighters, "If I had a Hammer," RCA Victor

Scott Joplin, "Himself," Nonsuch Records

Eastman Wind Ensemble, "Music of the Civil War," "Listen to the Mockingbird," Mercury Records

Belgian Band Organ, "Rio Grande," Audio Fidelity, AFSD 5975

"Old Time Circus Calliope," "Marching Through Georgia," Audio Fidelity, AFSD 6127

"Trumpet Fair Organ," "Sadie Mae," "Under the Anhauser Busch," Audio Fidelity, AFSD 6181

Quote — *Music Educator's Journal,* Vol. 64, No. 4, Dec. 1977, "A Phonograph Album," p. 52.

Quote — "Voices of the Past," Center for Cassette Studies, Inc., Thomas Alva Edison

"Voices of the Past," Center for Cassette Studies, Inc., Thomas Alva Edison

Quote — *Music Educator's Journal,* Vol. 64, No. 4, Dec. 1977, "A Phonograph Album," p. 59

Victor Talking Machine Records, "Turkey in the Straw," 1915

"The Nude Carmen," Mercury, SRM-I-604

Benny Goodman, "King of Swing, Vol. I," "Ridin' High," Columbia, CL 817

Glen Gray, "Sounds of the Great Bands," "720 in the Books," Capital Records, W 1022

Jimmy Dorsey, "Dixie by Dorsey," "South Rampart Street Parade," Columbia, CL 608

Doris Day, "Greatest Hits," "Everybody Loves a Lover," Columbia, CL 1210

Stan Kenton, "Lush Interlude," Concerto to End All Concertos, Capital Records, T 1130

"Rock Begins, Vol. I," "Shake, Rattle, and Roll," Joe Turner, ATCO, SD 33-314

"Rock Begins, Vol. I," "There Goes My Baby," The Drifters, ATCO, SD 33-314

Don Ellis, "Electric Bath," "Open Beauty," Columbia, CS 9585

"Rock Begins, Vol. I," "Tweedle-Dee," LaVerne Baker, ATCO, SD 33-314

Emerson, Lake, and Palmer, "Pictures at an Exhibition"

Quote—Paul Ackerman, jacket notes, "Rock Begins, Vol. I," ATCO, SD 33-314

"Electronic Music," Lewin-Richter, "Study No. 1," Turnabout, TV 30045

Disneyland, "Main Street Electrical Parade," "Fanfare and Ostinato," WD-4

"Switched-Off Bach," Glen Gould, Piano, "Two Part Invention in F," Columbia, MS 7241

"Switched-On Bach," Walter Carlos, "Two Part Invention in F," Columbia, MS 7194

"Country Moog," "Switched on Nashville," Gil Trythall, Athena, 6003

Tomita, "Golliwog's Cake Walk," by Claude Debussy, RCA, ARL 1-0488

Thelma Houston, "I Got the Music in Me," title song, Sheffield Lab, SL7/SL8

The most important experimental group was Group 3 in that it was considered to be the primary experimental group, with all other groups functioning as controls. The scores for this group were: reading test, $M = 16.48$; music test, $M = 15.72$. Thus, when subjects were forced to complete two simultaneous (i.e., shared) tasks, their scores dropped appreciably when compared to the other groups. This finding was deemed to be the most important aspect of the study. In addition, subjects within this group indicated via the questionnaire that they found the simultaneous task of having to go back and forth between tasks to be highly frustrating and extremely difficult. Only 1 subject out of 50 was positive in stating, "Once I got used to it, I found it a pleasant challenge."

Results of the questionnaire given to Groups 3 and 4 indicated that 21% of the subjects usually study with music. All subjects within these groups recognized some of the music, but could list only 11% and 13%, respectively, of the selections played during the reading test. This is consistent with previous research (Wolfe, 1983), which suggests that familiarity does not affect academic performance. Subjects in Groups 3 and 4 were also asked if the music interfered with the reading test. A total of 48 subjects in Group 3 and 25 in Group 4 responded "Yes." In Group 6, subjects were specifically selected on the basis of *usually* versus *never* listening to music. Questionnaire results for this group were approximately the same as for the other groups:

Table 25.2

Reading and Music Test Score Means and Standard Deviations

	Group 1	Group 2	Group 3	Group 4	Group 5	Group 6
	Reading test: multiple-choice questions	Music test: multiple-choice aural listening to music examples with narration	Reading test and music test with music	Reading test and background music from music test	Music test: multiple-choice written narrative, *No* music examples	Reading test and varied background music
Experiment 1 $N = 300$	$M = 31.74$ SD 6.87 $n = 50$	$M = 18.94$ SD 2.27 $n = 50$	$M = 16.48$ SD 6.35; $M = 15.72$ SD 3.14; $n = 50$	$M = 31.04$ SD 7.17 $n = 50$	$M = 9.18$ SD 3.17 $n = 50$	$M = 31.78$ SD 8.51 $n = 50$ *Yes*—I usually study with music $M = 33.92$; $SD = 8.15$ $n = 25$ *No*—I never study with music $M = 29.64$; $SD = 8.47$ $n = 25$
	Reading test	Music test (same as Group 2 above)	Replicated reading test	Replicated music test with music		
Experiment 2 $N = 50$	$M = 31.63$ SD 6.78	$M = 18.96$ SD 2.62	$M = 31.32$ SD 7.45	$M = 18.84$ SD 2.26		

all subjects recognized some of the music, with only 10% correct selections listed. Most importantly, total *reading* scores were almost identical for Groups 4 and 6 and even Group 1 that did not have music. It is interesting to note, however, that in Group 6, which was selected on the basis of "Yes, I *usually* study with music" versus "No, I *never* study with music," a difference in reading scores is observed (*Yes*, $M = 33.92$; *No*, $M = 29.64$). Also, while all of the subjects who never studied with music found it distracting, 18 of 25 subjects who usually study with music also found it distracting. It should be remembered that music for Group 6 was varied individually and chosen by the experimenter. Many subjects complained that "this is not my type of music." This is an area that warrants additional research.

Experiment 2

Method

In a design that used subjects as their own controls, a second experiment was completed that attempted to increase scores by having subjects simultaneously deal with familiar material. Subjects in this experiment either took the reading test during one 40-minute period and then on a subsequent day took the music listening test or vice versa (split half rotation). Then, all 50 subjects took the exact same tests simultaneously during a third day (40-minute period). The design of this experiment was structured to determine if, having previously gone through the music and academic material, subjects would be able to increase their score(s). Also, because materials were identical to those used in the previous experiment, comparisons could also be made between experiments.

Results

Results of the second experiment replicated almost exactly those two groups in the previous study that completed the reading test (Experiment 2, $M = 31.63$ vs. Experiment 1, $M = 31.74$) and the music test (Experiment 2, $M = 18.96$ vs. Experiment 1, $M = 18.94$). It is interesting that when subjects attempted both tasks simultaneously the scores for each of the two shared tasks were almost exactly the same as they had been for the two tasks independently (see Table 25.2). Therefore, it did not seem that subjects were able to increase their scores, though there was also not a consequential drop. It would appear that, even having gone through the material and therefore having the advantage of remembering the two tasks, subjects could not increase performance. When these subjects are compared to Group 3 of Experiment 1, it is evident that their total scores were substantially higher.

Also, as in Group 3, subjects indicated via the questionnaire that they found it difficult and highly distracting. A questionnaire was given to this group that specifically asked subjects what strategy(s) they used to complete the two tasks. All subjects who responded ($n = 39$) indicated that they went to the other task when they were dealing with material that they remembered. Typical responses were, "I read the paragraph until I thought I needed to listen to the music, then I marked the music test and went back to the GRE" or "Once I made a decision on one test, I would go to the other."

Discussion

A broad overview of these studies would indicate that, when a task requires an individual to attend to music in some manner, this attention occupies a high degree of participant involvement, thus creating a reduction in other behavior. Alternately, in a situation where music becomes a competing factor in relationship to another task (such as reading), the music may actually be phased out of awareness in order for the person to attend to the primary task.

This research is consistent with other studies which suggest that there is really no such thing as simultaneous focus of attention, although opposing models have been proposed (Allport, Antonis, & Reynolds, 1972; Martin, 1977). If replication upholds these data, then implications in the areas of music education and therapy seem manifold. The most obvious is that music which is used as "background" might actually inhibit discriminatory listening. Also, perhaps the entire area of what constitutes appropriate music pairing needs attention in relationship to dance, movies, studying, and so on.

The questionnaire responses concerning what aspect of the music seemed to interfere most indicated that changes in volume, tempo, and instrumentation, including vocal text, were, in that order, most distracting. Attention to music *changes* might suggest that it is this aspect of background music that does or does not determine focus of attention. Indeed, music played at a soft or moderate volume without any abrupt changes may provide a pleasant sound environment in such places as department stores, supermarkets, restaurants, and places of employment without disrupting primary functions of work tasks, decision making and/or interpersonal conversations. People seem to adapt to certain continuous, predictable noises (Broadbent, 1971), and this may be the case with the ongoing nature of background music.

Certain music can mask other environmental sounds and may even facilitate concentration compared to more distracting music or ambient noise. When music becomes distracting, for example, due to its perceived change in loudness, tempo, or text, it might demand a momentary awareness. If the change becomes too demanding, it may be controlled by manipulating the volume level of the sound source or escaping from or avoiding that particular music or music environment. Yet, this may not be possible in educational settings and might actively interfere with student learning. Conducting music lessons in a quiet environment to minimize stimulation from other events while concentrating on appropriate musical tasks would seem most desirable.

Even those subjects who perceived the music as most distracting had reading scores that were not adversely affected when compared to other subjects. The inconsistency between self-reported attitudes concerning distractibility and performance scores has been previously reported (Moller, 1980; Slater, 1968; Smith & Morris, 1976; Williams, 1961; Wolfe, 1983). This psychological component may be important in other ways. The psychological cost of having to force attention could be detrimental when structuring teaching/learning situations.

It would appear that most subjects were aware of the background music to some degree, based on the recognition of the musical selections. Many were able to identify correctly at least two or three of the selections. Attending to and hearing a short musical phrase of a particular sound track may serve as an adequate prompt for correct recognition, requiring only momentary attentiveness to the background environment. Or some other aspect within the total environment might momentarily capture attention. Regardless, it would seem that humans are capable of "timesharing" quite effectively. This aspect, however, might indicate a greater need for music educators to focus attention rather than encouraging conflicting attentiveness.

Part VI
Conclusion

26 The Blind Musicians and the Elephant

Jere L. Forsythe

"The Blind Men and the Elephant"

by John Godfrey Saxe (1816–1887)

It was six men of Indostan
  To learning much inclined,
Who went to see the Elephant
  (Though all of them were blind),
That each by observation
  Might satisfy his mind.

The first approached the Elephant,
  And happening to fall
Against his broad and sturdy side,
  At once began to bawl:
"God bless me! but the Elephant
  Is very like a WALL!"

The second, feeling of the tusk,
  Cried, "Ho! what have we here
So very round and smooth and sharp?
  To me 'tis mighty clear
This wonder of an Elephant
  Is very like a SPEAR!"

The third approached the animal
  And happening to take

The squirming trunk within his hands,
Thus boldly up and spake:
"I see," quoth he, "the Elephant
Is very like a SNAKE!"

The fourth reached out an eager hand,
And felt about the knee
"What most this wondrous beast is like
Is mighty plain," quoth he:
"Tis clear enough the Elephant
Is very like a TREE!"

The fifth who chanced to touch the ear,
Said: "E'en the blindest man
Can tell what this resembles most;
Deny the fact who can,
This marvel of an Elephant
Is very like a FAN!"

The sixth no sooner had begun
About the beast to grope,
Than seizing on the swinging tail
That fell within his scope,
"I see," quoth he, "the Elephant
Is very like a ROPE!"

And so these men of Indostan
Disputed loud and long,
Each in his own opinion
Exceeding stiff and strong,
Though each was partly in the right,
And all were in the wrong!

* * *

A major challenge facing music educators today is to reconcile the diverse perspectives that surround and define the total profession. Considering the enormity of the undertaking, the "blind men and the elephant" metaphor is no exaggeration. One is justifiably overwhelmed, if not discouraged, by the limits of our understanding in the face of immense uncertainties. This is especially distressing when one is in need of answers for Monday morning. But where does one turn for those answers? What "anatomical perspective" provides the best approach to understanding? Of course, we may be forced to concede that no "best" approach exists but rather, indeed, that each will always be partly "in the right" though all remain "in the wrong."

More important, it may be necessary to foster a healthy tolerance for some uncertainty while still maintaining vigilance in our pursuit of understanding. This is not an unrealistic position to take. It is achieved, in part, by determining the differences among the various modes of understanding and then by recognizing the strengths and weaknesses associated with each. In higher education, this discriminating perspective is called a "scholarly attitude" and its purpose is to encourage a balance between advocacy and inquiry, between confidence and uncertainty. Music educators should reaffirm endorsement of a variety of "modes of inquiry," for this commitment is fundamental to an enlightened profession.

Developing a scholarly attitude does not mean abandoning personal biases or becoming dispassionate about all aspects of the profession. Rather, it is a posture through which one respects and values diversity while being able to justify allegiance to a particular perspective at a given time. That is, one might shift from one to another, circumstantially, but acknowledgment of this change should be forthcoming. Considering the complexity of issues and the myriad of influences impinging on the thoughts, actions, and feelings of music educators, becoming a discriminating observer seems especially critical today. Developing a satisfactory means of coping with diversity is important personally and professionally. In short, one's perspective influences one's ability to meet new demands and to grow.

Although numerous dimensions of the professional "anatomy" comprise music education, the following four sources of influence appear to have a prevailing impact upon the ideas and practice of music education: (1) personal experiences of teachers at every level of learning; (2) contributions of experts who have achieved status or recognition within the profession; (3) ideas of philosophers and theorists; and (4) findings derived through empirical investigations. These categorical generalizations will, of course, overlap to some extent. Nonetheless, the differentiations should prove useful even as the reciprocity among them is examined. Any analysis of the strengths and weaknesses of each must take into account the interconnections, if not the interdependence, of all modes, for herein lies the essence of understanding the total "elephant."

Personal Experiences. Clearly, a dominant force in the lives of music educators at every level is personal experience. After all, this is the most intimate, subjective, and pervasive basis for knowing anything. Therefore, relying upon it extensively is understandable and necessary. It is especially important as a source of influence upon teaching practices in classrooms. The teaching profession is replete with cliches that endorse this mode of knowing (e.g., "There's no substitute for experience." "Experience is the best teacher." "The only way to learn to teach is to teach.").

In a very realistic sense, teachers are obliged to proceed in teaching on a kind of "trial and error" basis. There is little time, or inclination, to consult all other sources, in proportion to the complexity of the tasks involved in daily teaching. Dependence upon one's own devices is both desirable and necessary—desirable when one is successful and necessary regardless.

At the same time, even first-year teachers do not enter classrooms like blind men groping about the elephant, hoping to emerge triumphantly from a series of random efforts. Each of us brings to our personal initiative a synthesis of previous influences, including elements from all modes of knowing. One of the most powerful is the personal experiences of colleagues, in which we may participate vicariously, either through observation or through hearing verbal descriptions (e.g., stories about teaching experiences told in college classrooms, teachers' lounges, etc.). Many teachers are also protégés of their mentors and seek to emulate a model. The notion that we "teach as we were taught" gives testament to this influence. Sometimes the effects of university-level teacher educators can be limited because of the impact of strong mentors, some of whom may even disdain the value of anything but experience ("What do those professors know anyhow?"). Ironically, many teacher educators emphasize their own personal experiences as a basis for teacher preparation.

Of course, a major strength of personal experience is the practical knowledge gained through it. Practicing teachers face reality daily as rehearsals, lessons, and student problems return with imminent regularity. Understandably, any input resulting from the other modes will receive its most challenging test on this "front line" of education. An educational theory, no matter how intellectually engaging, or a scientific finding, no matter how objectively derived, will have little impact upon the profession unless translated into useful aspects of the classroom.

Another important strength associated with personal experience is the deep personal satisfaction that often accompanies individual initiative and creativity. (In some instances even surviving may be an accomplishment!) Self-reliance is admired in our society and respect is given to those who seem to have "learned on their own." A certain "psychological ownership" and confidence is generated by direct experience when one is successful, and this may even lead to strong personal beliefs and assertions. Failure creates the opposite. Both results are related to the potential shortcomings of reliance upon personal experience.

In many ways, teaching can be a very lonely pursuit. Despite influences from other sources, teachers must rely largely on personal experiences, and this carries certain risks. One danger is that teachers might inordinately accept particular ideas, attitudes, and approaches that seem to be "working." Thus they become reluctant to explore alternate ones that might prove even better (e.g., "I've done it this way for years and it works."). Similarly, they may reject new ideas prematurely because they do not produce immediate results (e.g., "Oh, I tried that once. It didn't work.").

Development of successful teaching techniques, a meaningful philosophy, and appropriate attitudes often takes years of diligent effort. Teachers are obliged and free to do so, but self-deception must be avoided in the subjective domain of personal experience. Even the influence of close colleagues could be adverse when ideas are accepted or rejected too readily, so caution and concern are necessary (though without cold skepticism or pessimism). Passionate advocacy is not incompatible with openness. Professional growth depends upon one's inclination toward asking questions and seeking input, even when it concerns a "sacred" belief about the elephant.

Another weakness of the personal experience mode is that dissemination within the profession is relatively limited. Although some efforts have been made to increase public sharing of ideas through publications, the effects are undetermined. On the other hand, when a very successful teacher surfaces publicly, the potential for influence may be escalated, especially if the individual contributes openly through workshop presentations, articles, and so forth. If this contribution is convincing, widely recognized, and sustained for a long period of time, the individual will be considered as an expert.

Expert Opinion. The music education profession is blessed with many notable experts who have achieved status and recognition for their contributions. (None will be named for fear of omissions.) Often in great demand as clinicians, these individuals provide a rich resource for teachers at every level of learning. One of their strengths is their visibility because literally thousands of teachers attend their workshops and clinics. They provide not only a wealth of ideas, but they can also be inspiring. How often we see teachers so excited by a workshop or clinic that they vow, with renewed vigor, to return to their classroom a changed teacher, ready to share that borrowed spark with their students.

Often this reaction is attributable to the ability of experts to provide practical and useful information enthusiastically, convincingly, and even entertainingly. Although allusions may be made to some theoretical framework, or even research findings, the emphasis is often upon successful ideas drawn from the master teachers' own experiences. Although they may become associated with a college or university, their doctoral degrees, if possessed, are not the source of their credibility, especially with practicing teachers. Rather, the strength of their influence seems to lie in their ability to relate to the experiences of teachers while providing inspirational models. They are individuals who have emerged from the personal experience mode successfully and eminently. Their contributions are often the hallmarks of the profession, and pursuits within all the other modes can be influenced by their ideas.

Despite respectful advocacy of experts as a source of influence, a "scholarly attitude" invites a few cautionary considerations. The most obvious reservation is, of course, that their ideas may not be applicable in certain situations. In view of the tremendous diversity of schools, student backgrounds, teacher personalities, and resources, teachers must be discriminating in their response to experts. Numerous factors will affect the potential for incorporating the views of experts, and naive acceptance may lead to disappointing results. For example, it is unlikely that teachers will be able to duplicate, in any precise manner, a teaching approach demonstrated by an expert in one workshop. At best, these instances seem only to entice further pursuit, which make them no less worthwhile. Yet, to assimilate an influence in any significant way will take years of practiced emulation. To respond otherwise may even be an insult to the scope of an expert's contribution. Inspiration may initiate desires, but reinforcement will be needed for long-term effects. Moreover, one may even wonder whether being overly enthralled is always beneficial, as the following poem suggests:

> Oh Thou awe struck student of "The Master,"
> Does your mental state help you to learn faster?
> Or instead of more effort inspiring,
> Lead you to thoughts of early retiring?

In a similar vein, it is a poignant irony that teachers hold independence as a primary goal for their students, yet many appear too much in need of their own guru. A wise man once said: "Everyone wants disciples but no one wants to be surrounded by anyone dumb enough to be one" (Lewis Pankaskie, personal communication, Tallahassee, Florida). Thus, care should be taken in weighing the influence of experts. To partake of this influence yet to remain "one's own person," pursuit of an additional dimension seems necessary for independence—that which comes from analyzing and understanding all experiences from a theoretical and philosophical perspective.

The Philosophical-Theoretical Mode. Most music educators recognize the importance of the intellectual dimension of professional endeavors. Even the most pragmatic practitioners, for example, know the value of philosophical foundations, especially when called upon to defend a program that is threatened with elimination. The demand for relevance and practicality does not circumvent the need for enlightened thinking. Moreover, although the routines of active teaching may not be ideally conducive to reflective thought, numerous opportunities are provided for reconsideration of the philosophical and theoretical underpinnings of one's activities. Serving on a committee to develop a curriculum guide, for example, requires a balanced perspective between theory and practice. Attending conferences, reading articles, and taking university courses can provide occasions for reflection and analysis. Ideas are important because they give meaning, purpose, direction, and momentum to one's endeavors. Socrates felt the "unexamined life is not worth living"; an unexamined life of teaching will not be very satisfying and, ultimately, not very successful.

One of the strengths of philosophical and theoretical ideas is that they usually represent a synthesis of respected ideas from related disciplines (e.g., psychology, aesthetics, epistemology, and education). Gifted writers are able to draw upon these rich resources and formulate relevant notions for music education. The results are often compelling, stimulating, and useful. They may provide a framework for articulating a clearer understanding of the profession and a guide by which to make decisions. They may also provide an inspiring set of ideals to which the profession aspires, and they become a source of intriguing ideas for empirical investigation. Philosophy and theory both emanate from and lead toward research and practice in music education.

Another strength is that the method employed in developing philosophical and theoretical principles is a rather systematic one, which relies upon reason, logic, argument, and clarity of thought. The impact of intellectuals depends upon their ability to articulate ideas clearly, precisely, and convincingly. It is an admirable contribution and a necessary component of the music education enterprise. Insufficient commitment to the intellectual domain can lead to vulnerability, mimicry, naive discipleship, and dependency. In short, one must be a "thinker" and a "doer."

Several cautions are suggested by a "scholarly attitude" toward philosophy and theory. The most obvious weakness associated with this mode comes in the acid test of applicability. Although some philosophers and theorists may not feel obliged to reconcile their contributions in this manner, a rather large constituency in music education will judge ideas accordingly. That is, they will want to know if a particular idea is useful or not. That practical perspective is inevitable and justifiable, for without some translation into the "real world," philosophical and theoretical discourse might be regarded as an "academic" exercise. If this were to occur pervasively, adjunct but separate disciplines might even evolve almost inadvertently, perpetuated by intellectuals writing elegant thoughts to one another. Some would argue that this is not altogether undesirable, but generation of new parts of the anatomy, either by design or mutation, might result in a strange-looking elephant.

When an idea is "untestable," either in classrooms or experiments, a different manifestation of this mode is indeed created. Music education can enjoy its share of "unicorns" so long as one acknowledges certain assumptions. Beautiful ideas can be seductive and engaging, luring us into accepting them axiomatically. A "model" for learning, for example, may prove so intellectually convincing that it becomes intrinsically valued and considerable time is spent renewing one's faith in its constructs rather than in testing its validity in classrooms or even laboratories. Freud seems to have done this with his theory of sexual repression because he interpreted increasing numbers of behaviors as being symptomatic of this inner struggle. Behaviorists fall victim to this tautological tendency toward a unified theory when asserting that a reinforcer is a reinforcer because it reinforces. Breaking out of these closed systems may be difficult, but the demand for relevance makes it necessary.

In summary, the purpose of philosophy and theory is to provide the profession with intellectual foundations that illuminate our understanding of the processes of teaching and learning music. Although intellectual ideas may have a certain intrinsic integrity, their ultimate value will be judged according to their impact upon the evolution of music education.

Empirical Investigation. The importance of research is widely recognized in music education. The need for an objective means of developing a knowledge base is evident, and research is commonly viewed as a respectable and necessary approach. Although the methods of research may vary according to the nature of the problem, a reasonable range of acceptable approaches has evolved within the profession. The result is an intriguing mosaic of research findings reflecting a diversity of interests and approaches to problems in music education.

Interest in research has burgeoned in recent decades. In the late 1950s and early 1960s research sessions at MENC national conventions were sparsely attended because research was apparently viewed as a rather esoteric activity, pursued largely by strange individuals who seemed to like sitting in small, smoke-filled rooms listening to the droning of long papers. The situation is dramatically different today. Research "poster" sessions at professional conferences are heavily attended, not only by doctoral students and researchers, but by practitioners as well. This transition is the result of years of effort by researchers, many of whom pioneered the struggle to gain acceptance for this unique aspect of music education. Concurrent with this effort was the proliferation of graduate programs as well as doctoral degrees nationally and the establishment of a distinguished journal, the *Journal of Research in Music Education*. It gave the profession a scholarly format, similar to that available in other disciplines, and it also provided a visible endorsement of the various research modes of inquiry within the profession.

One of the strengths of the research dimension in music education is that it reflects the profession's commitment to the scholarly traditions so respected in other fields, and this is most tangibly represented within a scholarly journal.

Research is the profession's noblest attempt to seek verifications and, to some extent, generalizations, of those theories, opinions, and personal experiences generated from the other modes of inquiry. It is an organic and continuing process that demands a delicate balance between conclusion and uncertainty, belief and doubt. A "scholarly attitude" is historically associated with this mode, and no graduate education program would be complete without instruction in research methods. Likewise, no professional "anatomy" would be complete without a thorough understanding of this important dimension.

Due in part to the ongoing nature of research, one of the shortcomings related to research is that findings often appear tentative if not equivocal. Although this can be frustrating at times, it does not follow that "the only thing of which we are certain is that we are certain of nothing." Rather, one simply learns to view results with discretion and perspective. A related concern is that, in the interest of control, some types of research may at times appear to yield relatively inconsequential results. A certain amount of patient faith is required in the same way that the pieces of a mosaic are put into place. The relative historical youth of research in music education and the constant reminders of remaining questions accentuate this feeling of incompletion. But this process characterizes the evolution of knowledge in any discipline.

Another concern is dissemination. Despite the quality and quantity of current knowledge, it is often difficult to incorporate findings into the mainstream of music education. This may be attributable not to lack of generalizability of the results but to limitations in the means of conveying findings on a wide basis. For example, relatively few practitioners will seek information in research journals, even though useful knowledge can be found there. Dissemination through workshops is helpful but still limited in breadth of influence. A major challenge for researchers today is to find ways to contribute to the needs of the profession without jeopardizing the standards of intellectual inquiry that characterize the scholarly tradition. Reciprocity will be reinforced by having researchers respond more directly to the immediate needs of the profession and by having the profession, particularly as represented by practitioners, become more tolerant and understanding of the tentative nature of the research process. In a compelling sense, research provides a universal means through which the profession can seek unity by embodying the essence of the other modes of inquiry.

Each of the modes described above must be viewed in terms of its contribution to the total anatomy of the profession. A "scholarly attitude" requires a discriminating perspective achieved by recognizing differences and understanding various strengths and weaknesses associated with each mode. This does not suggest that one should simplistically conclude that all modes are really "saying the same thing." An eclectic view cannot be justified when it is burdened with inconsistencies or incompatibilities. A better view is the "partly right-partly wrong" dichotomy, for this acknowledges respect yet admits inconclusiveness. Thus, this attitude leads to the pursuit of understanding while accepting limitations. Professional unity may lie in the appreciation of this diversity.

References

Abeles, H. F. (1973). Development and validation of a clarinet performance adjudication scale. *Journal of Research in Music Education, 21,* 246–275.

Abeles, H. F., & Porter, S. Y. (1978). The sex-stereotyping of musical instruments. *Journal of Research in Music Education, 26*(2), 65–75.

Alley, J. M. (1978). Competency based evaluation of a music therapy curriculum. *Journal of Music Therapy, 15,* 9–14.

Alley, J. M. (1980). The effect of self-analysis of videotapes on selected competencies of music therapy majors. *Journal of Music Therapy, 17,* 113–132.

Alley, J. M. (1982). The effect of videotape analysis on music therapy competencies: An observation of simulated clinical activities. *Journal of Music Therapy, 19,* 141–160.

Alpert, J. I. (1980). The effect of disc jockey, peer, and music teacher approval of music on music selection and preference. *Dissertation Abstracts International, 40,* 5641A. (University Microfilms Order No. 8009822).

Alpert, J. I. (1982). The effect of disc jockey, peer, and music teacher approval of music on music selection and preference. *Journal of Research in Music Education, 30,* 173–186.

Allport, D. A., Antonis, B., & Reynolds, P. (1972). On the division of attention: A disproof of the single channel hypothesis. *Quarterly Journal of Experimental Psychology, 24,* 225–235.

Apel, W. (Ed.). (1969). *Harvard dictionary of music* (2nd ed., pp. 181, 791–792, 836–837 [excerpts]). Cambridge, MA: Belknap Press of Harvard University Press.

Arenson, M. (1982). The effect of a competency-based computer program on the learning of fundamental skills in a music theory course for non-majors. *Journal of Computer-Based Instruction, 9,* 55–58.

Arwood, B., Williams, R. L., & Long, J. D. (1974). The effects of behavior contracts and behavior proclamations on social conduct and academic achievement in a ninth-grade English class. *Adolescence, 9,* 425–436.

Astin, A. W. (1975). *Preventing students from dropping out.* San Francisco: Jossey-Bass.

Astin, A. W. (1977). *Four critical years: Effect of college on beliefs, attitudes, and knowledge.* San Francisco: Jossey-Bass.

Austen, M. P. (1977). The effects of music on the learning of random shapes and syllables with the institutionalized severely mentally retarded adolescent. *Contributions to Music Education, 5,* 54–68.

Avner, R. A. (1980). *A basic statistical service package.* Minneapolis: Control Data Corporation.

Baird, J. (1958). Music teaching competencies. *Journal of Research in Music Education, 6,* 25–31.

Baker, D. S. (1980). The effect of appropriate and inappropriate in-class song performance models on performance preference of third- and fourth-grade students. *Journal of Research in Music Education, 28,* 1–17.

Ballard, K. D., & Glynn, T. (1975). Behavioral self-management in story writing with elementary school children. *Journal of Applied Behavior Analysis, 8*, 387–398.

Bamberger, J. (1974). *What's in a tune?* Boston: MIT Artificial Intelligence Laboratory. (ERIC Document Reproduction Service No. ED 118 369).

Bartlett, J. D. (1977). Remembering environmental sounds: The role of verbalization at input. *Memory and Cognition, 5*(4), 404–414.

Baugh, J. C., & Baugh, J. R. (1965). The effects of four types of music on the learning of nonsense syllables. *Journal of Music Therapy, 2*(2), 69–72.

Baumann, V. H. (1960). Teenage music preferences. *Journal of Research in Music Education, 8*, 75–84.

Becker, W. C., & Engelmann, S. (1976). *Analysis of achievement data on six cohorts of low-income children from 20 school districts in the University of Oregon direct instruction follow through model.* Eugene: University of Oregon. (ERIC Document Reproduction Service No. ED 145 922).

Becker, W. C., Engelmann, S., & Thomas, D. R. (1971). *Teaching: A course in applied psychology.* Chicago: Science Research Associates.

Bennett, S. (1976). The process of musical creation: Interviews with eight composers. *Journal of Research in Music Education, 24*, 3–13.

Berliner, D. C., & Rosenshine, B. (1976). *The acquisition of knowledge in the classroom: Beginning teacher evaluation study* (Technical Report IV-1). San Francisco: Far West Laboratory for Educational Research and Development. (ERIC Document Reproduction Service No. ED 146 158).

Bettinson, G. (1976, March). *The relationship between the conservation of certain melodic materials and standard Piagetian tasks.* Paper presented at the Music Educators National Conference, Atlantic City.

Bibzak, R. F. (1975, December). The grading game in instrumental music: Alternative ways to beat it. *The School Musician, 47*, 36–37.

Birch, T. E. (1962). Musical taste as indicated by records owned by college students with varying high school music preferences. *Missouri Journal of Research in Music Education, 1*, 53–54.

Blacking, J. (1973). *How musical is man?* Seattle: University of Washington Press.

Bolstad, O. D., & Johnson, S. M. (1972). Self-regulation in the modification of disruptive classroom behavior. *Journal of Applied Behavior Analysis, 5*, 443–454.

Bonanno, D., Dougherty, N., & Feigley, D. (1978). Competency by contract: An alternative to traditional competency testing techniques. *Journal of Physical Education and Recreation, 49*, 49–51.

Borst, J. M., & Cooper, F. S. (1957). Speech research devices based on a channel Vocoder. *Journal of the Acoustical Society of America, 29*, 777.

Botvin, G. J. (1974). Acquiring conservation of melody and crossmodal transfer through successive approximation. *Journal of Research in Music Education, 22*, 226–233.

Bower, G. H., & Holyoak, K. (1973). Encoding and recognition memory for naturalistic sounds. *Journal of Experimental Psychology, 101*, 360–366.

Boyle, J. D., Hosterman, G. L., & Ramsey, D. S. (1981). Factors influencing pop music preferences of young people. *Journal of Research in Music Education, 29*, 47–55.

Brand, M. (1977). Effectiveness of simulation techniques in teaching behavior management. *Journal of Research in Music Education, 25,* 131–138.

Braswell, C., Decuir, A., & Maranto, C. D. (1980). Ratings of entry level skills of music therapy clinicians, educators, and interns. *Journal of Music Therapy, 17,* 50–69.

Braswell, C., Maranto, C. D., & Decuir, A. (1979). A survey of clinical practice in music therapy, Part II: Clinical practice, educational and clinical training. *Journal of Music Therapy, 16,* 50–69.

Broadbent, D. E. (1971). *Decision and stress.* New York: Academic Press.

Broden, M., Hall, R. V., & Mitts, B. (1971). The effect of selfrecording on the classroom behavior of two eighth grade students. *Journal of Applied Behavior Analysis, 4,* 191–199.

Brophy, J. (1981). Teacher praise: A functional analysis. *Review of Educational Research, 51,* 5–32.

Brophy, J. E., & Evertson, C. M. (1974). *Process-product correlations in the Texas teacher effectiveness study: Final report.* Austin, TX: Research and Development Center for Teacher Education. (ERIC Document Reproduction Service No. ED 091 394).

Brophy, J., & Evertson, C. (1976). *Learning from teaching: A developmental perspective.* Boston: Allyn & Bacon.

Brophy, J., & Good, T. L. (1984). *Looking in classrooms.* New York: Harper & Row.

Brophy, J., Rohrkemper, M., Rashid, H., & Goldberger, M. (1983). Relationships between teachers' presentations of classroom tasks and students' engagement in those tasks. *Journal of Educational Psychology, 75,* 544–552.

Brown, A. (1978a). *The effect of videotaped feedback on music teaching skills.* Paper presented at the National Symposium in Music Behavior, Atlanta.

Brown, A. (1978b). Effects of television on student music selection, music skills, and attitudes. *Journal of Research in Music Education, 26,* 445–455.

Brown, A., & Alley, J. M. (1983). Multivariate analysis of degree persistence of undergraduate music education majors. *Journal of Research in Music Education, 31,* 271–281.

Brown, R. W., & Lennenberg, E. H. (1954). A study in language and cognition. *Journal of Abnormal and Social Psychology, 49,* 454–462.

Brownstein, S. C., & Weiner, M. (1982). *Barron's how to prepare for the Graduate Record Examination* (6th ed.). Woodbury, NY: Barron's Educational Series, Inc.

Burkett, L., & Darst, P. (1979). How effective is contract teaching in theory class? *Journal of Physical Education and Recreation, 50,* 86–87.

Campbell, D. T., & Stanley, J. C. (1963). *Experimental and quasi-experimental designs for research.* Chicago: Rand McNally & Co.

Canelos, J. J., Murphy, B. A., Blombach, A. K., & Heck, W. C. (1980). Evaluation of three types of instructional strategy for learner acquisition of intervals. *Journal of Research in Music Education, 28,* 243–249.

Cartwright, J., & Huckaby, G. (1972). Intensive preschool language program. *Journal of Music Therapy,* 9(3), 147–155.

Cassity, M. D. (1976). The influence of a music therapy activity upon peer acceptance, group cohesiveness, and interpersonal relationships of adult psychiatric patients. *Journal of Music Therapy, 13,* 66–76.

Chalmers, B. A. (1978). The development of a measure of attitude toward instrumental music style. *Journal of Research in Music Education, 26,* 90–96.

Chang, H. W., & Trehub, S. (1977). Auditory processing of relational information by young infants. *Journal of Experimental Child Psychology, 24,* 324–331.

Charboneau, M. L. (1981). The effect of bell-playing instruction and music listening on kindergarten students' preferences and attitudes. *Dissertation Abstracts International, 42,* 591A. (University Microfilms No. 8114197).

Chomsky, N., & Halle, M. (Eds.). (1968). *The sound pattern of English.* New York: Harper & Row.

Ciminillo, L. M. (1980). Discipline: The school's dilemma. *Adolescence, 15,* 1–12.

Clark, M. S., Milberg, S., & Erber, R. (1984). Effects of arousal on judgments of others' emotions. *Journal of Personality and Social Psychology, 46,* 551–560.

Cochran, D. J. (1980). Contracting in consultation: Training guidelines and examples. *Counselor Education and Supervision, 20,* 125–131.

Codding, P. A. (1983, November). *The effects of pitch discrimination training on guitar tuning accuracy and time.* Paper presented at the meeting of the National Association for Music Therapy, New Orleans.

Conklin, D. N. (1983). A study of computer-assisted instruction in nursing education. *Journal of Computer-Based Instruction, 4,* 131–144.

Cope, G., & Hannah, W. (1975). *Revolving college doors: The causes and consequences of dropping out.* New York: John Wiley.

Corder, B. F., Haizlip, T., Whiteside, R., & Vogel, M. (1980). Pre-therapy training for adolescents in group psychotherapy: Contracts, guidelines, and pre-therapy preparation. *Adolescence, 15,* 699–706.

Cossairt, A., Hall, V., & Hopkins, B. L. (1973). The effects of experimenter's instructions, feedback, and praise on teacher praise and student attending behavior. *Journal of Applied Behavior Analysis, 6,* 89–100.

Darrow, A. A. (1984). A comparison of rhythmic responsiveness in normal and hearing impaired children and an investigation of the relationship of rhythmic responsiveness to the suprasegmental aspects of speech perception. *Journal of Music Therapy, 21*(2), 48–66.

Deikman, A. J. (1973). Bimodal consciousness. In Ornstein, R. E. (Ed.), *The nature of human consciousness: A book of readings* (pp. 67–86). New York: Viking Press.

Dennis, C. C. (1977). The conditioning of a pitch response using uncertain singers. In Madsen, C. K., Greer, R. D., & Madsen, C. H., Jr. (Eds.), *Research in music behavior: Modifying music behavior in the classroom* (pp. 139–150). New York: Teachers College Press.

Deutsch, D. (1982). *The psychology of music.* New York: Academic Press.

Dillon, J. (1981). Duration of response to teacher questions and statements. *Contemporary Educational Psychology, 6,* 1–11.

Dimitroff, J. F. (1974). Student persistence. *College and University, 49,* 553–567.

DiSilvestro, F. R., & Markowitz, H. (1982). Contracts and completion rates in correspondence study. *Journal of Educational Research, 75,* 218–221.

Donington, R. (1960). *Tempo and rhythm in Bach's organ music* (p. 13). London: Hinrichsen Edition, Ltd.

Dorhout, A. J. (1980). An investigation into the nature of tempo perception. *Disser-*

tation Abstracts International, 40, 5354A–5355A. (University Microfilms No. 8007367).

Dorow, L. G. (1977). The effect of teacher approval/disapproval ratios on student music selection and concert attendance. *Journal of Research in Music Education, 25,* 32–40.

Dowling, W. J. (1982). Melodic information processing and its development. In Deutsch, D. (Ed.), *The psychology of music* (pp. 413–429). New York: Academic Press.

Dowling, W. J., & Bartlett, J. C. (1981). The importance of interval information in longterm memory for melodies. *Psychomusicology, 1,* 30–49.

Drake, A. H. (1968). An experimental study of selected variables in the performance of musical durational notation. *Journal of Research in Music Education, 16,* 329–338.

Duke, R. A., & Prickett, C. A. (1982). *The effect of pitch discrimination training on guitar students' tuning accuracy.* Unpublished manuscript, The Florida State University, Tallahassee.

Eckland, B. K. (1964). College dropouts who came back. *Harvard Educational Review, 34,* 402–420.

Eisenstein, S. R. (1974). Effect of contingent guitar lessons on reading behavior. *Journal of Music Therapy, 11,* 138–146.

Eisenstein, S. R. (1979). Grade/age level and the reinforcement value of the collective properties of music. *Journal of Research in Music Education, 27,* 76–86.

Ellis, H. C. (1978). *Human learning, memory and cognition* (2nd. ed.). Dubuque, IA: Wm. C. Brown Company, Publishers.

Etzkorn, P. K. (1964). The relationship between musical and social patterns in American popular music. *Journal of Research in Music Education, 12,* 279–286.

Everitt, B. S. (1977). *The analysis of contingency tables.* New York: Halsted Press.

Farnsworth, P. R. (1969). *The social psychology of music* (2nd. ed.). Ames, IA: Iowa State Press.

Feather, N. T., & Simon, J. G. (1975). Reactions to male and female success and failure in sex-linked occupations: Impressions of personality, causal attributions, and perceived likelihood of different consequences. *Journal of Personality and Social Psychology, 31,* 20–31.

Feinberg, S. (1973). A creative problem-solving approach to the development of perceptive music listening in the secondary school music literature class. *Dissertation Abstracts International, 34*(2), 806A. (University Microfilms No. 73-18, 722).

Ferencz, G. J. (1983). Part I: Four movements in literary forms (original composition); Part II: Rhythmic proportion and tempo: An inquiry into temporal displacement in artistic performance and its relationship to tempo. *Dissertation Abstracts International, 43,* 2149A. (University Microfilms No. DEP82-27956).

Fetters, W. B. (1977). *Withdrawal from institutions of higher education: An appraisal with longitudinal data involving diverse institutions.* National Longitudinal Study, National Center for Educational Statistics. Washington, DC: United States Office of Education.

Fishbein, M. (1967). Attitude and the prediction of behavior. In Fishbein, M. (Ed.), *Readings in attitude theory and measurement* (pp. 447–492). New York: Wiley.

Fixen, D. L., Phillips, E. L., & Wolf, M. M. (1972). Achievement place: The reliability of self-reporting and peer-reporting and their effects on behavior. *Journal of Applied Behavior Analysis, 5,* 19–32.

Fleming, J. L. (1953). The determination of musical experiences designed to develop musical competencies required of elementary school teachers in Maryland. *Journal of Research in Music Education, 1,* 59–67.

Flohr, J. (1979). Musical improvisation behavior in young children. *Dissertation Abstracts International, 40*(10), 5355A. (University Microfilms No. 8009033).

Flohr, J. W. (1982, February). *A comparison of relative and harmonic tuning for guitar.* Paper presented at the meeting of the Texas Music Educators' Association, San Antonio.

Flohr, J. W., & Brown, J. (1979). The influence of peer imitation on expressive movement to music. *Journal of Research in Music Education, 27,* 143–148.

Flowers, P. J. (1982, October). *Attention to elements of music and effect of instruction in vocabulary on written descriptions of music by children and undergraduates.* Paper presented at the Fifth National Symposium for Research in Music Behavior, Tallahassee.

Flowers, P. J. (1983). The effect of instruction in vocabulary and listening on nonmusicians' descriptions of changes in music. *Journal of Research in Music Education, 31,* 179–190.

Fonagy, I., & Magdics, K. (1972). Emotional patterns in intonation and music. In Bolinger, D. (Ed.), *Intonation* (pp. 286–312). Baltimore: Penguin Books.

Forsythe, J. L. (1975). The effect of teacher approval, disapproval, and errors on student attentiveness: Music versus classroom teachers. In Madsen, C. K., Greer, R. D., & Madsen, C. H., Jr. (Eds.), *Research in music behavior* (pp. 49–55). New York: Teachers College Press.

Forsythe, J. L. (1977). Elementary student attending behavior as a function of classroom activities. *Journal of Research in Music Education, 25,* 228–239.

Forsythe, J. L., & Kelly, M. (1985). *The effects of visual-spatial added cues on melodic discrimination among fourth-grade pupils.* Unpublished manuscript, Ohio State University, Columbus.

Framer, E. M., & Sanders, S. H. (1980). The effects of family contingency contracting on disturbed sleeping behaviors in a male adolescent. *Journal of Behavior Therapy and Experimental Psychiatry, 11,* 235–237.

Freeman, P. (1981). *Discrimination of tempo changes in recorded piano music.* Unpublished master's thesis, McGill University, Montreal.

Friedrich, O. (1984, December 10). Trapped in a musical elevator. *Time,* pp. 110–116.

Frye, D., Rawling, P., Moore, C., & Meyers, I. (1983). Object-person discrimination and communication at 3 and 10 months. *Developmental Psychology, 19,* 303–309.

Fuego, V., Saudargas, R. A., & Bushell, D. (1975). Two types of feedback in teaching swimming skills to handicapped children. *Perceptual and Motor Skills, 40,* 963–966.

Fullard, W. G., Jr. (1977). Pitch discrimination in elementary school children as a function of procedure and age. In Madsen, C. K., Greer, R. D., & Madsen, C.

H., Jr. (Eds.), *Research in music behavior* (pp. 151–164). New York: Teachers College Press.

Fuller, F., & Manning, A. (1973). Self-confrontation reviewed: A conceptualization for video playback in teacher education. *Review of Educational Research, 43,* 469–520.

Furman, C. E. (1984). Behavior checklists and videotapes versus standard instructor feedback in the development of a music teaching competency. *Dissertation Abstracts International, 45*(9), 2793A. (University Microfilms No. DA8427300).

Furman, C. E., & Greenfield, D. G. (1983). *The effect of videotapes and behavior checklists on guitar performance.* Unpublished manuscript, The Florida State University, Tallahassee.

Gall, M. D., Ward, B. A., & Berliner, D. C. (1978). Effects of questioning techniques and recitation on student learning. *American Educational Research Journal, 15,* 175–199.

Galloway, H. F. (1975). A comprehensive bibliography of music referential to communicative development, processing disorders, and remediation. *Journal of Music Therapy, 12*(4), 164–196.

Garafalo, R. J., & Whaley, G. (1979). Comparison of the unit study and traditional approaches for teaching music through school band performance. *Journal of Research in Music Education, 27,* 137–142.

Garretson, R. L. (1970). *Conducting choral music* (3rd. ed.). Boston: Allyn & Bacon.

Geringer, J. M. (1976). Tuning preferences in recorded orchestral music. *Journal of Research in Music Education, 24,* 169-176.

Geringer, J. M. (1977). An assessment of children's musical instrument preferences. *Journal of Music Therapy, 14,* 172–179.

Geringer, J. M. (1978). Intonational performance and perception of ascending scales. *Journal of Research in Music Education, 26,* 32–40.

Geringer, J. M. (1982, July). *Verbal and operant music listening preferences in relationship to age and musical training.* Paper presented at the International Society of Music Educators Ninth International Seminar on Research in Music Education, London.

Geringer, J. M. (1983). The relationship of pitch-making and pitch-discrimination abilities of preschool and fourth-grade students. *Journal of Research in Music Education, 31,* 93–99.

Geringer, J. M., & McManus, D. (1979). A survey of musical taste in relationship to age and musical training. *College Music Symposium, 19,* 69–76.

Geringer, J. M., & Madsen, C. K. (1981). Verbal and operant discrimination/preference for tone quality and intonation. *Psychology of Music, 9,* 26–30.

Geringer, J. M., & Madsen, C. K. (1984). Pitch and tempo discrimination in recorded orchestral music among musicians and non-musicians. *Journal of Research in Music Education, 32*(3), 195–204.

Geringer, J. M., & Madsen, C. K. (1985, March). *Pitch and tempo preferences in recorded popular music.* Paper presented at the Research in Music Behavior Symposium, Fort Worth.

Geringer, J. M., & Nelson, J. K. (1979). Effects of background music on musical task performance and subsequent music preference. *Perceptual and Motor Skills, 49*, 39–45.

Geringer, J. M., & Nelson, J. K. (1980). Effects of guided listening on music achievement and preference of fourth graders. *Perceptual and Motor Skills, 51*, 1282.

Glynn, E. L., Thomas, J. D., & Shee, S. M. (1973). Behavioral self-control of on-task behavior in an elementary classroom. *Journal of Applied Behavior Analysis, 6*, 105–113.

Goldman, G. (1978). Contract teaching of academic skills. *Journal of Counseling Psychology, 25*, 320–324.

Gonzo, C., & Forsythe, J. (1976). Developing and using videotapes to teach rehearsal techniques and principles. *Journal of Research in Music Education, 24*, 32–41.

Good, T., & Brophy, J. (1974). Changing teacher and student behavior: An empirical investigation. *Journal of Educational Psychology, 66*, 390–405.

Goodwin, A. W. (1980). An acoustical study of individual voices in choral blend. *Journal of Research in Music Education, 28*(2), 119–128.

Gorder, W. (1976). An investigation of divergent production abilities as constructs of musical creativity. *Dissertation Abstracts International, 37*, 171A. (University Microfilms No. DCJ76-16136).

Gorder, W. D. (1980). Divergent production abilities as constructs of musical creativity. *Journal of Research in Music Education, 28*, 34–42.

Gordon, E. (1979). *Primary measures of musical audiation*. Chicago: GIA Publications.

Gordon, M. (1979). Instrumental music instruction as a contingency for increased reading behavior. *Journal of Research in Music Education, 27*, 87–102.

Grashel, J. W. (1979). Strategies for using popular music to teach form to intermediate instrumentalists. *Journal of Research in Music Education, 27*, 185–191.

Greenfield, D. G. (1978). Evaluation of music therapy practicum competencies: Comparison of self and instructor ratings of videotapes. *Journal of Music Therapy, 15*, 15–20.

Greenfield, D. G. (1980). The use of visual feedback in training music therapy competencies. *Journal of Music Therapy, 17*, 94–102.

Greenfield, D. G. (1982). *Behavior observations by computer in music therapy research.* Paper presented at the meeting of the National Association for Music Therapy, Baltimore.

Greenwald, M. A. (1978). The effectiveness of distorted music versus interrupted music to decrease self-stimulatory behaviors in retarded adolescents. *Journal of Music Therapy, 15*, 58–66.

Greer, R. D. (1978, November). *An operant approach to motivation and affect: Ten years of research in music learning.* Paper presented at the National Symposium on the Applications of Psychology to the Teaching and Learning of Music, Ann Arbor, MI.

Greer, R. D. (1980). *Design for music learning.* New York: Teachers College Press.

Greer, R. D. (1981). An operant approach to motivation and affect: Ten years of research in music learning. In Music Educators National Conference (MENC)

(Ed.), *Documentary report of the Ann Arbor symposium: National symposium on the applications of psychology to the teaching and learning of music* (pp. 101–121). Reston, VA: MENC.

Greer, R. D., Dorow, L., & Hanser, S. (1973). Music discrimination training and the music selection behavior of nursery and primary level children. *Council for Research in Music Education, 35*, 30–43.

Greer, R. D., Dorow, L. G., & Randall, A. (1974). Music listening preferences of elementary school children. *Journal of Research in Music Education, 22*, 284–291.

Greer, R. D., Dorow, L. G., Wachhaus, G., & White, E. R. (1973). Adult approval and students' music selection behavior. *Journal of Research in Music Education, 21*, 345–354.

Greer, R. D., Dorow, L., & Wolpert, R. (1978, April). *The effect of taught music effect on the learning ability of young children at cognitive tasks*. Paper presented at the Music Educators National Conference, Chicago.

Groisser, P. L. (1964). *How to use the fine art of questioning*. New York: Teacher's Practical Press.

Groves, W. C. (1966). Rhythmic training and its relationship to the synchronization of motor rhythm responses. *Dissertation Abstracts International, 27*, 702A. (University Microfilms No. 66-07037).

Hadding-Koch, K., & Studdert-Kennedy, M. (1964). An experimental study of some intonation contours. *Phonetica, 11*, 175–185.

Hair, H. I. (1977). Discrimination of tonal direction on verbal and nonverbal tasks by first-grade children. *Journal of Research in Music Education, 25*, 197–210.

Hair, H. I. (1981). Verbal identification of music concepts. *Journal of Research in Music Education, 29*, 11–21.

Hair, H. I. (1982a). Microcomputer tests of aural and visual directional patterns. *Psychology of Music, 10*(2), 26–31.

Hair, H. I. (1982b). Music terminology of children, college students, and faculty: Applications for computer-assisted lessons. In *Proceedings of the Association for the Development of Computer-Based Instructional Systems* (pp. 222–225). Vancouver, B.C.

Hair, H. I., & Graham, R. M. (1983). A comparison of verbal descriptors used by TMR students and music therapists. *Journal of Music Therapy, 20*(2), 59–68.

Hall, R. V. (1974). *Managing behavior, Part 1: Behavior modification: The measurement of behavior.* Lawrence, KS: H&H Enterprises.

Hall, R. V., & Hall, M. C. (1982). *How to negotiate a behavioral contract*. Lawrence, KS: H&H Enterprises.

Hall, S. M., Cooper, J. L., Burmaster, S., & Polk, A. (1977). Contingency contracting as a therapeutic tool with methadone maintenance clients: Six single subject studies. *Behavior Research and Therapy, 15*, 438–441.

Hanser, S. B., & Furman, C. E. (1980). The effect of videotape-based feedback versus field-based feedback on the development of applied clinical skills. *Journal of Music Therapy, 17*, 103–112.

Harding, R. E. M. (1938). *Origins of musical time and expression*. Cambridge, MA: Harvard University Press.

Harris, V. W., Bushell, D., Sherman, J. A., & Kane, J. F. (1975). Instructions, feedback, praise, bonus payments, and teacher behavior. *Journal of Applied Behavior Analysis, 8*, 462.

Hasselbring, T. S., & Duffus, N. A. (1981). Using micro-computer technology in music therapy for analyzing therapist and client behavior. *Journal of Music Therapy, 18*, 156–165.

Hayes, S. C., & Cavoir, N. (1977). Multiple tracking and the reactivity of self-monitoring: I. Negative behaviors. *Behavior Therapy, 8*, 819–831.

Herbert, E. W., & Baer, D. M. (1972). Training parents as behavior modifiers. *Journal of Applied Behavior Analysis, 5*, 139–149.

Hersen, M., & Barlow, D. H. (1982). *Single case experimental designs: Strategies for studying behavior change*. New York: Pergamon Press.

Hitchcock, A. (1942). *The value of terminology in children's descriptions of changes in pitch direction*. Unpublished master's thesis, University of Minnesota, Minneapolis.

Hodges, D. A. (Ed.). (1980). *Handbook of music psychology*. Lawrence, KS: National Association for Music Therapy.

Hoffer, C. R. (1965). *Teaching music in the secondary schools*. Belmont, CA: Wadsworth Publishing Company.

Hofstetter, F. T. (1981). Computer-based aural training: The GUIDO system. *Journal of Computer-Based Instruction, 7*, 84–92.

Hollander, M., & Wolfe, D. A. (1973). *Nonparametric statistical methods*. New York: John Wiley & Sons.

Hornberger, R. H. (1960). The projective effects of fear and sexual arousal on the ratings of pictures. *Journal of Clinical Psychology, 16*, 328–331.

Horton, G. O. (1975). Generalization of teacher behavior as a function of subject matter specific discrimination training. *Journal of Applied Behavior Analysis, 8*, 311–319.

Hosford, R. D., & Johnson, M. E. (1983). A comparison of self-observation, self-modeling, and practice without video feedback for improving counselor interviewing behavior. *Counselor Education & Supervision, 23*, 62–70.

House, A. E., & Kinscherf, B. M. (1979). Effects of intrinsic and experimenter-induced motivation for change on accuracy of self-monitoring. *Psychological Reports, 45*, 667–670.

Hull, C. H., & Nie, N. H. (1981). *SPSS update 7–9*. New York: McGraw-Hill.

Hylton, J. (1983). A survey of choral education research: 1972–1981. *Bulletin of the Council for Research in Music Education, 76*, 1–29.

Iffert, R. E. (1957). *Retention and withdrawal of college students* (Bulletin #1). Washington, DC: U.S. Government Printing Office.

Isen, R. E., & Shalker, T. E. (1982). The effect of feeling state on evaluation of positive, neutral, and negative stimuli: When you "accentuate the positive," do you "eliminate the negative"? *Social Psychology Quarterly, 45*, 58–63.

Jacobson, N. S. (1977). Problem solving and contingency contracting in the treatment of marital discord. *Journal of Consulting and Clinical Psychology, 45*, 92–100.

Jamison, R. N., & Lovatt, K. F. (1983). Classroom delinquency, achievement, and computer assisted instruction. *Journal of Computer-Based Instruction, 9*, 145–147.

Jellison, J. A. (1976). Accuracy of temporal order recall for verbal and song digit-spans presented to right and left ears. *Journal of Music Therapy, 13*, 114–129.

Jellison, J. A. (1979). The music therapist in the educational setting: Developing and implementing curriculum for the handicapped. *Journal of Music Therapy, 16*, 128–137.

Jellison, J. A., & Miller, N. (1982). Recall of digit and word sequences by musicians and non-musicians as a function of spoken or sung input and task. *Journal of Music Therapy, 14*(4), 194–209.

Johnson, S. M., & White, G. (1971). Self-observation as an agent of behavioral change. *Behavior Therapy, 2*, 488–497.

Jones, D. (1909). *Intonation curves.* Berlin: B. G. Teubner.

Jones, E. E., & Goethals, G. R. (1972). Order effects in impression formation: Attribution context and the nature of the entity. In Jones, E. E., et al. (Eds.), *Attribution: Perceiving the causes of behavior.* Morristown, NJ: General Learning Press.

Jones, E. E., Goethals, G. R., Kennington, G. E., & Severance, J. J. (1972). Primacy and assimilation in the attribution process: The stable entity proposition. *Journal of Personality and Social Psychology, 40*, 250–274.

Jones, E. E., Worchel, S., Goethals, G. R., & Grumet, J. F. (1971). Prior expectancy and behavioral extremity as determinants of attitude attribution. *Journal of Experimental Social Psychology, 7*, 59–80.

Jones, M. (1979). Using a vertical-keyboard instrument with the uncertain singer. *Journal of Research in Music Education, 27*, 173–184.

Jones, M. A., Magura, S., & Shyne, A. W. (1981). Effective practice with families in protective and preventive services: What works? *Child Welfare, 60*, 67–80.

Kantorski, V. (1983). *Vocal and instrumental pitch-matching abilities of beginning string instrumentalists.* Unpublished manuscript, Center for Music Research, The Florida State University, Tallahassee.

Karma, K. (1979). Musical, spatial, and verbal abilities. *Bulletin of the Council of Research in Music Education, 59*, 50–53.

Katz, P. A. (1963). Effects of labels on children's perception and discrimination learning. *Journal of Experimental Psychology, 66*, 423–428.

Katz, P. A. (1973). Stimulus predifferentiation and modification of children's racial attitudes. *Child Development, 44*, 232–237.

Katz, P. A., Albert, J., & Atkins, M. (1971). Mediation and perceptual transfer in children. *Developmental Psychology, 4*, 268–276.

Katz, P. A., & Seavey, C. (1973). Labels and children's perceptions of faces. *Child Development, 44*, 770–775.

Katz, P. A., & Zigler, E. (1969). Effects of labels on perceptual transfer: Stimulus and developmental factors. *Journal of Experimental Psychology, 80*, 73–77.

Kazdin, A. E. (1974). Reactive self-monitoring: The effects of response desirability, goal setting, and feedback. *Journal of Consulting and Clinical Psychology, 42*, 704–716.

Kelley, M. L., & Stokes, T. F. (1982). Contingency contracting with disadvantaged youths: Improving classroom performance. *Journal of Applied Behavior Analysis, 15*, 447–454.

Kelly, D. T. (1961). A study of the musical preferences of a select group of adolescents. *Journal of Research in Music Education, 9,* 118–124.

Kessen, W., Levine, J., & Wendrich, K. A. (1979). The imitation of pitch in infants. *Infant Behavior and Development, 2,* 93–99.

Keston, M. J., & Pinto, I. M. (1955). Possible factors influencing musical preference. *Journal of Genetic Psychology, 86,* 101–113.

Killian, J. N. (1981). Effect of instructions and feedback on music teaching skills. *Journal of Music Therapy, 18,* 166–180.

Killian, J. N. (1985). Operant preference for vocal balance in four-voice chorales. *Journal of Research in Music Education, 33,* 55–67.

Kirkpatrick, R. (1984). *Interpreting Bach's well-tempered clavier.* New Haven, CT: Yale University Press.

Kostka, M. J. (1984a). An investigation of reinforcements, time use, and student attentiveness in piano lessons. *Journal of Research in Music Education, 32,* 113–122.

Kostka, M. J. (1984b). *A comparison of three approaches to music listening for fourth- and fifth-grade students.* Paper presented at the meeting of the Texas Music Educators Association, Ft. Worth.

Kratus, J. (1985). *The musical contents of children's original songs.* Unpublished doctoral dissertation, Northwestern University, Evanston, IL.

Kruse, L. C., & Barger, D. M. F. (1982). Development and implementation of a contract grading system. *Journal of Nursing Education, 21,* 31–37.

Kuhn, T. L. (1974). Discrimination of modulated beat tempo by professional musicians. *Journal of Research in Music Education,* 22(4), 270–277.

Kuhn, T. L. (1975). The effect of teacher approval and disapproval on attentiveness, musical achievement, and attitude of fifth grade students. In Madsen, C. K., Greer, R. D., & Madsen, C. H., Jr. (Eds.), *Research in music behavior* (pp. 40–48). New York: Teachers College Press.

Kuhn, T. L. (1976). *Reliability of a technique for assessing musical preferences in young children.* Paper presented at the meeting of the Music Educators National Conference, Atlantic City.

Kuhn, T. L. (1977). Effects of dynamics, halves of exercise, and trial sequences on tempo accuracy. *Journal of Research in Music Education, 25,* 222–227.

Kuhn, T. L. (1980). Instrumentation for the measurement of music attitudes. *Contributions to Music Education, 8,* 2–38.

Kuhn, T. L. (1985, March). *The effect of tempo, meter, and melodic complexity on the perception of tempo.* Paper presented at the Sixth National Symposium for Research in Music Behavior, Ft. Worth.

Kuhn, T., & Gates, E. (1975). Effect of notational values, age, and example length on tempo performance accuracy. *Journal of Research in Music Education, 23,* 203–210.

Kuhn, T. L., Shehan, P. K., & Sims, W. L. (1980, November). *Relationships among bipolar verbal music preference descriptors and time spent listening to three simultaneously available music selections.* Paper presented at the National Symposium for Research in Music Behavior, New York.

Lader, C. E. (1977). *The effect of differential treatment on the intonation of string instrumentalists.* Unpublished master's thesis, The Florida State University, Tallahassee.

Lavin, B. (1980). Can computer-assisted instruction make a difference? *Teaching Sociology, 7,* 163–179.

Lawrence, D. M. (1979). Role of verbal representations in testing recognition of naturalistic sound. *Perceptual and Motor Skills, 48,* 443–446.

Leahy, R. (1980). Writing made possible: A contract approach. *Improving college and university teaching, 28,* 155–157.

Leben, W. R. (1976). The tones in English intonation. *Linguistic Analysis, 2*(1), 69–107.

LeBlanc, A. (1979). Generic style music preferences of fifth-grade students. *Journal of Research in Music Education, 27,* 255–270.

LeBlanc, A. (1981). Effects of style, tempo, and performing medium on children's music preference. *Journal of Research in Music Education, 29,* 143–156.

LeBlanc, A. (1984). Selecting a response mode in preference research. *Contributions to Music Education, 11,* 1–14.

LeBlanc, A., & Cote, R. (1983). Effects of tempo and performing medium on children's music preference. *Journal of Research in Music Education, 31,* 57–66.

LeBlanc, A., & McCrary, J. (1983). Effect of tempo on children's music preference. *Journal of Research in Music Education, 31,* 283–294.

Lehiste, I. (1970). *Suprasegmentals.* Cambridge, MA: MIT Press.

Lehiste, I., & Peterson, G. E. (1961). Some basic considerations in the analysis of intonation. *Journal of the Acoustical Society of America, 33*(4), 419–425.

Leon, P. R., & Martin, P. (1972). Machines and measurements. In Bolinger, D. (Ed.), *Intonation* (pp. 30–51). Baltimore: Penguin Books.

Leonhard, C., & Colwell, R. J. (1976). Research in music education. *Bulletin of the Council for Research in Music Education, 49,* 1–30.

Lieberman, P. (1976). *Intonation, perception, and language.* Cambridge, MA: MIT Press.

Lipinski, D. P., Black, J. L., Nelson, R. O., & Ciminero, A. R. (1975). The influence of motivational variables on the reactivity and reliability of self-recording. *Journal of Consulting and Clinical Psychology, 43,* 637–645.

Lipinski, D. R., & Nelson, R. O. (1974). The reactivity and unreliability of self-recording. *Journal of Consulting and Clinical Psychology, 42,* 118–123.

List, G. (1972). Speech melody and song melody in central Thailand. In Bolinger, D. (Ed.), *Intonation* (pp. 263–281). Baltimore: Penguin Books.

Lord, A. S., & Palmer, R. (1982). Teaching psychiatric/mental health nursing via the contract for learning activities. *Journal of Nursing Education, 21,* 23–28.

Lozanov, G. (1979). *Suggestology and outlines of suggestopedy.* New York: Gordon & Breech.

Luiten, J., Ames, W., & Ackerson, G. (1980). A meta-analysis of the effects of advance organizers on learning and retention. *American Educational Research Journal, 17,* 211–218.

Lux, J. E. (1979). Contracting to demonstrate teacher competencies. *Journal of Teacher Education, 30,* 9–12.

Madsen, C. H., Jr., & Madsen, C. K. (1983). *Teaching/discipline: A positive ap-*

proach for educational development (3rd. ed.). Raleigh: Contemporary Publishing.

Madsen, C. K. (1979). Modulated beat discrimination among musicians and nonmusicians. *Journal of Research in Music Education*, *27*(1), 57–67.

Madsen, C. K. (1981a). *Music therapy: A behavioral guide for the mentally retarded*. Washington, DC: National Association for Music Therapy.

Madsen, C. K. (1981b). Music lessons and books as reinforcement alternatives for an academic task. *Journal of Research in Music Education*, *29*, 103–110.

Madsen, C. K. (1983). Ideas versus behavior: Comparison of children and adults' ability to specify measurable behavior. *Journal of Music Therapy*, *20*, 170–178.

Madsen, C. K., & Alley, J. M. (1979). The effect of reinforcement on attentiveness: A comparison of behaviorally trained music therapists and other professionals with implications for competency-based academic preparation. *Journal of Music Therapy*, *16*, 70–82.

Madsen, C. K., Dorow, L. G., Moore, R. S., & Womble, J. U. (1976). Effect of music via television as reinforcement for correct mathematics. *Journal of Research in Music Education*, *24*, 51–59.

Madsen, C. K., & Duke, R. A. (1985a). Perception of approval/disapproval in music. *Bulletin of the Council for Research in Music Education*, *85*, 119–130.

Madsen, C. K., & Duke, R. A. (1985b). Observation of teacher/student interactions in music: Observer perceptions versus actual events. *Journal of Research in Music Education*, *33*(3), 205–214.

Madsen, C. K., Duke, R. A., & Geringer, J. M. (1984). Pitch and tempo discrimination in recorded band music among wind and percussion musicians. *Journal of Band Research*, *20*(1), 20–29.

Madsen, C. K., & Forsythe, J. L. (1973). Effect of contingent music listening on increases of mathematical responses. *Journal of Research in Music Education*, *21*, 176–181.

Madsen, C. K., & Geringer, J. M. (1976). Preferences for trumpet tone quality versus intonation. *Bulletin of the Council for Research in Music Education*, *46*, 13–22.

Madsen, C. K., & Geringer, J. M. (1983). Attending behavior as a function of in-class activity in university music classes. *Journal of Music Therapy*, *20*(1), 30–38.

Madsen, C. K., Greer, R. D., & Madsen, C. H., Jr. (Eds.). (1975). *Research in music behavior*. New York: Teachers College Press.

Madsen, C. K., & Kuhn, T. L. (1978). *Contemporary music education*. Arlington Heights, IL: AHM Publishing.

Madsen, C. K., & Madsen, C. H., Jr. (1968). Music as a behavior modification technique for changing client behavior. *Journal of Music Therapy*, *5*, 72–76.

Madsen, C. K., & Madsen, C. H., Jr. (1978). *Experimental research in music*. Raleigh: Contemporary Publishing.

Madsen, C. K., Madsen, C. H., Jr., & Michel, D. E. (1975). The use of music stimuli in teaching language discrimination. In Madsen, C. K., Greer, R. D., & Madsen, C. H., Jr. (Eds.), *Research in music behavior* (pp. 182–190). New York: Teachers College Press.

Madsen, C. K., & Moore, R. S. (Eds.). (1978). *Experimental research in music: Workbook in design and statistical tests*. Raleigh: Contemporary Publishing.

Madsen, C. K., & Staum, M. J. (1983). Discrimination and interference in the recall of melodic stimuli. *Journal of Research in Music Education, 31,* 15–31.

Madsen, C. K., & Wolfe, D. E. (1979). The effect of interrupted music and incompatible responses on bodily movement and music attentiveness. *Journal of Music Therapy, 16,* 17–30.

Madsen, C. K., & Yarbrough, C. (1980). *Competency-based music education.* Englewood Cliffs, NJ: Prentice-Hall.

Mann, R. A. (1972). The behavior-therapeutic use of contingency contracting to control an adult behavior problem: Weight control. *Journal of Applied Behavior Analysis, 5,* 99–109.

Marchand, D. J. (1975). A study of two approaches to developing expressive performance. *Journal of Research in Music Education, 23,* 14–22.

Martin, M. (1977). Reading while listening: A linear model of selective attention. *Journal of Verbal Learning and Verbal Behavior, 16,* 453–463.

Mather, J., Nixon, J., & Corbet, D. (1978). Contracts can motivate physical underachievers. *Journal of Physical Education and Recreation, 49,* 23–24.

McCadden, J., & Despard, D. (1980). Contracting for success with special needs students. *VocEd, 55,* 46–48.

McDermott, P. A., & Watkins, M. W. (1983). Computerized versus conventional remedial instruction for learning-disabled pupils. *Journal of Special Education, 17,* 81–88.

McDonald, D. (1974). Environment: A factor in conceptual listening skills of elementary school children. *Journal of Research in Music Education, 22,* 205–214.

McGinnis, E. (1928). Seashore's measures of musical ability applied to children of pre-school age. *American Journal of Psychology, 40,* 620–623.

McKeown, B. (1975). *Guitar songbook with instruction.* Boston: Houghton Mifflin.

Merriam, A. P. (1964). *The anthropology of music.* Chicago: University of Chicago Press.

Meyer, L. B. (1956). *Emotion and meaning in music.* Chicago: University of Chicago Press.

Michel, D. E. (1971). Self-esteem and academic achievement in black junior high students: Effects of automated guitar instruction. *Bulletin of the Council for Research in Music Education, 24,* 15–23.

Miller, A. G. (1976). Constraint and target effects on the attribution of attitudes. *Journal of Experimental Social Psychology, 12,* 325–339.

Miller, N. (Ed.). (1984). *Bilingualism and language disability.* San Diego: College-Hill Press.

Milliman, R. E. (1982). Using background music to affect the behavior of supermarket shoppers. *Journal of Marketing, 46,* 86–91.

Mills, S. R., Rice, C. T., Berliner, D. C., & Rousseau, E. W. (1980). The correspondence between teacher questions and student questions in classroom discourses. *Journal of Experimental Education, 48,* 194–204.

Moller, L. E. (1980). Performance of musicians under noise. *Perceptual and Motor Skills, 50,* 301–302.

Moore, R. S. (1976a). Effect of differential teaching techniques on achievment, attitude, and teaching skills. *Journal of Research in Music Education, 24,* 129–141.

Moore, R. S. (1976b). The effects of videotaped feedback and self-evaluation forms on teaching skills, musicianship, and creativity of prospective elementary teachers. *Bulletin of the Council for Research in Music Education, 47,* 1–7.

Moore, R. S. (1981). Comparative use of teaching time by American and British elementary music specialists. *Bulletin of the Council for Research in Music Education, 66-67,* 62–68.

Moore, R. S. (1983). *Effects of age and gender on the vocal range of musically-talented children.* Paper presented at the Fifth National Symposium on Research in Music Behavior, Tallahassee.

Moore, R. S., & Kuhn, T. L. (1975). The effect of different behavioral techniques on teaching and musicianship skills of prospective elementary teachers: Six studies. In Madsen, C. K., Greer, R. D., & Madsen, C. H., Jr. (Eds.), *Research in music behavior* (pp. 56–65). New York: Teachers College Press.

Moorhead, G., & Pond, D. (1941–44). *Music of young children* (Vols. 1–3). Santa Barbara, CA: Pillsbury Foundation for Advancement of Music Education.

Morgan, B. J., & Lindsley, O. R. (1966). Operant preference for stereophonic over monophonic music. *Journal of Music Therapy, 3,* 135–143.

Morrissey, R. J. (1971). Attrition in probationary freshmen. *Journal of College Student Personnel, 12,* 279–285.

Mueller, K. H. (1956). Studies in music appreciation. *Journal of Research in Music Education, 4,* 3–25.

Munro, J. D. (1981). Utilization of written contracts to increase client self-determination. *Mental Retardation, 19,* 65–67.

Murray, H. A. (1933). The effect of fear upon estimates of the maliciousness of other persons. *Journal of Social Psychology, 4,* 310–339.

Murray, K. C. (1975). The effect of teacher approval/disapproval on musical performance, attentiveness, and attitude of high school choruses. In Madsen, C. K., Greer, R. D., & Madsen, C. H., Jr. (Eds.), *Research in music behavior* (pp. 165–180). New York: Teachers College Press.

Napoli, D. J. (1978). *Elements of tone, stress, and intonation.* Washington, DC: Georgetown Press.

Nelson, C. M., & McReynolds, W. T. (1971). Self-recording and control of behavior: A reply to Simkins. *Behavior Therapy, 2,* 594–597.

Nelson, R. O., & Hayes, S. C. (1981). Theoretical explanations for reactivity in self-monitoring. *Behavior Modification, 5,* 3–14.

Nolin, W. H. (1973). Attitudinal growth patterns toward elementary school music experiences. *Journal of Research in Music Education, 21,* 123–134.

Norcross, K. J. (1958). Effects on discrimination performance of similarity of previously acquired stimulus names. *Journal of Experimental Psychology, 56,* 305–309.

Norcross, K. J., & Spiker, C. C. (1957). The effects of type of stimulus pretraining on discrimination performance in preschool children. *Child Development, 28,* 79–84.

Norton, D. (1979). Relationship of music ability and intelligence to auditory and visual conservation of the kindergarten child. *Journal of Research in Music Education, 27,* 3–13.

Norton, D. (1980). Interrelationships among music aptitude, IQ, and auditory conservation. *Journal of Research in Music Education, 28,* 207–217.

Novak, G., & Hammond, J. M. (1983). Self-reinforcement and descriptive praise in maintaining token economy reading performance. *Journal of Educational Research, 76*, 186–189.

Obenshain, K. (1980). Practice problems? Make a contract. *Clavier, 19*, 47–50.

Ollendick, T. H. (1981). Self-monitoring and self-administered overcorrection: The modification of nervous tics in children. *Behavior Modification, 5*, 75–84.

Olson, G. (1978). Intersensory and intrasensory transfer of melodic contour perception by children. *Journal of Research in Music Education, 26*, 41–47.

Olson, G. (1981). Perception of melodic contour through intrasensory matching and intersensory transfer by elementary school students. *The Journal of Educational Research, 74*(5), 358–362.

Paduano, M. A. (1979). Introducing independent study into the nursing curriculum. *Journal of Nursing Education, 18*, 34–47.

Pagliaro, L. A. (1983). CAI in pharmacology: Student academic performance and instructional interactions. *Journal of Computer-Based Instruction, 4*, 131–144.

Palmer, W. (Ed.). (1981). *The well-tempered clavier, by J. S. Bach, Book I* (p. 218). Sherman Oaks, CA: Alfred Publishing.

Pantage, T. J., & Creedon, C. F. (1978). Studies of college attrition: 1950–1975. *Review of Education Research, 48*, 49–101.

Pascarella, E. T., & Terenzini, P. T. (1979). Student-faculty informal contact and college persistence: A further investigation. *Journal of Educational Research, 72*, 214–218.

Patterson, G. R. (1971). *Families*. Champaign, IL: Research Press.

Pedersen, D. M., & Pedersen, N. O. (1970). The relationship between pitch recognition and vocal pitch production in sixth grade students. *Journal of Research in Music Education, 18*, 265–272.

Pessemier, E. A. (1960). An experimental method for estimating demand. *Journal of Business, 33*, 373–383.

Petzold, R. G. (1966). *Auditory perception of musical sounds by children in the first six grades* (Cooperative Research Project No. 1051). Madison, WI: University of Wisconsin.

Pfeil, C. I. (1972). Creativity as an instructional mode for introducing music to non-music majors at the college level. *Dissertation Abstracts International, 33*, 2415A. (University Microfilms No. 72-30028).

Pflederer, M., & Sechrest, L. (1968). Conservation-type responses of children to musical stimuli. *Bulletin of the Council for Research in Music Education, 13*, 19–36.

Pick, A. D. (1979). Listening to melodies: Perceiving events. In Pick, A. D. (Ed.), *Perception and its development: A tribute to Eleanor J. Gibson* (pp. 145–165). Hillsdale, NJ: Erlbaum.

Pickett, J. M. (1980). *The sounds of speech communication*. Baltimore: University Park Press.

Piper, R. M., & Shoemaker, D. M. (1973). Formative evaluation of a kindergarten music program based on behavioral objectives. *Journal of Research in Music Education, 21*, 145–152.

Polczynski, J. J., & Shirland, L. E. (1977). Expectancy theory and contract grading combined as an effective motivational force for college students. *Journal of Educational Research, 70*, 238–241.

Pond, D. (1981). A composer's study of young children's innate musicality. *Bulletin of the Council for Research in Music Education, 68,* 1–12.

Porter, S. Y. (1977). The effect of multiple successive approximation on pitch-matching behaviors of uncertain singers. *Journal of Research in Music Education, 25,* 68–82.

Price, H. E. (1983). The effect of conductor academic task presentation, conductor reinforcement, and ensemble practice on performers' musical achievement, attentiveness, and attitude. *Journal of Research in Music Education, 31,* 245–257.

Prickett, C. A. (1983a, February). *The consistency of observer reliability: Self with instructor, self with classmate.* Paper presented at the meeting of the Southern Division, Music Educators National Conference, Louisville.

Prickett, C. A. (1983b). The effect of self-monitoring on positive comments given by music students coaching peers. *Dissertation Abstracts International, 44,* 2080A. (University Microfilms No. DA8325683).

Quinto, F., & McKenna, B. (1977). *Alternatives to standardized testing.* Washington, DC: National Education Association.

Radocy, R. E., & Boyle, J. D. (1979). *Psychological foundations of musical behavior.* Springfield, IL: Charles C. Thomas.

Ramist, L. (1981). *College student attrition and retention* (College Board Report No. 81-1). New York: College Entrance Examination Board.

Ray, W. J., Morell, M., Frediani, A. W., & Tucker, D. (1976). Sex differences and lateral specialization of hemispheric functioning. *Neuropsychologia, 14*(3), 391–394.

Realon, R. E., Lewallen, J. D., & Wheeler, A. J. (1983). Verbal feedback vs. verbal feedback plus praise: The effects on direct-care staff 's training behavior. *Mental Retardation, 21,* 209–212.

Redfield, D., & Rousseau, E. (1981). A meta-analysis of experimental research on teacher questioning behavior. *Review of Educational Research, 51,* 237–245.

Rees, A. L. W. (1977). Techniques for presenting songs. *English Language Teaching Journal, 31*(3), 226–233.

Reimer, B. (1967). *Development and trial in a junior and senior high school of a two-year curriculum in general music.* Cleveland: Case Western Reserve University. (ERIC Document Reproduction Service No. ED 017 526).

Riegle, R. P. (1978). The limits of contracting. *High School Journal, 61,* 13–19.

Robinson, R., & Winold, A. (1976). *The choral experience: Literature, materials, and methods.* New York: Harper & Row.

Roe, P. F. (1983). *Choral music education.* Englewood Cliffs, NJ: Prentice-Hall.

Rogers, V. R. (1957). Children's musical preferences as related to grade level and other factors. *Elementary School Journal, 57,* 433–435.

Romanek, M. L. (1974). A self-instructional program for musical concept development in preschool children. *Journal of Research in Music Education, 22,* 129–135.

Rose, T. L., Koorland, M. A., Lessen, E. I., & Reid, B. A. (1978). Improving practicum performance: The case contract. *Contemporary Education, 50,* 18–23.

Rosenshine, B. V. (1968). To explain: A review of research. *Educational Leadership, 26,* 303–309.

Rosenshine, B. V. (1979). Content, time, and direct instruction. In Peterson, P. L.,

& Walberg, H. T. (Eds.), *Research on teaching* (pp. 28–56.) Berkeley, CA: McCutchan Publishing.

Rosenthal, R. K. (1981). A data-based approach to elementary general music teacher preparation. *Dissertation Abstracts International, 43,* 2902A. (University Microfilms No. DEP82-29036).

Ross, A. W. (1976). Success in a behavioral weight loss program as a function of contingency contracting. *Dissertation Abstracts International, 37,* 1927B. (University Microfilms No. DCJ76-21912).

Ross, S. L. (1975, September). An objective grading system for band-orchestra directors. *The Instrumentalist, 30,* 28.

Rost, W. J. (1976). The identification of elementary school children's musical concepts as a function of two types of musical literature and environment. *Bulletin of the Council for Research in Music Education, 48,* 36–42.

Rowe, M. (1974). Pausing phenomena: Influence on the quality of instruction. *Journal of Psycholinguistic Research, 3,* 203–224.

Rubin-Rabson, G. (1940). The influence of age, intelligence, and training of reactions to classic and modern music. *Journal of General Psychology, 22,* 413–429.

Sadker, M., & Sadker, D. (1985). Sexism in the school room of the '80's. *Psychology Today, 19*(3), 54–57.

Salzberg, R. S. (1977). The effects of visual stimulus and instruction on intonation and accuracy of string instrumentalists. *Dissertation Abstracts International, 38,* 5323A. (University Microfilms No. 78-1512).

Salzberg, R. S., & Salzberg, C. L. (1981). Praise and corrective feedback in the remediation of incorrect left-hand positions of elementary string players. *Journal of Research in Music Education, 29,* 125–134.

Santogrossi, D.A., O'Leary, K. D., Romanczyk, R. G., & Kaufman, K. F. (1973). Self-evaluation by adolescents in a psychiatric hospital school token program. *Journal of Applied Behavior Analysis, 6,* 277–287.

Saudargas, R. A. (1972). Setting criterion rates of teacher praise: The effects of videotape feedback on a behavior analysis followthrough classroom. In Semb, G. (Ed.), *Behavior analysis and education* (pp. 253–261). Lawrence, KS: University of Kansas.

Saxon, W. (1979). Behavioral contracting: Theory and design. *Child Welfare, 58,* 523–529.

Schevill, H. S. (1969). Hierarchical processes in pitch delineation at the second grade level. *Dissertation Abstracts International, 31,* 308A. (University Microfilms No. 70-13160).

Schevill, H. S. (1971). *Perceived order of auditory and visual stimuli in children* (Final Report BR-1-1-043 October). San Francisco: Institute of Medical Sciences. (Eric Document Reproduction No. Ed 057 923).

Schiffenbauer, A. (1974). Effect of observers' emotional state on judgments of the emotional state of others. *Journal of Personality and Social Psychology, 30,* 31–35.

Schneider, D. J., Hastorf, A. H., & Ellsworth, P. C. (1979). *Person perception* (2nd. ed.). Reading, MA: Addison-Wesley.

Schoolcraft, V., & Delaney, C. (1982). Contract grading in clinical evaluation. *Journal of Nursing Education, 21,* 6–14.

Schuck, R. (1981). The impact of set induction on student achievement and retention. *Journal of Educational Research, 74*, 227–232.

Schukert, R. F., & McDonald, R. L. (1968). An attempt to modify the musical preferences of preschool children. *Journal of Research in Music Education, 16*, 39–44.

Scott, C. R. (1978, April). *Pitch concept formation in preschoolers: Its measurement.* Paper presented at the Music Educators National Conference, Chicago.

Seashore, C. (1938). *The psychology of music.* New York: McGraw-Hill.

Sexton, V. S. (1965). Factors contributing to attrition in college populations: Twenty-five years of research. *Journal of General Psychology, 72*, 301–326.

Seymour, F. W., & Stokes, T. F. (1976). Self-recording in training girls to increase work and evoke staff praise in an institution for offenders. *Journal of Applied Behavior Analysis, 9*, 41–54.

Sheeder, D. (1976). Teaching English through music. *Overseas Family,* 26–27.

Shehan, P. (1981). A comparison of mediation strategies in paired-associate learning for children with learning disabilities. *Journal of Music Therapy, 18*(3), 120–127.

Shuter-Dyson, R., & Gabriel, C. (1981). *The psychology of musical ability* (2nd ed.). London: Methuen.

Simons, G. M. (1976). *Simons measurements of music listening skills.* Chicago: Stoelting.

Sims, W. (1980). Effects of pitch and rhythm on the short-term memorization of nonsense syllable sequences by college students. *Contributions to Music Education, 8*, 73–91.

Slater, B. R. (1968). Effects of noise on pupil performance. *Journal of Educational Psychology, 59*, 239–243.

Smaby, M. H., & Tamminen, A. W. (1981). Classroom crisis intervention through contracting: A moral development model. *The School Counselor, 28*, 257–266.

Smith, C., & Morris, L. (1976). Effects of stimulative and sedative music on cognitive and emotional components of anxiety. *Psychological Reports, 38*, 1187–1193.

Smith, L., & Land, M. (1981). Low-inference verbal behaviors related to teacher clarity. *Journal of Classroom Interaction, 17*, 37–42.

Solomon, A. L. (1980). Music in special education before 1930: Hearing and speech development. *Journal of Research in Music Education, 28*(3), 236–242.

Spiker, C. C. (1963). Verbal factors in the discrimination learning of children. In Wright, J. C., & Kagan, J. (Eds.), *Basic cognitive processes in children.* Monograph of the Society for Research in Child Development, 28(2, Whole).

Spiker, C. C., & Norcross, K. J. (1962). Effects of previously acquired stimulus names on discrimination performance. *Child Development, 33*, 859–864.

Spradling, R. (1979). *The use of contingency contracting to increase the efficiency of practice time management in instrumental music majors.* Paper presented at the National Association for Music Therapy Convention, Dallas.

Spradling, R. L. (1980). The effect of timeout from performance on attentiveness and attitude of university band students. *Dissertation Abstracts International, 41*, 2989A. (University Microfilms No. DEN81-00653).

Staum, M. J. (1979). Music in the remediation of auditory perceptual deficits. *Contributions to Music Education, 7*, 21–40.

Stegall, J. R., Blackburn, J. E., & Coop, R. H. (1978). Administrators' ratings of

competencies for an undergraduate music education curriculum. *Journal of Research in Music Education, 26,* 3–15.
Stephens, L. F., & Motes, S. G. (1980). Contract learning. *Journalism Educator, 35,* 48–49.
Stratton, V. N., & Zalanowski, A. (1984). The effect of background music on verbal interaction in groups. *Journal of Music Therapy, 21*(1), 16–26.
Strenta, A., & Kleck, R. E. (1982). Perceptions of feedback: Investigating "kind" treatment of the handicapped. *Personality and Social Psychology Bulletin, 8,* 706–711.
Stuart, M. (1979). The use of videotape recordings to increase teacher trainees' error detection skills. *Journal of Research in Music Education, 27,* 14–19.
Stuart, R. (1971). Behavioral contracting with families of delinquents. *Journal of Behavior Therapy and Experimental Psychiatry, 2,* 1–11.
Summerskill, J. (1962). Dropouts from college. In Sanford, N. (Ed.), *The American college* (pp. 627–655). New York: John Wiley.
Sutherland, M. (1982). Performance contracting in school health. *Health Education, 13,* 45–46.
Swan, H. (1973). The development of a choral instrument. In Decker, H. A., & Herford, J. (Eds.), *Choral conducting: A symposium* (pp. 4–55). Englewood Cliffs, NJ: Prenctice-Hall.
Taebel, D. (1974, March). *The effect of various instructional modes on children's performance of music concept tasks.* Paper presented at the Music Educators National Conference, Anaheim, CA.
Taynor, J., & Deaux, K. (1973). When women are more deserving than men: Equity, attribution, and perceived sex differences. *Journal of Personality and Social Psychology, 28,* 360–367.
Thomas, D. R. (1972). Self-monitoring as a technique for modifying teaching behaviors. *Dissertation Abstracts International, 33,* 3809A. (University Microfilms No. 72-19947).
Thompson, K. P. (1972). Relative effectiveness on aural perception of televised verbal descriptions and visual representations of selected musical events. *Contributions to Music Education, 1,* 68–83.
Thurman, V. L. (1976). *A frequency and time description of selected rehearsal behaviors used by five choral conductors.* Paper presented at the Music Educators National Conference, Atlantic City.
Tobin, K., & Capie, W. (1982). Relationships between classroom process variables and middle-school science achievement. *Journal of Educational Psychology, 74,* 441–454.
Tyson, J. A., & Wall, S. M. (1983). Effect of inconsistency between counselor verbal and nonverbal behavior on perceptions of counselor attributes. *Journal of Counseling Psychology, 30,* 433–437.
Uhrbrock, R. S. (1961). Music on the job: Its influence on worker morale and production. *Personnel Psychology, 14,* 9–38.
Upper, D., Lochman, J. E., & Aveni, C. A. (1977). Using contingency contracting to modify the problematic behaviors of foster home residents. *Behavior Modification, 1,* 405–416.
Utley, E. (1973). The development of a musical perception test free of technical vo-

cabulary for use in grades six through twelve. *Bulletin of the Council for Research in Music Education, 35,* 44–52.

Vance, B. (1976). Using contracts to control weight and to improve cardiovascular physical fitness. In Krumboltz, J. D., & Thoreson, C. E. (Eds.), *Counseling methods* (pp. 527–541). New York: Holt, Rinehart, & Winston.

Van Houten, R., & Sullivan K. (1975). Effects of an audio cueing system on the rate of teacher praise. *Journal of Applied Behavior Analysis, 8,* 197–201.

Van Zee, N. (1976). Responses of kindergarten children to musical stimuli and terminology. *Journal of Research in Music Education, 24,* 14–21.

Vaughn, M. M. (1971). Music as a model and metaphor in the cultivation and measurement of creative behavior in children. *Dissertation Abstracts International, 32,* 5833A. (University Microfilms No. 72-11056).

Wagner, M. J. (1975). Effect of music and biofeedback on alpha brainwave rhythms and attentiveness. *Journal of Research in Music Education, 23,* 3–13.

Wagner, M. J. (1977). *Introductory musical acoustics.* Raleigh: Contemporary Publishing.

Wagner, M. J. (Speaker). (1978). *A forty minute audio presentation tracing one hundred years of science and sound.* Miami: Florida International University.

Wagner, M. J., & Altman, R. (1984). Music learning and brainwave biofeedback. *Update,* 2(3), 19–23.

Wagner, M. J., & Menzel, M. (1978). The effect of music listening and attentiveness training on the EEG's of musicians and non-musicians. *Journal of Music Therapy, 14*(4), 151–164.

Wagner, M. J., & Strul, E. P. (1979). Comparisons of beginning versus experienced elementary music educators in the use of teaching time. *Journal of Research in Music Education, 27,* 113–125.

Wagner, M. J., & Tilney, G. (1983). The effect of "superlearning techniques" on the vocabulary acquisition and alpha brainwave production of language learners. *TESOL Quarterly, 17,* 5–17.

Wang, C. C. (1983). Discrimination of modulated music tempo by music majors. *Journal of Research in Music Education, 31,* 49–55.

Wang, C. C., & Salzberg, R. S. (1984). Discrimination of modulated music tempo by string students. *Journal of Research in Music Education, 32,* 123–131.

Wapnick, J. (1976). A review of research on attitude and preference. *Bulletin of the Council for Research in Music Education, 48,* 1–20.

Wapnick, J. (1980a). The perception of musical and metronomic tempo change in musicians. *Psychology of Music, 8,* 3–12.

Wapnick, J. (1980b). Pitch, tempo, and timbral preferences in recorded piano music. *Journal of Research in Music Education, 28,* 43–58.

Webster, P. (1977). A factor of intellect approach to creative thinking in music. *Dissertation Abstracts International, 38,* 3136A. (University Microfilms No. DCJ77-26619).

Webster, P. (1983). An assessment of musical imagination in young children. In Tallarico, P. (Ed.), *Bowling Green State University Symposium on Music Teaching and Research,* Vol. 2 (pp. 100–123). Bowling Green, OH: Bowling Green State University.

Webster, P. R., & Schlentrich, K. (1982). Discrimination of pitch direction by preschool children with verbal and non-verbal tasks. *Journal of Research in Music Education, 30,* 151–162.

Webster, P. R., & Zimmerman, M. P. (1983). Conservation of rhythmic and tonal patterns of second through sixth grade children. *Bulletin of the Council for Research in Music Education, 73,* 28–49.

Weiss, R. L., Birchler, G. R., & Vincent, J. P. (1974). Contractual models for negotiation training in marital dyads. *Journal of Marriage and the Family, 36,* 321–331.

Welch, G. F. (1984). *Variability of practice and knowledge of results as factors in learning to sing in-tune.* Paper presented at the meeting of the International Society for Music Education, Victoria, B.C.

Weltens, B., & deBot, K. (1984). Visual feedback of intonation, II: Feedback delay and quality of feedback. *Language and Speech, 27*(1), 79–88.

Williams, H. M., Sievers, C., & Hattwick, M. (1932). The measurement of musical development. *University of Iowa Studies in Child Welfare, 7*(1), 1–191.

Williams, T. B. (1961). A study of the effect of music as a distraction on the mental test performance of certain eleventh grade students. *Dissertation Abstracts International, 22,* 168. (University Microfilms No. 61-2728, 150).

Willingham, W. W., & Breland, H. M. (1982). *Personal qualities and college admissions.* New York: College Entrance Examination Board.

Wilson, R. W., & Eisenhauer, V. J. (1982). Cognitive results of health behavior contracting. *Health Education, 13,* 21–23.

Winne, P. (1979). Experiments relating teacher's use of higher cognitive questions to student achievement. *Review of Educational Research, 49,* 13–49.

Winner, E. (1982). *Invented worlds: The psychology of the arts.* Cambridge, MA: Harvard University Press.

Wolfe, D. E. (1980). The effect of automated interrupted music on head posturing of cerebral palsied individuals. *Journal of Music Therapy, 17,* 184–206.

Wolfe, D. E. (1981). Training abusive parents in effective child management. *Behavior Modification, 5,* 320–335.

Wolfe, D. E. (1982). The effect of interrupted and continuous music on bodily movement and task performance of third-grade students. *Journal of Music Therapy, 19,* 74–85.

Wolfe, D. E. (1983). Effects of music loudness on task performance and self-report of college-aged students. *Journal of Research in Music Education, 31,* 191–201.

Wolfe, D. E. (1984). Improve practice with motivational contracts. *Music Educators Journal, 71,* 34–41.

Wolfe, D. E., & Jellison, J. A. (1984). (Written practice and teaching units: Pretest/posttest scores). Unpublished raw data.

Woods, H. B. (1979a). *Intonation.* Monograph from Workshop "Contact Canada." Quebec, Canada: Canadian Government Publishing Center.

Woods, H. B. (1979b). *Rhythm and unstress.* Monograph from Workshop "Contact Canada." Quebec, Canada: Canadian Government Publishing Center.

Worby, D. (1979). Independent learning: The use of the contract in an English program. *Lifelong Learning, 2,* 32–34, 42.

Wright, C., & Nuthall, G. (1970). The relationships between teacher behavior and pupil achievement in three experimental elementary science lessons. *American Educational Research Journal, 7,* 477–492.

Wysocki, T., Hall, G., Iwata, B., & Riordan, M. (1979). Behavioral management of exercise: Contracting for aerobic points. *Journal of Applied Behavior Analysis, 12,* 55–64.

Yank, S. E. (1975). The effect of multiple discrimination training on the pitch-matching behaviors of uncertain singers. *Dissertation Abstracts International, 36,* 25A. (University Microfilms No. 75-15, 766).

Yarbrough, C. (1975). Effect of magnitude of conductor behavior on students in selected mixed choruses. *Journal of Research in Music Education, 23,* 134–146.

Yarbrough, C. (1976). *The effect of videotaped observation and self-evaluation on rehearsal behavior of student conductors.* Paper presented at the Music Educators National Conference, Atlantic City.

Yarbrough, C. (1978). *Competency-based conducting: An exploratory study.* Unpublished manuscript, Syracuse University, Syracuse, NY.

Yarbrough, C. (1985). *The effect of musical excerpts on tempo discriminations and preferences of musicians and non-musicians.* Paper presented at the Sixth National Symposium for Research in Music Behavior, Fort Worth.

Yarbrough, C., & Price, H. E. (1981). Prediction of performer attentiveness based on rehearsal activity and teacher behavior. *Journal of Research in Music Education, 29,* 209–217.

Yarbrough, C., & Price, H. E. (1982, November). *The effect of instruction and repeated listening on behavioral preference, behavioral intent, verbal opinion, and ratings of familiarity and complexity.* Paper presented at the National Symposium for Research in Music Behavior, Tallahassee.

Yarbrough, C., Wapnick, J., & Kelly, R. (1979). Effect of videotape feedback techniques on performance, verbalization, and attitude of beginning conductors. *Journal of Research in Music Education, 27,* 103–112.

Young, R. W. (1976). *Making sense out of cents.* Oak Brook, IL: C. G. Conn, Ltd.

Youngberg, L., & Jones, D. (1980). Performance contracts help teach tumbling. *Journal of Physical Education and Recreation, 51,* 63.

Zaporozhets, A. V., & Elkonin, D. B. (Eds.). (1971). *The psychology of preschool children* (J. Shybut, & S. Simon, Trans.). Cambridge, MA: MIT Press.

Zimmerman, M. P., & Sechrest, L. (1970). Brief focused instruction and musical concepts. *Journal of Research in Music Education, 18,* 25–36.

Zurcher, W. (1975). The effect of model-supportive practice on beginning brass instrumentalists. In Madsen, C. K., Greer, R. D., & Madsen, C. H., Jr. (Eds.), *Research in music behavior* (pp. 131–138). New York: Teachers College Press.

Zurcher, W. (1980). A credit system for the Baldwin Junior High School band. In Greer, R. D., *Design for music learning* (pp. 150–157). New York: Teachers College Press.

Zurcher, W., & Greer, R. D. (1980). *The overjustification hypothesis and choice of high and low preference music and non-music activities over an extended time period in a junior high band program.* Paper presented at the Fourth National Symposium in Research in Music Behavior, New York.

Zwissler, R. N. (1971). An investigation of the pitch discrimination skills of first-grade children identified as accurate singers and those identified as inaccurate singers. *Dissertation Abstracts International, 32/07,* 4056A. (University Microfilms No. 72-02947).

Contributors

Amy Brown, School of Music, The Florida State University, Tallahassee
Peggy A. Codding, School of Music, Ohio University, Athens
Alice-Ann Darrow, Department of Music Education and Music Therapy, The University of Kansas, Lawrence
Robert A. Duke, Department of Music, The University of Texas at Austin
Patricia J. Flowers, School of Music, Ohio State University, Columbus
Jere L. Forsythe, School of Music, Ohio State University, Columbus
Charles E. Furman, Department of Music, The University of Minnesota, Minneapolis
John M. Geringer, Department of Music, The University of Texas at Austin
Dianne G. Greenfield, School of Music, The Florida State University, Tallahassee
Harriet I. Hair, School of Music, The University of Georgia, Athens
Bernard J. Harding, Department of Music, Florida International University, Miami
Judith A. Jellison, Department of Music, The University of Texas at Austin
Janice N. Killian, Carrollton–Farmers Branch Independent School District, Carrollton, Texas
Terry L. Kuhn, School of Music, Kent State University, Kent, Ohio
Clifford K. Madsen, School of Music, The Florida State University, Tallahassee
Randall S. Moore, School of Music, The University of Oregon, Eugene
Harry E. Price, School of Music, The University of Alabama, Tuscaloosa
Carol A. Prickett, School of Music, The University of Alabama, Tuscaloosa
Wendy L. Sims, Department of Music, The University of Missouri, Columbia
Jayne M. Standley, School of Music, The Florida State University, Tallahassee
Myra J. Staum, College of Music, Willamette University, Salem, Oregon
Michael J. Wagner, Department of Music, Florida International University, Miami
Joel Wapnick, Department of Music, McGill University, Montreal
Peter Webster, Department of Music, Case Western Reserve University, Cleveland
David E. Wolfe, Department of Music, Utah State University, Logan
Cornelia Yarbrough, School of Music, Louisiana State University, Baton Rouge
William Zurcher, Baldwin Harbor Junior High School, Baldwin Harbor, New York

Index of Citations